HUGH JOHNSON'S
POCKET
ENCYCLOPEDIA
OF WINE
1988

A Fireside Book
Published by Simon & Schuster, Inc.
New York London Toronto Sydney Tokyo

KEY TO SYMBOLS

r.	red	
p.	rosé	(in brackets) means relatively unimportant
w.	white	
br.	brown	
sw.	sweet	
s/sw.	semi-sweet	
dr.	dry	
sp.	sparkling	

★	plain, everyday quality
★★	above average
★★★	well known, highly reputed
★★★★	grand, prestigious, expensive
☐	usually particularly good value in its class

83 84 etc.
    recommended years which may be currently available.

82′ etc. Vintage regarded as particularly successful for the property in question.

80 etc. years in **bold** should be ready for drinking (the others should be kept). Where both reds and whites are indicated the red is intended unless otherwise stated.
N.B. German vintages are codified by a different system. See note on p. 100.

D.Y.A. drink the youngest available

NV vintage not normally shown on label

Cross-references are in SMALL CAPS

See p. 5 for extra explanation

A quick-reference vintage chart for France and Germany appears on p. 192.

© 1977 Mitchell Beazley Publishers
Text © Hugh Johnson 1977, 1978, 1979, 1980, 1981, 1982, 1983, 1984, 1985, 1986, 1987
First edition published 1977
Revised editions published 1978, 1979, 1980, 1981, 1982, 1983, 1984, 1985, 1986, 1987
© 1987 Mitchell Beazley Publishers
A FIRESIDE BOOK
Published by Simon & Schuster, Inc.
Simon & Schuster Building
1230 Avenue of the Americas
New York, New York 10020

ISSN 0893-259X

Editors Alison Franks, Kathie Gill
Production Androulla Pavlou
Senior Executive Editor Chris Foulkes
Filmsetting by Vantage Photosetting Co. Ltd. Eastleigh and London
Printed in Hong Kong by Mandarin Offset

Contents

Introduction

The emphasis in this eleventh edition of what has become a much-consulted little book has been on refining and deepening the information it contains without expanding its content. This edition is the same length as the last, but contains references to some 200 more wines, vineyards and wine-makers. All the existing references have been updated. Having revised the book already nine times, this time I asked independent assessors to read each section carefully and advise me on its failings. With their findings in mind I then set about the further telescoping of what were already pretty terse entries. I hope that my meaning remains clear despite this further compression – and that next year I shall be indulged with a few more pages again, because the number of wines on offer continues to grow apace.

I described this book in its original Introduction as an exercise in crowding angels on a pinhead, or students into a telephone box. That was in 1977, when I thought it was pretty ingenious to use symbols and a few abbreviations to make a pocketable encyclopedia. Looking back at the first edition I realize that I was hardly squeezing at all compared with later efforts. Experience has taught me how to get angels to stand on other angels' shoulders, how to pick pygmy students, starve them and then shove like a Tokyo train-filler.

We are indeed spoilt for choice today: Australia and New Zealand, the Pacific North-West and now increasingly the Eastern United States are adding their contributions of excellent quality to the regions already recognized around the world. Italy, Spain and Portugal continue to chase France, while France somehow manages to hang on to the lead.

The arrangement of the book is intended to be as helpful as possible when you are buying a bottle, whether you are on the nursery slopes or an old hand with a bad memory. You are faced with a list of wines or an array of bottles in a restaurant, wine merchant's or bottle store. Your mind goes blank. You fumble for your little book. All you need to establish is what country a wine comes from. Look up the principal words on the label in the appropriate country's section. You will find enough potted information to let you judge whether this is the wine you want.

Specifically, you will find information on the colour and type of wine, its status or prestige, whether it is usually particularly good value, which vintages are good and which are ready to drink — and often considerably more . . . about the quantity made, the grapes used, ownership and the rest. Hundreds of cross-references help you delve further.

How to read an entry

The top line of most entries consists of the following information in an abbreviated form.

1. Which part of the country in question the wine comes from. (References to the maps in this book.)
2. Whether it is red, rosé or white (or brown/amber), dry, sweet or sparkling, or several of these.
3. Its general standing as to quality: a necessarily rough and ready guide based principally on an ascending scale:

   ⋆ plain, everyday quality
   ⋆⋆ above average
   ⋆⋆⋆ well known, highly reputed
   ⋆⋆⋆⋆ grand, prestigious, expensive

So much is more or less objective. Additionally there is a subjective rating: a box round the stars of any wine which in my experience is usually particularly good (which means good value) within its price range. There are good everyday wines as well as good luxury wines. The box system helps you find them.

4. Vintage information: which were the more successful of the recent vintages which *may* still be available. And of these which are ready to drink this year, and which will probably improve with keeping. Your first choice for current drinking should be one of the vintage years printed in **bold** type. Buy light-type years for further maturing.

The German vintage information works on a different principle: see the Introduction to Germany, page 100.

Acknowledgements

This store of detailed recommendations comes partly from my own notes and partly from those of a great number of kind friends. Without the generous help and co-operation of every single member of the wine trade I have approached, I could not have attempted it. I particularly want to thank the following for giving me material help with research or in the areas of their special knowledge.

Rodrigo Alvarado
Burton Anderson
Anthony Barton
Jean-Claude Berrouet
Tim Bleach
Michael Broadbent M.W.
Alain de Courseulles
Terry Dunleavy
Len Evans
Dereck Foster
Chris Foulkes
Jean-Paul Gardère
Rosemary George M.W.
James Halliday
Robert Hart M.W.
Peter Hasslacher
Ian Jamieson M.W.
Graham Knox
Matt Kramer
Tony Laithwaite

Miles Lambert-Gócs
Tim Marshall
Patrick Matthews
Christian Moueix
David Peppercorn M.W.
István Pusztai
Alain Querre
Jan and Maite Read
Belle Rhodes
Dr. Bernard Rhodes
Dr. Bruno Roncarati
Peter M.F. Sichel
Steven Spurrier
Serena Sutcliffe M.W.
Hugh Suter M.W.
Bob Thompson
Peter Vinding-Diers
Manfred Völpel
James Walker
David Wolfe

Grape varieties

The most basic of all differences between wines stems from the grapes they are made of. Centuries of selection have resulted in each of the long-established wine-areas having its favourite single variety, or a group of varieties whose juice or wine is blended together. Red burgundy is made of one grape, the Pinot Noir; red Bordeaux of three or four: two kinds of Cabernet, Merlot, Malbec and sometimes others. The laws say which grapes must be used, so the labels do not mention them.

So in newer regions the choice of a grape is the planter's single most crucial decision. Where he is proud of it, and intends his wine to have the character of a particular grape, the variety is the first thing he puts on the label. Hence the useful, originally Californian, term "varietal wine" — meaning, in principle, *one* variety.

A knowledge of grape varieties, therefore, is the single most helpful piece of knowledge in finding wines you will like wherever they are grown. Learn to recognize the characters of the most important. At least seven—Cabernet, Pinot Noir, Riesling, Sauvignon Blanc, Chardonnay, Gewürztraminer and Muscat—have memorable tastes and smells distinct enough to form international categories of wine. To these you might add Merlot, Syrah, Semillon . . .

Further notes on grapes will be found in the sections on Germany, Italy, central and south-east Europe, South Africa, etc.

The following are the best and/or commonest wine grapes.

Grapes for white wine

Aligoté

Burgundy's second-rank white grape. Crisp (often sharp) wine, needs drinking young. Perfect for mixing with cassis (blackcurrant liqueur) to make a "Kir".

Blanc Fumé

Another name for SAUVIGNON BLANC, referring to the "smoky" smell of the wine, particularly on the upper Loire (Sancerre and Pouilly). Makes some of California's best whites.

Bual

Makes top-quality sweet Madeira wines.

Chardonnay

The white burgundy grape, one of the grapes of Champagne, and the best white grape of California and more recently Australia. Gives dry wine of rich complexity, especially when aged some months in new barrels. Italy, Spain, New Zealand, Bulgaria, the Pacific north-west all also now make good Chardonnays.

Chasselas

A prolific and widely grown early-ripening grape with little flavour, also grown for eating. Best known as Fendant in Switzerland, Gutedel in Germany. Perhaps the same as Hungary's Leanyka and Romania's Feteasca.

Chenin Blanc

The leading white grape of the middle Loire (Vouvray, Layon, etc.). Wine can be dry or sweet (or very sweet), but always retains plenty of acidity—hence its popularity in California, where it can make fine wine, but is rarely so used. See also STEEN.

Clairette

A dull neutral grape formerly used in the s. of France.

Fendant

See CHASSELAS

Folle Blanche

High acid and little flavour makes it ideal for brandy. Known as Gros Plant in Brittany, Picpoul in Armagnac. Perhaps at its best in California.

Furmint

A grape of great character: the trade mark of Hungary both in Tokay and as vivid vigorous table wine with an appley flavour. Called Sipon in Yugoslavia.

Gewürztraminer (or Traminer)

The most pungent wine grape, distinctively spicy to smell and taste, with flavours often identified as being like rose petals or grapefruit. Wines are often rich and soft, even when fully dry. Best in Alsace; also good in Germany, eastern Europe, Australia, California, New Zealand.

Grüner Veltliner

An Austrian speciality. Round Vienna and in the Wachau and Weinviertel can be delicious: light but dry and lively. For drinking young.

Italian Riesling

Grown in n. Italy and all over central eastern Europe. Much inferior to German or Rhine Riesling with lower acidity, but a fair all-round grape. Alias Wälschriesling, Olaszreisling (but no longer legally labelled "Riesling").

Kerner

The most successful of a wide range of recent German varieties, largely made by crossing Riesling and Sylvaner (but in this case Riesling and [red] Trollinger). Early-ripening, flowery wine with good acidity. Popular in RHEINPFALZ, RHEINHESSEN, etc.

Malvasia

Known as Malmsey in Madeira, Malvasia in Italy, Malvoisie in France. Alias Vermentino. Also grown in Greece, Spain, W. Australia, eastern Europe. Makes rich brown wines or soft whites with superb potential, not often realized.

Müller-Thurgau

Dominant variety in Germany's Rheinhessen and Rheinpfalz; a cross between Riesling and Sylvaner. Ripens early to make soft flowery wines to drink young. Makes good sweet wines but dull dry ones. Grows well in New Zealand, Austria, England.

Muscadet (alias Melon de Bourgogne)

Makes light, very dry wines round Nantes in Brittany. They should not be sharp, but faintly salty, savoury and v. refreshing.

Muscat (many varieties)

Universally grown easily recognized pungent grape, mostly made into perfumed sweet wines, often fortified (as in France's VIN DOUX NATURELS). Muscat d'Alsace is unusual in being dry.

Palomino

Alias Listan. Makes all the best sherry.

Pedro Ximénez

Said to have come to s. Spain from Germany. Makes very strong wine in Montilla and Malaga. Used in blending sherry. Also grown in Australia, California, South Africa.

Pinot Blanc

A close relation of CHARDONNAY without its strength of character. Grown in Champagne, Alsace (increasingly), n. Italy (good sparkling wine), s. Germany, eastern Europe. Called Weissburgunder in German. California's 'Pinot Blanc' is apparently actually Muscadet.

Pinot Gris

Makes rather heavy, even "thick", full-bodied whites with a certain spicy style. Known as Tokay in Alsace, Tocai in n.e. Italy and Yugoslavia, Ruländer in Germany.

Pinot Noir

Superlative black grape (see under Grapes for red wine) used in Champagne and occasionally elsewhere (e.g. California) for making white wine, or a very pale pink "vin gris".

Riesling

Germany's finest grape, now planted round the world. Wine of brilliant sweet/acid balance, flowery in youth but maturing to subtle oily scents and flavours. Successful in Alsace (for dry wine), Austria, parts of eastern Europe, Australia (where it is widely grown), California, South Africa. Often called White, Johannisberg or Rhine Riesling.

Sauvignon Blanc

Very distinctive aromatic, herby and sometimes smoky scented wine, can be austere (on the upper Loire) or buxom (in Sauternes, where it is combined with SEMILLON, and parts of California). Also called Fumé Blanc or vice versa.

Scheurebe

Spicy-flavoured German Riesling × Silvaner cross, very successful in Rheinpfalz, esp. for Ausleses.

Semillon

The grape contributing the lusciousness to great Sauternes; subject to "noble rot" in the right conditions. Makes soft dry wine of great potential. Traditionally called "Riesling" in parts of Australia. Old Hunter Valley Semillon can be great wine.

Sercial

Makes the driest Madeira: where they claim it is really Riesling.

Seyval Blanc

French-made hybrid between French and American vines. Very hardy and attractively fruity. Popular and successful in the eastern States and England.

Steen South Africa's most popular white grape: good, lively, fruity wine. Said to be the Chenin Blanc of the Loire.

Sylvaner (Silvaner)

Germany's workhorse grape: wine rarely better than pleasant except in Franconia. Good in the Italian Tyrol and useful in Alsace. Very good as "Johannisberg" in Switzerland.

Tokay

See PINOT GRIS. Also a table grape in California and a supposedly Hungarian grape in Australia. The wine Tokay is made of FURMINT.

Traminer

See GEWÜRZTRAMINER

Trebbiano

Important grape of central Italy, used in Orvieto, Chianti, Soave, etc. Also grown in s. France as Ugni Blanc, and Cognac as "St-Emilion". Thin, neutral wine, really needs blending.

Ugni Blanc

See TREBBIANO

Verdelho

Madeira grape making excellent medium-sweet wine.

Verdicchio

Gives its name to good dry wine in central Italy.

Vernaccia

Grape grown in central and s. Italy and Sardinia for strong lively wine inclining towards sherry.

Viognier

Rare but remarkable grape of the Rhône valley, grown at Condrieu to make very fine soft and fragrant wine.

Welschriesling (or Wälschriesling)

See ITALIAN RIESLING

Weissburgunder

See PINOT BLANC

Grapes for red wine

Barbera
> One of several productive grapes of n. Italy, esp. Piemonte, giving dark, fruity, often sharp wine. Useful in blends in California.

Brunello
> S. Tuscan form of SANGIOVESE, splendid at Montalcino.

Cabernet Franc
> The lesser of two sorts of Cabernet grown in Bordeaux; the Cabernet of the Loire making Chinon, etc., and rosé.

Cabernet Sauvignon
> Grape of great character; spicy, herby and tannic. The first grape of the Médoc, also makes the best Californian, Australian, South American and eastern European reds. Its red wine always needs ageing and usually blending. Makes v. aromatic rosé.

Carignan
> By far the commonest grape of France, covering hundreds of thousands of acres. Prolific with dull but harmless wine. Also common in North Africa, Spain and California.

Cinsaut
> Common bulk-producing grape of s. France; in S. Africa crossed with PINOT NOIR to make Pinotage.

Dolcetto Source of soft, seductive dry red in Piemonte.

Gamay
> The Beaujolais grape: light very fragrant wines at their best young. Makes even lighter wine on the Loire and in Switzerland and Savoie. Known as Napa Gamay in California.

Gamay Beaujolais
> Not Gamay but a variety of PINOT NOIR grown in California.

Grenache
> Useful grape for strong and fruity but pale wine: good rosé. Grown in s. France, Spain, California. Usually blended.

Grignolino
> Makes one of the good cheap table wines of Piemonte.

Malbec (also called Cot)
> Minor in Bordeaux, major in Cahors and Argentina.

Merlot
> Adaptable grape making the great fragrant and rich wines of Pomerol and St-Emilion, an important element in Médoc reds, soft and strong in California, lighter but good in n. Italy, Italian Switzerland, Yugoslavia, Argentina, etc.

Nebbiolo (also called Spanna and Chiavennasca)
> Italy's best red grape, the grape of Barolo, Barbaresco, Gattinara and Valtellina. Intense, nobly fruity and perfumed wine but very tannic, taking years to mature.

Pinot Noir
> The glory of Burgundy's Côte d'Or, with scent, flavour, texture and body unmatched anywhere. Less happy elsewhere; makes light wines of no great distinction in Germany, Switzerland, Austria, Hungary. The great challenge to the winemakers of California and Australia. Shows great promise in Oregon.

Sangiovese
> The main red grape of Chianti and much of central Italy.

Spätburgunder
> German for PINOT NOIR, but a v. pale shadow of burgundy.

Syrah (alias Shiraz)
> The best Rhône red grape, with tannic purple wine, which can mature superbly. Very important as "Shiraz" in Australia.

Tempranillo
> The characteristic fine Rioja grape, called Ull de Lebre in Catalonia, Cencibel in La Mancha. Early-ripening.

Zinfandel
> Fruity adaptable grape peculiar to California. Also makes white.

Wine & Food

There are no rules or statutes about what wine goes with what food, but there is a vast body of accumulated experience which it is absurd to ignore, even while trying out new ideas.

This list of dishes and appropriate wines records many of the conventional combinations and suggests others that I personally have found good. But it is only a list of ideas intended to help you make quick decisions. Any of the groups of recommended wines could have been extended almost indefinitely, drawing on the whole world's wine list. In general I have stuck to the wines that are widely available, at the same time trying to ring the changes so that the same wines don't come up time and time again—as they tend to do in real life.

The stars refer to the rating system used throughout the book: see opposite Contents.

Before the Meal—Aperitifs

The traditional apéritif wines are either sparkling (epitomized by champagne) or fortified (epitomized by sherry). They are still the best, but avoid peanuts with them, they destroy wine flavours. Eat almonds instead. The current fashion for a glass of white wine before eating calls for something light and stimulating, dry but not acid, with a degree of character, such as:

France:
> Alsace Edelzwicker, Riesling or Sylvaner; Chablis; Muscadet; Sauvignon de Touraine; Graves Blanc; Mâcon Blanc; Crépy. Bugey, Haut-Poitou.

Germany:
> Any Kabinett wine or QbA. Choose a 'halbtrocken'—nearly dry.

Italy:
> Soave; Orvieto Secco; Frascati; Gavi; Pinot Bianco; Montecarlo; Vernaccia; Tocai; Lugano; Albana di Romagna.

Spain:
> Rioja Blanco Marqués de Caceres or Faustino V, or Albariño. But fino sherry, Manzanilla or Montilla is even better.

Portugal:
> Any vinho verde; Bucelas.

Eastern Europe:
> Leanyka, Welschriesling, Riesling, Chardonnay.

U.S.A.:
> Californian "Chablis"; Chenin Blanc; Riesling; French Colombard; Fumé Blanc; Gewürztraminer, or a good "house blend"; Riesling or Semillon from the Pacific north-west.

Australia:
> Barossa or Coonawarra Riesling. Houghton's white Burgundy.

South Africa:
> Steen is ideal.

England:
> Almost any is ideal.

References to these wines will be found in national A–Z sections.

First courses

Aïoli
> A thirst-quencher is needed with so much garlic. ★→★★ white Rhône, or Frascati, or Verdicchio, and mineral water.

Antipasto (see also Hors d'oeuvre)
> ★★ dry or medium white, preferably Italian (e.g. Soave) or light red, e.g. Valpolicella, Bardolino or young ★ Bordeaux.

Artichoke

    ★ red or rosé.

    vinaigrette ★ young red, e.g. Bordeaux, Côtes-du-Rhône.

    hollandaise ★ or ★★ full-bodied dry or medium white, e.g. Mâcon Blanc, Rheinpfalz, or a California "house blend".

Asparagus

    ★★→★★★ white burgundy or Chardonnay, or Corsican rosé.

Assiette anglaise (assorted cold meats)

    ★★ dry white, e.g. Chablis, Muscadet, Silvaner, Riesling.

Avocado

    with prawns, crab, etc. ★★→★★★ dry to medium white, e.g. Rheingau or Rheinpfalz Kabinett, Graves, California or Australian Chardonnay or Sauvignon, Cape Steen, or dry rosé.

    vinaigrette ★ light red, or manzanilla sherry.

Bisques

    ★★ dry white with plenty of body: Pinot Gris, Chardonnay. Fino sherry, or Montilla.

Bouillabaisse

    ★→★★ very dry white: Muscadet, Alsace Sylvaner, Entre-Deux-Mers, Pouilly Fumé, Cassis, Tuscan Trebbiano, Grechetto.

Carpaccio

    Seems to work well with the flavour of most wines, including ★★★ reds.

Caviare

    ★★★ champagne or iced vodka (or both).

Cheese fondue

    ★★ dry white: Fendant or Johannisberg du Valais, Grüner Veltliner, Alsace Riesling, N.Z. Sauvignon Blanc.

Chicken Liver Pâté

    Appetizing dry white, e.g. ★★ white Bordeaux, or light fruity red; Beaujolais, Gamay de Touraine, young Chianti or Valpolicella.

Clams and Chowders

    ★★ big-scale white, not necessarily bone dry: e.g. Rhône, Pinot Gris, Dry Sauternes, Napa Chardonnay.

Consommé

    ★★→★★★ medium-dry sherry, dry Madeira, Marsala, Montilla.

Crudités

    ★→★★ light red or rosé, e.g. Côtes-du-Rhône, Beaujolais, Minervois, Chianti, Zinfandel.

Eggs (see also Soufflés)

    These present difficulties: they clash with most wines and spoil good ones. So ★→★★ of whatever is going.

Empanadas

    ★→★★ Chilean or Argentine Cabernet, Zinfandel.

Escargots

    ★★ red or white of some substance: e.g. Burgundy, Côtes-du-Rhône, Chardonnay, Shiraz, etc.

Foie gras

    ★★★→★★★★ white. In Bordeaux they drink Sauternes. Others prefer vintage champagne or a late-harvest Gewürztraminer.

Gazpacho

    Sangria (see Spain) is refreshing, but to avoid too much liquid intake dry Manzanilla or Montilla is better.

Grapefruit

    If you must start a meal with grapefruit try port, Madeira or sweet sherry with it.

Gravlax

    Akvavit, or Grand Cru Chablis, or Californian or Australian Chardonnay.

Ham, raw

    See Prosciutto.

Herrings, raw or pickled
>Dutch gin or Scandinavian akvavit, and cold beer.

Hors d'oeuvres (see also Antipasto)
>★→★★ clean fruity sharp white: Sancerre or any Sauvignon, Alsace Sylvaner, Muscadet, Cape Steen—or young light red Bordeaux, Rhône or equivalent.

Mackerel, smoked
>★★→★★★ full-bodied tasty white: e.g. Gewürztraminer, Tokay d'Alsace or Chablis Premier Cru. Or Manzanilla sherry.

Mayonnaise
>Adds richness that calls for a contrasting bite in the wine. Côte Chalonnaise whites are good.

Melon
>Needs a strong sweet wine: ★★ Port, Bual Madeira, Muscat, Oloroso sherry or Vin doux naturel.

Minestrone
>★ red: Grignolino, Chianti, Zinfandel, Shiraz, etc.

Mushrooms à la Greque
>Robola from California or any hefty dry white, or fresh young red.

Omelettes
>See observations under Eggs.

Onion/Leek tart
>★→★★★ fruity dry white, e.g. Alsace Pinot Gris or Riesling. Mâcon-Villages of a good vintage, Jurançon, California or Australian Riesling.

Pasta
>★→★★★ red or white according to the sauce or trimmings, e.g.
>**with seafood sauce (vongole, etc.)** Verdicchio, Soave, Sauvignon.
>**meat sauce** Chianti, Montepulciano d'Abruzzo.
>**tomato sauce** Barbera or Sicilian or Yugoslav red.
>**cream sauce** Orvieto, Frascati or Italian Chardonnay.

Pâté
>★★ dry white: e.g. Mâcon-Villages, Graves, Fumé Blanc.

Peppers or aubergines (egg-plant), stuffed
>★★ vigorous red: e.g. Chianti, Dolcetto, Zinfandel.

Pizza
>Any ★★ dry Italian red or a ★★ Rioja, Australian Shiraz or California Zinfandel. Or Corbières or Roussillon.

Prawns or Shrimps
>★★→★★★ dry white: burgundy or Bordeaux, Chardonnay or Riesling. ("Cocktail sauce" kills any wine.)

Prosciutto with melon
>★★→★★★ full-bodied dry or medium white: e.g. Orvieto or Frascati, Pomino, Fendant, Grüner Veltliner, Alsace or California Gewürztraminer, Australian Riesling.

Quiches
>★→★★ dry white with body (Alsace, Graves, Sauvignon) or young red (e.g. Beaujolais-Villages), according to the ingredients.

Ratatouille
>★★ vigorous young red, e.g. Chianti, Zinfandel, Bulgarian or young red Bordeaux.

Salade niçoise
>★★ very dry not too light or flowery white, e.g. white (or rosé) Rhône or Corsican, Catalan white, Dão, California Sauvignon.

Salads
>As a first course, especially with blue cheese dressing, any dry and appetizing white wine. After a main course: no wine.
>N.B. Vinegar in salad dressings destroys the flavour of wine. If you want salad at a meal with fine wine, dress the salad with wine or a little lemon juice instead of vinegar.

Salami
>★→★★ powerfully tasty red or rosé: e.g. Barbera, young Zinfandel, Tavel or Ajaccio rosé, young Bordeaux.

Salmon, smoked

A dry but pungent white, e.g. fino sherry, Alsace Gewürz-traminer, Chablis Grand Cru. Vernaccia di San Gimignano.

Soufflés

As show dishes these deserve ★★→★★★ wines.

Fish Dry white, e.g. burgundy, Bordeaux, Alsace, Chard, etc.

Cheese Red burgundy or Bordeaux, Cabernet Sauvignon, etc.

Taramasalata

Calls for a rustic southern white of strong personality; not necessarily the Greek Retsina. Fino sherry works well.

Terrine

As for pâté, or the equivalent red; e.g. Beaune, Mercurey, Beaujolais-Villages, fairly young ★★ St-Emilion, California Cabernet or Zinfandel, Bulgarian or Chilean Cabernet, etc.

Tomato sauce (on anything)

The acidity of tomato sauce is no friend to fine wines. ★★ red will do. Try Chianti.

Trout, smoked

Sancerre, Pouilly Fumé, or California Fumé Blanc. Or Rully.

Fish

Abalone

★★→★★★ dry or medium white: e.g. Sauvignon Blanc, Chardon-nay, Pinot Grigio, Muscadet sur Lie.

Bass, striped

Same wine as for sole.

Cod A good neutral background for fine dry or medium whites, e.g. ★★→★★★ Chablis, Meursault, cru classé Graves, German Kabinett or dry Spätleses and their equivalents.

Coquilles St. Jacques

An inherently slightly sweet dish, best with medium-dry whites.

in cream sauces ★★★ German wines or a -Montrachet.

grilled or fried Hermitage Blanc, Gewürztraminer, California Chenin Blanc, Riesling or champagne.

Crab, cold, with salad

★★★ California or Rheinpfalz Riesling Kabinett or Spätlese.

Crab, softshell

★★★ Chardonnay.

Eel, jellied

NV champagne or a nice cup of tea.

smoked Either strong or sharp wine, e.g. fino sherry or Bourgogne Aligoté. Or schnapps.

Fish and Chips, fritto misto (or tempura)

★ white Bordeaux, Orvieto Secco, Koshu.

Haddock

★★→★★★ dry white with a certain richness: e.g. Meursault, California or Australian Chardonnay.

Herrings

Need a white with some acidity to cut their richness. Burgundy Aligoté or Gros Plant from Brittany or dry Sauvignon Blanc.

Kippers: a good cup of tea, preferably Ceylon (milk, no sugar).

Lamproie à la Bordelaise

★★ young red Bordeaux, St-Emilion, Pomerol or Fronsac.

Lobster or Crab

salad ★★→★★★★ white. Non-vintage champagne, Alsace Riesl-ing, Chablis Premier Cru, Condrieu.

richly sauced Vintage champagne, fine white burgundy, cru classé Graves, California or Australian Chardonnay, Rheinpfalz Spätlese, Hermitage Blanc.

Mackerel
  ★★ hard or sharp white: Sauvignon Blanc from Bergerac or Touraine, Gros Plant, vinho verde, white Rioja.

Mullet, red
  ★★ Mediterranean white, even Retsina, for the atmosphere.

Mussels
  ★→★★ Gros Plant, Muscadet, California "Chablis".

Oysters
  ★★→★★★ white. Champagne (non-vintage), Chablis or (better) Chablis Premier Cru, or Muscadet or Entre-Deux-Mers.

Salmon, fresh
  ★★★ fine white burgundy: Puligny- or Chassagne-Montrachet, Meursault, Corton-Charlemagne, Chablis Grand Cru, California, Idaho or Australian Chardonnay, or Rheingau Kabinett or Spätlese, California Riesling or equivalent.

Sardines, fresh grilled
  ★→★★ very dry white: e.g. vinho verde, Dão, Muscadet.

Scallops
  See Coquilles St. Jacques.

Shad ★★→★★★ white Graves or Meursault or Hunter Semillon.

Shellfish (general)
  Dry white with plain boiled shellfish, richer wines with richer sauces.

Shrimps, potted
  Fino sherry, Chablis, Gavi or New York Chardonnay.

Skate with black butter
  ★★ white with some pungency (e.g. Alsace Pinot Gris) or a clean one like Muscadet.

Sole, Plaice, etc.
  plain, grilled or fried An ideal accompaniment for fine wines: ★ up to ★★★★ white burgundy, or its equivalent.
  with sauce Depending on the ingredients: sharp dry wine for tomato sauce, fairly rich for Sole véronique, etc.

Sushi (and sashimi)
  Sparkling wines, incl. Californian, or Calif. or Australian Chardonnay or Sauvignon. Chablis Grand Cru.

Trout Delicate white wine, e.g. ★★★ Mosel.
  Smoked, a full-flavoured ★★→★★★ white: Gewürztraminer, Pinot Gris, Rhine Spätlese or Australian Hunter white.

Turbot
  Fine rich dry white, e.g. ★★★ Meursault or its California, Australian or New Zealand equivalent. Viognier from Condrieu.

Meat, Poultry, etc.

Barbecues
  ★★ red with a slight rasp, therefore young. Shiraz, Chianti, Zinfandel, Turkish Buzbag.

Beef, boiled
  ★★ red: e.g. Bordeaux (Bourg or Fronsac), Côtes-du-Rhône-Villages, Australian Shiraz or good Mâcon-Villages white.

Beef, roast
  An ideal partner for fine red wine. ★★→★★★★ red of any kind.

Beef stew
  ★★→★★★ sturdy red, e.g. Pomerol or St-Emilion, Hermitage, Shiraz, Calif. or Oregon Pinot Noir.

Beef Strogonoff
  ★★→★★★ suitably dramatic red: e.g. Barolo, Brunello, Valpolicella, Amarone, Hermitage, late-harvest Zinfandel.

Cassoulet
  ★★ red from s.w. France, e.g. Madiran, Cahors or Corbières, or Barbera or Zinfandel.

Chicken or Turkey, roast (or guinea fowl)

Virtually any wine, including your very best bottles of dry or medium white and finest old reds.

Chili con carne

★→★★ young red: e.g. Bull's Blood, Chianti, Mountain Red.

Chinese food

Canton or **Peking style** ★★→★★★★ dry to medium-dry white: e.g. Yugoslav "Riesling", Mâcon-Villages, California Chardonnay. Or NV Champagne.

Szechuan style Very cold beer.

Choucroute

Alsace Pinot Gris.

Cold meats

Generally taste better with full-flavoured white wine than red.

Confit d'Oie

★★→★★★ rather young and tannic red Bordeaux helps to cut the richness. Alsace Tokay or Gewürztraminer matches it.

Coq au Vin

★★→★★★★ red burgundy. In an ideal world one bottle of Chambertin in the dish, two on the table.

Corned beef hash

★★ Zinfandel, Chianti, Côtes-du-Rhône red.

Curry ★→★★ medium-sweet white, very cold: e.g. Orvieto abboccato, certain California Chenin Blancs, Yugoslav Traminer.

Duck or Goose

★★★ rather rich white, e.g. Rheinpfalz Spätlese or Alsace Réserve Exceptionelle, or ★★★ Bordeaux or burgundy.

Wild Duck ★★★ big-scale red: e.g. Hermitage, Châteauneuf-du-Pape, Calif. or S. African Cabernet, Australian Shiraz.

Frankfurters

★→★★ German or Austrian white, or Beaujolais. Or beer.

Game birds

Young birds plain roasted deserve the best red wine you can afford. With older birds in casseroles ★★→★★★ red, e.g. Gevrey-Chambertin, Pommard, Grand Cru St-Emilion, Napa Cab.

Game pie

(Hot) ★★★ red wine. (Cold) Equivalent white.

Goulash

★★ strong young red: e.g. Zinfandel, Bulgarian Cabernet.

Grouse See under Game birds

Ham ★★→★★★ fairly young red burgundy, e.g. Volnay, Savigny, Beaune, Corton, or a slightly sweet German white, e.g. a Rhine Spätlese, or a Tuscan red, or a lightish Cabernet.

Hamburger

★→★★ young red: e.g. Beaujolais, Corbières or Minervois, Chianti, Zinfandel, Kadarka from Hungary.

Hare Jugged hare calls for ★★→★★★ red with plenty of flavour: not-too-old burgundy or Bordeaux. The same for saddle.

Kebabs

★★ vigorous red: e.g. Greek Demestica, Turkish Buzbag, Bulgarian or Chilean Cabernet, Zinfandel.

Kidneys

★★→★★★ red: Pomerol or St-Emilion, Rhône, Barbaresco, Rioja, California, Spanish or Australian Cabernet.

Lamb cutlets or chops

As for roast lamb, but less grand.

Lamb, roast

One of the traditional and best partners for very good red Bordeaux—or its Cabernet equivalents from the New World.

Liver

★★→★★★ young red: Beaujolais-Villages, St-Joseph, Médoc, Italian Merlot, Zinfandel, Oregon Pinot Noir.

Meatballs

$\star\star\to\star\star\star$ red: e.g. Mercurey, Madiran, Rubesco, Dão, Bairrada, Zinfandel or Cabernet.

Mixed Grill

A fairly light easily swallowable red; $\star\star$ red Bordeaux from Bourg, Fronsac or Premières Côtes; Chianti; Bourgogne Passe-tout-grains.

Moussaka

$\star\to\star\star$ red or rosé: e.g. Naoussa, Chianti, Corbières, Côtes de Provence, Ajaccio or Patrimonio, California Burgundy.

Oxtail $\star\star\to\star\star\star$ rather rich red: e.g. St-Emilion or Pomerol, Burgundy, Barolo or Chianti Classico, Rioja Reserva, California or Coonawarra Cabernet or a dry Riesling Spätlese.

Paella $\star\star$ Young Spanish r., dry w. or rosé, e.g. Penedés or Rioja.

Partridge, pheasant

See under Game birds.

Pigeons or squabs

$\star\star\to\star\star\star\star$ red Bordeaux, Chianti Classico, Californian or Australian Cabernet.

Pork, roast

Pork is a good, rich, neutral background to very good white or red wine.

Rabbit $\star\to\star\star\star$ young red: Italian for preference.

Ris de veau See Sweetbreads.

Risotto

Pinot Grigio from Friuli, Gavi, youngish Semillon.

Sauerkraut Lager.

Sausages

The British banger requires a 3-year-old N. Italian Merlot. (A red wine, anyway.)

Shepherd's Pie

$\star\to\star\star$ rough and ready red seems most appropriate, but no harm would come to a good one.

Steak and Kidney Pie or Pudding

Red Rioja Reserva or mature $\star\star\to\star\star\star$ Bordeaux.

Steaks

Au poivre a fairly young $\star\star\star$ Rhône red or Cabernet.

Tartare $\star\star$ light young red: Beaujolais, Bergerac, Valpolicella.

Filet or Tournedos $\star\star\star$ red of any kind (but not old wines with Béarnaise sauce).

T-bone $\star\star\to\star\star\star$ reds of similar bone-structure: e.g. Barolo, Hermitage, Australian Cabernet or Shiraz.

Fiorentina (bistecca) Chianti Classico Riserva.

Ostrich South African Pinotage.

Stews and Casseroles

A lusty full-flavoured red, e.g. young Côtes-du-Rhône, Corbières, Barbera, Shiraz, Zinfandel, etc.

Sweetbreads

These tend to be a grand dish, suggesting a grand wine, e.g. $\star\star\star$ Rhine Riesling or Franken Silvaner Spätlese, or well-matured Bordeaux or Burgundy, depending on the sauce.

Tongue Ideal for favourite bottles of any red or white.

Tripe $\star\to\star\star\star$ red: Corbières, Mâcon Rouge, etc., or rather sweet white, e.g. Liebfraumilch. Better: W. Australian "white Burgundy".

Veal, roast

A good neutral background dish for any fine old red which may have faded with age, or a $\star\star\star$ German white.

Venison

$\star\star\star$ big-scale red (Rhône, Bordeaux of a grand vintage) or rather rich white (Rheinpfalz Spätlese or Tokay d'Alsace).

Vitello tonnato

Light red (Valpolicella, Beaujolais) served cool.

Wiener Schnitzel

　　★★→★★★ light red from the Italian Tyrol (Alto Adige) or the Médoc: or Austrian Riesling, Grüner Veltliner or Gumpolds-kirchener.

Cheese

　　Very strong cheese completely masks the flavour of wine. Only serve fine wine with mild cheeses in peak condition.

Bleu de Bresse, Dolcelatte, Gorgonzola, Stilton

　　Need emphatic accompaniment: young ★★ red wine (Barbera, Dolcetto, Moulin-à-Vent, etc.) or sweet white — or port.

Cream cheeses: Brie, Camembert, Bel Paese, Edam, etc.

　　In their mild state marry with any good wine, red or white.

English cheeses

　　Can be either mild or strong and acidic. The latter need sweet and strong wine.

　　Cheddar, Cheshire, Wensleydale, Gloucester, etc. If mild, claret. If strong, ruby, tawny or vintage-character (not vintage) port, old dry oloroso sherry, or a very big red: Hermitage, Châteauneuf-du-Pape, Barolo, etc.

Goat cheeses

　　★★→★★★ white wine of marked character, either dry (e.g. Sancerre) or sweet (e.g. Monbazillac, Sauternes).

Hard Cheese, Parmesan, Gruyère, Emmenthal old Gouda

　　Full-bodied dry whites, e.g. Tokay d'Alsace or Vernaccia, or fino or amontillado sherry.

Roquefort, Danish Blue

　　Are so strong-flavoured that only the youngest, biggest or sweetest wines stand a chance. Old dry sherries have the necessary horse-power.

Desserts

Apple pie, apple strudel

　　★★→★★★ sweet German, Austrian or Hungarian white.

Apples, Cox's Orange Pippins

　　Vintage port (55, 60, 63, 66, 70, 75).

Bread and butter pudding

　　10-y-o. Barsac from a good château.

Cakes Bual or Malmsey Madeira, Oloroso or cream sherry.

Cheesecake

　　★★→★★★ sweet white from Vouvray or Coteaux du Layon.

Chocolate cake, mousse, soufflés

　　Huxelrebe Auslese or California orange muscat.

Christmas pudding, mince pies

　　Sweet champagne or Asti Spumante, or cream sherry.

Creams and Custards

　　★★→★★★ Sauternes, Monbazillac or similar golden white.

Crème brûlée

　　The most luxurious dish, demanding ★★★→★★★★ Sauternes or Rhine Beerenauslese, or the best Madeira or Tokay.

Crêpes Suzette

　　Sweet champagne or Asti Spumante.

Fruit flans (i.e. peach, raspberry)

　　★★★ Sauternes, Monbazillac or sweet Vouvray or Anjou.

Fruit, fresh

　　Sweet Coteaux du Layon white, light sweet muscat (e.g. California).

Raspberries

　　(no cream, little sugar) Excellent with fine reds.

Rhubarb

　　Rhubarb wine, I suppose.

Fruit salads, orange salad

 No wine.

Nuts Oloroso sherry, Bual, Madeira, vintage or tawny port, Vinsanto.

Sorbets, ice-creams

 No wine.

Stewed fruits, i.e. apricots, pears, etc.

 Sweet Muscatel: e.g. Muscat de Beaumes de Venise, Moscato di Pantelleria or from Tarragona.

Strawberries and cream

 ★★★ Sauternes or Vouvray Moelleux.

Wild strawberries Serve with ★★★ red Bordeaux poured over them and in your glass (no cream).

Summer Pudding

 Fairly young Sauternes of a good vintage (e.g. 75, 76, 79, 80).

Treacle Tart

 Too sweet for any wine but a treacly Malmsey Madeira.

Trifle No wine: should be sufficiently vibrant with sherry.

Sweet Soufflés

 Sweet Vouvray or Coteaux du Layon. Sweet Champagne.

Zabaglione

 Light gold Marsala.

Savouries

Generally highly seasoned, these are not ideal partners for the last glass of a fine wine. But **Cheese straws** make an admirable meal-ending with a final glass (or bottle) of a particularly good red wine.

Temperature

No single aspect of serving wine makes or mars it so easily as getting the temperature right. White wines almost invariably taste dull and insipid served warm and red wines have disappointingly little scent or flavour served cold. The chart below gives an indication of what is generally found to be the most satisfactory temperature for serving each class of wine.

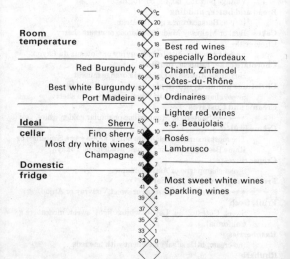

	°F	°C	
	68	20	
Room	66	19	
temperature	64	18	Best red wines
	63	17	especially Bordeaux
Red Burgundy	62	16	Chianti, Zinfandel
	59	15	Côtes-du-Rhône
Best white Burgundy	57	14	
Port Madeira	55	13	Ordinaires
	54	12	Lighter red wines
Ideal Sherry	52	11	e.g. Beaujolais
cellar Fino sherry	50	10	Rosés
Most dry white wines	48	9	Lambrusco
Champagne	46	8	
Domestic	45	7	
fridge	43	6	Most sweet white wines
	41	5	Sparkling wines
	39	4	
	37	3	
	35	2	
	33	1	
	32	0	

A little learning . . .

The last fifteen years have seen a revolution in wine technology. They have also heard a revolution in wine-talk—and the beginnings of a reaction. Attempts to express the characters of wine used to get no further than such vague terms as "fruity" and "full-bodied". Then came the demand for sterner, more scientific, stuff: the jargon of laboratory analysis. This hard-edge wine-talk is very briefly explained below.

The most frequent references are to the ripeness of grapes at picking; the resultant alcohol and sugar content of the wine; various measures of its acidity; the amount of sulphur dioxide used as a preservative, and the amount of "dry extract"—the sum of all the things that give wine its characteristic flavours.

Currently the fashion is for analogues with a quasi-poetic effect: "Scents of apricots, raspberries, leather; flavours of plum and truffle, shading to tar with a hint of fish-glue". Anybody can play. Few can play well.

The **sugar** in wine is mainly glucose and fructose, with traces of arabinose, xylose and other sugars that are not fermentable by yeast, but can be attacked by bacteria. Each country has its own system for measuring the sugar content or ripeness of grapes, known as the "**must-weight**". The chart below relates the three principal ones (German, French and American) to each other, to specific gravity, and to the potential alcohol of the wine if all the sugar is fermented.

Specific Gravity	°O °Oechsle	Baumé	Brix	% Potential Alcohol v/v
1.065	65	8.8	15.8	8.1
1.070	70	9.4	17.0	8.8
1.075	75	10.1	18.1	9.4
1.080	80	10.7	19.3	10.0
1.085	85	11.3	20.4	10.6
1.090	90	11.9	21.5	11.3
1.095	95	12.5	22.5	11.9
1.100	100	13.1	23.7	12.5
1.105	105	13.7	24.8	13.1
1.110	110	14.3	25.8	13.8
1.115	115	14.9	26.9	14.4
1.120	120	15.5	28.0	15.0

Residual sugar is the sugar left after fermentation has finished or been artificially stopped, measured in grammes per litre.

Alcohol content (mainly ethyl alcohol) is expressed as a percentage by volume of the total liquid.

Acidity is both fixed and volatile. **Fixed acidity** consists principally of tartaric, malic and citric acids which are all found in the grape, and lactic and succinic acids, which are produced during fermentation. **Volatile acidity** consists mainly of acetic acid, which is rapidly formed by bacteria in the presence of oxygen. A small amount of volatile acidity is inevitable and attractive. With a larger amount the wine becomes "pricked"—i.e. starts to turn to vinegar.

Total acidity is fixed and volatile acidity combined. As a rule of thumb for a well-balanced wine it should be in the region of 1 gramme/thousand for each 10°Oechsle (see above).

pH is a measure of the strength of the acidity, rather than its volume. The lower the figure the more acid. Wine normally ranges in pH from 2.8 to 3.8. Winemakers in hot climates can have problems getting the pH low enough. Lower pH gives better colour, helps prevent bacterial spoilage, allows more of the SO_2 to be free and active as a preservative.

Sulphur dioxide (SO_2) is added to prevent oxidation and other accidents in wine-making. Some of it combines with sugars, etc., and is known as "bound". Only the "**free SO_2**" that remains in the wine is effective as a preservative. **Total SO_2** is controlled by law according to the level of residual sugar: the more sugar the more SO_2 needed.

France

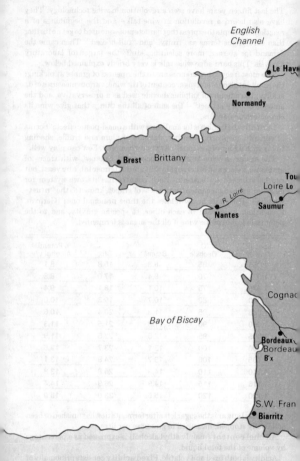

English Channel

Le Hav

Normandy

Brest • Brittany

R. Loire

Nantes

Tou

Loire Lo

Saumur

Cognac

Bay of Biscay

Bordeaux
Bordeau
B'x

S.W. Fran

Biarritz

Spain

France makes every kind of wine, and invented most of them. Tens of thousands of properties make wine of all complexions over a large part of her surface. This is a guide to the best known of them and their producers: the essential information in identifying good, authentic wines.

All France's best wine regions (producing about 20% of all her wine) have Appellations Contrôlées, which may apply to a single small vineyard or a whole large district. The system varies from region to region, with Burgundy on the whole having the smallest and most precise appellations, grouped into larger units by complicated formulae, and Bordeaux having the widest and most general appellations, in which it is the particular property (or "château") that matters. In between lie an infinity of variations.

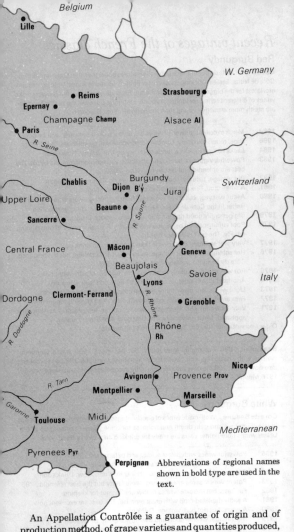

Abbreviations of regional names shown in bold type are used in the text.

An Appellation Contrôlée is a guarantee of origin and of production method, of grape varieties and quantities produced, but only partially one of quality. All "A.C." wines are officially tasted, but many of shoddy quality get through the net.

Appellations therefore help to identify a wine and indicate that it comes from a major area. They are the first thing to look for on a label. But the next is the name of the maker.

Wine regions without the overall quality and traditions required for an appellation can be ranked as Vins Délimités de Qualité Supérieure (VDQS), or (a third rank, created largely to encourage the improvement of mediocre wines in the south of France) Vins de Pays. VDQS wines are almost always good value, on the Avis principle. Vins de Pays are increasingly worth trying. They include some brilliant originals and often offer France's best value for money.

Recent vintages of the French classics

Red Burgundy

Côte d'Or Côte de Beaune reds generally mature sooner than the bigger wines of the Côte de Nuits. Earliest drinking dates are for lighter commune wines: Volnay, Beaune, etc. latest for the biggest wines of Chambertin, Romanée, etc. Different growers make wines of different styles, for longer or shorter maturing, but even the best burgundies are much more attractive young than the equivalent red Bordeaux.

1986	Much excellent, powerful wine; but some, picked too early, will be poor.
1985	Ripe, round and juicy. Concentrated wines will be splendid. '89–2000.
1984	Lacks natural ripeness; tends to be dry and/or watery. Now–'92.
1983	Powerful, vigorous, tannic and attractive vintage, compromised by rot. The best are splendid, but be careful. Now–2000.
1982	Big vintage, pale but round. Best in Côte de Beaune. Drink soon.
1981	A small crop, ripe but picked in rain. Disappointing.
1980	A late, wet year, but attractive wines from the best growers who avoided rot. Better in the Côte de Nuits. Keep (only) the best another year or two.
1979	Big generally good ripe vintage with weak spots. Drink up.
1978	Poor summer saved by miraculous autumn. A small vintage of outstanding quality. The best will live 15 years.
1977	Very wet summer. Better wine than expected, but drink up.
1976	Hot summer, excellent vintage. As usual great variations, but the best (esp. Côte de Beaune) rich and long-lived—to 1990.
1975	Rot was rife, particularly in the Côte de Beaune. Mostly very poor.
1974	Another big wet vintage; even the best light and lean. Drink up.
1973	Light wines, but many fruity and delicate. Most are already too old.
1972	Firm and full of character, ageing well. Few need keeping longer now.
1971	Very powerful and impressive wines, not as long-lasting as they first appeared. Most now ready. The best have 4 or 5 years ahead.

Older fine vintages: '69, '66, '64, '62, '61, '59 (all mature).

Beaujolais 1986 was highly satisfactory, but not great. 1985 was a wonderful vintage, with Crus to keep still. 1984 was fair, but should be drunk. 1983 was excellent, also now ready. 1982 is now too old. Generally avoid older vintages except possibly 1976 Moulin à Vent.

White Burgundy

Côte de Beaune Well-made wines of good vintages with plenty of acidity as well as fruit will improve and gain depth and richness for some years—anything up to ten. Lesser wines from lighter years are ready for drinking after two or three years.

1986	Powerful wines with better acidity and balance than '85.
1985	Very ripe; many wines are too soft; be careful. Now–'95.
1984	Some well-balanced wines; most rather lean or hollow. Drink soon.
1983	Potent wines; some exaggerated, some faulty but the best splendid. –'95.
1982	Fat, tasty but delicate whites of low acidity, not for keeping.
1981	A sadly depleted crop with great promise. The best are excellent now.
1980	A weak, but not bad, vintage. Drink up.
1979	Big vintage. Overall good and useful, not great. Drink soon.
1978	Very good wines, firm and well-balanced. Keep only the best.
1977	Rather light; some well-balanced and good. Drink up.
1976	Hot summer, rather heavy wines; good but not for keeping longer.
1975	Whites did much better than reds. Chablis best, but all now ready.
1974	Never exciting. Avoid now.
1973	Very attractive, fruity, typical and plentiful. Drink up.
1972	High acidity, but plenty of character. All are now ready to drink.
1971	Great power and style, some almost too rich, but the best have good balance. Small crop. Top wines are now wonderful.

The white wines of the Mâconnais (Pouilly-Fuissé, St Véran, Macon-Villages) follow a similar pattern, but do not last as long. They are more appreciated for their freshness than their richness.

Chablis Grand Cru Chablis of vintages with both strength and acidity can age superbly for up to ten years. Premiers Crus proportionately less. Drink other Chablis young.

1986	A splendid, big vintage. Now–1995.
1985	Good but often low-acid wines. The best Grands and Premiers Crus will age 6 years.
1984	A small vintage. Most too feeble to last.
1983	Superb vintage if not over-strong. The best will improve until '93.
1982	Charming light wines. Good value. Not to keep.
1981	Small, concentrated and fine harvest. Keeping well. –'90.
1980	More successful than the rest of Burgundy. Drink up.
1979	Very big crop. Good easy wines, not for storing. Drink soon.
1978	Excellent wines now passing their peak.

Red Bordeaux

Médoc/red Graves For some wines bottle-age is optional: for these it is indispensable. Minor châteaux from light vintages need only two or three years, but even modest wines of great years can improve for fifteen years or so, and the great châteaux of these years need double that time.

1986	Another splendid (and huge) heatwave harvest. Most will probably be superior to '85.
1985	Very good vintage, in a heatwave. Some great wines. '89–2010.
1984	Only fair. Little Merlot but good ripe Cabernet. Generally overpriced. –'95?
1983	A classic vintage: abundant tannin with fruit to balance it. –2010.
1982	Made in a heatwave. Huge rich strong wines which promise a long life. Only open petits châteaux now.
1981	Admirable despite rain. Not rich, but balanced and fine. Now–'98.
1980	Small, late harvest, ripe but rained-on. Many delicious light wines but few exciting ones. Drink now–'90.
1979	Abundant harvest of good average quality. Now–'95.
1978	A miracle vintage: magnificent long warm autumn saved the day. Some superb wines. Now–2000.
1977	Pleasant light wine, many better than 1974. Now–'87.
1976	Excessively hot, dry summer; rain just before vintage. Generally very good, maturing rather quickly. Now–'95.
1975	A very fine vintage, with deep colour, high sugar content and (sometimes excessive) tannin. For long keeping. "Petits Châteaux" are now ready.
1974	Oceans of disappointing light wines. Be very careful.
1973	A huge vintage, attractive young and still giving pleasure. Now or soon.
1972	High acidity from unripe grapes. Now.
1971	Small crop. Less fruity than '70 and less consistent. All are ready to drink.
1970	Big excellent vintage with scarcely a failure. Now–'95.
1969/68	Avoid them both.
1967	Never seductive, but characterful in its maturity. Drink soon.
1966	A very fine vintage with depth, fruit and tannin. Now–'90.

Older fine vintages: '62, '61, '59, '55, '53, '52, '50, '49, '48, '47, '45, '29, '28.

St-Emilion/Pomerol

1986	A prolific vintage; quality depends on the grower's restraint.
1985	One of the great years, with a long future. –2010.
1984	A sad story. Most of the crop wiped out in spring. Not for laying down.
1983	Conditions were ideal. Some growers prefer this vintage to 1982.
1982	Enormously rich and concentrated wines, most excellent. –2000+.
1981	A very good vintage, if not as great as it first seemed. Now–'95+.
1980	A poor Merlot year; very variable quality. Choose carefully. Soon.
1979	A rival to '78; in most cases even better. Now–'95.
1978	Fine wines, but some lack flesh. Now–'92.
1977	Very wet summer. Mediocre with few exceptions. Drink up.
1976	Very hot, dry summer and early vintage, but vintage rain made complications. Some excellent but not for very long life. Drink from now on.
1975	Most St-Emilions good, the best superb. Frost in Pomerol cut crops and made splendid concentrated wine. Now–2000.
1974/73/72	All need drinking soon, if at all.
1971	On the whole better than Médocs but generally now ready.
1970	Glorious weather and beautiful wines with great fruit and strength throughout the district. Very big crop. Now–'90s.

Older fine vintages: '67, '66, '64, '61, '59, '53, '52, '49, '47, '45.

Ackerman-Laurance

The oldest champagne-method house of the Loire, at SAUMUR. Fine *Crémant* de Loire.

Ajaccio Corsica r. p. or w. dr. [★→★★] 84 85' 86

The capital of Corsica. A.C. for some v. good SCIACARELLO.

Aligoté Second-rank burgundy white grape and its wine, often agreeably sharp and fruity and with considerable local character when young. BOUZERON (A.C.) makes the best.

Aloxe-Corton B'y. r. or w. ★★★ 69 71 76 78 79 80 82 83 84 85 86

Northernmost village of CÔTE DE BEAUNE: best v'yds.: CORTON (red) and CORTON-CHARLEMAGNE (white). Village wines (called Aloxe-Corton) are lighter but can be v.g. value.

Alsace Al. w. or (r.) [★★] 71 76 81 82 83' 84 85' 86

Aromatic, fruity dry white of Germanic character from French Rhineland. Normally sold by grape variety (RIESLING, GEWÜRZ-TRAMINER, etc.). Matures well up to 5, even 10, years.

Alsace Grand Cru [★★★] 71 76 81 82 83' 84 85 86

Appellation restricted to about 30 of the best named v'yds.

Alsace Grand Vin or Réserve

Wine with minimum 11° natural alcohol.

Amance, Marcel See MAUFOUX, PROSPER

Ampeau, Robert

Leading grower and specialist in MEURSAULT, POMMARD, etc.

Anjou Lo. (r.) p. or w. (sw. dr. or sp.) [★→★★★] 76 78 81 82 83 84 85 86

Very various Loire wines, incl. good CABERNET rosé, luscious COTEAUX DU LAYON. Maturity depends on style.

Anjou-Côteaux de la Loire

A.C. for CHENIN BLANC whites, incl. the notable SAVENNIÈRES.

Appellation Contrôlée ("A.C." or "A.O.C.")

Government control of origin and production of all the best French wines (see France Introduction).

Apremont Savoie w. dr. [★★] D.Y.A.

One of the best villages of SAVOIE for pale delicate whites, recently including CHARDONNAY.

Arbin Savoie r. ★★ Drink at 1–2 years

Deep-coloured lively red of Mondeuse grapes, like a good LOIRE Cabernet.

Arbois Jura r. p. or w. (dr. sp.) ★★ D.Y.A.

Various good and original light wines; speciality VIN JAUNE.

l'Ardèche, Coteaux de Central France r. (w. dr.) [★→★★] D.Y.A.

Light country reds, the best made of SYRAH. A useful change from BEAUJOLAIS. Also remarkable burgundy-like CHARDONNAY from LOUIS LATOUR.

Armagnac

Region of s.w. France famous for its excellent brandy, a fiery spirit of rustic character. The red wine of the area is MADIRAN.

Auxey-Duresses B'y. r. or w. [★★→★★★] 76 78 79 82 83 85 86

Second-rank (but v. pretty) CÔTE DE BEAUNE village: has affinities with VOLNAY and MEURSAULT. Best estates: Duc de Magenta, Prunier, Roy, HOSPICES DE BEAUNE Cuvée Boillot.

Avize Champ. ★★★★

One of the best white-grape villages of CHAMPAGNE.

Ay Champ. ★★★★

One of the best black-grape villages of CHAMPAGNE.

Ayala NV "Château d'Ay" 75 76 79 and Blanc de Blancs 79

Once-famous Ay-based old-style champagne concern. To watch.

Bandol Prov. r. p. or (w.) ★★★ 76 78 80 81 82 83 84 85

Little coastal region near Toulon with strong tasty reds from the Mourvèdre grape; esp. Ch. Vannières, Domaine Tempier.

Banyuls Pyr. br. sw. ★★ normally NV

One of the best VIN DOUX NATURELS (fortified sweet red wines) of the s. of France. Not unlike port.

Bar-sur-Aube Champ
> Secondary area to the s. Some good lighter wines.

Barancourt Cramant NV, Cramant Grand Cru **76 78 79 80** 81, Bouzy
Brut, Bouzy **81**, Rosé NV
> Grower at Bouzy making fine full-bodied champagnes. Pricey.

Barsac B'x. w. sw. **★★→ ★★★** **70 71 75 76′ 78 79′ 80 81 82 83′ 84 85**
> Neighbour of SAUTERNES with similar superb golden wines, often
> less rich and more racy. Top ch'x.: CLIMENS and COUTET.

Barton & Guestier
> Bordeaux shipper since 18th century, now owned by Seagram's.

Bâtard-Montrachet B'y. w. dr. **★★★★** **71 76 78 81 82 83 84 85 86**
> Neighbour of MONTRACHET, the top white burgundy. Should be
> v. long-lived and intense in flavour. Top growers incl. LEFLAIVE,
> BOUCHARD PÈRE, Gagnard, Morey.

Baumard, Domaine des
> Leading grower of Anjou wine, especially SAVENNIÈRES and
> COTEAUX DU LAYON (Clos Ste Catherine).

Béarn s.w. France r. p. or w. dr. **★** D.Y.A.
> Minor appellation of growing local (Basque country) interest,
> esp. wines from the coop. of Sallies de Béarn-Bellocq.

Beaujolais B'y. r. (p. w.) **★** D.Y.A.
> The simple appellation of the big Beaujolais region: light short-
> lived fruity red.

Beaujolais de l'année
> The Beaujolais of the latest vintage, until the next.

Beaujolais Primeur (or Nouveau)
> The same made in a hurry (often only 4 – 5 days fermenting) for
> release at midnight on the third Wednesday in November. Often
> crude and sharp. BEAUJOLAIS-VILLAGES *should* be a better bet.

Beaujolais Supérieur B'y. r. (w.) **★** D.Y.A.
> Beaujolais 1° of natural alcohol stronger than the 9° minimum.
> Since sugar is almost always added this means little.

Beaujolais-Villages B'y. r. **★★ 85 86**
> Wine from the better (northern) half of Beaujolais, stronger and
> tastier than plain Beaujolais. The 9 (easily) best "villages" are
> the "crus": FLEURIE, BROUILLY, etc. Of the 30 others the best lie
> around Beaujeu. The crus cannot be released "en primeur"
> before December 15th. They are best kept till spring (or longer).

Beaumes de Venise Rh. (r. p.) br. sw. **★★★** NV
> Sometimes France's best dessert MUSCAT, from the s. Côtes-du-
> Rhône; can be high-flavoured, subtle, lingering (e.g. Domaine de
> Coyeux). The red and rosé from the cooperative are also good.

Beaune B'y. r. or (w. dr.) **★★★ 71 76 78′ 80 82 83′ 84** 85 86
> Middle-rank classic burgundy. Négociants' "CLOS" wines
> (usually "Premier Cru") are often best. "Beaune du Château" is
> a (good) brand of BOUCHARD PÈRE. V'yds incl.: Grèves,
> Bressandes, Teurons, Marconnets, Fèves.

Becker, Caves J.
> Proud old family at Zellenberg, ALSACE.

Bégadan
> Leading village of the n. MEDOC, with commendable coop (Cave
> St. Jean), and ch'x incl. La Tour de By, Vieux-Ch-Landon,
> Greysac, Laujac, Patache d'Aux.

Bellet Prov. p. r. w. dr. **★★★**
> Highly fashionable, much above average, local wine from near
> Nice. Small production. Generally overpriced.

Bergerac Dordogne r. or w. sw. or dr. **★★** **82 83 84** (w.) 85
> Light-weight, often tasty, Bordeaux-style. Drink young, the
> white very young. See also Pécharmant.

Besserat de Bellefon Cuvée Blanc de Blancs, NV, **71 73 75 77 78 79** 82,
Rosé **79**, Brut Intégral **79**
> Rising champagne house for fine light wines, esp. CRÉMANT.

Beyer, Leon

Ancient ALSACE family wine business at Eguisheim making forceful dry wines that need ageing at least 2–3 yrs.

Bichot, Maison Albert

BEAUNE-based grower and merchant. V'yds in CHAMBERTIN, CLOS DE VOUGEOT, RICHEBOURG, etc., and Domaine Long-Depaquit in CHABLIS. Said to be the biggest B'y exporter.

Billecart-Salmon NV **75 76 78 79** 82, Rosé NV

Good small champagne house. Fresh-flavoured wines.

Bize, Simon

Admirable grower at SAVIGNY-LES-BEAUNE.

Blagny B'y. r. or w. dr. |****→*****| **76 78 81** w. **82 83 84** (w.) **85 86**

Hamlet between MEURSAULT and PULIGNY-MONTRACHET; affinities with both and VOLNAY for reds. Ages well. Growers incl. LATOUR, AMPEAU, Matrot.

Blanc de Blancs

Any white wine made from (only) white grapes, esp. CHAMPAGNE, which is usually made of black and white. *Not* an indication of quality.

Blanc de Noirs White (or sl. pink or 'blush') wine made from black grapes.

Blanck, Marcel

High-quality Alsace grower at Kientzheim.

Blanquette de Limoux Midi w. dr. sp. |******| normally NV

Good bargain sparkler from near Carcassonne made by a version of the MÉTHODE CHAMPENOISE. Very dry and clean.

Blaye B'x. r. or w. dr. ***→**** **81 82 83** 85 86

Your daily Bordeaux from e. of the Gironde. PREMIÈRES CÔTES DE BLAYE are better.

Boisset, Jean Claude

Dynamic Burgundy merchant/grower at NUITS ST GEORGES.

Bollinger NV "Special Cuvée", Grande Année **69 70 73 75 76 79** 82, Année Rare **73 75**, Rosé 81 82

Top champagne house, at AY. Dry full-flavoured style. Luxury wines "R.D." **73 75 76** and "Vieilles Vignes Françaises" **69 70 75 79 80** 81 from ungrafted vines.

Bommes

Village of SAUTERNES. Best ch'x.: LATOUR-BLANCHE, LAFAURIE-PEYRAGUEY, etc.

Bonneau du Martray, Domaine

Major producer (with 22 acres) of CORTON-CHARLEMAGNE of the highest quality; also admirable red CORTON.

Bonnes Mares B'y. r. |********| **66 69 71 76** 78' **79 80 82** 83' 84 85 86

37-acre Grand Cru between CHAMBOLLE-MUSIGNY and MOREY-SAINT-DENIS. Sometimes (not often) better than CHAMBERTIN.

Bonnezeaux Lo. w. sw. |*******|**76 78 81 82 84** 85 86

Unusual fruity/acidic wine from CHENIN BLANC grapes, the best of COTEAUX DU LAYON.

Bordeaux B'x. r. or (p.) or w. *** 81 82 83** 85 (for ch'x. see p. 54)

Basic catch-all appellation for low-strength Bordeaux wine.

Bordeaux Supérieur ***→****

Ditto, with slightly more alcohol.

Bordeaux Côtes-de-Francs B'x. r. or w. dr. |*****| **82 83** 85 86

Fringe Bordeaux from east of ST-EMILION. Increasingly attractive light wines, esp. from ch'x Puygueraud, de Belcier.

Borie-Manoux

Admirable Bordeaux shippers and château-owners, owned by the Castéja family. Ch'x. incl. BATAILLEY, HAUT BAGES-MON-PELOU, DOMAINE DE L'EGLISE, TROTTEVIEILLE, BEAU-SITE.

Bouchard Aîné

Famous and long-established burgundy shipper and grower with 62 acres in BEAUNE, MERCUREY, etc.

Bouchard Père et Fils
    Important burgundy shipper (est. 1731) and grower with 209 acres of excellent v'yds., mainly in the CÔTE DE BEAUNE, and cellars at the Château de Beaune. Reliable quality.

Bourg B'x. r. or (w. dr.) ★★ 81 82 83 85 86
    Meaty, un-fancy claret from e. of the Gironde. CÔTES DE BOURG are better.

Bourgogne B'y. r. (p.) or w. dr. ★★ 83 85 86
    Catch-all appellation for burgundy, but with theoretically higher standards than basic BORDEAUX. Light but often good flavour. BEAUJOLAIS crus can also be sold as Bourgogne.

Bourgogne Grand Ordinaire B'y. r. or (w.) ★ D.Y.A.
    The lowest burgundy appellation for Gamay wines. Rare.

Bourgogne Passe-tout-grains B'y. r. or (p.) 🔲 Age 1–2 years
    Often enjoyable junior burgundy. ⅓ PINOT NOIR and ⅔ GAMAY grapes mixed in the vat. Not as "heady" as BEAUJOLAIS.

Bourgueil Lo. r. ★★★ 76′ 81 82 83′ 85 86
    Normally delicate fruity CABERNET red from Touraine, the best from St. Nicolas de Bourgueil. Rich in exceptional years.

Bouvet-Ladubay Major producer of sparkling SAUMUR, controlled by TAITTINGER. Excellent CREMANT de Loire.

Bouzeron Village of the CÔTE CHALONNAISE distinguished for the only single-village appellation ALIGOTÉ.

Bouzy Rouge Champ. r. ★★★ 82 83 85 86
    Still red wine from famous black-grape CHAMPAGNE village. Like light burgundy, ageing early.

Brédif, Marc
    One of the most important growers and traders of VOUVRAY.

Brouilly B'y. r. ★★★ 85 86
    One of the 9 best CRUS of BEAUJOLAIS: fruity, round, refreshing. One year in bottle is enough. Ch. de la Chaize is top estate.

Brut Term for the driest wines of CHAMPAGNE until recently, when some completely unsweetened wines have become available as "Brut Intégrale", "Brut non-dosé", "Brut zéro" etc.

Bugey Savoie w. dr. or sp. ★→ ★★ D.Y.A.
    District with a variety of light sparkling, still or half-sparkling wines. Grapes incl. Roussette (or Roussanne) and v.g. CHARD.

Buzet s.w. France r. or w. dr. ★★ 81 82 83 85 86
    Good Bordeaux-style wines from just s.e. of Bordeaux. Promising area with well-run cooperative. Best wine: Cuvée Napoleon.

Cabernet See Grapes for red wine

Cabernet d'Anjou Lo. p. ★→ ★★ D.Y.A.
    Delicate, often rather sweet, grapy rosé.

Cahors s.w. France r. ★→ ★★ 75 78 79 80 81 82 83 85′ 86
    Traditionally hard "black" wine, now made more like Bordeaux, but can be full-bodied and increasingly distinct. Top growers: Baldés, Jouffreau, Vigouroux (esp. Ch. de Haute-Serre), Ch. de Caix, Ch. Larroze.

Cairanne Rh. r. p. or w. dr. ★★ 80 81 82 83 84 85 86
    Village of CÔTES-DU-RHÔNE-VILLAGES. Good solid wines, esp. from Dom. Rabasse-Charavin.

Calvet Famous old shippers of Bordeaux and Burgundy, now owned by Whitbread.

Canard-Duchêne NV Brut, rosé and Charles VII.
    NV, Vintage Charles VII and (sometimes) Coteaux Champenois. High quality champagne house owned by VEUVE CLICQUOT.

Canon-Fronsac B'x. r. ★★★ 70 75 78 79 81 82 83′ 85 86
    Tannic, often full-flavoured reds of increasing quality and style from small area w. of POMEROL. Ch'x. include Canon, Canon-Moueix, Canon de Brem, Coustolle, Junayme, Mazeris-Bellevue, Moulin-Pey-Labrie, Toumalin, Vraye-Canon-Boyer. Bottle-age is important. See also FRONSAC.

Cantenac B'x. r. ★★★

Village of the HAUT-MÉDOC entitled to the Appellation MAR-GAUX. Top ch'x. include PALMER, BRANE-CANTENAC, etc.

Cap Corse Corsica w. dr. br; ★★→★★★

The wild north cape of the island. Splendid muscat and rare dry VERMENTINO white.

Caramany Pyr. r. (w. dr.) ⬚ 82 83 84 85 86

New appellation for part of CÔTES DE ROUSSILLON-VILLAGES.

Cassis Prov. (r. p.) w. dr. ★★ D.Y.A.

Seaside village e. of Marseille known for its lively dry white, exceptional for Provence (e.g. Domaine du Paternel). Not to be confused with cassis, a blackcurrant liqueur made in Dijon.

Castellane, de

Long-established Épernay champagne house. Good wines incl. Maxim's house champagne.

Cave Cellar, or any wine establishment.

Cave coopérative

Wine-growers' cooperative winery. Coops now account for 56% of French production and have 245,000 members. Almost all are now well run, well equipped and making some of the best wine of their areas.

Cépage Variety of vine, e.g. CHARDONNAY, MERLOT.

Cérons B'x. w. dr. or sw. ★★ 79 80 81 83 84 85

Neighbour of SAUTERNES with some good sweet-wine ch'x, e.g. Ch. de Cérons et de Calvimont.

Chablis B'y. w. dr. ★★ 85 86

Distinctive full-flavoured greeny gold wine. Made only of CHARDONNAY in n. Burgundy. Top growers incl. Raveneau, Dauvissat, LAROCHE, Pic, Févre, etc. All the best Chablis is either Premier Cru or Grand Cru.

Chablis Grand Cru B'y. w. dr. ★★★★ 78 81 82 83 84 85 86

Strong, subtle and altogether splendid. One of the great white burgundies. There are seven v'yds: Blanchots, Bougros, Clos, Grenouilles, Preuses, Valmur, Vaudésir. See also MOUTONNE.

Chablis Premier Cru B'y. w. dr. ★★★ 81 83 84 85 86

Second-rank but often excellent and more typical of Chablis than Grands Crus. Best v'yds incl.: Côte de Lechet, Fourchaume, Mont de Milieu, Montée de Tonnerre, Montmains, Vaillons.

Chai Building for storing and maturing wine, esp. in Bordeaux.

Chambertin B'y. r. ★★★★ 69 71 76 78 79 80 82 83 84 85 86

32-acre Grand Cru giving the meatiest, most enduring and often the best red burgundy, 15 growers, incl. ROUSSEAU, BOUCHARD PÈRE, Camus, Damoy, Tortochot, Rebourseau, Trapet.

Chambertin-Clos-de-Bèze B'y. r. ★★★★ 76 78 79 80 81 82 83 84 85

37-acre neighbour of CHAMBERTIN. Similarly splendid wine. Ten growers incl. CLAIR-DAU, DROUHIN, Damoy, ROUSSEAU.

Chambolle-Musigny B'y. r. (w.) ★★★ 76 78 79 80 82 83 84 85 86

420-acre CÔTE DE NUITS village with fabulously fragrant, complex wine. Best v'yds.: MUSIGNY, part of BONNES-MARES, Les Amoureuses, Les Charmes. Growers incl.: DE VOGÜÉ, DROUHIN, FAIVELEY, Roumier, Mugnier, Hudelot-Noëllat.

Champagne

Sparkling wine from 60,000 acres 90 miles e. of Paris, made by the MÉTHODE CHAMPENOISE. Wines from elsewhere, however good, cannot be Champagne. (See also names of brands.)

Champagne, Grande The appellation of the best area of COGNAC.

Champigny See Saumur

Chandon de Briailles, Domaine

Small burgundy estate at SAVIGNY. Makes v.g. CORTON.

Chanson Père et Fils

Growers (with 110 acres) and traders in fine wine at BEAUNE. Reds can be pale but generally develop well.

Chante-Alouette

A famous brand of white HERMITAGE from CHAPOUTIER.

Chantovent Major brand of VIN DE TABLE, largely from MINERVOIS.

Chapelle-Chambertin B'y. r. ★★★ 76 78 80 82 83′ 85 86

13-acre neighbour of CHAMBERTIN. Wine not so meaty.

Chapoutier

Long-established growers and traders of fine Rhône wines.

Charbaut, A. et Fils NV, Blanc de Blancs, Rosé NV, 73 76 79

ÉPERNAY Champagne house. Clean light wines. Good 'rosé'.

Chardonnay See Grapes for white wine

Charmes-Chambertin B'y. r. ★★★ 71 76 78 79 80 82 83′ 85 86

76-acre neighbour of CHAMBERTIN. Growers incl. Bachelet, Castagnier, Roty, ROUSSEAU.

Chartron & Trebuchet

Recent company with good burgundies, esp. Domaine Chartron's PULIGNY-MONTRACHET, Clos de la Pucelle.

Chassagne-Montrachet B'y. r. or w. dr. ★★★ →★★★★ 76 78 80 r.
81 w. 82 83 84 85 86

750-acre CÔTE DE BEAUNE village with superlative rich dry whites and sterling hefty reds. Best v'yds.: MONTRACHET, BÂTARD-MONTRACHET, CRIOTS-BÂTARD-MONTRACHET, Ruchottes, Caillerets, Boudriottes (r. w.), Morgeot (r., w.), CLOS-ST-JEAN (r.). Growers incl. RAMONET-PRUDHON, Morey, MAGENTA, DELAGRANGE-BACHELET, Gagnard-Delagrange, Niellon.

Chasseloir, Domaine du

The HQ of the firm of Chéreau-Carré, makers of several excellent domaine MUSCADETS.

Château

An estate, big or small, good or indifferent, particularly in Bordeaux. In Burgundy the term "domaine" is used. For all Bordeaux ch'x see pp. 54–72.

Château-Chalon Jura w. dr. ★★★

Unique strong dry yellow wine, almost like *fino* sherry. Usually ready to drink when bottled (at about 6 years).

Château Corton-Grancey B'y. r. ★★★ 76 78 79 82 83 85 86

Famous estate at ALOXE-CORTON, the property of Louis LATOUR. Impressive wine.

Château d'Arlay

Major JURA estate; 160 acres in skilful hands.

Château de Beaucastel Rh. r. ★★★ 76 78′ 79 80 81 83 84 85

One of the biggest (173 acres) and best-run estates of CHÂTEAUNEUF-DU-PAPE.

Château de la Chaize B'y. r. ★★★ 85 86

The best known estate of BROUILLY, with 200 acres.

Château de la Maltroye B'y. r. w. dr. ★★★

Sometimes excellent 32-acre estate at CHASSAGNE-MONTRACHET.

Château de Meursault B'y. r. w. ★★★

100-acre estate owned by PATRIARCHE with good v'yds in MEURSAULT, VOLNAY, POMMARD, BEAUNE. Splendid cellars open to the public for tasting. Vaut le détour.

Château de Panisseau Dordogne w. dr. ★★ D.Y.A.

Leading estate of BERGERAC: good dry SAUVIGNON BLANC.

Château de Selle Prov. r. p. or w. dr. ★★

Estate near Cotignac, Var. Well-known and typical wines.

Château des Fines Roches Rh. r. ★★★ 78 79 80 81 83 84 85

Large (112 acres) and distinguished estate in CHÂTEAUNEUF-DU-PAPE. Strong old-style wine.

Château du Nozet Lo. w. dr. ★★★ 85 86

Biggest and best-known estate of Pouilly (FUMÉ) sur Loire. Top wine, Baron de L., can be wonderful.

Château Fortia Rh. r. ★★★ 79 80 81 83 84 85 86

First-class property in CHÂTEAUNEUF-DU-PAPE. Traditional methods. The owner's father, Baron Le Roy, also fathered the APPELLATION CONTRÔLÉE system.

Château-Grillet Rh. w. dr. ★★★★ 82 83 84 85 86

3½-acre v'yd. with one of France's smallest appellations. Intense, fragrant, expensive. Drink fairly young.

Château-Gris B'y. r. ★★★ 78 82 83 85 86

Well-known estate at NUITS-ST-GEORGES, linked with BICHOT.

Châteaumeillant Lo. r. p. or w. dr. ★ D.Y.A.

Small VDQS area near SANCERRE. Light GAMAY and P. NOIR.

Châteauneuf-du-Pape Rh. r. (w. dr.) ★★★ 78 79 80 82 83 84 85

7,800 acres near Avignon. Best estate ("domaine") wines are dark, strong, long-lived. Others may be light and/or disappointing. The white can be heavy: most now made to D.Y.A.

Château Rayas Rh. r. (w. dr.) ★★★ 78 80 81 83 84 85 86

Famous old-style property in CHÂTEAUNEUF-DU-PAPE.

Château Simone Prov. r. p. or w. dr. ★★ Age 2-3 yrs.

Well-known property in Palette; the only one with a name in this appellation near Aix-en-Provence.

Château Vignelaure Prov. r. ★★ 78 79 80 81 82 84 85 86

135-acre Provençal estate near Aix making good Bordeaux-style wine with CABERNET, Syrah and Grenache grapes.

Chatillon-en-Diois Rh. r. p. or w. dr. ★ D.Y.A.

Small Appellation e. of the Rhône near Die. Adequate GAMAY reds; white (some Aligoté) mostly made into CLAIRETTE DE DIE.

Chave, Gérard

To many the top grower of HERMITAGE, red and white.

Chavignol

Village of SANCERRE with famous v'yd., Les Monts Damnés. Chalky soil gives vivid wines that age well.

Chénas B'y. r. ★★★ 83 85 86

Good Beaujolais cru, neighbour to MOULIN-À-VENT and JULIENAS. One of the weightier Beaujolais.

Chenin Blanc

See Grapes for white wine (p. 6).

Chevalier-Montrachet B'y. w. dr. ★★★★ 71 78 81 82 83 84 85 86

17-acre neighbour of MONTRACHET with similar luxurious wine, perhaps a little less powerful. Includes Les Demoiselles (LATOUR, JADOT). Growers incl. BOUCHARD PÈRE, LEFLAIVE, Niellon.

Cheverny Lo. r. p. or w. dr. (sp.) ★→★★ D.Y.A.

Loire VDQS from near Chambord. CHENIN BL. or SAUV. BL. whites, GAMAY, P. NOIR or CAB reds; generally light but fresh and tasty.

Chignin Savoie w. dr. ★ D.Y.A.

Light soft white of Jacquère grapes.

Chinon Lo. r. ★★★ 76 82 83' 85 86

Delicate fruity CABERNET FRANC from TOURAINE. Drink cool when young. Exceptional vintages age like Bordeaux.

Chiroubles B'y. r. ★★★ 85 86

Good but tiny Beaujolais cru next to FLEURIE; freshly fruity silky wine for early drinking.

Chorey-lès-Beaune B'y. r. ★★ 83 85 86

Minor appellation on flat land n. of BEAUNE notable for one fine grower: TOLLOT-BEAUT.

Chusclan Rh. r. p. or w. dr. ★ 83 84 85 86

Village of CÔTE-DU-RHÔNE-VILLAGES. Good middle-weight wines from the cooperative.

Cissac HAUT-MÉDOC village just w. of PAUILLAC.

Clair-Daü

First-class 100-acre burgundy estate of the northern CÔTE DE NUITS, with cellars at MARSANNAY. Merged in 1986 with JADOT.

Clairet Very light red wine, almost rosé.

Clairette

Mediocre white grape of the s. of France. Gives neutral wine.

Clairette de Bellegarde Midi w. dr. ★ D.Y.A.

Plain neutral white from near Nîmes.

Clairette de Die Rh. w. dr. or s./sw. sp. ☐ ★★ ☐ NV

Popular dry or (better) semi-sweet rather MUSCAT-flavoured sparkling wine from the e. Rhône, or straight dry CLAIRETTE white, surprisingly ageing well 3–4 years.

Clairette du Languedoc Midi w. dr. ★ D.Y.A.

Plain neutral white from near Montpellier.

La Clape Midi r. p. or w. dr. ☐ ★→★★ ☐

Full-bodied VDQS wines from between Narbonne and the sea. The red gains character after 2–3 years, the white even longer. V.g. rosé.

Claret Traditional English term for red BORDEAUX.

Climat Burgundian word for individual named v'yd., e.g. Beaune Grèves, Chambolle-Musigny les Amoureuses.

Clos A term carrying some prestige, reserved for distinct, usually walled, v'yds., often in one ownership. Frequent in Burgundy and Alsace. Les Clos is Chablis's Grandest Cru.

Clos-de-Bèze See Chambertin-Clos-de-Bèze.

Clos de la Roche B'y. r. ☐ ★★★ ☐ 71 76 78 79 80 82 83' 84 85 86

38-acre Grand Cru at MOREY-ST-DENIS. Powerful complex wine like CHAMBERTIN. Producers incl. BOUCHARD PÈRE, Ponsot, DUJAC, ROUSSEAU, Rémy, Castagnier.

The Confrèrie des Chevaliers du Tastevin is Burgundy's wine fraternity and the most famous of its kind in the world. It was founded in 1933 by a group of Burgundian patriots, headed by Camille Rodier and Georges Faiveley, to rescue their beloved Burgundy from a period of slump and despair by promoting its inimitable products. Today it regularly holds banquets with elaborate and sprightly ceremonial for 600 guests at its headquarters, the Cistercian château in the Clos de Vougeot. The Confrèrie has branches in many countries and members among lovers of wine all over the world.

Clos des Lambrays B'y. r. ★★★ 78 83 85 86

15-acre Grand Cru v'yd. at MOREY-ST-DENIS. Changed hands in 1979 after a shaky period. Young vines need time.

Clos des Mouches B'y. r. or w. dr. ★★★

Splendid Premier Cru v'yd. of BEAUNE owned by DROUHIN.

Clos de Tart B'y. r. ★★★ 71 76 78 79 80 82 83' 84 85

18-acre Grand Cru at MOREY-ST-DENIS owned by MOMMESSIN. At best wonderfully fragrant, whether young or old.

Clos de Vougeot B'y. r. ★★★ 71 76 78 80 82 83 84 85 86

124-acre CÔTE-DE-NUITS Grand Cru with many owners. Bewilderingly variable, occasionally sublime. Maturity depends on the grower's technique and his position on the hillside.

Clos du Chêne Marchand

Well-known v'yd. at Bué, SANCERRE.

Clos du Roi B'y. r. ★★★

Part of the Grand Cru CORTON. Also a Premier Cru of BEAUNE.

Clos St Denis B'y. r. ☐ ★★★ ☐ 76 78 79 80 82 83' 84 85 86

16-acre Grand Cru at MOREY-ST-DENIS. Splendid sturdy wine.

Clos St Jacques B'y. r. ★★★ 71 76 78 79 80 82 83' 84 85 86

17-acre Premier Cru of GEVREY-CHAMBERTIN. Excellent powerful velvety wine, often better (and dearer) than some of the CHAMBERTIN Grands Crus. Main grower: ROUSSEAU.

Clos St Jean B'y. r. ☐ ★★★ ☐ 76 78 79 80 82 83' 84 85 86

36-acre Premier Cru of CHASSAGNE-MONTRACHET. Very good red, more solid than subtle.

Cognac Town and region of western France and its brandy.

Collioure Pyr. r. ⭐ `80 81 82 83 84 85 86`
Strong dry RANCIO red from BANYULS area. Small production.

Condrieu Rh. w. dr. ⭐⭐⭐⭐ D.Y.A.
Outstanding soft fragrant white of great character (and price) from the Viognier grape. The leading growers are Vernay, Ch. du Rozay and DELAS. Ch-GRILLET is similar.

Corbières Midi r. or (p.) or (w.) `★→★★` `85 86`
Good vigorous bargain reds, steadily improving and now rewarded with A.C. Rarely disappointing at their price.

Cordier, Ets D.
Important Bordeaux shipper and château-owner, including Ch'x. GRUAUD-LAROSE, TALBOT, CANTEMERLE, MEYNEY.

Cornas Rh. r. `★★→★★★` `78 79 80 81 82 83′ 84 85 86`
Expanding 400-acre district s. of HERMITAGE. Typical sturdy Rhône wine of v.g. quality from the SYRAH grape. Needs ageing.

Corse The island of Corsica. Strong wines of all colours. Better appellations incl. PATRIMONIO, Sartène, AJACCIO, CAP CORSE.

Corton B'y. r. `★★★★` `71 76′ 78′ 80 82 83′ 84 85 86`
The only Grand Cru red of the CÔTE DE BEAUNE. 200 acres in ALOXE-CORTON incl. les Bressandes and le CLOS DU ROI. Rich powerful wines should be long-lived. Many good growers.

Corton-Charlemagne B'y. w. dr. ⭐⭐⭐⭐ `78 79 80 81 82 83 84 85 86`
The white section (one-third) of CORTON. Rich spicy lingering wine. Behaves like a red wine and ages magnificently. Top growers: BONNEAU DU MARTRAY, LATOUR, JADOT.

Coste, Pierre Influential wine-broker and -maker of LANGON.

Costières du Gard Midi r. p. or w. dr. ★→★★ D.Y.A.
VDQS of moderate (improving) quality from the Rhône delta.

Coteaux Champenois Champ. r. (p.) or w. dr. ⭐⭐⭐
The appellation for non-sparkling champagne. Vintages follow those for Champagne. Do not pay inflated prices.

Coteaux d'Aix-en-Provence Prov r. p. or w. dr. ★→★★
An appellation on the move. The established Ch. de VIGNELAURE is challenged by the extravagant Domaine Val-Joannis. V.g. wines. Also Ch'x Fonscolombe, Calissanne.

Coteaux d'Ancenis r. p. w. dr. ⭐ D.Y.A.
Light Cabernet and Gamay reds and pinks; sharpish whites from MUSCADET country.

Coteaux de la Loire Lo. w. dr. sw. `★★→★★★` `79 81 82 83 84 85 86`
Forceful and fragrant CHENIN BLANC whites from Anjou. The best are in SAVENNIERES. Excellent as an apéritif.

Coteaux de l'Aubance Lo. p. or w. dr./sw. ⭐⭐ D.Y.A.
Light and typical minor ANJOU wines. The best are MOELLEUX.

Coteaux de Pierrevert Rh. r. p. or w. dr. or sp. ⭐ D.Y.A.
Minor southern VDQS from nr. Manosque. Well-made coop wine mostly rosé, with fresh whites.

Coteaux de Saumur Lo. w. dr./sw. ⭐⭐ D.Y.A.
Pleasant dry or sweetish fruity CHENIN BLANC.

Coteaux des Baux-en-Provence Prov. r. p. or w. dr. ★→★★ NV
Neighbour of COTEAUX D'AIX, without the excitement.

Coteaux du Giennois r. w. dr. ⭐
Minor Loire area n. of SANCERRE. Light GAMAY and PINOT NOIR, SAUVIGNON and CHENIN BLANC.

Coteaux du Languedoc Midi r. p. or w. dr. `★→★★` D.Y.A.
Scattered better-than-ordinary Midi areas with VDQS status. The best (e.g. Faugères, St Saturnin, LA CLAPE, ST CHINIAN, Quatourze, St-Georges-d'Orques, Cabrières) age for 1 yr or two.

Coteaux du Layon Lo. w. s./sw. or sw. ⭐⭐ `78 81 82 83 84 85 86`
District centred on Rochefort, s. of Angers, making sweet CHENIN BLANC wines above the general Anjou standard. "C. du L-Chaume" is a higher appellation.

Coteaux du Loir Lo. r. p. or w. dr./sw. ★★ 78 82 83 84 85 86
Small region n. of Tours. Occasionally excellent wines. Best v'y'd.: JASNIERES. The Loir is a tributary of the Loire.

Coteaux du Lyonnais Rh. r. p. (w. dr.) ★ D.Y.A.
Junior Beaujolais, and whites in keeping, from nr. Lyon. Best *en* PRIMEUR.

Coteaux du Tricastin Rh. r. p. or w. dr. ★★ D.Y.A.
Fringe CÔTES-DU-RHÔNE of increasing quality from s. of Valence. Pierre Labeye is the chief producer. Attractive PRIMEUR red.

Coteaux du Vendomois Lo. r. p. or w. dr. ★ D.Y.A.
Fringe Loire from n. of Blois. Mainly GAMAY.

Côte(s)
Means hillside; generally a superior vineyard to those on the plain. Many appellations start with either Côtes or Coteaux, which means the same thing. In ST-EMILION it distinguishes the valley slopes from the higher plateau.

Côte Chalonnaise B'y. r. w. dr. sp. ★★→★★★
Lesser-known v'y'd. area between BEAUNE and MÂCON. See Mercurey, Givry, Rully, Montagny. Alias 'Région de Mercurey'.

Côte de Beaune B'y. r. or w. dr. ★★→★★★★
Used geographically: the southern half of the CÔTE D'OR. Applies as an appellation only to parts of BEAUNE.

Côte de Beaune-Villages B'y. r. or w. dr. ★★ 78 80 83 85
Regional appellation for secondary wines of the classic area. They cannot be labelled "Côte de Beaune" without either "Villages" or the village name.

Côte de Brouilly B'y. r. ★★★ 83 85 86
Fruity, rich, vigorous Beaujolais cru. One of the best. Leading estates: Ch. Thivin, Domaine de Chavanne.

Côte de Nuits B'y. r. or (w. dr.) ★★→★★★★
The northern half of the CÔTE D'OR. Nearly all red wine.

Côte de Nuits-Villages B'y. r. (w.) ★★ 78 80 83 85
A junior appellation, rarely seen but worth investigating.

Côte d'Or
Département name applied to the central and principal Burgundy v'y'd. slopes, consisting of the CÔTE DE BEAUNE and CÔTE DE NUITS. The name is not used on labels.

Côte Rôtie Rh. r. ★★★ 78 79 80 82 83' 84 85 86
Potentially the finest Rhône red, from just s. of Vienne; achieves complex delicacy with age. Top growers include JABOULET, CHAPOUTIER, VIDAL-FLEURY, Jasmin, Guigal, Jamet.

Côtes d'Auvergne Central France r. p. or (w. dr.) ★ D.Y.A.
Flourishing small VDQS area near Clermont-Ferrand. Red (at best) like light BEAUJOLAIS. Chanturgues is the best known.

Côtes de Blaye B'x. w. dr. ★ D.Y.A.
Run-of-the-mill Bordeaux white from BLAYE.

Côtes de Bordeaux Saint-Macaire B'x. w. dr./sw. ★ D.Y.A.
Run-of-the-mill Bordeaux white from east of SAUTERNES.

Côtes de Bourg B'x. r. ★→★★ 78 79 81 82 83 85 86
Appellation used for many of the better reds of BOURG. Ch'x incl. de Barbe, La Barde, du Bousquet, La Croix de Millorit, de la Grave, Grand-Jour, Font Guilhem, Guerry, Rousset, Lalibarde, Lamothe, Mendoce, Falfas, Peychaud, de Thau.

Côtes de Castillon B'x. r. ★→★★ 78 79 81 82 83 85 86
Flourishing region east of St. Emilion. Similar wines, though a touch lighter. Ch'x incl. Fonds-Rondes, Haut-Tuquet, Lardit, PITRAY, Ste Colombe, Moulin-Rouge, Rocher-Bellevue.

Côtes de Duras Dordogne r. or w. dr. ★ 82 83 85 86
Neighbour to BERGERAC. Similar light wines; the white best.

Côtes de Francs See Bordeaux—Côtes de Francs.

Côtes de Fronsac See FRONSAC.

Côtes de Montravel Dordogne w. dr./sw. ⭐ NV
> Part of BERGERAC; trad. medium-sw. wine, now often dry.

Côtes de Provence Prov. r. p. w. dr. ⭐→⭐⭐
> The wine of Prov; still often with more alcohol than character.
> Standards are rapidly improving. 60% is rosé, 30% red.

Côtes de Saint-Mont s.w. France r. w. dr. p. ⭐
> Promising VDQS from the Gers, not unlike MADIRAN.

Côtes de Thongue Midi r. w. dr. ⭐ D.Y.A.
> Above-average *vins de pays* from the HÉRAULT.

Côtes de Toul E. France r. p. or w. dr. ⭐ D.Y.A.
> Very light wines from Lorraine; mainly VIN GRIS (rosé).

Côtes du Forez Central France r. or p. ⭐ D.Y.A.
> Light Beaujolais-style red, can be good in warm years.

Côtes du Frontonnais s.w. France r. or p. ⭐→⭐⭐ D.Y.A.
> The local wine of Toulouse, gaining admirers elsewhere. Ch.
> Bellevue-la-Forêt makes outstanding silky red.

Côtes du Haut-Roussillon s.w. France br. sw. ⭐→⭐⭐ NV
> Area for VINS DOUX NATURELS n. of Perpignan.

Côtes du Jura Jura r. p. or w. dr. (sp.) ⭐ D.Y.A.
> Various light tints and tastes. ARBOIS is theoretically better.

Côtes du Luberon Rh. r. p. or w. dr. sp. ⭐→⭐⭐ D.Y.A.
> Improving country wines from northern Provence; especially
> the reds of La Vieille Ferme, and Ch. de Sannes.

Côtes du Marmandais Dordogne r. p. or w. dr. ⭐ D.Y.A.
> Light wines from s.e. of Bordeaux. The coop at Cocumont makes
> most of the best.

Côtes-du-Rhône Rh. r. p. or w. dr. ⭐→⭐⭐ 85 86
> The basic appellation of the Rhône valley. Best drunk young —
> even as PRIMEUR. Wide variations of quality due to grape
> ripeness, therefore rising with alcohol %. See CÔTES-DU-RHÔNE-
> VILLAGES.

Côtes-du-Rhône-Villages Rh. r. p. or w. dr. ⭐→ ⭐⭐ 83 84 85 86
> The wine of the 17 best villages of the southern Rhône.
> Substantial and on the whole reliable. Sometimes delicious.

Côtes du Roussillon Pyr. r. p. or w. dr. ⭐→⭐⭐ 81 82 83 84 85 86
> Country wine of e. Pyrenees. The hefty reds are best and can be
> very tasty. Some whites are sharp VINS VERTS.

Côtes du Roussillon-Villages Pyr. r. ⭐⭐ 81 82 83 84 85 86
> The best reds of the region, incl. CARAMANY and LATOUR DE
> FRANCE.

Côtes du Ventoux Prov. r. (w. dr.) ⭐⭐ 83 84 85 86
> Booming appellation for tasty reds between the Rhône and
> Provence.

Côtes du Vivarais Prov. r. p. or w. dr. ⭐ NV
> Pleasant country wines from s. Massif Centrale. Like light
> CÔTES-DU-RHÔNE.

Côtes Roannaises Central France r. ⭐ D.Y.A.
> Minor GAMAY region high up the LOIRE.

Coulée de Serrant Lo. w. dr./sw. ⭐⭐⭐ 76 78 79 81 82 83 84 85 86
> 10-acre v'yd. on n. bank of LOIRE at SAVENNIERES, Anjou.
> Intense strong fruity/sharp wine, good as an aperitif. Ages well.

Crémant In Champagne means "Creaming"—i.e. half-sparkling.
> Since 1975 an appellation for high-quality champagne-method
> sparkling wines from Alsace, the Loire and Bourgogne—often a
> notable bargain.

Crémant de Loire w. dr. sp. ⭐⭐ NV
> High-quality sparkling wine from ANJOU and TOURAINE.

Crépy Savoie w. dr. ⭐⭐ D.Y.A.
> Light, Swiss-style white from s. shore of Lake Geneva.
> "Crépitant" has been coined for its faint fizz.

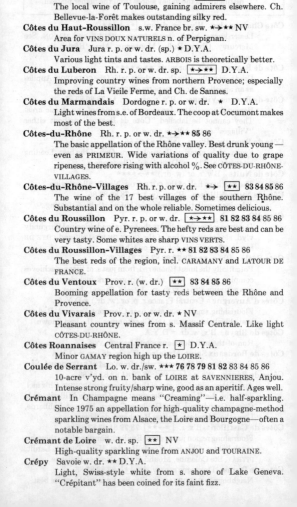

Criots-Bâtard-Montrachet B'y. w. ★★★ 76 78 79 81 82 83 84 85 86
4-acre neighbour to BÂTARD-MONTRACHET. Similar wine.

Crozes-Hermitage Rh. r. or (w. dr.) ⭐⭐ 78 80 82 83 84 85 86
Larger and less distinguished neighbour to HERMITAGE. Robust and often excellent reds, but choose carefully.

Cru "Growth", as in "first-growth"—meaning vineyard.

Cru Bourgeois
General term for MÉDOC châteaux below CRU CLASSÉ.

Cru Bourgeois Supérieur (Cru Grand Bourgeois)
Official rank one better than the last. Aged in barrels.

Cru Classé
Classed growth. One of the first five official quality classes of the Médoc, classified in 1855. Also any classed growth of another district (e.g. Graves, St-Emilion, Sauternes).

Cru Grand Bourgeois Exceptionnel
Official rank above CRU BOURGEOIS SUPÉRIEUR, immediately below CRU CLASSÉ. Several fine châteaux are unofficially acknowledged (and labelled) as Exceptionnel.

Cruse et Fils Frères
Long-established Bordeaux shipper famous for fine wine. Owner of Ch. D'ISSAN.

Cubzac, St.-André-de B'x. r. or w. dr. ★ 82 83 85 86
Town 15 miles n.e. of Bordeaux, centre of the minor Cubzaguais region. Sound reds have the appellation Bordeaux. Estates include: Ch. du Bouilh, Ch. de Terrefort-Quancard, Ch. Timberlay, Domaine de Beychevelle.

Cussac Village just s. of ST. JULIEN. Appellation Haut-Médoc.

Burgundy boasts one of the world's most famous and certainly its most beautiful hospital, the Hospices de Beaune, founded in 1443 by Nicolas Rolin, Chancellor to the Duke of Burgundy, and his wife Guigone de Salins. The hospital he built and endowed with vineyards for its income still operates in the same building and still thrives, tending the sick of Beaune without charge, on the sale of its wine. Many growers since have bequeathed their land to the Hospices. Today it owns 125 acres of prime land in Beaune, Pommard, Volnay, Meursault, Corton and Mazis-Chambertin. The wine is sold by auction every year on the third Sunday in November.

Cuve Close
Short-cut method of making sparkling wine in a tank. The sparkle dies away in the glass much quicker than with MÉTHODE CHAMPENOISE wine.

Cuvée The quality of wine produced in a "cuve" or vat. Also a word of many uses, incl. "blend". In Burgundy interchangeable with "Cru". Often just refers to a "lot" of wine.

d'Angerville, Marquis
Famous burgundy grower with immaculate estate in VOLNAY.

Degré alcoolique
Degrees of alcohol, i.e. percent by volume.

De Ladoucette
Leading producer of POUILLY-FUMÉ, based at Ch. DE NOZET. Luxury brand "Baron de L.". Also SANCERRE Comte Lafond.

Delagrange-Bachelet
One of the leading proprietors in CHASSAGNE-MONTRACHET.

Delas Frères
Long-established and excellent firm of Rhône-wine specialists at Tournon, v'yds. at CÔTE RÔTIE, HERMITAGE, CORNAS, CONDRIEU, etc. Owned by DEUTZ.

Delorme, André
Leading merchants and growers of the CÔTE CHALONNAISE. Specialists in sparkling wine and excellent RULLY.

De Luze, A. et Fils
> Bordeaux shipper and owners of Ch'x. CANTENAC-BROWN and
> PAVEIL DE LUZE; owned by Rémy-Martin of Cognac.

Demi-Sec   "Half-dry": in practice more than half-sweet.

Depagneux, Jacques de Cie
> Well-regarded merchants of BEAUJOLAIS.

Deutz   Brut NV and 75 76 79 81 82, Rosé 82, Blanc de Blancs 78 79 81 82
> One of the best of the smaller champagne houses. Full-flavoured
> wines. Luxury brand: Cuvée William Deutz (75 79)

Domaine
> Property, particularly in Burgundy.

Domaine de Belair
> An attractive light-weight branded red Bordeaux. D.Y.A.

Domaine de l'Eglantière
> Important CHABLIS estate. See DURUP.

Domaine du Vieux Télégraphe   Rh. r. w. dr. ★★★ 76 78 79 81 83 84 85
> A leader in fine modern CHÂTEAUNEUF-DU-PAPE for long ageing.

Dom Pérignon   70 71 73 75 76 78 80 and Rosé 75 78
> Luxury brand of MOËT ET CHANDON, named after the legendary
> Abbey cellarmaster who 'invented' champagne.

Dopff "au Moulin"
> Ancient family wine-house at Riquewihr, Alsace. Best wines:
> Riesling Schoenenbourg, Gewürztraminer Eichberg. Pioneers of
> sparkling wine in Alsace.

Dopff & Irion
> Another excellent Riquewihr (ALSACE) business. Best wines
> include Muscat les Amandiers, Riesling de Riquewihr.

Doudet-Naudin
> Burgundy merchant and grower at Savigny-lès-Beaune. V'yds.
> incl. BEAUNE CLOS DU ROI.

Dourthe Frères
> Well-reputed Bordeaux merchant representing a wide range of
> ch'x., mainly good Crus Bourgeois, incl. Ch'x. MAUCAILLOU,
> TRONQUOY-LALANDE, BELGRAVE. "Beau-Mayne" is their reli-
> able branded Bordeaux.

Doux   Sweet.

Drouhin, J. et Cie
> Prestigious Burgundy grower (130 acres) and merchant. Offices
> in BEAUNE, v'yds. in BEAUNE, MUSIGNY, CLOS DE VOUGEOT,
> CHABLIS, etc. Drouhin also owns Jaffelin et Cie.

Duboeuf, Georges
> Top-class BEAUJOLAIS merchant at Romanèche-Thorin. The
> leader of the region.

Duclot, Ets
> Bordeaux merchant specializing in the top growths. Controlled
> by MOUEIX.

Dufouleur Frères
> Growers and merchants of toothsome burgundy at NUITS-ST-
> GEORGES and MERCUREY.

Dujac, Domaine
> Fashionable burgundy grower at MOREY-ST-DENIS with v'yds in
> that village, ECHÉZEAUX, BONNES-MARES, GEVREY-CHAMBER-
> TIN, etc. His best wines are splendidly vivid.

Durup, Jean
> One of the biggest Chablis growers with 140 acres, including the
> DOMAINE DE L'EGLANTIERE and Ch. de Maligny.

Echézeaux   B'y. r.   ★★★★   76 78′ 79 80 82 83′ 84 85 86
> 74-acre Grand Cru between VOSNE-ROMANÉE and CLOS DE
> VOUGEOT. Can be superlative fragrant burgundy without great
> weight e.g. from Mugneret, Gouroux, DOM DE LA ROMANÉE-
> CONTI, Jacqueline Jayer.

Edelzwicker Alsace w. ★ D.Y.A.
> Light white from mixture of grapes, often fruity and good.

Entre-Deux-Mers B'x. w. dr. ★ D.Y.A.
> Standard dry white Bordeaux from between the Garonne and Dordogne rivers. Often a good buy, esp. "La Gamage", Ch. ST. BONNET.

Eschenauer, Louis
> Famous Bordeaux merchants, owners of Ch'x. RAUSAN-SEGLA and SMITH-HAUT-LAFITTE, DE LAMOUROUX and LA GARDE in GRAVES. Controlled by John Holt, part of the Lonrho group.

l'Etoile Jura w. dr./sw/sp. ★★
> Sub-region of the Jura known for stylish whites, incl. VIN JAUNE like CHÂTEAU-CHALON and good sparkling.

Faiveley, J.
> Family-owned growers (with 182 acres) and merchants at NUITS-ST-GEORGES, with v'yds. in CHAMBERTIN-CLOS-DE-BÈZE, CHAMBOLLE-MUSIGNY, CORTON, NUITS, MERCUREY (150 acres). Consistent high quality recently.

Faller, Théo
> Top ALSACE grower at the Domaine Weinbach, Kaysersberg.

Faugères Midi r. (p. or w. dr.) ★→★★ 82 83 84 85 86
> Isolated village of the COTEAUX DU LANGUEDOC making above-average wine. Became Appellation Contrôlée in 1982.

Feuillate, Nicolas NV Brut, Rosé
> Champagne marque popular in restaurants. Rosé esp. good.

Fèvre, William
> Conservative Chablis grower with the biggest Grand Cru holding (40 acres). His label is Domaine de la Maladière.

Fitou Midi r. ★★ 82 83 84 85 86
> Superior CORBIÈRES red; powerful and ages well.

Fixin B'y. r. ★★ 76 78 80 82 83' 84 85 86
> A worthy and under-valued neighbour to GEVREY-CHAMBERTIN. Often splendid reds. Best v'yds.: Clos du Chapitre, Les Hervelets, Clos Napoléon.

Fleurie B'y. r. ★★★ 83 84 85
> The epitome of a BEAUJOLAIS cru: fruity, scented, silky, racy.

Frais Fresh or cool.

Frappé Ice-cold.

Froid Cold.

Fronsac B'x. r. ★→★★ 75 78 79 81 82 83 85 86
> Pretty hilly area of good reds just w. of St-Emilion. Ch'x incl. Dalem, La Dauphine, Mayne-Vieil, la Rivière, de Carles, La Valade, Villars. See also CANON-FRONSAC.

Frontignan Midi br. sw. ★ NV
> Strong sweet and liquorous muscat wine.

Gagnard-Delagrange, Jacques
> Estimable small (13-acre) grower of CHASSAGNE-MONTRACHET, including some LE MONTRACHET.

Gaillac s.w. France r. p. or w. dr./sw. or sp. ★
> Ancient area showing signs of new life after generations of dullness. Slightly fizzy "Perlé" is good value. Reds can age well.

Gallaire B'x. r. ★★ D.Y.A.
> Very attractive fruity young Bordeaux from SICHEL.

Gamay See Grapes for red wine

Geisweiler et Fils
> One of the bigger merchant-houses of Burgundy. Cellars and 50 acres of v'yds. at NUITS-ST-GEORGES. Also 150 acres at Bevy in the HAUTES CÔTES DE NUITS and 30 in the CÔTE CHALONNAISE.

Gevrey-Chambertin B'y. r. ★★★ 76 78 79 80 82 83 85
> The village containing the great CHAMBERTIN and many other noble v'yds, as well as a considerable number more commonplace.

Gewürztraminer

The speciality grape of ALSACE: perfumed and spicy, whether dry or sweet.

Gigondas Rh. r. or p. ★★ 78 80 81 83 84 85 86

Worthy neighbour to CHÂTEAUNEUF-DU-PAPE. Strong, full-bodied, sometimes peppery wine, esp. Dom. du Pesquier.

Gilbey, S.A.

British firm long-established as Bordeaux merchants at Ch. LOUDENNE in the MÉDOC. Now owned by International Distillers and Vintners.

Gisselbrecht, Louis

High-quality Alsace shippers at Dambach-la-Ville.

Givry B'y. r. or w. dr. ★★ 83 84 85 86

Underrated village of the CÔTE CHALONNAISE: light but tasty and typical burgundy.

Gosset NV, 73 75 76 78 79 80 81 "Grande Réserve" and Rosé NV

Small, very old champagne house at Ay. Fine full wines (esp. Grande Réserve). Now linked with Philiponnat.

Gouges, Henri

Worthy burgundy grower of NUITS-ST-GEORGES. Good reds and very rare white "La Perrière".

Goulaine, Château de

The ceremonial showplace of MUSCADET; a noble family estate and its appropriate wine.

Goulet, Georges NV, rosé 76 79, Crémant Blanc de Blancs 79 and 71 73 75 76 79 81

High-quality Reims champagne house. Abel Lepitre is a cheaper range. Luxury brand: Cuvée du Centenaire 74 76 79.

Goût

Taste, e.g. "goût anglais"—as the English like it (i.e. dry).

Grand Cru

One of the top Burgundy v'yds. with its own Appellation Contrôlée. Similar in Alsace but more vague elsewhere. In ST-EMILION the third rank of château, numbering about 200.

Grand Roussillon Midi br. sw. ★★ NV

Broad appellation for muscat and other sweet fortified wines ("Vins Doux Naturels") of eastern Pyrenees.

Grands-Echézeaux B'y. r. ★★★★ 69 71 76 78 79 80 82 83 84 85

Superlative 22-acre Grand Cru next to CLOS DE VOUGEOT.

Gratien, Alfred and Gratien & Meyer

Excellent smaller champagne house (fine, very dry, long-lasting wine 73 76 79 82) and its counterpart at SAUMUR on the Loire.

Graves B'x. r. or w. ★→★★★★

Large region s. of Bordeaux city. Its best wines are red, but the name is used chiefly for its dry or medium whites.

Graves-Léognan

New A.O.C. for part of n. Graves, incl. six communes.

Graves-Pessac

New appellation for the three northernmost GRAVES communes.

Graves de Vayres B'x r. or w. ★

Part of ENTRE-DEUX-MERS; of no special character.

Les Gravières B'y. r. ★★★

Famous Premier Cru v'yd. of SANTENAY. Incl. Clos des Tavannes.

Griotte-Chambertin B'y. r. ★★★ 69 71 76 78' 79 80 82 83' 84 85 86

14-acre Grand Cru adjoining CHAMBERTIN. Similar wine, but less masculine and more "tender". Growers incl. DROUHIN.

Gros Plant du Pays Nantais Lo. w. ★ D.Y.A.

Junior cousin of MUSCADET, sharper and lighter; made of the COGNAC grape also known as Folle Blanche, Ugni Blanc etc.

Haut-Benauge B'x. w. dr. ★ D.Y.A.

Appellation for a limited area within ENTRE-DEUX-MERS.

Hautes-Côtes de Beaune B'y. r. or w. dr. `★★` 83 85 86
Appellation for a dozen villages in the hills behind the CÔTE DE BEAUNE. Light wines, worth investigating.

Hautes-Côtes de Nuits B'y. r. or w. dr. `★★` 78 83 85 86
The same for the CÔTE DE NUITS. An area on the way up.

Haut-Médoc B'x. r. ★★→★★★ 66 70 75 76 78 79 80 81 82 83 84 85 86
Big appellation including all the best areas of the Médoc. Most of the zone has communal appellations (e.g. MARGAUX, PAUILLAC). Some fine ch'x (e.g. LA LAGUNE) are simply A.C. Haut-Médoc.

Haut-Montravel Dordogne w. sw. ★ 81 82 83 85 86
Medium-sweet BERGERAC.

Haut Poitou Lo. (r.) w. d.r. `★→★★` D.Y.A.
Up-and-coming VDQS area south of ANJOU. Cooperative makes v. good whites, incl. CHARDONNAY and SAUVIGNON BLANC.

Heidsieck, Charles NV, rosé 81 and 73 75 76 79 81
Major champagne house of Reims, family-owned, now controlled by Remy Martin; also Trouillard and de Venoge, Luxury brands: Cuvée Champagne Charlie 79 81.

Heidsieck, Monopole NV, rosé and 73 75 76 79 82
Important champagne merchant and grower of Reims now owned by MUMM. V.g. luxury brand: Diamant Bleu (76 79).

Henriot NV, Blanc de Blancs Crémant Brut Souverain NV; Brut Rosé 81; Cuvée Baccarat 79; and 79
Old family champagne house now owned by Veuve Clicquot. Very big dry style. Luxury brand: Réserve Baron Philippe de Rothschild.

Hérault Midi
The biggest v'yd. *département* in France with 400,000 hectares of vines. Chiefly vin ordinaire.

Hermitage Rh. r. or w. dr. `★★★` 71 76 78′ 79 80-82 83′ 84 85 86
The "manliest" wine of France. Dark, powerful and profound. Needs long ageing. The white is heady and golden; now usually made for early drinking, though the best wines mature for many years. Top growers: CHAVE, JABOULET, CHAPOUTIER, Grippat.

Hospices de Beaune
Hospital in BEAUNE, with excellent v'yds. in MEURSAULT, POMMARD, VOLNAY, BEAUNE, CORTON, etc. See panel on page 35.

Huet, Gaston
Top VOUVRAY grower and mayor of the commune.

Hugel Père et Fils
The best-known ALSACE growers and merchants. Founded at Riquewihr in 1639 and still in the family. Best wines: Cuvées Exceptionnelles, Selections de Grains Nobles.

Imperiale Bordeaux bottle holding 8½ normal bottles (5 litres).

Irancy B'y. r. or (p.). `★★` 78 83 85 86
Good light red made near CHABLIS of PINOT NOIR and "César". The best vintages are long-lived and mature well. To watch.

Irouléguy s.w. France r.p. (or w. dr.) ★★ D.Y.A.
Agreeable local wines of the Basque country.

l'Isle de Beauté Name given to VINS DU PAYS from CORSICA.

Jaboulet, Paul
Old family firm at Tain, leading growers of HERMITAGE (esp. "La Chapelle" `★★★★`) and merchants in other RHÔNE wines.

Jaboulet-Vercherre et Cie
Well-known Burgundy merchant-house with v'yds. (34 acres) in POMMARD, etc., and cellars in Beaune. Middling wines.

Jadot, Louis
Much-respected top-quality Burgundy merchant-house with v'yds (50 acres) in BEAUNE, CORTON, etc.

Jaffelin see Drouhin.

Jardin de la France
Name given to VINS DU PAYS of the LOIRE.

Jasnières Lo. (r.) (p.) or w. dr. ★★★ 71 76 78 79 80 82 83 84 85 86
Rare VOUVRAY-like wine of n. Touraine.

Jeroboam
In Bordeaux a 6-bottle bottle, or triple magnum; in Champagne a double magnum.

Juliénas B'y. r. ★★★ 85 86
Leading cru of Beaujolais: vigorous fruity wine.

Jura See Côtes de Jura

Jurançon s.w. France w. sw. or dr. ★★ 78 79 81 82 83 84 85
Unusual high-flavoured and long-lived speciality of Pau in the Pyrenean foothills. Ages well for several years. Top growers: Barrère, Chigné, Guirouilh, Lamouroux.

Kressman, E.S. & Cie
Family-owned Bordeaux merchants and owners of Ch. LATOUR-MARTILLAC in GRAVES. "Monopole Rouge" is very good.

Kriter Popular low-price sparkling wine processed in Burgundy by PATRIARCHE.

Krug "Grande Cuvée" (NV), 64 66 69 71 73 75 76 79 81, Rosé and Clos du Mesnil 79
Small but very prestigious champagne house known for full-bodied very dry wine of the highest quality.

Kuentz-Bas
High-quality ALSACE grower and merchant at Husseren-les-Châteaux.

Labarde
Village just s. of MARGAUX and included in that appellation. Best ch.: GISCOURS.

Labouré-Gontard
Producer of high-quality CRÉMANT de Bourgogne at NUITS.

Labouré-Roi
Good little merchant at NUITS-ST-GEORGES, esp. for MEURSAULT.

Lafon, Domaine des Comtes
31-acre top-quality Burgundy estate in VOLNAY, MEURSAULT and LE MONTRACHET. Excellent '83s.

Lalande de Pomerol B'x. r. ⬚★★⬚ 75 76 78 79 81 82 83 85 86
Neighbour to POMEROL. Wines similar but considerably less fine. Top ch'x, Les Annereaux, Les Hauts-Conseillants, Les Hauts-Tuileries, Moncets, Tournefeuille, Belair, Siaurac.

Langlois-Château
Producer of sparkling SAUMUR, controlled by BOLLINGER.

Langon The principal town of the s. GRAVES/SAUTERNES district.

Lanson Père et Fils Black Label NV, rosé NV, Red Label 75 76 79 81 82
Important Champagne house, cellars at Reims. Luxury brand: Noble Cuvée 81. Black Label is a reliable fresh N.V.

Laroche
Important (160 acres) grower and merchant of CHABLIS, incl. Domaine Laroche, La Jouchère. Labels incl. Bacheroy-Josselin. Also owns the Château de PULIGNY-MONTRACHET.

Latour, Louis
Top Burgundy merchant and grower with v'yds. (120 acres) in CORTON, BEAUNE, etc. Among the best, esp. for white wines.

Latour de France r. (w. dr.) ★→★★ 81 82 83 84 85 86
New appellation in CÔTES DE ROUSSILLON-VILLAGES.

Latricières-Chambertin B'y. r. ★★★ 71 76 78 79 80 82 83' 84 85 86
17-acre Grand Cru neighbour of CHAMBERTIN. Similar wine, but lighter and "prettier".

Laudun Rh. r. p. or w. dr. ⬚★⬚
Village of CÔTES-DU-RHÔNE-VILLAGES. Attractive wines from the cooperative incl. fresh whites.

Laugel, Michel
One of the biggest ALSACE merchant-houses, at Marlenheim.

Laurent-Perrier NV, rosé brut and **71 73 75 76 78 79**

Highly successful young champagne house at Tours-sur-Marne. Luxury brand: Cuvée Grande Siècle. Ultra Brut is just that.

Leflaive, Domaine

Perhaps the best of all white burgundy growers at PULIGNY-MONTRACHET. Best v'yds: Clavoillons, Pucelles, Bienvenue-, Chevalier-Montrachet.

Léognan B'x.

Leading village of the GRAVES. Best ch'x.: DOMAINE DE CHEVALIER, MALARTIC-LAGRAVIÈRE and HAUT-BAILLY.

Leroy

Important burgundy merchants at AUXEY-DURESSES with superb stocks of old wines. Part-owners and distributors of the DOMAINE DE LA ROMANÉE-CONTI.

Lichine, Alexis et Cie

Post-war Bordeaux merchants, proprietors of Ch. LASCOMBES.

Burgundy: a grower's own label

MISE EN BOUTEILLES AU DOMAINE **NUITS ST GEORGES** **LES PRULIERS** APPELLATION CONTRÔLÉE DOMAINE HENRI GOUGES A NUITS GEORGES, CÔTE D'OR	Domaine is the burgundy equivalent of château. The Appellation Contrôlée is Nuits St Georges. The individual v'yd. in Nuits is called Les Pruliers. The name and address of the grower/producer. (The word propriétaire is often also used.)

A merchant's label

SANTENAY **LES GRAVIERES** APPELLATION CONTRÔLÉE PROSPER MAUFOUX NEGOCIANT À SANTENAY	The village. The vineyard. The wine qualifies for the Appellation Santenay. Prosper Maufoux is a Négociant, or merchant, who bought the wine from the grower to mature, bottle and sell.

Lie, sur

"On the lees." Muscadet is often bottled straight from the vat, without 'racking' or filtering (or so its makers say), for maximum freshness.

Limoux Pyr. r. or w. dr. [******] D.Y.A.

The non-sparkling version of BLANQUETTE DE LIMOUX and a remarkable fresh claret-like red: Anne des Joyeuses.

Lirac Rh. r. p. or (w. dr.) ** 81 83 84 85

Neighbouring village to TAVEL. Similar wine; the red becoming more important than the rosé, esp. Ch. de Segriés.

Listel Midi r. p. w. dr. [***→****] D.Y.A.

Vast estate on the sandy beaches of the Golfe du Lion. Owned by the giant Salins du Midi, making very pleasant light "vins des sables". Domaine du Bosquet is a light fruity red.

Listrac B'x. r. **→ [*******]

Village of HAUT-MÉDOC next to MOULIS. Best ch'x.: FOURCAS-HOSTEN, FOURCAS-DUPRÉ, CLARKE.

Loire The major river of n.w. France. See under wine and regional names.

Long-Depaquit

V.g. CHABLIS domaine (esp. MOUTONNE), owned by BICHOT.

Loron et Fils

Big-scale burgundy grower and merchant, specialist in BEAUJOLAIS and sound *vins de table*.

Loupiac B'x. w. sw. ★★ **76 79 80 81 83 84** 85 86
Neighbour to SAUTERNES with similar but less good wine. Top ch'x: Loupiac-Gaudiet, de Ricaud.

Ludon
HAUT-MÉDOC village s. of MARGAUX. Best ch.: LA LAGUNE.

Lugny ("Macon-Lugny") B'y. r. w. dr. sp. ★★ **85 86**
Village next to VIRÉ with active and good co-operative. Wine of Les Genevrières v'yd. is sold by LOUIS LATOUR.

Lupé-Cholet et Cie
Merchants and growers at NUITS-ST-GEORGES controlled by BICHOT. Best estate wines: Château Gris and Clos de Lupé.

Lussac-Saint-Emilion B'x. r. ★★ **78 79 81 82** 83 85 86
N-e. neighbour to ST-EMILION. Top ch'x incl. Lyonnat, Tour de Grenot. Coop (at PUISSEGUIN) makes "Roc de Lussac".

Macau
HAUT-MÉDOC village s. of MARGAUX. Best ch.: CANTEMERLE.

macération carbonique
Traditional technique of fermentation with whole bunches of unbroken grapes in a vat full of carbon dioxide. Fermentation inside each grape eventually bursts it, giving vivid and very fruity mild wine for quick consumption. Esp. in BEAUJOLAIS; now much used in the Midi and elsewhere.

Machard de Gramont
Burgundy family estate: cellars in NUITS and v'yds. in NUITS, SAVIGNY, BEAUNE, POMMARD. Extremely well-made reds.

Mâcon B'y. r. (p.) or w. dr. ★★ 85 86
Southern district of sound, usually unremarkable, reds and tasty dry (CHARDONNAY) whites. Wine with a village name (e.g. Mâcon-Prissé) is better. POUILLY-FUISSÉ is best appellation of the region. See also Mâcon-Villages.

Mâcon-Lugny See Lugny

Mâcon Supérieur
The same but slightly better, from riper grapes.

Mâcon-Villages B'y. w. dr. ★★→★★★
Increasingly well-made and typical white burgundies. Mâcon-Prissé, MÂCON-VIRÉ, MÂCON-LUGNY are examples.

Mâcon-Viré See Mâcon-Villages and Viré

Madiran s.w. France r. ★★ **75 76 78 79 81 82 83 84 85 86**
Dark vigorous fragrant red from ARMAGNAC. Well worth ageing. Top growers: Dom. de Bouscassé, Peyros, Laplace, Barréjat.

Magenta, Duc de
Burgundy estate (30 acres) based at CHASSAGNE-MONTRACHET, managed by JADOT.

Magnum A double bottle (1.5 litres).

Mähler-Besse
First-class Dutch wine-merchants in Bordeaux, with a majority share in Ch. PALMER. Brands incl. Cheval Noir.

Maire, Henri
The biggest grower and merchant of the JURA wines.

Marc Grape skins after pressing; also the strong-smelling brandy made from them. (cf. Italian "Grappa").

Marcillac s.w. France r.p. ★ D.Y.A.
Good rustic VDQS from the coop.

Margaux B'x. r. ★★→★★★★ **66 70 71 75 76 78 79 80** 81 82 83' 84 85 86
Village of the HAUT-MÉDOC making the most "elegant" red Bordeaux. The name includes CANTENAC and several other villages as well. Top ch'x. include MARGAUX, LASCOMBES, etc.

Margnat Major producer of everyday VIN DE TABLE.

Marque déposée Trade mark.

Marsannay B'y. (r.) or p. ★★★ **78 80** 83 85 86 (rosé D.Y.A.)
Village near Dijon with excellent light red and delicate PINOT NOIR rosé, perhaps the best rosé in France.

Mas de Daumas Gassac Midi r. ★★★ 80 81 82 83 84 85 86
 The outstanding estate of the Midi, producing huge Bordeaux-like wines on apparently unique soil. Alarming quality.

Maufoux, Prosper
 Family firm of burgundy merchants at SANTENAY. Reliable wines with good keeping qualities. Alias Marcel Amance.

Maury Pyr. r. sw. ★→★★ NV
 Red VIN DOUX NATUREL from ROUSSILLON.

Mazis (or Mazy) Chambertin B'y. r. ★★★ 76 78 80 82 83 85 86
 30-acre Grand Cru neighbour of CHAMBERTIN. Lighter wine.

Médoc B'x. r. ★★ 78 79 81 82 83 84 85 86
 Appellation for reds of the less good (n.) part of Bordeaux's biggest and best district. HAUT-MÉDOC is better.

Meffre, Gabriel
 The biggest southern Rhône estate, based at GIGONDAS. Includes Ch. de Vaudieu, CHÂTEAUNEUF-DU-PAPE.

Ménétou-Salon Lo. r. p. or w. dr. ★★ D.Y.A.
 Attractive light wines from w. of SANCERRE. SAUVIGNON white; PINOT NOIR red.

Mercier et Cie NV, Extra Rich and Rosé 80 81 and 73 75 76 78 80 81
 One of the biggest champagne houses, at Epernay. Controlled by MOËT & CHANDON.

Mercurey B'y. r. or w. dr. ★★ 78 83 84 85 86
 Leading red-wine village of the CÔTE CHALONNAISE. Good middle-rank burgundy. Growers incl. Ch. de Chamirey.

Métaireau, Louis
 The ring-leader of a group of top Muscadet growers. Expensive well-finished wines.

méthode champenoise
 The traditional laborious method of putting the bubbles in champagne by refermenting the wine in its bottle.

Meursault B'y. (r.) w. dr. ★★★ 78 81 82 83 84 85 86
 CÔTE DE BEAUNE village with some of the world's greatest whites: rich, savoury, dry but mellow. Best v'yds. incl. Perrières, Genevrières, Charmes. Top growers incl: AMPEAU, COCHE-DURY, Delagrange, LAFON, LATOUR, MAGENTA, CH. DE MEURSAULT, P. Morey, G. ROULOT. See also Blagny.

Meursault-Blagny See Blagny

Midi General term for the south of France, where standards have risen consistently in recent years.

Minervois Midi r. or (p.) (w.) or br. sw. ★→★★ 83 84 85 86
 Hilly VDQS area with some of the best wines of the Midi: lively and full of flavour. Also sweet MUSCAT de St. Jean de M.

mise en bouteilles au château, au domaine
 Bottled at the château, at the property or estate. N.B. dans nos caves (in our cellars) or dans la région de production (in the area of production) are often used although they mean little.

Moelleux Mellow. Used of the sweet wines of VOUVRAY, etc.

Moët & Chandon NV, rosé 81, Dry Imperial 71 73 75 76 78 80 81 82
 The biggest champagne merchant and grower, with cellars in Epernay and sparkling wine branches in Argentina, Brazil and California. Consistent quality. Luxury brand: DOM PÉRIGNON.

Moillard
 Big firm of growers and merchants in NUITS-ST-GEORGES, recently revitalized and making fine CÔTE DE NUITS wines.

Mommessin, J. Major BEAUJOLAIS merchant. Owner of CLOS DE TART.

Monbazillac Dordogne w. sw. ★★ 71 75 76 78 79 80 81 83 85 86
 Golden SAUTERNES-style wine from BERGERAC. Ages well. Ch. Monbazillac is best known.

Mondeuse Savoie r. ★★ D.Y.A.
 Red grape of SAVOIE. Good, vigorous, deep-coloured wine.

Mongeard-Mugneret
> 40-acre VOSNE-ROMANÉE estate. Fine ECHEZEAUX, VOUGEOT, etc.

Monopole   Vineyard in single ownership.

Montagne-Saint-Emilion   B'x. r. **★★** 75 76 78 79 81 82 83 85 86
> North-east neighbour of ST-EMILION with similar wines, becoming more important with each year. Top ch'x: Calon, St-André-Corbin, Vieux-Ch-St-André, Roudier, Teyssier, des Tours.

Montagny   B'y. w. dr. **★★** →★★★ 83 85 86
> CÔTE CHALONNAISE village between MÂCON and MEURSAULT, both geographically and gastronomically.

Montée de Tonnerre   B'y. w. dr. **★★★**
> Famous and excellent PREMIER CRU of CHABLIS.

Monthelie   B'y. r. **★★★** 78 80 82 83 84 85 86
> Little-known neighbour and almost equal of VOLNAY. Excellent fragrant reds. Best estate: Château de Monthélie.

Montlouis   Lo. w. sw./dr. **★★** 75 76 78 81 82 83' 84 85 86
> Neighbour of VOUVRAY. Similar sweet or dry long-lived wine.

Montrachet   B'y. w. dr. **★★★★** 69 71 73 76 78 79 80 81 82 83 84 85 86
> 19-acre Grand Cru v'yd. in both PULIGNY and CHASSAGNE-MONTRACHET. Potentially the greatest white burgundy: strong, perfumed, intense, dry yet luscious. (The "ts" are silent.)

Montravel   See Côtes de Montravel

Mont-Redon, Domaine de   Rh. r. (w. dr.) **★★★** 78 79 80 81 83 85 86
> Outstanding 235-acre estate in CHÂTEAUNEUF-DU-PAPE. Relatively early-maturing wines.

Moreau et Fils
> CHABLIS merchant and grower with 175 acres. Also major table-wine producer. Best wine: Clos des Hospices (Grand Cru).

Morey-Saint-Denis   B'y. r. **★★★** 71 76 78 79 80 82 83 84 85 86
> Small village with four Grands Crus between GEVREY-CHAMBER-TIN and CHAMBOLLE-MUSIGNY. Glorious wine, often overlooked.

Morgon   B'y. r. **★★★** 83 85 86
> The "firmest" cru of BEAUJOLAIS, needing time to develop its rich and savoury flavour.

Moueix, J-P et Cie
> The leading proprietor and merchant of St-Emilion and Pomerol. Ch'x. incl. MAGDELAINE, LAFLEUR-PETRUS, and part of PETRUS. Now also has a venture in California, see DOMINUS.

Moulin-à-Vent   B'y. r. **★★★** 83 84 85 86
> The "biggest" and best wine of Beaujolais; powerful and long-lived, eventually tasting more like CÔTE D'OR wine.

Moulis   B'x. r. **★★→★★★**
> Village of the HAUT-MÉDOC with its own appellation and several Crus Exceptionnels: CHASSE-SPLEEN, POUJEAUX-THEIL, MAUCAILLOU, etc. Wines are growing steadily finer.

Mousseux   Sparkling.

Mouton Cadet
> Best-selling brand of blended red and white Bordeaux.

Moutonne
> CHABLIS GRAND CRU *honoris causa*, owned by BICHOT.

Mumm, G. H. & Cie   NV "Cordon Rouge", rosé 79, Crémant de Cramant (NV) and 69 71 73 75 76 79 82
> Major champagne grower and merchant owned by Seagram's. Luxury brand: René Lalou (79). The Cramant is superb.

Muscadet   Lo. w. dr. **★★** D.Y.A.
> Popular, good-value, often delicious dry wine from round Nantes in s. Brittany. Should never be sharp. Perfect with fish.

Muscadet de Sèvre-et-Maine
> Wine from the central and usually best part of the area.

Muscat   Distinctively perfumed grape and its (usually sweet) wine, made dry in ALSACE.

Muscat de Beaumes de Venise
    One of the best French muscats (see Beaumes de Venise).

Muscat de Frontignan Midi br. sw. ** D.Y.A.
    Sweet Midi muscat.

Muscat de Lunel Midi br. sw. ** NV
    Ditto. A small area but good.

Muscat de Mireval Midi br. sw. ** NV
    Ditto, from near Montpellier.

Muscat de Rivesaltes Midi br. sw. * NV
    Sweet muscat from a big zone near Perpignan.

Musigny B'y. r. (w. dr.) **** 69 71 76 78 79 80 82 83 84 85 86
    25-acre Grand Cru in CHAMBOLLE-MUSIGNY. Often the best, if
    not the most powerful, of all red burgundies (and a little white).
    Best growers: DE VOGÜÉ, DROUHIN, Mugnier.

Nature Natural or unprocessed, esp. of still champagne.

Néac B'x. r. **
    Village n. of POMEROL. Wines sold as LALANDE-DE-POMEROL.

Négociant-éleveur
    Merchant who "brings up" (i.e. matures) the wine.

Nicolas, Ets.
    Paris-based wholesale and retail wine merchants controlled by
    Rémy-Martin. One of the biggest in France and one of the best.

Nuits-St-Georges r. **→ *** 69 71 76 78' 80 82 83' 84 85 86
    Important wine-town: wines of all qualities, typically sturdy and
    full-flavoured. Name can be shortened to "Nuits". Best v'yds.
    incl. Les St-Georges, Vaucrains, Les Pruliers, Clos des Corvées,
    Les Cailles, etc. Many growers and merchants.

Oisly et Thesée, Vignerons de
    Go-ahead cooperative in e. TOURAINE (Loire), experimenting
    successfully with superior grapes, esp. SAUV. BL. Good value.

Ott, Domaine
    Important producer of high-quality PROVENCE wines.

Pacherenc-du-Vic-Bilh S.W. France w. sw. * NV
    Rare minor speciality of the ARMAGNAC region.

Paillard, Bruno NV, Crémant Bl. de Bls, Rosé, 75 76 79
    Small but prestigious young Champagne house with excellent
    silky vintage and NV wines at fair prices.

Palette Prov. r. p. or w. dr. **
    Near Aix-en-Provence. Aromatic reds and good rosés.

Parigot-Richard
    Producer of high-quality CRÉMANT DE BOURGOGNE at SAVIGNY.

Pasquier-Desvignes
    Very old firm of Beaujolais merchants at St Lager, BROUILLY.

Patriarche
    One of the bigger firms of burgundy merchants. Cellars in
    Beaune; also owns Ch. DE MEURSAULT (100 acres), KRITER, etc.

Patrimonio Corsica r.w. dr. p **→ ***
    Wide range from dramatic chalk hills in n. Corsica. Fragrant
    reds, crisp whites, fine V.D.N. Top grower: Gentile.

Pauillac B'x. r. **→ **** 66 70 71 73 75 76 78 79 81 82 83 84 85 86
    The only village in Bordeaux (HAUT-MÉDOC) with three first-
    growths (Ch'x. LAFITE, LATOUR, MOUTON) and many other fine
    ones, famous for high flavour but very various in style.

Pécharmant Dordogne r. ** 82 83 85 86
    Usually better-than-typical light BERGERAC red, with more
    "meat". Top estate: Ch. de Tiregand.

Pelure d'oignon "Onion skin"—tawny tint of certain rosés.

Perlant or Perlé Very slightly sparkling.

Pernand-Vergelesses B'y. r. or (w. dr.) *** 78 80 81 82 83 84 85 86
    Village next to ALOXE-CORTON containing part of the great
    CORTON and CORTON-CHARLEMAGNE v'yds. and one other top
    v'yd.: Ile des Vergelesses.

Perrier, Joseph   NV, rosé and **71 73 75 76 79** 82
Family-run champagne house with considerable v'yds. at Chalon-s-Marne. Consistent light and fruity style.

Perrier-Jouet   NV, Blason de France NV, **71 73 75 76 79** 82
Excellent champagne-growers and makers at Epernay now linked with MUMM. Luxury brands: Belle Epoque **79** (in a painted bottle), Blason de France (NV). Also Belle Epoque Rosé **79** 82.

Pétillant   Slightly sparkling.

Petit Chablis   B'y. w. dr. **★★ 85 86**
Wine from fourth-rank CHABLIS v'yds. Lacks great character.

Piat Père et Fils
Important growers and merchants of BEAUJOLAIS and MÂCON wines at Mâcon, now controlled by Grand Metropolitan Ltd. V'yds. in MOULIN-À-VENT, also CLOS DE VOUGEOT. BEAUJOLAIS, MÂCON-VIRÉ in special Piat bottles maintain a fair standard.

Pic, Albert
Fine   CHABLIS   producer,   controlled   by   DE LADOU-CETTE.

Picpoul-de-Pinet   Midi w. dr. ★ NV
Rather dull very dry southern white, best v. cold on the spot.

Pineau de Charente
Strong sweet apéritif made of white grape juice and Cognac.

Pinot   See Grapes for white and red wine.

Piper-Heidsieck   NV, rosé **79**, Vintage **71 73 75 76 79** 82, Année Rare **76**, Brut Sauvage **79**
Champagne-makers of old repute at Reims.

Pol Roger   NV, rosé **75 79**, Blanc de Blancs **79** and **71 73 75 76 79**
Excellent champagne house at Epernay. Particularly good non-vintage White Foil. Luxury cuvée: "Sir Winston Churchill".

"Noble rot" (in French *pourriture noble*, in German *Edelfäule*, in Latin *Botrytis cinerea*) *is a form of mould that attacks the skins of ripe grapes in certain vineyards in warm and misty autumn weather.*

Its effect, instead of rotting the grapes, is to wither them. The skin grows soft and flaccid, the juice evaporates through it, and what is left is a super-sweet concentration of everything in the grape except its water content.

The world's best sweet table wines are all made of nobly rotten grapes. They occur in good vintages in Sauternes, the Rhine, the Mosel (where wine made from them is called Trockenbeerenauslese), in Tokaji in Hungary, in Burgenland in Austria, and occasionally elsewhere — California included. The danger is rain on pulpy grapes already far gone in noble rot. All too often, particularly in Sauternes, the grower's hopes are dashed by a break in the weather.

Pomerol   B'x. r. ★★→★★★★ **70 71 75 76 78 79 81 82** 83 85 86
The next village to ST-EMILION: similar but more "fleshy" wines, maturing sooner, reliable and delicious. Top ch. PETRUS, LA FLEUR-PETRUS, VIEUX-CH-CERTAN, LATOUR À POMEROL, etc..

Pommard   B'y. r. ★★★ **69 71 76 78 80 82** 83 84 85 86
The biggest and best-known village in Burgundy. No superlative wines, but many warmly appealing ones. Best v'yds.: Rugiens, Épenots and HOSPICES DE BEAUNE cuvées.

Pommery & Greno   NV, NV rosé and **71 73 75 76 78 79 80 81** 82
Very big CHAMPAGNE growers and merchants at Reims, revitalized by new owners. Luxury brand: Louise Pommery **80**.

Pouilly-Fuissé   B'y. w. dr. ★★→★★★ **83 84 85** 86
The best white of the MÂCON area. At its best (e.g. Ch. Fuissé, Vieilles Vignes) excellent, but almost always far over-priced.

Pouilly-Fumé   Lo. w. dr. ★★→★★★ **85 86**
"Gun-flinty", fruity, often sharp pale white from the upper Loire, next to SANCERRE. Grapes must be SAUVIGNON BLANC. Good vintages improve for 2–3 yrs.

Pouilly-Loché   B'y. w. dr. **★★**
Neighbour of POUILLY-FUISSÉ. Similar wine but little of it.

Pouilly-Sur-Loire Lo. w. dr. ★ D.Y.A.
> Inferior wine from the same v'yds. as POUILLY-FUMÉ, but different grapes (CHASSELAS).

Pouilly-Vinzelles B'y. w. dr. `★★` 85 86
> Neighbour of POUILLY-FUISSÉ. Similar wine, worth looking for.

Pousse d'Or, Domaine de la
> 32-acre estate in POMMARD, SANTENAY, and (esp.) VOLNAY where its "monopoles", "Bousse d'Or" and "60 Ouvrées" are justly famous.

Preiss Zimmer, Jean
> Old-established Alsace wine-merchants at Riquewihr.

Premières Côtes de Blaye B'x. r. w. dr. ★→★★ 78 81 82 83 85 86
> Restricted appellation for better reds of BLAYE. Ch'x. include Barbé, Charron, Bourdieu, l'Escadre, Segonzac, Le Menaudat.

Premier Cru
> First-growth in Bordeaux (see page 54), but the second rank of v'yds. (after Grand Cru) in Burgundy.

Premières Côtes de Bordeaux B'x. r. (p.) or w. dr. or sw. ★→★★
> Large area east of GRAVES: a good bet for quality and value, though never brilliant. Ch'x incl. Laffitte (sic), Gardera, Fayau, Haut-Brignon, REYNON, Tanesse.

Prieur, Domaine Jacques
> 35-acre estate all in top Burgundy sites, incl. Premier Cru MEURSAULT, VOLNAY, PULIGNY- and CHEVALIER-MONTRACHET.

Primeur
> Early wine (like early vegetables); esp. of BEAUJOLAIS.

Prissé See Mâcon-Villages

Propriétaire-récoltant Owner–manager.

Provence See Côtes de Provence

Puisseguin-Saint-Emilion B'x. r. `★★` 81 82 83 85 86
> Eastern neighbour of ST-EMILION; wines similar — not so fine but often good value. Ch'x incl. Laurets, Guibeau, Puisseguin, Soleil, Teyssier. Also "Roc de Puisseguin" from coop.

Puligny-Montrachet B'y. w. dr. (r.) ★★★ 78 81 82 83 84 85 86
> Bigger neighbour of CHASSAGNE-MONTRACHET with equally glorious rich dry whites. Best v'yds.: MONTRACHET, CHEVALIER-MONTRACHET, BATÂRD-MONTRACHET, Bienvenue-Bâtard-Montrachet, Les Combettes, Clavoillon, Pucelles, Champ-Canet, etc. Top growers incl: AMPEAU, BOUCHARD PÈRE, CHARTRON, LEFLAIVE, SAUZET.

Quarts de Chaume Lo. w. sw. ★★★ 75 76 78 82 83 84 85 86
> Famous 120-acre plot in COTEAUX DU LAYON. CHENIN BLANC grapes. Long-lived, intense, rich golden wine, esp. Ch. La Suronde.

Quatourze Midi r. (p.) or w. dr. ★ 83 84 85 86
> Minor VDQS area near Narbonne.

Quincy Lo. w. dr. ★★ 85 86
> Small area making v. dry SANCERRE-style wine of SAUV. BL.

Ramonet-Prudhon
> One of the leading proprietors in CHASSAGNE-MONTRACHET with 34 acres. Sometimes excellent whites, and red Clos St-Jean.

Rancio
> Term for the tang of wood-aged fortified wine, esp. BANYULS and other VINS DOUX NATURELS. A fault in table wines.

Rasteau Rh. r. (p. w. dr.) or br. sw. ★★ NV
> Village of s. Rhône valley. Very sound reds. Good strong sweet dessert wine is the local speciality.

Ratafia de Champagne
> Sweet apéritif made in Champagne of ⅔ grape juice and ⅓ brandy.

Récolte Crop or vintage.

Reine Pédauque, La
> Burgundy growers and merchants at ALOXE-CORTON.

Remoissenet Père et Fils
>Fine Burgundy merchants (esp. for white wines) with a tiny estate at BEAUNE.

Rémy Pannier Important Loire-wine merchants at SAUMUR.

Reuilly Lo. (r.p.) w. dr. **★★ 85 86**
>Neighbour of QUINCY with similar wine; also good PINOT GRIS.

Riceys, Rosé des
>Minute appellation in southern CHAMPAGNE for a notable PINOT NOIR rosé. Principal producer: A. Bonnet.

Richebourg B'y. r. **★★★★ 66 69 70 71 76 78 79 80 81 82 83 84 85 86**
>19-acre Grand Cru in VOSNE-ROMANÉE. Powerful, perfumed, fabulously expensive wine, among Burgundy's best.

Riesling See Grapes for white wine

Rivesaltes Midi r.w. dr. br. sw. **★★ NV**
>Fortified sweet wine, some muscat-flavoured, from e. Pyrenees. An ancient tradition still very much alive, if struggling.

La Roche-aux-Moines Lo. w. dr./sw. **★★★ 75 76 78 79 81 82 83 85 86**
>60-acre v'yd. in Savennières, Anjou. Intense strong fruity/sharp wine ages well.

Rodet, Antonin
>Substantial Burgundy merchant and a well-known grower of MERCUREY (Ch. de Chamirey).

Roederer, Louis Brut Premier NV, Rosé 75 and **71 73 75 76 78 79** 81
>One of the best champagne-growers and merchants at Reims. V. reliable non-vintage wine with plenty of flavour. Luxury brand: Cristal Brut 79 (in white glass bottles).

La Romanée B'y. r. **★★★★ 71 76 78 80 82 83 84 85 86**
>2-acre Grand Cru in VOSNE-ROMANÉE just uphill from ROMANÉE-CONTI, distributed by BOUCHARD.

Romanée-Conti B'y. r. **★★★★ 66 71 73 76 78 79 80 81 82 83 84 85 86**
>4½-acre Grand Cru in VOSNE-ROMANÉE. The most celebrated and expensive red wine in the world. Sometimes the best.

Romanée-Conti, Domaine de la
>The grandest estate of Burgundy, owning the whole of ROMANÉE-CONTI and LA TÂCHE and major parts of RICHEBOURG, GRANDS ECHÉZEAUX, ECHÉZEAUX and ROMANÉE-ST-VIVANT (under Marey-Monge label). Also a very small part of LE MONTRACHET.

Romanée-St-Vivant B'y. r. **★★★★ 71 76 78 79 80 82 83 84 85 86**
>23-acre Grand Cru in VOSNE-ROMANÉE. Similar to ROMANÉE-CONTI but lighter and less sumptuous.

Ropiteau
>Burgundy wine-growers and merchants at MEURSAULT. Specialists in MEURSAULT and CÔTE DE BEAUNE wines.

Rosé d'Anjou Lo. p. ★ D.Y.A.
>Pale, slightly sweet, rosé. Cabernet d'Anjou *should* be better.

Rosé de Loire Lo. p. dr. ★→★★ D.Y.A.
>Appellation for dry Loire rosé (Anjou is sweet).

Roty, Joseph Small grower of classic GEVREY-CHAMBERTIN.

Rousseau, Domaine A.
>Major burgundy grower famous for CHAMBERTIN, etc. of highest quality. Only avoid his '82s.

Roussette de Savoie Savoie w. dr. ★★ D.Y.A.
>The tastiest of the fresh whites from s. of Geneva.

Roussillon
>See Côtes du Roussillon. "Grands Roussillons" are VINS DOUX NATURELS.

Ruchottes-Chambertin B'y. r. **★★★ 71 73 76** 78 **79 80** 82 83 84 85
>7½-acre Grand Cru neighbour of CHAMBERTIN. Similar splendid long-lasting wine.

Ruinart Père et Fils NV, rosé and Bl. de Blancs **71 73 75 76 78 79**
>The oldest champagne house, now belonging to Moët-Hennessy. Luxury brand: Dom Ruinart, Blanc de Blancs **79**.

Rully B'y. r. or w. dr. or (sp.) ⟦★★⟧ 83 84 w. 85 86
    Village of the CÔTE CHALONNAISE famous for sparkling burgundy. Still reds and white light but tasty and good value.

Saint-Amour B'y. r. ★★ 85 86
    Northernmost cru of BEAUJOLAIS: light, fruity, irresistible.

Saint-Aubin B'y. (r.) or w. dr. ⟦★★⟧ 83 85 86
    Little-known neighbour of CHASSAGNE-MONTRACHET, up a side-valley. Not top-rank, but typical and good value. Also sold as CÔTE-DE-BEAUNE-VILLAGES.

Saint Bris B'y. (r.) w. dr. ⟦★⟧ D.Y.A.
    Village w. of CHABLIS known for its fruity ALIGOTÉ, making good sparkling burgundy, but chiefly for SAUVIGNON de ST BRIS.

Saint Chinian Midi r. ⟦★→★★⟧ 83 84 85 86
    Hilly area of growing reputation in the COTEAUX DU LANGUEDOC. Appellation Contrôlée since 1982. Tasty reds.

Sainte Croix-du-Mont B'x. w. sw. ⟦★★⟧ 71 75 76 79 80 81 83 84 86
    Neighbour to SAUTERNES with similar golden wine. No superlatives but well worth trying, esp. Ch. Loubens. A bargain.

Sainte-Foy-Bordeaux B'x.
    Part of ENTRE-DEUX-MERS, more akin to BERGERAC.

Saint-Emilion B'x. r. ★★→★★★★ 70 71 75 76 78 79 80 81 82 83 85 86
    The biggest (13,000 acres) top-quality Bordeaux district; solid, rich, tasty wines from hundreds of ch'x., incl. CHEVAL-BLANC, AUSONE, CANON, MAGDELAINE, FIGEAC, etc. Also a v.g. coop.

Saint-Estèphe B'x. r. ⟦★★⟧ →★★★★ 75 78 79 80 81 82 83 84 85 86
    Northern village of HAUT-MÉDOC. Solid, satisfying, occasionally superlative wines. Top ch'x.: CALON-SÉGUR, COS D'ESTOURNEL, MONTROSE, etc., and many notable CRUS BOURGEOIS.

St-Gall
    Brand-name used by Union-Champagne the very good champagne-growers' Cooperative at AVIZE.

Saint-Georges-Saint-Emilion B'x. r. ⟦★★⟧ 81 82 83 85 86
    Part of MONTAGNE-ST-EMILION. with high standards. Best ch'x.: ST-GEORGES, Belair-Montaiguillon, Marquis-St-Georges, Tour-du-Pas-St-Georges.

Saint-Joseph Rh. r. (p. or w. dr.) ⟦★★⟧ 76 78 79 80 82 83 85 86
    Northern Rhône appellation of second rank but reasonable price. Substantial wine often better than CROZES-HERMITAGE.

Saint-Julien B'x. r. ★★★→★★★★ 70 75 76 78 79 80 81 82' 83' 84 85 86
    Mid-Médoc village with a dozen of Bordeaux's best ch'x., incl. three LÉOVILLES, BEYCHEVELLE, DUCRU-BEAUCAILLOU, GRUAUD-LAROSE, etc. The epitome of well-balanced red wine.

Saint-Laurent
    Village next to SAINT-JULIEN. Appellation HAUT-MÉDOC.

Saint-Nicolas-de-Bourgueil Lo. r. ★★ 82 83 84 85 86
    The next village to BOURGUEIL: the same light but lively and fruity CABERNET red.

Saint-Péray Rh. w. dr. or sp. ★★ NV
    Rather heavy white from the n. Rhône, much of it made sparkling. A curiosity worth investigating.

Saint Pourçain Central France r. p. or w. dr ⟦★⟧ D.Y.A.
    The agreeable local wine of Vichy, rather chic in Paris. Made from GAMAY and/or PINOT NOIR, the white from Tressalier, CHARDONNAY or SAUVIGNON BLANC.

Saint Romain B'y. r. w. dr. ⟦★★⟧ 83 85 86
    Overlooked village just behind the CÔTE DE BEAUNE. Value, esp. for young whites. Top grower: Thévenin.

Saint-Sauveur
    HAUT-MÉDOC village just w. of PAUILLAC.

Saint-Seurin-de-Cadourne
    HAUT-MÉDOC village just n. of SAINT-ESTÈPHE.

Saint-Véran B'y. w. dr. `**` 83 84 85

Next-door appellation to POUILLY-FUISSÉ. Similar but better value: real character from the best slopes of MÂCON-VILLAGES.

Salins du Midi, Domaine Viticole See Listel

Salon Le Mesnil 61 64 66 69 71 73 76 79

The original Blanc de Blancs champagne, from Le Mesnil. Fine very dry wine with extraordinary keeping qualities.

Sancerre Lo. (r. p.) or w. dr. `***` 85 86

Very fragrant and fresh SAUVIGNON white almost indistinguishable from POUILLY-FUMÉ, its neighbour over the Loire. Drink young. Also light P. NOIR red (best drunk at 2–3 yrs) and rosé.

Santenay B'y. r. or (w. dr.) `***` 71 76 78 79 80 82 83 84 85 86

Very worthy, rarely rapturous, sturdy reds from the s. of the CÔTE DE BEAUNE. Best v'yds.: Les Gravières, Clos de Tavannes, La Comme. Top grower: DOMAINE DE LA POUSSE D'OR.

Saumur Lo. r. p. or w. dr. and sp. `*→` `**`

Big versatile district in ANJOU, with fresh fruity whites, v. g. CRÉMANT pale rosés and increasingly good CABERNET reds, the best from Saumur-Champigny, esp. Ch. de Chaintres.

Sauternes B'x.w. sw. `**` `→****` 67 71 75 76 78 79 80 81 82 83 84 85 86

District of 5 villages (incl. BARSAC) making France's best sweet wine: strong (14% + alcohol) luscious and golden, demanding, to be aged. Top ch'x.: D'YQUEM, SUDUIRAUT, COUTET, CLIMENS, GUIRAUD, etc. Also dry wines which cannot be sold as Sauternes.

Sauvignon Blanc See Grapes for white wine

Sauvignon-de-St-Bris B'y. w. dr. `**` D.Y.A.

A baby VDQS cousin of SANCERRE from near CHABLIS. To try.

Sauvion et Fils

Ambitious and well-run MUSCADET house, based at the Ch. de Cléray. Top wine: Cardinal Richard.

Sauzet, Etienne

White burgundy estate at PULIGNY-MONTRACHET. Recent quality patchy.

Savennières Lo. w. dr./sw. `***` 75 76 78 81 82 83 84 85 86

Small ANJOU district of pungent, long-lived whites, incl. COULÉE DE SERRANT, LA ROCHE AUX MOINES, Clos du Papillon.

Savigny-lès-Beaune B'y. r. or (w. dr.) `***` 76 78 80 82 83 85 86

Important village next to BEAUNE, with similar well-balanced middle-weight wines, often deliciously delicate and fruity. Best v'yds.: Marconnets, Dominode, Serpentières, Vergelesses, les Guettes. Top growers incl: BIZE, Girard-Vollot, TOLLOT-BEAUT.

Savoie E. France r. or w. dr. or sp. `**` D.Y.A.

Alpine area with light dry wines like some Swiss wine or minor Loires. CRÉPY, SEYSSEL and APREMONT are best known whites, ROUSSETTE is often more interesting. Also MONDEUSE red.

Schlumberger et Cie

ALSACE grower-merchants of luscious wines at Guebwiller.

Schröder & Schyler

Old family firm of Bordeaux merchants, owners of CH. KIRWAN.

Sciacarello

Red grape of Corsica's best red and rosé, e.g. AJACCIO, Sartène.

Sec Literally means dry, though champagne so-called is medium-sweet (and better at breakfast and tea-time than Brut).

Selection de Grains Nobles

Description coined by HUGEL for Alsace equivalent to German BEERENAUSLESE. "Grains nobles" are individual grapes with "noble rot" (see page 46).

Sèvre-et-Maine

The *département* containing the best v'yds. of MUSCADET.

Seyssel Savoie w. dr. or sp. `**` NV

Delicate pale dry white making admirable sparkling wine.

Sichel & Co.

Two famous merchant houses. In Bordeaux owners of Ch. D'ANGLUDET and part-owners of Ch. PALMER. In Germany, maker of BLUE NUN.

Soussans

Village just n. of MARGAUX, sharing its appellation.

Sylvaner

See Grapes for white wine

Syrah See Grapes for red wine

La Tâche B'y. r. ★★★★ 62 69 70 71 73 76 78 79 80 81 82 83 84 85 86

15-acre Grand Cru of VOSNE-ROMANÉE and one of the best v'yds. on earth: dark, perfumed and luxurious wine. Owned by the DOMAINE DE LA ROMANÉE-CONTI.

Taittinger NV, Collection Brut 78 and 71 73 75 76 78 79 80 82

Fashionable champagne growers and merchants of Reims with a light touch. Luxury brand: Comtes de Champagne 76 79 (also v.g. rosé 79).

Tastevin, Confrérie des Chevaliers du

Burgundy's colourful and successful promotion society. Wine carrying their Tastevinage label has been approved by them and will usually be of a fair standard. A tastevin is the traditional shallow silver wine-tasting cup of Burgundy. See panel, page 31.

Tavel Rh. p. ★★★ D.Y.A.

France's most famous, though not her best, rosé, strong and dry, starting vivid pink and fading to orange. Avoid orange bottles.

Tête de Cuvée

Archaic term vaguely used of the best wines of an appellation.

Thénard, Domaine

The major grower of GIVRY, but best known for his substantial portion (4.5 acres) of LE MONTRACHET.

Thevenet, Jean

A master maker of white Mâcon-Clessé (Domaine de la Bon Gran) at Quintaine-Clessé, near LUGNY.

Thorin, J.

Grower and major merchant of BEAUJOLAIS, at Pontanevaux, owner of the Château des Jacques, MOULIN À VENT.

Thouarsais, Vin de Lo. r. ⬜★ D.Y.A.

Light GAMAY VDQS area south of SAUMUR.

Tokay d'Alsace See Pinot Gris under Grapes for white wine

Tollot-Beaut

Stylish burgundy grower with some 50 acres in the CÔTE DE BEAUNE, incl. CORTON, BEAUNE, Grèves, SAVIGNY (Les Champs Chevrey) and at Chorey-lès-Beaune where he is based.

Tortochot, Domaine

25-acre estate based at GEVREY-CHAMBERTIN. Classic wines.

Touraine Lo. r. p. w. dr./sw./sp. ⬜★→★★★

Big mid-Loire province with immense range of wines, incl. dry white SAUVIGNON, dry and sweet CHENIN BLANC (e.g. VOUVRAY), red CHINON and BOURGUEIL, light red CABERNETS, GAMAYS and rosés. Cabernets, Sauvignons and Gamays of good years are bargains. Amboise, Azay-le-Rideau and Mesland are sub-sections of the appellation.

Trimbach, F. E.

Distinguished ALSACE grower and merchant at Ribeauvillé. Best wines (incl. the austere Riesling Clos Ste. Hune) mature magnificently.

Tursan s.w. France r. p. w. dr. ★

Emerging VDQS in the Landes. Sound reds.

Vacqueyras Rh. r. ⬜★★ 78 80 82 83 84 85 86

Prominent village of s. CÔTES-DU-RHÔNE, neighbour to GIGON-DAS; comparable with CHÂTEAUNEUF-DU-PAPE but less heavy and more "elegant".

Valençay Lo. w. dr. ★ D.Y.A.

Neighbour of CHEVERNY: similar pleasant sharpish wine.

Val-Joannis, Ch. de Prov. r. p. w. dr. ★★

Impressive new estate making v.g. AIX wines.

Varichon & Clerc

Principal makers and shippers of SAVOIE sparkling wines.

Varoilles, Domaine des

Burgundy estate of 30 acres, principally in GEVREY-CHAMBER-TIN. Wines with great keeping qualities.

Vaudésir B'y. w. dr. ★★★★ 78 81 83 84 85 86

Arguably the best of the 7 Grands Crus of CHABLIS (but then so are the others).

VDQS Vin Délimité de Qualité Supérieure (see p. 21).

Vendange Vintage.

Vendange tardive

Late vintage. In ALSACE equivalent to German AUSLESE.

Veuve Clicquot NV ("Yellow label") NV Demi-Sec (White Label) and (Gold Label) 73 75 76 78 79 80 and rosé.

Historic champagne house of the highest standing, now owned by Louis Vuitton (luggage!). Full-bodied wines. Cellars at Reims. Luxury brand: La Grande Dame 79.

Vidal-Fleury, J.

Long-established shippers and growers of top Rhône wines.

Vieilles Vignes

"Old vines" — therefore the best wine. Used for such wine by BOLLINGER, DE VOGÜÉ and others.

Viénot, Charles

Grower-merchant of good burgundy, at NUITS. 70 acres in Nuits, CORTON, RICHEBOURG, etc.

Vignoble Area of vineyards.

Vin de garde

Wine that will improve with keeping. The serious stuff.

Vin de l'année

This year's wine. See Beaujolais, Beaujolais-Villages.

THE COLOUR OF AGE

One very easy way of gauging the maturity of a red wine without opening the bottle is simply to hold the neck of the bottle up to a bright light. If the colour of the wine in the neck is deep red the wine is almost certainly still young and vigorous. If it appears a light orange colour, the wine is fully mature and should be drunk. If possible, compare a very fine Bordeaux and a simple one at, say, ten years old to see the difference: the better wine will look much darker.

Vin de paille

Wine from grapes dried on straw mats, consequently very sweet, like Italian passito. Especially in the JURA.

Vin de Pays

The junior rank of country wines (see Introduction). Well over 100 are now operational. Don't turn up your nose.

Vin de Table

Standard everyday table wine, not subject to particular regulations about grapes and origin. Choose the previous entry.

Vin Doux Naturel ("VDN")

Sweet wine fortified with wine alcohol, so the sweetness is "natural", not the strength. The most distinguished product of ROUSSILLON. A vin doux liquoreux is several degrees stronger.

Vin Gris

"Grey" wine is very pale pink, made of red grapes pressed before fermentation begins, unlike rosé, which ferments briefly before pressing. Oeil de Perdrix means much the same; so does "blush".

Vin Jaune Jura w. dr. ★★★

>Speciality of ARBOIS: odd yellow wine like fino sherry. Normally ready when bottled. The best is CHÂTEAU CHÂLON.

Vin nouveau See Beaujolais Nouveau

Vin vert

>A very light, acidic, refreshing white wine, a speciality of ROUSSILLON and v. necessary in summer in those parts.

Vinsobres Rh. r. (p. or w. dr.) ★★ 78 80 81 83 84 85 86

>Contradictory name of good s. Rhône village. Strong substantial reds which mature well.

Viré B'y. w. dr. ★★ 84 85

>One of the best white-wine villages of Mâcon. Good wines from coop, Ch. de Viré, Clos du Chapitre, JADOT.

Visan Rh. r. p. or w. dr. ★★ 83 84 85 86

>One of the better s. Rhône villages. Reds better than white.

Viticulteur Wine-grower.

Vogüé, Comte Georges de

>First-class 30-acre burgundy domaine at CHAMBOLLE-MUSIGNY. At best the ultimate MUSIGNY and BONNES MARES. Avoid '83s.

Volnay B'y. r. ★★★ 71 76 78 79 80 81 82 83 84 85 86

>Village between POMMARD and MEURSAULT: the best reds of the CÔTE DE BEAUNE, not strong or heavy but fragrant and silky. Best v'yds.: Caillerets, Clos des Ducs, Champans, Clos des Chênes, etc. Best growers: POUSSE D'OR, d'ANGERVILLE.

Volnay-Santenots B'y. r. ★★★

>Excellent red wine from MEURSAULT is sold under this name. Indistinguishable from VOLNAY.

Vosne-Romanée B'y. r. ★★★→★★★★ 71 76 78 79 80 81 82 83 84 85 86

>The village containing Burgundy's grandest Crus (ROMANÉE-CONTI, LA TÂCHE, etc.). There are (or rather should be) no common wines in Vosne.

Vougeot See Clos de Vougeot

Vouvray Lo. w. dr./sw./sp. ★★→★★★★ 71 76 78 79 82 83 84 85 86

>Small district of TOURAINE with very variable wines, at their best intensely sweet and almost immortal. Good dry sparkling.

"Y" (Pronounced ygrec) 78 79 80 84

>Brand name of powerful dry wine of great character, occasionally made at Ch. D'YQUEM.

Ziltener, André

>Swiss burgundy merchant with cellars in Gevrey-Chambertin. Reds especially good.

Zind-Humbrecht

>64-acre Alsace estate in Wintzenheim, Turckheim and Thann. First-rate individual v'yd wines (esp. Clos St. Urbain Riesling).

Châteaux of Bordeaux

Some 370 of the best-known Bordeaux châteaux are listed below, a–z. The vintage information has been entirely revised for the 1988 edition with the help of my friends and colleagues in Bordeaux and abroad, supplementing my own notes.

Vintages marked with an accent are judged to epitomize the qualities of the château in question. Whether each vintage will improve with keeping or should be drunk is indicated, as elsewhere, by the weight of type.

The information is complete up to the 1985 vintage (the most recent bottled), which was made in almost ideal conditions, culminating in a heatwave in late September. If there was a problem it was with the size of the crop, which means that however good the wines, few have either the fruity depth of the great '82s, or the classic structure of the '83s. It is a very good vintage, but will be a fairly fast-maturing one.

N.B. Many '84s are recommended here after careful assessment, but with a proviso: their original prices were much too high for a rather lean vintage. It is the least good vintage since 1980, particularly for Pomerol and St-Emilion. Bargain hard. Do not pay inflated prices. For the moment we are in a buyer's market.

1986 (not yet in bottle, therefore no individual recommendations yet) was an even bigger vintage than '85, but may well turn out to have more depth of fruit. In Sauternes it was a great success.

It should always be remembered that in Bordeaux the making of a vintage is only the preface to its history: opinions and reputations continue to alter until the last bottle has been drunk.

d'Agassac   Haut-Médoc r.   **★★**   75′ 78 79 80 81 82′ 83 84 85
14th-century moated fort with 86 acres. Same owners as Ch'x CALON-SÉGUR and DU TERTRE. Very tasty wines.

Andron-Blanquet   St-Est. r.   **★★** 82 83 85
Sister-château to COS LABORY. Can be a big rustic character.

L'Angélus   St-Em. r.   **★★** 75′ 76 78 79′ 80 81′ 82 83 85
Well-situated classed-growth of 57 acres on the St-Emilion Côtes w. of the town. More steady than exciting, but worth watching.

d'Angludet   Cant-Mar. r.   **★★**   70′ 75 76′ 78′ 79 80 81′ 82 83′ 84 85
75-acre British-owned Cru Exceptionnel of classed-growth quality. Lively fragrant Margaux of great style.

d'Archambeau   Graves r. and w. dr. (sw.)   **★★**
Up-to-date 54-acre property at Illats. V.g. fruity dry wine; now also good easy red.

D'Arche   Sauternes w. sw.   **★★** 78 79 80 81 82 83′ 85
Substantial second-rank classed-growth of 88 acres rejuvenated since 1980. Ch. d'Arche-Lafaurie was its second label until '81.

d'Arcins   Central Médoc r.   **★★**
185-acre property of the Castel family (cf. Castelvin); sister-château to neighbouring Barreyres (160 acres).

l'Arrosée   St-Em. r.   **★★**   78 79 81 82 83 85
Substantial 24-acre Côtes property. Serious wine with "stuffing", despite its name (which means watered).

Ausone   St-Em. r.   **★★★★** 70 71′ 75′ 76′ 78 79′ 80 81′ 82′ 83′ 84 85
Celebrated first-growth with 17 acres in the best position on the Côtes and famous rock-hewn cellars under the vineyard. Impresses more with each vintage. See also Ch. Belair.

Bahans-Haut-Brion   Gr. r.   **★★★** NV and 83
The second-quality wine of Ch. HAUT-BRION.

Balestard-la-Tonnelle   St-Em. r.   **★★**   70′ 75′ 76′ 78 79 81 82 83 85
Historic 30-acre classed-growth on the plateau near the town. Mentioned by the 15th-century poet Villon and still in the same family (which also owns Ch. CAP-DE-MOURLIN).

de Barbe   Côtes de Bourg r. (w.)   **★★**   79′ 81 82′ 83 85
The biggest (148 acres) and best-known ch. of the right bank of the Gironde. Good tasty, light but fruity, Merlot red.

Bastor-Lamontagne   Sauternes w. sw.   **★★**   76 79 80 82 83 85
Large "bourgeois" Preignac property; excellent rich wines.

Batailley   Pauillac r.   **★★★**   61 70 75′ 76 78′ 79′ 80 81 82′ 83 84 85
The bigger of the famous pair of fifth-growths (with HAUT-BATAILLEY) on the borders of Pauillac and St-Julien. 110 acres. Fine, firm strong-flavoured wine. Sold by BORIE-MANOUX.

Beaumont   Cussac, Haut-Médoc r.   **★★**   78′ 79 81 82 83 84 85
Considerable Cru Bourgeois, well-known in France for rather light but consistently attractive wines. In new hands since '79. Second label: Ch. Moulin d'Arvigny.

Beauregard   Pomerol r.   **★★★**   75′ 76 79′ 81 82′ 83 85
32-acre v'yd. with pretty 17th-century ch. near LA CONSEILLANTE. Well-made delicate "round" wines.

Beau Séjour-Bécot   St-Em. r.   **★★★** 75′ 76′ 78 79 80 81 82 83′ 85
Half of the old Beau Séjour Premier Grand Cru estate on the w. slope of the Côtes. Easy, tasty wines. 45 acres. Controversially demoted in class in '85. The Bécots also own CH. GRAND PONTET.

Beauséjour-Duffau-Lagarosse   St-Em. r.   **★★★** 70 75 76 78 79 80 81 82 83 85
The other half of the above, 17 acres in old family hands, making well-structured (not heavy) wine for long maturing.

Beau-Site   St-Est. r.   **★★**   70′ 75′ 76′ 78 79 80 81 82 83 84 85
55-acre Cru Bourgeois Exceptionnel in same hands as Ch'x BATAILLEY, TROTTEVIEILLE, etc. Regular quality and substance typical of St-Estèphe.

Belair St-Em. r. ★★★ **70 71 75' 76' 78 79' 80 82' 83' 85'**
Sister-ch. and neighbour of AUSONE with 34.5 acres on the Côtes. A very high standard in recent vintages (esp. '85). Makes a NV, "Roc-Blanquant", in magnums only.

de Bel-Air Lalande de Pomerol r. ★★ **75' 76 78 79 80 81 82' 83 85**
The best-known estate of this village just n. of Pomerol, with very similar wine. 25 acres.

Bel Air-Marquis d'Aligre Sou-Mar. r. ★★ **70' 75' 76 78 79 80 81 82' 83 84 85**
Cru Exceptionnel with 42 acres of old vines, now on fine form.

Belgrave St-Lau. r. ★★ **81 82 83 85**
Obscure fifth-growth in St-Julien's back-country. 107 acres. Acquired by DOURTHE in 1979. To watch.

Bel-Orme-Tronquoy-de-Lalande St-Seurin-de-Cadourne (Haut-Médoc) r. ★★ **70' 71 75' 76 78' 79' 81 82' 83 84 85**
Reputable 60-acre Cru Bourgeois n. of St-Estèphe. Old v'yd. producing tannic wines. Same owner as Ch. RAUZAN-GASSIES.

Berliquet St-Em. r. ★★ **79 80 81 82 83 85**
Tiny Grand Cru Classé recently v. well run (by the coop).

Beychevelle St-Jul. r. ★★★ **61 66 70' 75' 78 79 80 81 82' 83 84 85**
170-acre fourth-growth with the Médoc's finest mansion. Wine of more elegance than power, patchy to '82, now steady.

Bonnet Entre-Deux-Mers r. & w. dr. ★★ (w.) D. Y. A.
Big-scale producer of some of the Best Entre-Deux-Mers.

Bon-Pasteur Pom. r. ★★→★★★ **70 75 76 78 79 81 82 83 85**
Excellent very small property on the St-Emilion boundary. Concentrated, sometimes even creamy, wines.

Le Bourdieu Haut-Médoc r. ★★ **75' 78' 79 80 81 82 83 85**
Cru Bourgeois at Vertheuil with sister ch. Victoria (134 acres in all) known for well-made St-Estèphe-style wines.

A Bordeaux label

CHATEAU LANGOA-
BARTON

GRAND CRU CLASSE

APPELLATION ST-JULIEN
CONTROLEE

MIS EN BOUTEILLES AU
CHATEAU

1 A château is an estate, not necessarily with a mansion or a big expanse of vineyard.
2 Reference to the local classification. It varies from one part of Bordeaux to another.
3 The Appellation Contrôlée: look up St-Julien in the France A–Z.
4 "Bottled at the château"—now the normal practice with classed-growth wines.

Bourgneuf-Vayron Pomerol r. ★★→★★★ **75' 76 78 79 81 82 83 84 85**
22-acre v'yd. on chalky clay soil making fairly rich wines with good typically plummy Pomerol perfume.

Bouscaut Graves r. w. dr. ★★★ **70' 75' 76 78' 79 80 81 82' 83 84** (w.) **85**
Classed-growth at Cadaujac bought in 1980 by Lucien Lurton, owner of Ch. BRANE-CANTENAC, etc. 75 acres red (largely Merlot); 15 acres white. Never yet brilliant.

du Bousquet Côtes de Bourg r. ★★ **78 79 81 82 83 85**
Reliable estate with 148 acres making attractive solid wine.

Boyd-Cantenac Margaux r. ★★★ **75' 76' 78' 79 80 81 82' 83' 84 85**
44-acre third-growth regularly producing attractive wine; tending to improve. See also Ch. POUGET.

Branaire-Ducru St-Jul. r. ★★★ **70' 75' 76 78 79' 80 81 82' 83 84 85**
Fourth-growth of 125 acres producing notably spicy and flavoury wine: attractive and reliable.

Brane-Cantenac Cant-Mar. r. ★★★ 75' 76 78' 79 80 81 82' 83 85
 Big (211 acres) well-run second-growth. Fragrant, gamey wines occasionally sl. coarse. Same owners as Ch'x DURFORT-VIVENS, VILLEGEORGE, CLIMENS, BOUSCAUT, etc.

Brillette Moulis, Haut-Médoc r. ★★ 75 78 79 80 81' 82 83 84
 70-acre v'yd. Reliable and attractive; fulfilling high promise.

La Cabanne Pomerol r. 71 75' 76 78' 79 81 82' 83 85
 Highly-regarded 25-acre property near the great Ch. TROTANOY. Recently modernized; expect to hear more.

Cadet Piola St-Em. r. ★★ 70' 71 73 75' 76 78 79 81 82 83 85
 Reliable little property just n. of the town of St-Emilion. Ch. Faurie de Souchard has same owner; slightly less fine wine.

Caillou Sauternes w. sw. ★★ 83
 Well-run second-rank 37-acre vineyard for firm, fruity wine.

Calon-Ségur St-Est. r. ★★★ 70 75 76 78' 79' 80 81 82' 83 84 85
 Big (123-acre) third-growth of great reputation. A great classic for big hearty wines, but recently suffering in reputation.

Cambon-la-Pelouse Haut-Médoc r. ★★ 81 82 83 84 85
 Huge (145-acre) accessible Cru Bourgeois. A sure bet for fresh typical Médoc without wood ageing.

Camensac St-Lau. r. ★★ 75' 76 78' 79 80 81 82' 83 84 85
 149-acre fifth-growth, replanted in the '60s with new equipment and the same expert direction as LAROSE-TRINTAUDON. Good vigorous but not exactly classic wines.

Canon St-Em. r. ★★★ 70 71 75' 76 78 79' 80 81 82' 83' 84 85
 Famous first-classed-growth with 44+ acres on the plateau w. of the town. Conservative methods; very impressive wine.

Canon-la-Gaffelière St-Em. r. ★★ 75 78 79 81 82' 83 85
 47-acre classed-growth on the lower slopes of the Côtes in German ownership. Reliable lightish wines.

Canon-Moueix Fronsac r. ★★★ 83 85
 Revolutionary new Canon Fronsac made like a luxury Pomerol.

Cantemerle Macau r. ★★★ 66 70 75' 76 78 79 81 82 83' 84 85
 Superb estate at the extreme s. of the Médoc, with a romantic ch. in a wood and 100 acres of vines. Officially fifth-growth: potentially nearer second. Problems hampered quality in late '70s. A new broom (CORDIER) since 1981 is fulfilling potential.

Cantenac-Brown Cant-Mar. r. 61 70 75 76 78 79 80 81 82 83 84 85
 Formerly old-fashioned 77-acre third-growth, with very promising '82 and '83. Big wines. New owners in '87.

Capbern-Gasqueton St-Est. r. ★★ 75 76 78 79 80 81 82 83 84 85
 Good 85-acre Cru Bourgeois; same owner as CALON-SÉGUR.

Cap de Mourlin St-Em. r. ★★ 70' 75' 78 79' 80 81 82' 83 85
 Well-known 37-acre property of the Cap de Mourlin family, owners of Ch. BALESTARD. Classic St-Emilion.

Carbonnieux Graves r. and w. dr. ★★★ (r.) 78' 79 81 82 83 85
 Historic estate at Léognan making good fairly light wines by modern methods. The white is the better, up to 4-5 years.

La Cardonne Blaignan (Médoc) r. ★★ 78 79 81' 83 84 85
 Large (200+ acres) Cru Bourgeois in the n. Médoc bought in 1973 by the Rothschilds of LAFITE. A safe bet.

Les Carmes-Haut-Brion Graves r. ★★ 75 78 79 80 81' 82' 83 85
 Small neighbour of HAUT-BRION with high bourgeois standards.

Caronne-Ste-Gemme St-Lau. (Haut-Médoc) r. ★★→★★★ 75 76 78 79 80 81 82' 83 84 85
 Cru Bourgeois of 100 acres. Steady quality repays patience.

Chambert-Marbuzet St-Est. r. ★★ 78 79 80 81 82 83 84 85
 Tiny (20-acre) sister-ch. of HAUT-MARBUZET. Very good fruity wine aged in new oak matures quite fast.

du Castéra Médoc r. ★★ 75 78 79 81 82 83 84 85
 Historic property at St-Germain in the n. Médoc. Recent investment; to watch for tasty but not tannic wine.

Certan de May   Pomerol r.   ★★★ 70 71 75 76 78 79 81 82′ 83 85
  Neighbour of VIEUX-CHÂTEAU-CERTAN. Tiny property with full-
  bodied rich and tannic wine, recently flying high.

Certan-Giraud   Pomerol r.   ★★★ 71 75 76 78 79 81 82′ 83′ 85
  Small (17-acre) property next to the great Ch. PETRUS.

Chantegrive   Graves r. w. dr.   ★★ 84 85
  150-acre estate half white, half red; useful modern Graves. Other
  labels incl. Mayne-Levéque, Bon-Dieu-des-Vignes.

Chasse-Spleen   Moulis r.   ★★★ 70′ 71 75′ 76 78′ 79 80 81′ 82′ 83′ 84 85
  180-acre Cru Exceptionnel of classed-growth quality. Consistently good, usually outstanding, long-maturing wine. 2nd label:
  Ermitage de C-S.

Cheval Blanc   St-Em. r.   ★★★★ 66 70 75′ 76 78 79 80 81′ 82′ 83′ 84 85
  This and AUSONE are the "first-growths" of St-Emilion. Rich,
  full-blooded, intensely vigorous and perfumed, from 100 acres on
  the border of Pomerol.

Chicane   Graves r.   ★★
  Satisfying and reliable product of the Langon merchant Pierre
  Coste. Domaine de Gaillat is another. Drink at 2–6 years.

Cissac   Cissac r.   ★★ 70′ 75′ 76 78′ 79 80 81 82′ 83 84 85
  A pillar of the bourgeoisie. 80-acre Grand Bourgeois Exceptionnel with a steady record for tasty long-lived wine.

Citran   Avensan, Haut-Médoc r.   ★★ 70′ 75 78′ 81 82 83 85
  Grand Bourgeois Exceptionnel of 178 acres. Stylish wine.

Clarke   Listrac, Haut-Médoc r. (p.)   ★★→★★★ 78 79 80 81 82 83 84 85
  Huge (350-acre) Cru Bourgeois Rothschild development, incl.
  elaborate visitor facilities. Ch'x. Malmaison and Peyrelebade
  are second labels.

Clerc-Milon   Pauillac r.   ★★★ 75′ 76 78′ 79 80 81 82′ 83′ 84 85
  Forgotten little fifth-growth bought by Baron Philippe de
  Rothschild in 1970. Now 73 acres. Not normally thrilling, but a
  v.g. '83.

Climens   Sauternes w. sw.   ★★★ 71′ 75′ 76′ 78′ 79 80 81 82 83′ 84 85
  Famous 74-acre classed-growth at Barsac making some of the
  best and most stylish sweet wine in the world for a good 10 years'
  maturing. Same owner as Ch. BRANE-CANTENAC, etc.

Clinet   Pomerol r.   ★★ 70 71 75 76 78 79 81 83 85
  15-acre property in central Pomerol making tannic "Pauillac-
  style" wine. Some more flesh would help.

Clos l'Eglise   Pomerol r.   ★★★ 71 75 76 78 79′ 81 82′ 83 85
  14-acre v'yd in one of the best sites in Pomerol. Excellent wine
  without great muscle or flesh. The same family owns CH. PLINCE.

Clos Fourtet   St-Em. r.   ★★★ 70 75 78 79 80 81 82′ 83 85
  Well-known 42-acre first-growth on the plateau with cellars
  almost in the town. Back on form after a middling patch. Same
  owners as CLIMENS, BRANE-CANTENAC, etc.

Clos Haut-Peyraguey   Sauternes w. sw.   ★★ 78 79 80 81 82 83 85
  Tiny production of good medium-rich wine. The v.g. Cru
  Bourgeois Ch. Haut- Bommes is in the same hands.

Clos des Jacobins   St-Em. r.   ★★ 75′ 76 78 79 80 81 82′ 83′ 85
  Well-known and well-run little (18-acre) classed-growth owned
  by the shipper CORDIER. Wines of notable depth and style.

Clos du Marquis   St-Jul. r. ★★
  The second wine of LÉOVILLE-LASCASES.

Clos l'Oratoire   St-Em. r.   ★★ 78 79 80 81 82 83 85
  Richly typical Grand Cru. See also Ch. PEYREAU.

Clos René   Pomerol r.   ★★★ 70 71′ 75 76 78 79 80 81 82′ 83 85
  Leading ch. on the w. of Pomerol. 38 acres making powerful wine;
  eventually delicate. Also sold as Ch. Moulinet-Lasserre.

La Closerie-Grand-Poujeaux   Moulis (Haut-Médoc) r.   ★★
  Small but respected traditional middle-Médoc. To keep.

La Clotte St-Em. r. ☒ **75′ 76′ 78 79 81 82 83 85**

    Tiny Côtes Grand Cru with marvellously scented "supple" wine.

Colombier-Monpelou Pauillac r. ★★

    Reliable small Cru Bourgeois made to a high standard.

La Conseillante Pomerol r. ★★★ **70′ 71′ 75′ 76 78 79 80 81′ 82′ 83 84 85**

    29-acre classed-growth on the plateau between PETRUS and CHEVAL BLANC. Some of the noblest and most fragrant Pomerol, worthy of its superb position.

Corbin (Giraud) St-Em. r. ★★ **75 76 78 79 81 82′ 83′ 85**

    28-acre classed-growth in n. St-Emilion where a cluster of Corbins occupy the edge of the plateau. Can be very rich.

Corbin-Michotte St-Em. r. ☒ **70 71 75 76 78 79 81 82 83 85**

    Well-run 19-acre property; "generous" Pomerol-like wine.

Cos-d'Estournel St-Est. r. ★★★★ **61 66 70 71 73 75′ 76′ 78′ 79 80 81′ 82′ 83 84 85**

    140-acre second-growth with eccentric chinoiserie building overlooking Ch. LAFITE. Always full-flavoured, often magnificent, wine. Now regularly one of the best in the Médoc. Maître d'Estournel is a good blend.

Cos Labory St-Est. r. ☒ **75′ 76 78′ 79′ 80 81′ 82′ 83 84 85**

    Little-known fifth-growth neighbour of COS D'ESTOURNEL with 37 acres. Blunt fruity wines mature early. To watch.

Coufran St-Seurin-de-Cadourne (Haut-Médoc) r. ☒ **78′ 79 81 82′ 83 85**

    Coufran and Ch. VERDIGNAN, on the northern-most hillock of the Haut-Médoc, are under the same ownership. Coufran has mainly Merlot vines; soft lightish wine. 148 acres.

Couhins Graves (r.) w. dr. ★★ **81 82 83′ 84**

    17-acre v'yd. at Villenave-d'Ornon run by the State. Fine white (and a little red) for drinking young. Ch. Couhins-Lurton is another 15-acre part of the v'yd. making v.g. all-Sauvignon white.

La Couronne Pauillac r. ★★ **75 76 78 79 81′ 82′ 83**

    Excellent (very) small Cru Exceptionnel made at Ch. HAUT-BATAILLEY.

Coutet Sauternes w. sw. ★★★ **70′ 71′ 73 75′ 76 79 81 82 83′**

    Traditional rival to Ch. CLIMENS; 91 acres in Barsac. Often slightly less rich; at its best equally fine but recently less reliable. A dry GRAVES sold under the same name is not v. special.

Couvent des Jacobins St-Em. r. ☒ **75 76 78 79′ 80 81 82′ 83 85**

    Well-known vineyard of 22 acres adjacent to the town of St-Emilion to the east. Among the best of its kind.

Le Crock St-Est. r. ☒ **79 80 81 82 83 84 85**

    Well-situated Cru Bourgeois of 74 acres in the same family as Ch. LÉOVILLE-POYFERRÉ. Among the many excellent C.B's of the commune.

La Croix Pomerol r. ★★ **70′ 71′ 75′ 76 78 79′ 81 82′ 83 85**

    Well-reputed property of 32 acres. Appealing plummy Pomerol with a spine; matures well. Also La C.-St-Georges, La C.-Toulifaut and Clos des Lafitaines.

La Croix de Gay Pomerol r. ★★★ **70′ 71′ 75′ 76′ 78 79 81 82′ 83′ 85**

    30 acres in the best part of the commune. Recently on fine form. Has underground cellars, rare in Pomerol. "La Fleur de Gay" is the best selection.

Croizet-Bages Pauillac r. ☒ **70′ 75′ 76 78′ 79′ 80 81 82′ 83 84 85**

    52-acre fifth-growth (lacking a ch.) with the same owners as Château RAUZAN-GASSIES. Sturdy wines with growing finesse.

Croque-Michotte St-Em. r. ★★ **75 76 78 79 80 81 82′ 83 85**

    35-acre Pomerol-style classed-growth on the Pomerol border.

du Cruzeaux Graves r. w. dr. ★★

    100-acre GRAVES-LÉOGNAN v'yd. recently developed by André Lurton of LA LOUVIÈRE etc. V. high standards; to try.

Curé-Bon-la-Madeleine   St-Em. r. ★★★ 71´ 75 76´ 78 79 80 81 82´ 83 85
　　Small (12-acre) property among the best of the Côtes; between
　　AUSONE and CANON. Managed by MOUEIX.

Dassault   St-Em. r. ★★ 78 79 81 82 83 85
　　Consistent early-maturing middle-weight Grand Cru. 58 acres.

Dauzac   Lab-Mar. r. ★★→★★★ 70 75 76 78 79´ 80 81 82´ 83 84 85
　　Substantial fifth-growth near the river s. of Margaux. In new
　　hands and much improved since ´79. 120 acres.

Desmirail   Mar. r. ★★ → ★★★ 81 82 83´
　　Third-growth, now 45 acres. A long-defunct name recently
　　revived by the owner of BRANE-CANTENAC. Gentle, fragrant
　　wines.

Dillon   Haut-Médoc r. (w. dr.) ★★ 75´ 76 78´ 79´ 81 82 83 85
　　Local wine college of Blanquefort, just n. of Bordeaux. 85 acres.
　　Dry white: Ch. Lucas (D.Y.A.)

Doisy-Daëne   Barsac w. sw. and dr. ★★★ 75 76´ 78 79 80 81 82 83´ 84 85
　　Forward-looking 34-acre estate making crisp dry white (incl.
　　Riesling grapes) as well as notably fine sweet Barsac.

Doisy-Dubroca   Barsac w. sw. ★★ 71´ 75´ 76 78 79 80 81 83 85
　　Tiny (8½-acre) Barsac classed-growth allied to Ch. CLIMENS.

---

*Why do the Châteaux of Bordeaux have such a large section of this book
devoted to them? The reason is simple: collectively they form by far the
largest supply of high-quality wine on earth.*

*A single typical Médoc château with 150 acres (some have far more)
makes approximately 26,000 dozen bottles of identifiable wine a year — the
production of two or three Californian "boutique" wineries. The tendency
over the last two decades has been for the better-known châteaux to buy more
land. Many classed-growths have expanded by as much as 10 times since
they were classified in 1855.*

Doisy-Védrines   Sauternes w. sw. ★★★ 71 75´ 76´ 78 79 80 81 82´ 83´ 85
　　50-acre classed-growth at Barsac, near CLIMENS and COUTET.
　　Deliciously sturdy rich wines designed for a long life.

Domaine de Chevalier   Graves r. and w. dr. ★★★★ (r.)61 66 70´
　　71 75´ 76 78´ 79´ 80 81´ 82´ 83 84 85
　　Superb small estate of 36 acres at Léognan. The red is stern at
　　first, richly subtle with age. The white is delicate but matures to
　　rich flavours. (w. 75 76´ 78 79´ 81 82 83´ 84 85). Changed hands (but
　　not management) in 1983.

Domaine de l'Eglise   Pomerol r. ★★ 70 71 75 76 78 79´ 81 82´ 85
　　Small property: fragrant wine distributed by BORIE-MANOUX.

Domaine la Grave   Graves r. w. dr. ★★ 81 82 83 (w. 83) 84 85
　　Innovative little estate at Portets. Lively medal-winning reds
　　made for a long life. Oak-aged delicious whites.

Domaine de Toutigeac   Entre-Deux-Mers r. (w. dr.) ★
　　Enormous producer of useful Bordeaux at Targon.

La Dominique   St-Em. r. ★★★ 70 71´ 75 76 78 79 80 81 82´ 83 85
　　Fine 45-acre classed-growth next door to Ch. CHEVAL BLANC,
　　making wine almost as arresting.

Ducru-Beaucaillou   St-Jul. r. ★★★ 61 66 70´ 71 75´ 76 78´ 79 80 81
　　82´ 83´ 84 85
　　Outstanding second-growth; 120 acres overlooking the river.
　　The owner, M. Borie, makes classical "cedar-pencil" claret. See
　　also Grand-Puy-Lacoste, etc.

Duhart-Milon-Rothschild   Pauillac. ★★★75´ 76´ 78 79 80 81 82´ 83 85
　　Fourth-growth neighbour of LAFITE under the same man-
　　agement. Maturing vines; increasingly fine quality. 110 acres.

Durfort-Vivens   Margaux r. ★★★ 70 75 76 78´ 79´ 80 81 82´ 83 85
　　Relatively small (49-acre) second-growth owned by M. Lurton
　　of BRANE-CANTENAC. Recent wines (except ´84) have real finesse.

Dutruch-Grand-Poujeaux Moulis r. ★★ 70 73 75 76 78 79 80 81 82 83 84 85

One of the leaders of MOULIS; full-bodied, rich and tannic wines.

L'Eglise-Clinet Pomerol r. ★★★ 70 71 75 76 78 79 80 81 82 83 85

11 acres. Highly ranked; full, fleshy wine. Changed hands in '82; '83 augurs well for the future.

L'Enclos Pomerol r. ★★ 70 71 75 76 78 79 80 81 82 83 85

Respected 26-acre property on the w. side of Pomerol, near CLOS-RENÉ. Big, well-made, long-flavoured wine.

L'Evangile Pomerol r. ★★★ 70 71 73 75 76 78 79 80 81 82 83 85

33 acres between PETRUS and CHEVAL BLANC. Impressive wines. In the same area and class as LA CONSEILLANTE.

Fargues Sauternes w. sw. ★★★ 70 71 75 76 78 79 80 81 83 85

25-acre v'yd. in same ownership as CH. YQUEM. Fruity and extremely elegant but much lighter wines.

Ferrande Graves r. (w. dr.) ★★

Major estate of Castres with 100 + acres. Easy enjoyable red for early drinking.

Ferrière Margaux r. ★★ 70 75 78 79 81 82 83 85

Phantom third-growth of only 10+ acres. The wine is made at Ch. LASCOMBES.

Feytit-Clinet Pomerol r. ★★ 70 71 75 76 78 79 81 82 83 85

Little property next to LATOUR-POMEROL. Has made some fine big strong wines. Managed by J-P MOUEIX.

Fieuzal Graves r. and (w. dr.) ★★★ 75 76 78 79 80 81 82 83 84 85

56-acre classed-growth at Léognan. Finely made memorable wines of both colours.

Figeac St-Em. r. ★★★ 61 70 71 75 76 78 79 80 81 82 83 84 85

Famous first-growth neighbour of CHEVAL BLANC. Superb 98-acre v'yd. gives one of Bordeaux's most attractive rich but elegant wines, maturing relatively quickly.

Filhot Sauternes w. sw. and dr. ★★★ 71 75 76 78 79 80 81 82 83 85

Second-rank classed-growth with splendid ch., 148-acre v'yd. Good sw. wines for fairly early drinking, a little dry, and red.

La Fleur St-Em. r. ★★ 75 76 78 79 80 81 82 83 85

Very small Côtes estate producing luxuriously fruity wines.

La Fleur-Petrus Pomerol r. ★★★ 70 75 76 78 79 80 81 82 83 85

18-acre v'yd. flanking PETRUS and under the same MOUEIX management. Exceedingly fine plummy wines; Pomerol at its best and most stylish.

Fombrauge St-Em. r. ★★ 70 71 75 76 78 79 80 81 82 83 85

Major property of St-Christophe-des-Bardes, e. of St-Emilion, with 120 acres. Reliable St-Emilion making great efforts.

Fonbadet Pauillac r. ★★ 70 75 78 79 80 81 82 83 84 85

Cru Bourgeois of high repute with 38 acres next door to PONTET-CANET. Old vines and no oak give solid wine needing long bottle-age.

Fonplégade St-Em. r. ★★ 71 75 76 78 79 81 82 83 85

48-acre v'yd. on the Côtes w. of St.-Emilion in another branch of the MOUEIX family. Fragrant and appealing.

Fonréaud Listrac r. ★★ 70 75 76 78 79 80 81 82 83 84 85

One of the bigger (96 acres) and better Crus Bourgeois of its area, selling mainly in France and at the door.

Fonroque St-Em. r. ★★★ 70 71 75 76 78 79 80 81 82 83 85

48 acres on the plateau n. of St-Emilion, MOUEIX property. Big deep dark wine that needs time.

Les Forts de Latour Pauillac r. ★★★ 70 71 75 76 78 79 80 81 82

The second wine of Ch. Latour; well worthy of its big brother. Unique in being bottle-aged at least three years before release.

Fourcas-Dupré Listrac r. ★★ 70 75 76 78 79 80 81 82 83 84 85

A top-class 100-acre Cru Bourgeois Exceptionnel making consistent and elegant wine. To follow.

Fourcas-Hosten Listrac r. `**→***` 7075 76 78' 79 80 81 82' 83 84 85
96-acre Cru Bourgeois currently considered the best of its commune. Firm wine with a long life.

La Gaffelière St-Em. r. ★★★ 66 70 71 75' 76 78 79 80 81 82' 83' 84 85
61-acre first-growth at the foot of the Côtes below Ch. BEL-AIR. Its great years are wonderful; lesser years not thrilling.

La Garde Graves r. (w. dr.) `**` 75' 76' 78 79 81 82' 83' 84 85
Substantial ESCHENAUER property making reliably sound red.

Le Gay Pomerol r. ★★★ 70 71 75' 76' 78 79 81 82' 83' 85
Well-known 14-acre v'yd. on the northern edge of Pomerol. Same owner as Ch. LAFLEUR. MOUEIX management. Splendid wine.

Gazin Pomerol r. ★★★ 70' 71' 75' 76 78 81 82 83 85
Large property (for Pomerol) with 56 acres. Not quite as splendid as its position next to PETRUS.

Gilette Sauternes w. sw. ★★★ 49 55 59
Extraordinary small Preignac château which stores its rich wines in cask to a great age.

Giscours Lab-Mar. r. `***` 70 71' 75' 76 78' 79' 80 81' 82' 83 84 85
Splendid 182-acre third-growth s. of CANTENAC. Dynamically run and making excellent vigorous wine for long maturing.

du Glana St-Jul. r. ★★ 70' 75' 78 79 81 82' 83 85
Big Cru Bourgeois in centre of St-Julien. Undemanding quality.

Gloria St-Jul. r. `***` 66 70' 71 73 75' 76 78' 79' 80 81 82' 83 84 85
Outstanding Cru Bourgeois making wine of vigour and finesse, among good classed-growths in quality. 110 acres. The owner, Henri Martin, bought Ch. ST-PIERRE in 1982.

Grand-Barrail-Lamarzelle-Figeac St-Em. r. `**` 70 71 75 76 78 79 81 82' 83 85
48-acre property near FIGEAC, incl. Ch. La Marzelle. Well-reputed and popular, if scarcely exciting.

Grand-Corbin-Despagne St-Em. r. ★★ 70 75 78 79 81 82' 83 85
One of the biggest and best Grands Crus on the CORBIN plateau.

Grand-Pontet St-Em. r. ★★ 75 76 78 79 81 82' 83 85
Widely distributed 35-acre neighbour of Ch. BEAU SÉJOUR-BÉCOT, in the same hands since 1980. "Supple", smooth wine.

Grand-Puy-Ducasse Pauillac r. `***` 75 76 78 79 80 81 82' 83 84 85
Well-known little fifth-growth bought in '71, renovated and enlarged to 90 acres under expert management. A best buy.

Grand-Puy-Lacoste Pauillac r. `***` 70' 71 75 76 78' 79' 80 81' 82' 83 84 85
Leading fifth-growth famous for excellent full-bodied vigorous Pauillac. 110 acres among the "Bages" ch'x. s. of the town, owned by the Borie family of DUCRU-BEAUCAILLOU.

Gravas Sauternes w. sw. ★★
Small Barsac property; impressive firm wine.

La Grave Trigant de Boisset Pom. r. `***` 75' 76' 78 79 80 81 82' 83 85
Verdant ch. with small but first-class v'yd. owned by Christian MOUEIX. Firm, beautifully structured Pomerol.

Gressier Grand Poujeaux Moulis r. `***` 70 75' 76 78 79' 80 81 82 83' 84 85
Good Cru Bourgeois. Fine firm wine with a good track record.

Greysac Médoc r. ★★ 78 79' 80 81' 82 83 85
Elegant 140-acre property. Easy, early-maturing wines.

Gruaud-Larose St-Jul. r. `***` 70' 71 73 75' 76 78' 79 80 81 82' 83 84 85
One of the biggest and best-known second-growths. 189 acres making smooth rich stylish claret. Owned by CORDIER. The excellent second wine is called Sarget de Gruaud-Larose.

Guiraud Sauternes (r.) w. sw. (dr.) ★★★ 70' 76 78' 79' 80 81 82 83' 85
Newly restored classed-growth of top quality. 250 + acres. At best excellent sweet wine of great finesse and a small amount of red and dry white. The '83 should be superb in time.

La Gurgue Margaux r. ★★ 79 81 82 83′ 84 85′
> Small (30-acre) well-placed property with fine typical Margaux, recently bought by owners of Ch. CHASSE-SPLEEN. To watch.

Hanteillan Cissac r. ☐ ★★ ☐ 75 76 79′ 80 81 82′ 83 84 85
> Large (200 + acres) v'yd. renovated and enlarged since 1973. Admirable bourgeois wine. Ch. Larrivaux-Hanteillan is second quality.

Haut-Bages-Averous Pauillac r. ☐ ★★ ☐ 81 82 83 84 85
> The second wine of Ch. LYNCH BAGES. Delicious easy drinking.

Haut-Bages-Libéral Pauillac r. ★★ 75 76 78 80 81 82′ 83 84 85
> Lesser-known fifth-growth of 64 acres in same stable as CHASSE-SPLEEN since '83. The auguries are excellent.

Haut-Bages-Monpelou Pauillac r. ★★ 75′ 76 78 79 80 81 82′ 83 84 85
> 25-acre Cru Bourgeois stable-mate of CH. BATAILLEY on former DUHART-MILON land. Good-value Pauillac.

Haut-Bailly Graves r. ☐ ★★★ ☐ 70′ 75 78 79′ 80 81′ 82 83 84 85
> 60-acre est. at Léognan famous for ripe, round, sometimes "feminine" r. Graves, esp. since 1979. 2nd label: La Parde de H-B.

Haut-Batailley Pauillac r. ☐ ★★★ ☐ 70′ 75′ 76 78′ 79 80 81 82′ 83 84 85
> The smaller section of the fifth-growth Batailley estate: 49 acres. Often in a gentler vein than its sister ch., GRAND-PUY-LACOSTE.

Haut-Brignon 1ères Côtes r. & w. dr. ★
> Big producer of standard wines at Cénac, owned by a major Champagne coop.

Haut-Brion Pessac, Graves r. (w.) ★★★★ 61 62 64 66 70′ 71 75′ 76 78′ 79 80 81′ 82′ 83 84 85
> The oldest great ch. of Bordeaux and the only non-Médoc first-growth of 1855. 108 acres. Reds of singular balance, particularly good since 1975. A little full dry white in 76 78 79 81 83 84 85. See also BAHANS-HAUT-BRION.

Haut-Marbuzet St-Estèphe r. ☐ ★★ ☐ 75′ 76 78′ 79 80 81 82′ 83 84 85
> One of the best of many good St-Estèphe Crus Bourgeois. 100 acres. Ch'x Tour de Marbuzet, CHAMBERT-MARBUZET, MacCarthy-Moula in same hands. New oak gives them all classic style.

Haut-Pontet St-Em. r. ★★ 70 71 73 75 78 79 81 82′ 83 85
> 12-acre v'yd. of the Côtes well deserving its Grand Cru status.

Haut-Quercus St-Em. r. ★★
> Oak-aged cooperative wine to a very high standard.

Haut-Sarpe St-Em. r. ☐ ★★ ☐ 78 79 81 82 83′ 85
> Small Grand Cru Classé with a very fine château. Same owner as Ch. LA CROIX. To follow.

Haut-Ségottes St.-Em. r. ★★ 85′
> 22-acre Grand Cru resolutely run. To watch.

Hortevie St-Jul. r. ☐ ★★ ☐ 81 82 83 84 85
> One of the few St. Julien Crus Bourgeois. This tiny v'yd. and its sister TERREY-GROS-CAILLOU are shining examples.

Houissant St-Estèphe r. ★★ 78 79 80 81 82 83 84 85
> Typical robust well-balanced St-Estèphe Cru Bourgeois Exceptionnel, also called Ch. Leyssac; well known in Denmark.

d'Issan Cant-Mar. r. ☐ ★★★ ☐ 70 73′75′ 76′ 78 79′ 80 81 82′ 83′ 84 85
> Beautifully restored moated ch. with 75-acre third-growth v'yd. well known for fragrant, virile but delicate wine.

Kirwan Cant-Mar. r. ☐ ★★★ ☐ 75′ 76 78 79′ 80 81 82′ 83′ 84 85
> Well-run 86-acre third-growth owned by SCHRÖDER & SCHYLER. New planting of '60s was mature and results tasting v. good.

Labégorce Margaux r. ★★ 75′ 76 78 79 80 81′ 82′ 83′ 84 85
> Substantial 69-acre property north of Margaux with long-lived wines of true Margaux quality.

Labégorce-Zédé Margaux r. ☐ ★★ ☐ 75′ 76 78 79 80 81′ 82′ 83′ 84 85
> Outstanding Cru Bourgeois on the road n. from Margaux. 62 acres. Typical delicate fragrant Margaux, truly classic since '81. The same family as VIEUX-CHÂTEAU-CERTAN.

Lacoste–Borie   The second wine of Ch. GRAND-PUY-LACOSTE.

Lafaurie–Peyraguey   Sauternes w. sw. ★★★ 75′ 76′ 78′ 79 80 81 83′ 85
Fine classed-growth of only 49 acres at Bommes, belonging to
CORDIER. After a lean patch, good, rich and racy wines.

Lafite–Rothschild   Pauillac r. ★★★★ 61 70′ 75′ 76′ 78 79 80 81′ 82′ 83
First-growth of fabulous style and perfume in its great vintages,
which keep for decades. Off-form for several years but resplen-
dent since '76. Amazing circular cellars opened '87. 2nd wine:
Moulin des Carruades. 225 acres.

Lafleur   Pomerol r. ★★★ 70′ 71′ 73 75′ 76 78 79 80 81 82′ 83 85
Property of 12 acres just n. of PETRUS. Excellent wine of the finer,
less "fleshy" kind. Same owner as LE GAY. MOUEIX direction.

Lafleur–Gazin   Pomerol r. ★★ 70 71′ 75′ 76′ 78 79 81 82′ 83 85
Distinguished small MOUEIX estate on the n.e. border of Pomerol.

Lafon–Rochet   St-Est. r. ★★ 70′ 75′ 76 78 79 81 82 83 85
Fourth-growth neighbour of Ch. COS D'ESTOURNEL, restored
in the '60s. 110 acres. Rather hard dark full-bodied St-Estèphe.
Same owner as Ch. PONTET-CANET.

Lagrange   Pomerol r. ★★★ 70′ 71′ 75′ 76 78 79 80 81 82′ 83
20-acre v'yd. in the centre of Pomerol run by the ubiquitous
house of MOUEIX. Maturing vines are giving deeper flavour.

ARGUMENTS FOR AND AGAINST DECANTING
*Fierce arguments take place between wine-lovers over whether it is a
good or a bad thing to decant wine from its bottle into a carafe. The
argument in favour is that it allows the wine to "breathe" and its
bouquet to expand: against, that its precious breath is dissipated — or
at the least that it makes no difference.*

*Two additional practical reasons in favour concern old wine which
has deposited dregs, which can be left in the bottle by careful decanting,
and young wine being consumed before it is fully developed: thorough
aeration helps to create the illusion of maturity. An aesthetic one is that
decanters are handsome on the table.*

*Decanting is done by pouring the wine into another container very
steadily until any sediment reaches the shoulder of the bottle. To see the
sediment clearly hold the bottle's neck over a light-bulb or a candle.*

Lagrange   St-Jul. r. ★★★ 70′ 75′ 78 79′ 81 82 83 84 85
Run-down third-growth inland from St-Julien. Bought by
Suntory in 1982. 123 + acres, being extensively restored. To
watch. Second label: Les Fiefs de Lagrange (83′).

La Lagune   Ludon r. ★★★ 70′ 71 73′ 75′ 76′ 78′ 79 80 81 82′ 83 84 85
Well-run ultra-modern 160-acre third-growth in the extreme s.
of the Médoc. Attractively rich and fleshy wines; usually
brilliant quality.

Lalande–Borie   St-Jul. r. ★★ 78 79 81 82 83 84 85
A baby brother of the great DUCRU-BEAUCAILLOU created from
part of the former v'yd. of Ch. LAGRANGE.

Lamarque   Lamarque (Haut-Médoc) r. ★★ 75′ 78 79 80 81′ 82 83′ 85
Splendid medieval fortress of the central Médoc with 113 acres
giving admirable wine of high "Bourgeois" standard.

Lanessan   Cussac (Haut-Médoc) r. ★★ 70′ 75′ 76 78′ 79 80 81 82′ 83 84 85
Distinguished 108-acre Cru Bourgeois Exceptionnel just s. of
St-Julien. Same owner as PICHON-LONGUEVILLE-BARON.

Langoa–Barton   St-Jul. r. ★★★ 70′ 75′ 76 78′ 79 80 81 82′ 83 84 85
Fine 18th-century ch. housing the wine of third-growth Langoa
(49 acres) as well as second-growth LÉOVILLE-BARTON. The
wines are similar: Langoa slightly less potent.

Larcis–Ducasse   St-Em. r. ★★★ 70′ 71′ 75′ 76 78 79 80 81 82 83 85
The top property of St-Laurent, eastern neighbour of St-
Emilion, on the Côtes next to Ch. PAVIE. 30 acres. Coasting?

Larmande St-Em. r. ★★ **75' 78 79 80 81** 82 83 84 85
Substantial 54-acre property related to CAP-DE-MOURLIN.
Replanted and now making rich, strikingly scented wine.

Laroque St-Em. r. ★★ **70' 75' 76' 78 79 80** 81 82' 83 85
Important 108-acre v'yd. with an impressive mansion on the St-
Emilion côtes in St. Christophe.

Larose-Trintaudon St-Lau. (Haut-Médoc) r. │ ★★ │ **75' 78 79 80 81**
82 83 84 85
The biggest v'yd. in the Médoc: 388 acres. Modern methods
make reliable fruity and charming Cru Bourgeois wine.

Laroze St-Em. r. ★★ **71' 75' 76 78' 79 80** 81 82 83 85
Big v'yd. (74 acres) on the w. Côtes. Relatively light wines from
sandy soil; soon enjoyable. Sometimes excellent.

Larrivet-Haut-Brion Graves r. (w.) │ ★★ │ **75' 78** 79' 80 81 82' 83 84 85
Little property at Léognan with perfectionist standards.

Lascombes Margaux r. (p.) ★★★ **61 66 70' 75' 76 78 79** 81 82 83 84 85
240-acre second-growth owned by the British brewers Bass-
Charrington and lavishly restored. After a poor patch, new
vigour and skill. Second wine: Ch. Segonnes.

Latour Pauillac r. │ ★★★★ │ **61 62 64 66 67** 70' 71 73 75' **76' 77 78' 79' 80**
81 82' 83 84 85
First-growth. The most consistent great wine in Bordeaux, in
France and probably the world: rich, intense and almost
immortal in great years, almost always classical and pleasing
even in bad ones. British-owned. 150 acres. Second wine LES
FORTS DE LATOUR.

Latour à Pomerol Pomerol r. │ ★★★★ │ **70' 71' 75' 76' 78 79' 80** 81 82' 83 85
Top growth of 19 acres under MOUEIX management. Pomerol of
great power and perfume, yet also ravishing finesse.

Laujac Médoc r. ★★ **75' 78 81 82** 83 85
Cru Bourgeois in the n. Médoc owned by the CRUSE family. Well
known but scarcely outstanding. 62 acres.

des Laurets St-Em. r. ★★ **70' 75' 76 78 79 81** 82 83 85
Major property of Puisseguin and Montagne-St-Emilion (to the
e.) with 160 acres on the Côtes. Sterling wine.

Laville-Haut-Brion Graves w. dr. ★★★★ **71 75 78 79** 81 82 83' 84 85
A tiny production of one of the very best white Graves for long
maturing, made at Ch. LA MISSION-HAUT-BRION.

Léoville-Barton St-Jul. r. │ ★★★ │ **61 66 70' 71 74 75' 76 78' 79 80** 81 82'
83 84 85
90-acre portion of the great second-growth Léoville v'yd. in the
Anglo-Irish hands of the Barton family for over 150 years.
Powerful and classical claret, made by traditional methods at the
Bartons' third-growth Ch. LANGOA.

Léoville-Las Cases St-Jul. r. │ ★★★★ │ **61 64 66 67 70' 71 73** 75' **76**
78' **79 80** 81 82' 83 84 85
The largest portion of the old Léoville estate, 210 acres, with one
of the highest reputations in Bordeaux. Elegant, complex,
powerful but never heavy wines. Second label: Clos du Marquis.

Léoville-Poyferré St-Jul. r. ★★★ **70' 75' 76 78' 79 80** 81 82' 83 84 85
For years the least outstanding of the Léovilles; since 1980 again
living up to the great name. '82 is a triumph and '83 splendid. 156
acres. Second label: Ch. Moulin-Riche.

Lestage Listrac r. ★★ **75' 76 78' 79 80** 81 82' 83 84 85
130-acre Cru Bourgeois in same hands as Ch. FONRÉAUD. Light,
quite stylish wine.

Liot Barsac w. sw. ★★ **70' 71 75' 76 78 79' 80** 81 83 85
Consistent fairly light golden wines from 94 acres.

Liversan St-Sau. (Haut-Médoc) r. │ ★★ │ **75' 76 78 79 80** 81 82' 83 84 85
116-acre Grand Cru Bourgeois inland from Pauillac. Change of
regime in 1984 should maintain high standards. Ch. Fonpiqueyre
is the same wine in certain markets.

Livran   Médoc r. ★★ 75 76′ 78′ 79 81 82′ 83 85
> Big Cru Bourgeois at St-Germain in the n. Médoc. Consistent round wines (half Merlot).

Loudenne   St-Yzans (Médoc) r. ★★★ (r.) 75′ 78′ 79 80 81 82′ 83 84 85
> Beautiful riverside ch. owned by Gilbeys since 1875. Well-made Cru Bourgeois red and a very agreeable dry white from 120 acres. The white is best young.

Loupiac-Gaudiet   Loupiac w. sw.   ★★
> Reliable source of good-value almost-Sauternes, just across the river Garonne.

La Louvière   Graves r. and w. dr.   ★★   (r.) 75 78 79 80 81 82′ 83 84
> Noble 135-acre estate at Léognan. Excellent white for drinking fresh or maturing, and red recently of classed-growth standard.

de Lussac   St-Em. r. ★★ 75′ 78′ 79 81 82 83
> One of the best estates in Lussac-St-Emilion (to the n.e.).

Lynch-Bages   Pauillac r.   ★★★   61 66 70 75′ 76 78′ 79 80 81 82′ 83′ 84 85
> One of the biggest and best fifth-growths, closer to second- in quality. 200 acres making rich robust wine: delicious; occasionally great, with recent vintages esp. notable.

Lynch-Moussas   Pauillac r.   ★★   75′ 76 78 79 80 81 82′ 83 84 85
> Fifth-growth restored by the director of Ch. BATAILLEY since 1969. Now 60+ acres and new equipment are making serious wine, gaining depth as the young vines age.

du Lyonnat   Lussac-St-Em. r. ★★ 81 82
> 120-acre estate with well-distributed reliable wine.

Magdelaine   St-Em. r.   ★★★   70′ 71′ 73 75′ 76 78 79 80 81 82′ 83 85
> Leading first-growth of the Côtes, 28 acres next to AUSONE owned by J-P MOUEIX. Beautifully balanced wine. On top form.

Magence   Graves r. w. dr.   ★★   (r.)
> Go-ahead 45-acre property at St Pierre de Mons, in the s. of the Graves, well known for distinctly SAUVIGNON-flavoured very dry white that ages well, and fruity red for drinking in 4–6 yrs.

Malartic-Lagravière   Graves r. and (w. dr.)   ★★★   (r.) 70′ 75′ 76′ 78 79 80 81 82′ 83 (w.) 75 76 79 81′ 82 83 84 85
> Well-known Léognan classed-growth of 34 acres making well-structured red for long maturing and a very little excellent fruity SAUVIGNON white, hard to resist young.

Malescasse   Lamarque (Haut-Médoc) r. ★★ 75 78 79′ 80 81 82 83 85
> Renovated Cru Bourgeois with 100 acres in a good situation, owned by M. Tesseron of Ch. LAFON-ROCHET.

Malescot St-Exupéry   Margaux r.   ★★★   61 66 70′ 71 75′ 76 78′ 79′ 80 81 82′ 83′ 84 85
> Third-growth of 84 acres allied until 1979 with Ch. MARQUIS-D'ALESME. Long-maturing, eventually classically fragrant and stylish Margaux.

de Malle   Sauternes r. w. sw./dr. ★★★ (w. sw.) 70 71 75 76 78 79 80 81′ 82 83 85
> Famous and beautiful ch. with Italian gdns. at Preignac. 55 acres. Good sweet and dry w. and r. (Graves) Ch. de Cardaillan.

de Malleret   Haut-Médoc r. ★★
> Big well-run Cru Bourgeois at Le Pian near Bordeaux. Reliable quality.

Maquin-St-Georges   St-Em. r.   ★★   79 81 82 83 85
> Steady producer of delicious "satellite" St-Em. at St-Georges.

de Marbuzet   St-Est. r.   ★★   75 76 78 79 81 82 83 84 85
> Effectively the second label of Ch. COS D'ESTOURNEL, and correspondingly well made.

Margaux   Margaux r. (w. dr.) ★★★★ 61 66′ 70′ 75 76 78′ 79 80 81′ 82′ 83′ 84 85
> First-growth (with 209 acres of vines), the most delicate and finely perfumed of all in its best vintages. "Pavillon Rouge" (79′ 80 81 82′ 83′ 84 85) is the second wine. "Pavillon Blanc" is the best white (SAUVIGNON) wine of the Médoc, for 3–4 years ageing.

Marquis-d'Alesme Margaux r. ⋆⋆ 70' 71' 75' 78 79 80 81 82 83 84 85
Tiny (17-acre) third-growth, formerly made with Ch. MALES-COT; independent since '79. Finer than its reputation.

Marquis-de-Terme Margaux r. ⋆⋆⋆ 70' 75' 76 78' 79 80 81' 82 83 85
Renovated fourth-growth of 84 acres. Fragrant, fairly lean wines. Sells principally in France.

Martinens Margaux r. ⌈⋆⋆⌉ 75 76 78' 79' 80 81 82 83 84 85
75-acre Cru Bourgeois at Cantenac, recently much improved.

Maucaillou Moulis r. ⌈⋆⋆⌉ 70' 75' 76' 78 79 80 81 82 83' 84 85
130-acre Cru Bourgeois with v. high standards, property of DOURTHE family. Full, fruity. "Franc Caillou" is second wine.

Meyney St-Est. r.⋆⋆→⋆⋆⋆ 75' 78' 79 80 81 82' 83 84 85
Big (125-acre) riverside property next door to Ch. MONTROSE, one of many steady Crus Bourgeois in St-Estèphe. Owned by CORDIER. Second label: Prieur de Meyney.

Millet Graves r. w. dr. ⋆⋆ 78 79 81 82 83 85
160-acre estate at Portets; useful Graves.

La Mission-Haut-Brion Graves r. ⋆⋆⋆⋆ 61 64 66 71' 75' 76 78' 79 80 81 82' 83 84 85
Neighbour and long-time rival to Ch. HAUT-BRION, since 1984 in the same hands. Serious and grand old-style claret for long maturing. 30 acres. Ch. Latour-H-B is its second-quality wine.

Monbousquet St-Em. r. ⌈⋆⋆⌉ 75 76 78' 79' 80 81 82 83 84 85
Fine 75-acre estate in the Dordogne valley below St-Emilion. Attractive early-maturing wine from deep gravel soil.

Montrose St-Est. r. ⌈⋆⋆⋆⌉ 61 66 70' 75' 76 78' 79' 80 81 82' 83 84 85
158-acre family-run second-growth well known for deeply coloured, forceful, old-style claret. Recent vintages are lighter.

Moulin-à-Vent Moulis r. ⋆⋆ 70' 75' 76 78' 79 80 81 82' 83 84 85
60-acre property now in the forefront of this up-and-coming appellation. Lively, forceful wine.

Moulin des Carruades
The second-quality wine of Ch. LAFITE.

Moulin du Cadet St-Em. r. ⌈⋆⋆⌉ 71' 75' 76 78' 79 80 81 82' 83 84 85
First-class little v'yd. on the Côtes managed by MOUEIX.

Moulinet Pomerol r. ⋆⋆⋆ 75 76 78 79 81 82 83 85
One of Pomerol's bigger ch'x, 43 acres on lightish soil; wine ditto.

Mouton-Baronne-Philippe Pauillac r. ⋆⋆⋆ 70' 75' 76 78' 79 81 82' 83 84 85
Substantial fifth-growth with the enormous advantage of belonging to Baron Philippe de Rothschild, 125 acres making fine but much gentler, less rich and tannic wine than MOUTON.

Mouton-Rothschild Pauillac r. ⋆⋆⋆⋆ 61 66 67 70' 71 73 75' 76 78' 79 80 81 82' 83 84 85
Officially a first-growth since 1973, though for 20 years worthy of the title. 175 acres (87% CABERNET SAUVIGNON) making wine of majestic richness (82 is Imperial). Also the world's greatest museum of works of art relating to wine.

Nairac Sauternes w. sw. ⌈⋆⋆⌉ 73 75 76 78 79 80 81 82 83 85
Barsac classed-growth with perfectionist owner. Fascinating wines to lay down.

Nenin Pomerol r. ⋆⋆⋆ 67 70' 71' 75' 76 78 81 83 85
Well-known 66-acre estate; currently below par.

Olivier Graves r. and w. dr. ⋆⋆⋆ (r.) 78 79' 80 81 82 83 84 85
90-acre classed-growth, surrounding a moated castle at Léognan. 9,000 cases r., 12,000 w., both being upgraded from good to fine.

Les Ormes-de-Pez St-Est. r. ⌈⋆⋆⌉ 75' 76 78' 79 80 81' 82' 83' 84 85
Outstanding 72-acre Cru Bourgeois managed by Ch. LYNCH BAGES. Increasingly notable full-flavoured St-Estèphe.

Les Ormes Sorbet Medoc r. ⌈⋆⋆⌉ 78 79 81 82 83 85
Emerging smaller producer of good solid red at Couquèques.

Palmer Cant-Mar. r. ★★★★ 61 66 70 71′ 75′ 76 78′ 79 80 81′ 82 83′ 84 85
    The star ch. of CANTENAC; a third-growth often on a level just
    below the first-growths. Wine of power, flesh and delicacy. 110
    acres with Dutch, British and French owners.

Pape-Clément Graves r. and (w. dr.) ★★★ 70 73 75′ 76 78′ 79′ 80 81
    82′ 83 84 85
    Ancient v'yd. at Pessac, with record of seductive, scented reds,
    but recent vintages less even.

Patache d'Aux Bégadan (Médoc) r. ★★ 75′ 76′ 78 79′ 80 81 82′ 83′ 85
    90-acre Cru Bourgeois of the n. Médoc. Fragrant, lightish wine.

Paveil-de Luze Margaux r. ★★ 75′ 76′ 78 79 80 81 82′ 83 84 85
    Old family estate at Soussans. Small but highly regarded.

Pavie St-Em. r. ★★★ 70 71′ 75′ 76 78 79′ 80 81 82′ 83′ 84 85
    Splendidly sited first-growth of 100 acres on the slope of the Côtes.
    Typically rich and tasty St-Em., particularly since '82. The
    family owns the smaller Ch'x Pavie-Decesse and La Clusière.

Pavie-Macquin St-Em. r. ★★ 75 76 78 79 81 82 83 85
    Reliable small (25-acre) Côtes v'yd. e. of St-Emilion.

Pedesclaux Pauillac r. ★★ 70′ 71 75′ 76 78 79 80 81 82′ 83 84 85
    50-acre fifth-growth on the level of a good Cru Bourgeois. Solid
    strong wines loved by Belgians. Grand-Duroc-Milon and
    Bellerose are second labels.

Petit-Village Pomerol r. ★★★ 70 71′ 75′ 76′ 78 79 80 81 82′ 83 84 85
    One of the best-known little properties: 26 acres next to VIEUX-
    CH.-CERTAN, same owner as Ch. COS D'ESTOURNEL. Powerful
    plummy wine.

Petrus Pomerol r. ★★★★ 61 64 66 67 70′ 71′ 73 75′ 76′ 78 79′ 80 81
    82′ 83 85′
    The great name of Pomerol. 28 acres of gravelly clay giving the
    world's most massively rich and concentrated wine. 95% Merlot
    vines. Each vintage adds lustre. The price, too, is legendary.

Peyrabon St. Sauveur r. ★★ 75 76 78 79 80 81 82 83 84 85
    Serious 82-acre Cru Bourgeois popular in the Low Countries.

Peyreau St-Em. r. ★★
    Sister-ch. of CLOS L'ORATOIRE.

de Pez St-Est. r. ★★★ 66 70′ 71′ 73 75′ 76 78′ 79 80 81 82′ 83 84 85
    Outstanding Cru Bourgeois of 60 acres. As reliable as any of the
    classed growths of the village, and nearly as fine. Needs v. long
    storage.

Phélan-Ségur St-Est. r. ★★ 66 70′ 71 75′ 76′ 78 79 80 81 82′ 84
    Big and important Cru Bourgeois (125 acres) with some fine old
    vintages. New owners in 1985.

Pichon-Longueville-Baron Pauillac r. ★★★ 70′ 71 75 76 78′ 79′ 80
    81 82′ 83 84 85
    77-acre second-growth usually making fine sturdy Pauillac,
    recently on cracking form.

Pichon-Longueville, Comtesse de Lalande Pauillac r. ★★★★ 61 66
    70′ 71 73 75′ 76 78′ 79′ 80 81′ 82′ 83 84 85
    Second-growth neighbour to Ch. LATOUR. 148 acres. Consistent-
    ly among the very top performers; classic long-lived wine of
    fabulous breed, even in lesser years.

Pique-Caillou Graves r. ★★
    Little-known 40-acre neighbour of HAUT-BRION in the Bordeaux
    suburbs. Worth watching.

Pindefleurs St-Em. r. ★★ 75 76 78 79 81 82′ 83 85
    Up and coming 25-acre v'yd. on the St-Emilion plateau.

de Pitray Castillon r. ★★ 78 79 80 81 82 83 85
    Substantial (62 acre) v'yd. on the Côtes de Castillon e. of St-
    Emilion. Good light wines.

Plince Pomerol r. ★★ 75 76 78 79 80 81 82 83 85
    Reputable 20-acre property near Libourne. Attractive, perhaps
    rather simple wine from sandy soil.

La Pointe Pomerol r. ★★★ 70′ 71′ 75′ 76 78 79 81 82 83′ 85
Prominent 63-acre estate, well made, but relatively spare of flesh. Ch. LA SERRE is in the same hands.

Pontet-Canet Pauillac r. ★★★ 70 75′ 76 78′ 79′ 80 81′ 82′ 83′ 85
One of the biggest classed-growths. 182 acres, neighbour to MOUTON, potentially better than its official rank of fifth-growth, but dragged its feet for years. Current owners (same as LAFON-ROCHET) are trying hard. 2nd label: Les Hauts de Pontet.

Potensac Potensac (Médoc) r. ★★ 75′ 76 78′ 79 80 81 82′ 83 84 85
The best-known Cru Bourgeois of the n. Médoc. The neighbouring Ch'x. Lassalle and Gallais-Bellevue belong to the same family, the Delons, owners of LÉOVILLE–LASCASES. Class shows.

Pouget Margaux ★★ 70′ 75 76 78 79 80 81 82′ 83 85
19-acre v'yd. attached to Ch. BOYD-CANTENAC. In 1983 separate chais were built. Similar, rather lighter, wines.

Poujeaux (Theil) Moulis r. ★★ 70′ 71 75′ 76 79′ 80 81 82 83 84
Family-run Cru Exceptionnel of 120 acres selling its powerful, concentrated wine largely direct to an appreciative French public. 2nd label: La Salle de Poujeaux. Also Ch. Arnauld (83′).

Prieuré-Lichine Cant-Mar.r. ★★★ 70 75 76 78′ 79′ 80 81 82′ 83′ 84 85
143-acre fourth-growth brought to the fore by Alexis Lichine since 1952. Excellent full-bodied and fragrant Margaux.

Puy-Blanquet St-Em. r. ★★ 75′ 76 78 79 81 82′ 83 85
The major property of St-Etienne-de-Lisse, e. of St-Emilion, with over 50 acres. Typical full St-Em., if below the top class.

Puy-Razac St-Em. r. ★★ 75 76 78 79 80 81′ 82′ 83 85
Small property at the foot of the Côtes near Ch. PAVIE.

Puygueraud Côte de Francs r. ★★ 82 83 85
Leading ch. of this rising district. Wood-aged wines of surprising class.

Rabaud-Promis Sauternes w. sw. ★★ 71 75 76 78 79 81 83 85
74-acre classed-growth at Bommes. Little seen outside France.

Rahoul Graves r. and w. dr. ★★ (r.) 78′ 79 80 81 82 83 84 85 (w.) 82′ 83 84 85
37-acre v'yd. at Portets making particularly good wine from maturing vines; 80% red. White is aged in oak, too. Same Danish winemaker as DOMAINE LA GRAVE.

Ramage-la-Batisse Haut-Médoc r. ★★ 75′ 76 78 79 80 81 82 83′ 85
Outstanding Cru Bourgeois of 130 acres at St-Sauveur, west of Pauillac. Increasingly attractive since '80.

Rausan-Ségla Margaux r. ★★★ 61 70′ 75′ 76 78 79 80 81 82′ 83′ 84 85
94-acre second-growth; famous for its fragrance; a great Médoc name trying hard to regain its rank. Owned by ESCHENAUER.

Rauzan-Gassies Margaux r. ★★★ 61 75′ 76 78′ 79′ 80 81 82 83 85
74-acre second-growth neighbour of the last with little excitement to report for two decades, now seemingly perking up.

Raymond-Lafon Sauternes w. sw. ★★ 75 76 78 79 80′ 81′ 82 83 85
Serious Sauternes estate run by the manager of Ch. d'YQUEM. Splendid wines for long ageing. Among the top Sauternes today.

de Rayne-Vigneau Sauternes w. sw. ★★★ 67 71′ 76′ 78 81 83 85
164-acre classed-growth at Bommes. Standard sweet wine and a little dry, "Raynesec". New equipment in 1980.

Respide Graves (r.) w. dr. ★★ 81 82 83 84 85
One of the better white-wine ch'x. of s. Graves, at St Pierre de Mons. Full-flavoured wines.

Reynon lères Côtes de Bordeaux r. and w. dr. ★★
100 acres producing extraordinary dry white from very old Sauvignon vines ("Vieilles Vignes": 81 83′ 84 85). Also D.Y.A. white and serious red (79 81 82 83 85).

Reysson Vertheuil Haut-Médoc r. ★★ 81 82′ 83 84 85
Recently replanted, up-and-coming 120-acre Cru Bourgeois with the same owners as Ch. CHASSE-SPLEEN.

Ricaud Loupiac w. sw. (or dr.) or r. ★★ 81 82 83 85
Substantial grower of Sauternes-like dessert wine, just across the river. New owners are working hard.

Rieussec Sauternes w. sw. ★★★ 70 71 75′ 76′ 78 79 80 81′ 82 83 85
Worthy neighbour of Ch. D'YQUEM with 136 acres in Fargues, bought in 1984 by the (Lafite) Rothschilds. Not the sweetest; can be exquisitely fine. Also a dry wine: "R".

Ripeau St-Em. r. ★★ 75 78 79 81 82 83 85
Increasingly high-performance Grand Cru in the centre of the plateau. 49 acres.

La Rivière Fronsac r. ★★
The biggest and most impressive Fronsac property. Tannic wines repay long ageing.

de Rochemorin Graves r. (w. dr.) ★★ 81 82 83 84 85
An important restoration at Martillac by the owner of ch. LA LOUVIÈRE. 135 acres of new vines promise great things.

Romer du Hayot Sauternes w. sw. ★★ 79 80 81 82 83 85
A minor classed growth with a growing reputation.

Roquetaillade-la-Grange Graves r. w. dr. ★★
Substantial estate establishing a name for fine red (s.) Graves.

Roudier Montagne-St-Em. r. ★★
75-acre "satellite" St-Em. with the flavour of the real thing. Sister-ch. of BALESTARD.

Rouget Pomerol r. ★★ 70 71 75′ 76′ 78 79 81 82′ 83 85
Attractive old estate with rising standards on the n. edge of Pomerol. Good vintages need 10 years +.

Royal St-Emilion
Brand name of the important and dynamic growers' cooperative. See also HAUT QUERCUS, BERLIQUET.

Ruat-Petit-Poujeaux Moulis r. ★★ 79 80 81 82 83 84 85
45-acre v'yd. gaining in reputation for sound wine.

St-André Corbin St-Emilion r. ★★ 71 75′ 76′ 78 79′ 81 82′ 83 85
Considerable 54-acre property in Montagne-St-Emilion with a long record of above-average wines.

St. Bonnet Médoc r. ★★
Big n. Médoc estate at St. Christoly. V. flavoury wine.

St-Estèphe, Marquis de St-Est. r. ★
The growers' co-operative; over 200 members. Good value.

St-Georges St-Geo., St-Em. r. ★★ 70 75 76 78 79 80 81 82 83 85
Noble 18th-century ch. overlooking the St-Emilion plateau from the hill to the n. 125 acres; v. good wine sold direct to the public.

St. Georges-Côte-Pavie St. Em. r. ★★ 79 81 82 83 85
Perfectly placed little v'yd. on the Côtes. To watch.

Saint-Pierre St-Jul. r. ★★★ 70′ 71 75′ 76 78′ 79 80 81′ 82′ 83′ 84 85
Small (50-acre) fourth-growth many years in Belgian ownership; bought in 1982 by Henri Martin of Ch. GLORIA. A name to watch.

St-Pierre Graves (r.) w. dr. ★★ 81 83 84 85
Estate at St Pierre de Mons making classic Graves of notable character and flavour.

de Sales Pomerol r. ★★★ 70′ 71 75′ 76′ 78′ 79 80 81 82′ 83 85
The biggest v'yd. of Pomerol (116 acres), attached to the grandest château. Not poetry but excellent prose. Second labels: Ch. Chantalouette and Ch. du Delias.

Sénéjac Haut-Médoc r. (w. dr.) ★★ 75 76′ 78 79 80 81 82′ 83′ 85
43-acre Cru Bourgeois in s. Médoc run with increasing skill.

La Serre St-Em. r. ★★ 70 75′ 78 79 80 81 82 83 85
Well-run small Grand Cru with same owner as LA POINTE.

Sigalas-Rabaud Sauternes w. sw. ★★★ 71′ 75′ 76′ 78 79 81 82 83′ 85
The lesser part of the former Rabaud estate: 34 acres in Bommes, making first-class sweet wine.

Siran Lab-Mar. r. ★★★ **61 66 70 71**′ 75′ 78′ **79 80** 81′ 82′ 83 84 85
74-acre property of Cru Classé quality. Elegant, long-lived wines, consistently well made.

Smith-Haut-Lafitte Graves r. and (w. dr.) ★★★ (r.) **78 79** 81 82′ 83 84 85 (w.) D.Y.A.
Run-down old classed-growth at Martillac restored by ESCHENAUER in the '60s and '70s. 122 acres (14 of white). The white wine is light and fruity; the red dry. Recent efforts should improve it.

Sociando-Mallet Haut-Medóc r. ★★ **70 75** 78 79 81 82 83 84 85
Splendid Cru Grand Bourgeois at St-Seurin in the n. 65 acres. Dark dense wine for the patient.

Soutard St-Em. r. ★★ **70**′ **71** 75′ **76** 78′ **79 80** 81 82′ 83 85
Reliable 48-acre classed-growth n. of the town. Some vintages have been a bit "butch". A keeper.

Suduiraut Sauternes w. sw. ★★★ **67 70 76**′ **78 79 80** 81 82 83 85
One of the best Sauternes: of glorious creamy richness. Over 173 acres of the top class, under capable new management.

Taillefer Pomerol r. ★★ **70 73 75 76 78** 79 81 82′ 83 85
24-acre property on the edge of Pomerol owned by another branch of the MOUEIX family. Give it time.

Talbot St-Jul. r. (w.) ★★★ **66 70**′ **71** 75′ **76 78**′ **79 80** 81 82′ 83 84 85
Important 240-acre fourth-growth, sister-ch. to GRUAUD-LAROSE, wine similarly attractive rich, satisfying. (V.g.) second label: Connétable Talbot. A little white is called "Caillou Blanc".

Tayac Sou-Mar. r. ★★
Margaux's biggest Cru Bourgeois. Reliable if not noteworthy.

Terrefort-Quancard Bordeaux r. w. dr. ★★ **78 79 80** 81 82 83 85
Huge producer of good value wines at St-André-de-Cubzac. Rocky sub-soil contributes to surprising quality.

du Tertre Ar-Mar. r. ★★★ **70**′ **71**′ 75 **76 79**′ **80 81** 82′ 83 84 85
Fifth-growth, isolated s. of Margaux; restored to excellence by the owner of CALON-SEGUR. Fragrant and long-lived.

Tertre-Daugay St-Em. r. ★★★ **78 79** 81 82′ 83 85
Small, spectacularly sited, Grand Cru. Restored to excellence since '78 by the owner of LA GAFFELIÈRE.

Timberlay Bordeaux r. (w. dr.) ★ **81 82** 83 84 85
The biggest property of Cubzac; 185 acres. Pleasant light wines.

Toumilon Graves r. w. dr ★★
Notable ch. in St. Pierre de Mons. Fresh and charming r. and w.

La Tour-Blanche Sauternes w. sw. (r.) ★★★ **71** 75′ **76 78 79** 81′ 83′ 85
Top-rank 57-acre estate at Bommes with a state wine-growing school. Not among the leaders for a long time. But '83 is v.g.

La Tour-Carnet St-Lau. r. ★★ 75′ **76 78 79 80** 81 82′ 83 84 85
Fourth-growth reborn from total neglect in the '60s. Medieval tower with 79 acres just w. of St-Julien. Lightish, pretty wine.

La Tour de By Bégadan (Médoc) r. ★★ 75′ **76** 78′ **79**′ **80** 81 82′ 83 85
Very well-run 144-acre Cru Bourgeois in the n. Médoc increasing its reputation for sturdy, impressive yet appealing wine.

La Tour-de-Mons Sou-Mar. r. ★★ **70**′ **71**′ 75′ **78 79 80** 81 82′ 83 85
Distinguished Cru Bourgeois of 75 acres, three centuries in the same family. Sometimes excellent claret with a long life.

La Tour-du-Pin-Figeac St-Em. r. ★★
26-acre Grand Cru worthy of restoration.

La Tour-du-Pin-Figeac-Moueix St-Em. r. ★★★ **76 78 79** 81 82 83 85
Another 26-acre section of the same old property, owned by a branch of the famous MOUEIX family. Looking very good.

La Tour-Figeac St-Em. r. ★★ **70** 75 78 **79 80** 81 82′ 83
34-acre Grand Cru between Ch. FIGEAC and Pomerol, now showing the form that such a site suggests.

La Tour-Haut-Brion Graves r. ★★★ **70 75 76 78 79 80** 81 82′ 83 85
The second label of Ch. LA MISSION-HAUT-BRION. A plainer, harder, smaller-scale wine but with the same fine pedigree.

La Tour-Martillac   Graves r. and w. dr. ★★ (r.) 75' **78 79** 81 82' 83 84 85
Small but serious property at Martillac. 10 acres of white grapes; 37 of black. Quantity is sacrificed for quality. The owner, Jean Kressmann, is resurrecting the neighbouring Ch. Lespault.

La Tour St-Bonnet   Médoc r.   ★★   **75' 76 78' 79 80** 81 82' 83 85
Consistently well-made and typical n. Médoc from St-Christoly. 100 acres.

La Tour du Haut Moulin   Cussac (Haut-Médoc) r.   ★   78 79 81 82 83 85
Little-known 70-acre property; concentrated wines to age.

Tournefeuille   Lalande de Pomerol r.   ★★   71' 75' 76' 78 79 81' 82' 83 85
The star of Néac, overlooking Pomerol from the n. A small property (43 acres), but excellent long-lived wine.

des Tours   Montagne-St-Em. r. ★★ 75' 78 79 81 82 83 85
Spectacular ch. with modern 170-acre v'yd. Sound, easy wine.

Tronquoy-Lalande   St-Est. r. ★★ **70 71 75 76 78** 79 80 81 82' 83 85
40-acre Cru Bourgeois making typical high-coloured St-Estèphe needing long ageing. Distributed by DOURTHE.

Troplong-Mondot   St-Em. r.   ★★   **70' 71 75 76 78** 79 81 82' 83
One of the bigger Grand Crus of St-Emilion. 70 + acres well sited on the Côtes above Ch. PAVIE. To watch.

Trotanoy   Pomerol r.   ★★★★   **61 70 71' 73** 75' **76'** 78 79 80 81 82' 83
Perhaps the 2nd Pomerol after PETRUS, from the same stable. Only 27 acres but a glorious fleshy perfumed wine ('71 is famous).

Trottevieille   St-Em. r. ★★★ **70 71 75' 76 78** 79' **80** 81 82'
Grand Cru of 27 acres on the Côtes e. of the town, inexplicably-dragging its feet. Same owners as BATAILLEY.

Le Tuquet   Graves r. and w. dr. ★★ **76 78** 79 81 82 83
Big estate at Beautiran. Light fruity wines; the white better.

Verdignan   Médoc r.   ★★   **75 76 78 79 80** 81 82
Substantial Grand Bourgeois sister property to Ch. COUFRAN. More Cabernet than Coufran: Jack Sprat and his wife.

Vieux-Château-Certan   Pomerol r.   ★★★   **76 78 79 80** 81 82' 83 84 85
Traditionally rated close to PETRUS in quality, but totally different in style; almost Médoc build. 34 acres. Same (Belgian) family owns LABEGORCE-ZÉDÉ and another tiny Pomerol, Le Pin.

Vieux-Château-Landon   Médoc r. ★★ 81 82 83 85
Up-to-date grower of vigorous wine worth keeping 3–4 years.

Vieux-Château-St-André   St-Emilion r.   ★★   75' 76' 78 79' 81 82' 83 85
Small v'yd. in Montagne-St-Emilion owned by the leading wine-maker of Libourne. To follow.

Villegeorge   Avensan r.   ★★   **73'** 75' **76** 78' 79 **80** 81 82' 83
24-acre Cru Exceptionnel to the n. of Margaux with the same owner as Ch. BRANE-CANTENAC. Excellent full-bodied wine.

Villemaurine   St-Em. r.   ★★   **70' 71 75' 76 78** 79' **80** 81 82' 83 85
Small Grand Cru with splendid cellars well sited on the Côtes by the town. Firm wine with a high proportion of Cabernet. Recently v.g.

Vraye-Croix-de-Gay   Pomerol ★★★ **70' 71' 75' 76 78** 79 81 82' 83 85
Very small ideally situated v'yd. in the best part of Pomerol.

Yon-Figeac   St-Em. r.   ★★   **79** 81 82 83
59-acre Grand Cru to follow for savoury and scented wine.

d'Yquem   Sauternes w. sw. (dr.) ★★★★ 71' **73** 75' **76'** 77 **78 79 80** 81
The world's most famous sweet-wine estate. 250 acres making only 500 bottles per acre of very strong, intense, luscious wine kept 4 years in barrel. Most vintages improve at least 15 yrs. Also dry "Ygrec" in **78** 79 80 84.

More Bordeaux châteaux are listed under Canon-Fronsac, Côtes de Bourg, Cubzac, Fronsac, Côtes-de-Castillon, Lalande de Pomerol, Loupiac, Ste-Croix-du-Mont, Premières Côtes de Blaye, Premières Côtes de Bordeaux.

Switzerland

There are no great Swiss wines, but almost all (especially whites) are enjoyable and satisfying. Switzerland has some of the world's most efficient and productive vineyards. Costs are high and nothing less is viable. All the most important are lined along the south-facing slopes of the upper Rhône valley and Lake Geneva, respectively the Valais and the Vaud. For other areas see map. Wines are known by place-names, grape-names, and legally controlled type-names. All three, with those of leading growers and merchants, appear in the following list. On the whole, D.Y.A.

Aigle Vaud w. dr. ★★

   Principal town of CHABLAIS, between L. Geneva and the VALAIS. Dry whites of appropriately transitional style: at best strong and well balanced.

Amigne Traditional white grape of the VALAIS. Heavy but tasty wine, usually made dry.

Arvine Another old VALAIS white grape, similar to the last; perhaps better. Makes good dessert wine. Petite Arvine is similar.

Auvernier Neuchâtel r. p. w. dr. (sp.) ★★

   Village s. of NEUCHÂTEL known for PINOT NOIR, CHASSELAS and OEIL DE PERDRIX.

Blauburgunder

   One of the names given to the form of PINOT NOIR grown in German-speaking Switzerland.

Bonvin Old-established growers and merchants at SION.

Chablais Vaud (r.) w. dr. ★★

   The district between Montreux on L. Geneva and Martigny where the Rhône leaves the VALAIS. Good DORIN wines. Best villages: AIGLE, YVORNE, Bex.

Chasselas The principal white grape of Switzerland, neutral in flavour but taking local character. Known as FENDANT in VALAIS, DORIN in VAUD and PERLAN round Geneva.

Clevner (or Klevner)

   Another name for BLAUBURGUNDER.

Completer Rare Grisons (see map) grape giving liquorous wine.

Cortaillod Neuchâtel r. (p. w.) ★★

   Village near NEUCHÂTEL specializing in light PINOT NOIR reds.

Côte, La

   The n. shore of L. Geneva from Geneva to Lausanne. Pleasant DORIN and SALVAGNIN. Best villages incl. Féchy and Rolle.

Dézaley Vaud w. dr. ★★★

> Best-known village of LAVAUX, between Lausanne and Montreux. Steep s. slopes to the lake make fine, strong, fruity DORIN. Dézaley-Marsens is equally good.

Dôle Valais r. ★★

> Term for red VALAIS wine of PINOT NOIR or GAMAY or both grapes, reaching a statutory level of strength and quality.

Dorin Vaud w. dr. ★→★★

> The name for CHASSELAS wine in the VAUD, the equivalent of FENDANT from the VALAIS.

Epesses Vaud w. dr. and r. ★★

> Well-known lakeside village of LAVAUX. Good dry DORIN.

Ermitage

> VALAIS name for white wine from MARSANNE grapes. Rich, concentrated and heavy; usually dry.

Fendant Valais w. dr. ★→★★★

> The name for CHASSELAS wine in the VALAIS, where it reaches its ripest, strongest and smoothest. SION is the centre.

Flétri Withered grapes for making sweet wine, often MALVOISIE.

Gamay The Beaujolais grape; grown in French-speaking Switzerland.

Glacier, Vin du

> Almost legendary long-matured white stored at high altitudes. Virtually extinct today.

Goron

> Red VALAIS wine that fails to reach the DÔLE standard.

Hammel Major merchant and grower of LA CÔTE at Rolle.

Herrschaft Grisons r. (w. sw.) ★→★★★

> District near the border of Austria and Liechtenstein. Small amount of light PINOT NOIR reds and a few sweet whites.

Humagne

> Old VALAIS grape. Some red Humagne is sold: decent country wine. The strong white is a local speciality.

Johannisberg

> The Valais name for SYLVANER, which can make excellent stiff, dense and high-flavoured dry wine here, comparable to Frankenwein (see Germany).

Lavaux Vaud r. w. dr. ★→★★★

> The n. shore of L. Geneva between Lausanne and Montreux. The e. half of the VAUD. Best villages incl. DÉZALEY, EPESSES, Villette, Lutry, ST-SAPHORIN.

Légèrement doux

> Most Swiss wines are dry. Any with measurable sugar must be labelled thus or as "avec sucre résiduel".

Malvoisie

> VALAIS name for PINOT GRIS. Makes some wonderful late-picked sweet wines.

Mandement Geneva r. (p.) w. dr. ★

> Wine district just w. of Geneva, (see Vin-Union-Genève). Very light reds, chiefly GAMAY, and whites (PERLAN).

Marsanne

> The white grape of Hermitage on the French Rhône, used in the VALAIS to make ERMITAGE.

Merlot Bordeaux red grape (see Grapes for red wine) used to make the better wines of Italian Switzerland (TICINO). See also Viti.

Mont d'Or, Domaine du Valais w. dr. sw. ★★★★

> The best wine estate of Switzerland: 60 acres of steep hillside near SION. Good FENDANT, JOHANNISBERG, AMIGNE, etc., and real Riesling. Very rich concentrated wines.

Neuchâtel Neuchâtel r. p. w. dr. sp. ★→★★★

> City and the wine from the n. shore of its lake. Pleasant light PINOT NOIR and attractive sometimes sparkling CHASSELAS.

Nostrano

Word meaning "ours" applied to the lesser red wine of the TICINO, made from a mixture of native and Italian grapes, in contrast to MERLOT from Bordeaux.

Oeil de Perdrix

Pale rosé of PINOT NOIR.

Orsat Important and popular wine firm at Martigny, VALAIS.

Perlan Geneva w. dr. ★

The MANDEMENT name for the ubiquitous CHASSELAS, here at its palest, driest and least impressive.

Premier Cru

Any wine from the maker's own estate can call itself this.

Provins The excellent central cooperative of the VALAIS.

Rèze The grape, now very rare, used for VIN DU GLACIER.

Riesling-Sylvaner

Swiss name for MÜLLER-THURGAU, common in E. Switzerland (Thurgau), where it was bred by Dr. Müller. "A prophet is not without honour. . . ."

Rivaz Vaud r. w. dr. ★★

One of the better known villages of LAVAUX.

St-Saphorin Vaud w. dr. ★★

One of the principal villages of LAVAUX: wines drier and more austere than DÉZALEY or EPESSES.

Salvagnin Vaud r. ★→★★

Red VAUD wine of tested quality: the equivalent of DÔLE.

Savagnin Swiss name for the TRAMINER, called Païen in the VALAIS.

Schafiser Bern (r.) w. dr. ★→★★

The n. shore of L. Bienne (Bielersee) is well known for light CHASSELAS sold as either Schafiser or Twanner.

Schenk, S.A.

The biggest Swiss wine firm, based at Rolle in the VAUD, with 570 acres as well as other world-wide interests.

Sion Valais w. dr. ★→★★★

Centre of the VALAIS wine region, famous for its FENDANT.

Sierre

Important centre for some of the best VALAIS wines.

Spätburgunder

PINOT NOIR: by far the commonest grape of German-speaking Switzerland, making very light wines.

Testuz, V. and P.

Well-known growers and merchants at Dézaley, LAVAUX.

Ticino

Italian-speaking s. Switzerland. See Merlot, Viti, Nostrano.

Twanner See Schafiser

Valais

The Rhône valley between Brig and Martigny. Its n. side is an admirable dry sunny and sheltered v'yd., planted mainly to the CHASSELAS grape, which here makes its best wine.

Vaud The region of L. Geneva. Its n. shore is Switzerland's biggest v'yd. and in places as good as any. DORIN and SALVAGNIN are the main wines.

Vétroz Valais (r.) w. dr. ★★

Village near SION in the best part of the VALAIS.

Vevey Town near Montreux with a famous wine festival once every 30-odd years. The last was in 1977.

Vin-Union-Genève

Big growers' cooperative at Satigny in the MANDEMENT. Light reds and white PERLAN are Geneva's local wine.

Viti Ticino r. ★★

Legal designation of better-quality TICINO red, made of MERLOT and with at least 12% alcohol.

Yvorne Village near AIGLE with some of the best CHABLAIS v'yds.

Italy

Valle d'Aosta
Vd'A

Turin
Piemonte
Piem

Liguria

Genoa

The single most important fact for Italian wine in 1988 is the quality of the two vintages that are now generally coming into circulation. 1985 and 1986 were years to please almost everyone. The adulteration scandal that damaged confidence early in 1986 can safely be forgotten. In the late 80s the long process of the modernization of Italian wine has reached a new phase; that of confident consolidation by masters of their craft.

Underlying this confidence, however, there is a growing problem with the wine law itself. Like Germany, Italy is operating under a system that is restrictive in the wrong ways. Its DOC system is losing touch with the fast-moving realities of the modern wine world. A Denominazione di Origine Controllata (DOC) is defined in terms of tradition first, potential quality second, and actual tested quality scarcely at all.

In these circumstances it is the maker's name that matters most. Many of the best makers are turning their backs on regulations which they consider run counter to the best modern practice. In their place they are putting internal quality controls at much higher levels than the law could apply overall.

Meanwhile the DOC system remains, for all its faults, the only general key to the Italian wine maze. It is the approximate equivalent of France's Appellations Contrôlées, built up over the last 25 years. Most of Italy's worthwhile wines have defined areas and standards under the system. A few, like Chianti Classico, it must be said, had them long before. An increasing number, however, have not – and DOCs have been granted to many areas of only local interest: so the mere existence of a DOC proves little. The entries in this book ignore a number of unimportant DOCs and include considerably more non-DOCs. They also include a large number of grape-name entries.

Italian wines are named in a variety of ways: some geographical like French wines, some historical, some folklorical, and many of the best from their grapes. These include old "native" grapes such as Barbera and Sangiovese and more and more imported "international" grapes from France and Germany. Many of the DOCs, particularly in the north-east, are area names applying to widely different wines from more than a dozen different varieties. No overall comment on the quality of such a diversity is really possible, except to say that general standards are rising steadily and a growing number of producers are emerging as outstanding by international standards.

Trentino-Alto
-Adige Tr-Aad
● Bolzano
● Trento

Friuli-
Venezia
-Giulia
Fr-Vg

bardy

● Verona
Veneto Ven

● Trieste

● Venice

lia-Romagna
Ro

● Bologna

rence
uscany Tusc

Marches
Mar

● Siena

● Perugia

Umbria
Umbr

R. Tiber

Abruzzi Abr

● Rome

Latium
Lat

Molise M

Apulia Apu

Campania Camp

● Bari

● Naples

● Alghero

Basilicata
Bas

Sardinia
Sard

Calabria
Cal

● Cagliari

● Palermo
Marsala

Mt Etna ▲
Sicily Sic

The map is the key to the province
names used for locating each
entry.
Abbreviations of province names
shown in bold type are used in the
text.

The following abbreviations are
used in the Italian section:
Pa.   passito
Pr.   Province
Com.   commune
f.   fortified
See also key to symbols opposite
Contents

Abbazia di Rosazzo
>   Leading estate of COLLI ORIENTALI. White Ronco delle Acacie and red Ronco dei Roseti are v.g. single v'yd wines.

Abboccato Semi-sweet.

Aglianico del Vulture Bas. DOC r. (s/sw. sp.) ★★★ 75 77 78 79 81 82 85 86
>   Among the best wines of s. Italy. Ages well to rich aromas. Called Vecchio after 3 yrs., Riserva after 5. Top grower: Fratelli D'Angelo.

Alba Major wine-centre of PIEMONTE.

Albana di Romagna Em-Ro. DOCG w. dr. s/sw. (sp.) ★★ 85 86
>   Produced for several centuries in Romagna from Albana grapes. Cold fermentation now robs it of much character. Fattoria PARADISO makes some of the best.

Alcamo Sic. DOC w. dr. ★
>   Soft neutral whites from w. Sicily. Rapitalà is the best brand.

Aleatico Red, slightly muscat-flavoured grape, chiefly of the south.

Aleatico di Gradoli Lat. DOC r. sw. or f. ★★
>   Aromatic, fruity; alcohol 17.5%. Made near Viterbo.

Aleatico di Puglia Apu. DOC r. sw. or f. ★★
>   Aleatico grapes make good dessert wine over a large area. Two distinct types have 15% or 18.5% alcohol.

Alezio Apu. DOC (r.) p. dr. ★★ 83 85 86
>   Recent Salento DOC, esp. for powerful Negro Amaro rosé.

Allegrini
>   High-quality producer of Veronese wines, incl. VALPOLICELLA.

Alto Adige Tr-Aad. DOC r. p. w. dr. sw. sp. ★★ → ★★★
>   A DOC covering some 19 different wines, usually named after their grape varieties, in 33 villages round Bolzano.

Ama, Castello di
>   Modern CHIANTI CLASSICO estate nr. Gaiole. San Lorenzo is excellent top wine.

Amabile Semi-sweet, but usually sweeter than ABBOCCATO.

Amaro
>   Bitter. When prominent on a label the contents is a "bitters", not a wine.

Amarone See Recioto.

Antinori
>   A long-established Tuscan house of the highest repute producing first-rate CHIANTI and ORVIETO, now also distinguished for pioneering new styles: e.g. TIGNANELLO.

Artimino
>   Ancient hill-town and wine-estate west of Florence, best known for its CHIANTI plus CABERNET: DOC CARMIGNANO. Future uncertain.

Assisi Umbr. r. (w.dr.) ★★
>   Rosso di Assisi is a very attractive new red *vino di tavola*. Drink young and cool.

Asti Major wine-centre of PIEMONTE.

Asti Spumante Piem. DOC w. sp. ★★★ NV
>   Sweet and very fruity muscat sparkling wine. Low in alcohol.

Avignonesi
>   MONTEPULCIANO estate with range of good wines incl. VINO NOBILE, blended red Grifi, and superlative VINSANTO.

Azienda agricola (or agraria)
>   A farm producing various crops, often incl. wine.

Azienda vinicola
>   Wine firm using primarily bought-in grapes.

Azienda vitivinicola A (specialized) wine estate.

Badia a Coltibuono 71 75 78 79 80 81 82 83 85 86
>   Fine Chianti-maker at Gaiole with a restaurant and remarkable collection of old vintages.

Banfi See Villa Banfi.

Barbacarlo (Oltrepò Pavese) Lomb. DOC r. dr. or sw. ★★→★★★ 82
83 85 86
Delicately flavoured with bitter after-taste, made in the
Commune of Broni in the province of Pavia.

Barbaresco Piem. DOCG r. dr. ★★★→★★★★ 71 74 78 79 80 82 83 85 86
Neighbour of BAROLO from the same grapes but lighter, ageing
sooner. At best subtle and fine. At 4 yrs. becomes Riserva. Best
producers incl. GAJA, BRUNO GIACOSA, Marchesi di Gresy,
Produttori del B., Castello di Neive.

Barbera
Dark acidic red grape, a speciality of Piemonte also used in
Lombardy, Emilia-Romagna and other northern provinces. Its
best wines are:

Barbera d'Alba Piem. DOC r. dr. ★★ 79 80 82 83 85 86
Tasty, tannic, fragrant red. Superiore can age 7 years. Round
ALBA, NEBBIOLO is sometimes added to make a VINO DA TAVOLA.

Barbera d'Asti Piem. DOC r. dr. ★★ 79 80 82 83 85 86
To many the best of the Barberas; all Barbera grapes; grapy and
appetizing, young or aged up to 7 years.

Barbera del Monferrato Piem. DOC r. dr. ★ 82 83 85 86
From a large area in the Pr. of Alessandria and ASTI. Pleasant,
slightly fizzy, sometimes sweetish.

Bardolino Ven. DOC r. dr. (p.) ★★ D.Y.A.
Pale, light, slightly bitter red from e. shore of La Garda.
Bardolino Chiaretto is even paler and lighter.

Berlucchi, Guido
Italy's biggest producer of sparkling METHODO CLASSICO, at
FRANCIACORTA. Steady quality.

Barolo Piem. DOCG r. dr. ★★★→★★★★ 71 74 78 79 80 82 83 85 86
Small area s. of Turin with one of the highest-rated Italian red
wines, dark, rich, alcoholic (minimum 12°), dry but deep in
flavour. From NEBBIOLO grapes. Ages for up to 15 yrs, Riserva
after 5. Best producers incl. VIETTI, GIACOSA, COGNO, CONTERNO,
Pio Cesare, Marcarini, MASCARELLO, CERETTO, PRUNOTTO, COR-
DERO, RATTI. The coop "Terre de Barolo" is also v.g.

Bell 'Agio Brand of sweet white MOSCATO from BANFI.

Bertani
Well-known producers of quality Veronese wines (VALPOLI-
CELLA, SOAVE, etc.), including aged AMARONE.

Bianco White.

Bianco d'Arquata Umbr. w.dr. ★★ 83 84 85 86
A limpid and inspiring light and fruity white from near Perugia.

Bianco di Pitigliano Tusc. DOC w. dr. ★ D.Y.A.
A soft, fruity, lively wine made near Grosseto.

Bianco Vergine della Valdichiana Tusc. DOC w. dr. ★★ D.Y.A.
Pale dry light wine from Arezzo. But what music in the name.

Bigi, Luigi & Figlio
Famous producers of ORVIETO and other wines of Umbria and
Tuscany. Their Torricella v'yd produces v.g. dry Orvieto.

Biondi-Santi
The original producer of BRUNELLO with cellars in Montalcino
(Siena). His prices are outrageous.

Boca Piem. DOC r. dr. ★★ 79 80 82 83 85 86
From same grape as BAROLO in n. of PIEMONTE, Pr. of Novara. A
coming name.

Bolla
Famous Veronese firm producing VALPOLICELLA, SOAVE, etc.
Top wines: Jago, Castellaro.

Bonarda
Minor red grape widely grown in PIEMONTE and Lombardy.

Bonarda (Oltrepò Pavese)　Lomb. DOC r. dr. ★★ 82 83 85 86
　　　Soft, fresh, pleasant red from south of Pavia.

Bosca　Wine-producers from PIEMONTE known for their ASTI SPU-
　　　MANTE and Vermouths; also popular fizzy Caneï.

Boscarelli, Poderi
　　　Small estate with v.g. VINO NOBILE DI MONTEPULCIANO.

Botticino　Lomb. DOC r. dr. ★★ 82 83 85 86
　　　Strong, full-bodied rather sweet red from Brescia.

Brachetto d'Acqui　Piem. DOC r. sw. (sp.) ★ D.Y.A.
　　　Sweet sparkling red with pleasant muscat aroma.

Bramaterra　Piem. DOC r. dr.　★★　78 79 80 82 83 85 86
　　　A substantial and stylish recent addition to Piemonte's reds.
　　　Nebbiolo grapes predominate.

Breganze　Ven. DOC ★→★★ 79 80 82 83 85 86
　　　A catch-all for many varieties around Vicenza. CABERNET and
　　　PINOT BIANCO are best. Top producer: Maculan.

Bricco Manzoni　Piem. r.　★★★　79 80 82 83 85 86
　　　Excellent red of blended NEBBIOLO and BARBERA from Monforte
　　　d'Alba.

Brolio
　　　One of the oldest (c. 1200) and most famous CHIANTI CLASSICO
　　　estates, now owned by a British group. Good whites as well as red.

Brunello di Montalcino　Tusc. DOCG r. dr. ★★★★ 70 71 75 77 78 79
　　　80 81 82 83 85 86
　　　Italy's most celebrated red wine. Strong, full-bodied, high-
　　　flavoured and long-lived. After 5 yrs. is called Riserva. Produced
　　　for over a century 25 miles s. of Siena.

Buttafuoco　Lomb. ★★ 82 83 85 86
　　　A potent foaming red of BARBERA and other grapes, sold under
　　　the DOC OLTREPÒ PAVESE.

Ca' del Bosco
　　　FRANCIACORTA estate making some of Italy's v. best sparkling
　　　wine, CHARDONNAY, and excellent reds (Pinot Noir, "Zanella"
　　　and FRANCIACORTA).

Cabernet
　　　Bordeaux grape much used in n.e. Italy and increasingly in
　　　Tuscany and the south. See place names, e.g.:

Cacchiano, Castello di
　　　First-rate CHIANTI CLASSICO estate at Gaiole, owned by
　　　RICASOLI.

Calcinaia, Villa
　　　CHIANTI CLASSICO estate for centuries in the Capponi family.

Caldaro or Lago di Caldaro　Tr-Aad. DOC r. dr. ★→★★ D.Y.A.
　　　Alias KALTERESEE. Light, soft, slightly bitter-almond red.
　　　Classico from a smaller area is better. From south of Bolzano.

Caluso Passito　Piem. DOC w. sw. (f.) ★★ 74 76 78 79 80 82 85 86
　　　Made from selected Erbaluce grapes left to partly dry; delicate
　　　scent, velvety taste. From a large area in the provinces of Turin
　　　and Vercelli.

Cannonau di Sardegna　Sard. DOC r. (p.) dr. or s/sw. ★★ 83 84 85
　　　Cannonau is Sardinia's basic red grape; its wine often formidably
　　　strong (min. 13.5% alc.). Less potent Cannonaus without the
　　　DOC can be easier to like.

Cantina
　　　1. Cellar or winery. 2. Cantina Sociale = growers' co-op.

Capargo, Tenuta
　　　MONTALCINO estate with excellent BRUNELLO La Casa; also
　　　CHARDONNAY and red blend Ca'del Pazzo.

Capezzana, Tenuta di
　　　The Tuscan estate of the ancient Bonacossi family, producers
　　　of excellent CHIANTI MONTALBANO and CARMIGNANO. Also a
　　　Bordeaux-style red, GHIAIE DELLA FURBA.

Carpenè Malvolti
Leading producer of classic PROSECCO and other sp. wines at Conegliano, Veneto.

Capri Campania DOC r. w. p. ★★
Widely abused name of the famous island in the Bay of Naples. No guarantee of quality.

Carema Piem. DOC r. dr. ★★ 71 74 78 79 80 82 83 85 86
Old speciality of northern PIEMONTE. NEBBIOLO grapes traditionally fermented Beaujolais-style before crushing. (See France: Macération carbonique.) More conventional today.

Carmignano Tusc. DOC r. dr. (p. br.) [★★★] 78 79 80 81 82 83 85 86
Section of CHIANTI using 10% of CABERNET to make increasingly good, and some very fine, wine. See Capezzana.

Carso Fr.-VG. DOC r. w. dr. ★★ 85 86
New DOC near Trieste includes good MALVASIA. Terrano del C. in a soft REFOSCO-like red.

Casa fondata nel . . . Firm founded in . . .

Castel del Monte Apu. DOC r. p. w. dr. ★★ 79 81 83 84 85 86
Dry, fresh, well-balanced southern wines. The red becomes Riserva after 3 yrs. Rosé most widely known.

Castel San Michele Tr-Aad. r. dr. [★★] 79 81 82 83 85 86
A good red made of Cabernet and Merlot grapes by the Trentino Agricultural College near Trento.

CAVIT
CAntina VITicultori, a co-operative of co-operatives near Trento, producing large quantities of table and sp. wines.

Cellatica Lomb. DOC r. dr. ★★ 82 83 85 86
Light red with slightly bitter after-taste of Schiava grapes, from Brescia.

Cerasuolo Abr. DOC p. dr. ★★
The rosato version of MONTEPULCIANO D'ABRUZZO.

Ceretto High-quality grower of BARBARESCO, BAROLO, etc. Barb. is called Bricco Asili, Barolo Bricco Rocche (now Italy's most expensive wine).

Cerveteri Lat. DOC w. dr. s/sw. ★ 81 82 83 85 86
Sound wines produced n.w. of Rome between Lake Bracciano and the Tyrrhenian Sea.

Chardonnay
Has recently joined permitted varieties for several w. Italian DOCs. Some of the best (e.g. GAJA) are still only VINI DA TAVOLA.

Chianti Tusc. DOCG r. dr. [★→★★] 78 79 80 81 82 83 85 86
The lively local wine of Florence. Fresh but warmly fruity when young, still occasionally sold in straw-covered flasks. Variously age-worthy. Montalbano, Rufina and Colli Fiorentini, Senesi, Aretini, Colline Pisane are sub-districts.

Chianti Classico Tusc. DOCG r. dr. [★→★★★] 78 79 80 81 82 83 85 86
Senior Chianti from the central area. Many estates make fine powerful slightly astringent wine. Riservas (after 3 yrs.) often have the bouquet of age in oak. The neck-label is a black rooster.

Chianti Putto Tusc. DOCG r. dr. [★→★★★]
Often high-quality Chianti from a league of producers outside the Classico zone. Neck-label is pink and white cherub.

Chiaretto
Very light reds, almost rosé (the word means "claret") produced around Lake Garda. See Riviera del Garda.

Cinqueterre Lig. DOC w. dr. or sw. or pa. ★
Fragrant, fruity white made for centuries near La Spezia. The PASSITO is known as Sciacchetrà.

Cinzano
Major Vermouth company also known for its ASTI SPUMANTE from PIEMONTE.

Cirò Cal. DOC r. (p. w.) dr. ★★ 77 78 79 81 82 83 84 85 86

The wine of the ancient Olympic games. Very strong red, fruity white (to drink young).

Classico

Term for wines from a restricted, usually central, area within the limits of a DOC. By implication, and often in practice, the best of the region.

Clastidium Lomb. w. dr. ★★★ 78 82 83 85

Unique full-bodied oak-aged white of PINOTS NERO and GRIGIO. Ages splendidly.

Col Sandago

Up-to-date estate winery near Treviso (Veneto) with good reds, whites and sparkling Prosecco. Changes afoot here.

Collavini, Cantina

High-quality producers of COLLIO, COLLI ORIENTALI and GRAVE DEL FRIULI wines: PINOT GRIGIO, RIESLING, MERLOT, PINOT NERO and sparkling.

Colli Means "hills" in many wine-names.

Colli Albani Lat. DOC w. dr. or s/sw. (sp.) ★→★★ D.Y.A.

Soft fruity wine of the Roman hills.

Colli Berici Ven. DOC r. w. p. dr. ★★ 81 82 83 85 86

CABERNET is the best of several promising products of these hills south of Vicenza.

Colli Bolognesi Em-Ro. DOC r. p. w. dr. ★★ D.Y.A. (w.). 82 83 85 86

From the hills s.w. of Bologna. Six possible grape varieties.

Colli della Toscana Centrale

Several of the best Chianti makers are starting to use this name for table wines. (A future DOC? See PREDICATO.)

Colli del Trasimeno Umb. DOC r. w. dr. ★★ 82 83 85 86

Lively wines from the province of Perugia.

Colli Euganei Ven. DOC r. w. dr. or s/sw. (sp.) ★ 82 83 85 86

A DOC applicable to 7 wines produced s.w. of Padua. Red is adequate; white soft and pleasant. The table wine of Venice.

Colli Orientali del Friuli Fr-VG. DOC r. w. dr. or sw. ★★→ 82 83 84 85 86

12 different wines are produced under this DOC on the hills east of Udine and named after their grapes, esp v.g. whites.

Colli Piacentini Tusc. DOC r. p. w. dr. ★→★★

New DOC incl. traditional GUTTURNIO and Monterosso Val d'Arda among 11 types.

Collio (Goriziano) Fr-VG. DOC r. w. dr. ★★★→★★★ 82 83 84 85

12 different wines named after their grapes from a small area between Udine and Gorizia nr. the Yugoslav border. V.g. whites.

Colli Perugini Umbr. DOC r. p. w. ★ 82 83 85 86

New DOC for light wines in the hills of Perugia.

Coltassala Tusc. r.dr. ★★★ 80 81 82 83 85 86

Notable new "Bordeaux-style" red from the ancient CHIANTI CLASSICO estate of CASTELLO DI VOLPAIA at Radda.

Coltiva – Gruppo Italiano Vini

Complex of coops and wineries, now apparently the world's third largest producer.

Conterno, Aldo and Giacomo

Highly regarded growers of BAROLO, etc., have separate estates at Monforte d'Alba.

Contratto

Piemonte firm known for ASTI SPUMANTE, BAROLO, etc.

Copertino Apu. DOC r.dr. ★★ 82 83 84 85 86

Age-worthy dark red of Negroamaro grapes from the heel of Italy.

Cora A leading House producing ASTI SPUMANTE and Vermouth from PIEMONTE.

Cordero, Paolo, di Montezemolo Tiny producer of top-class Barolo.

Cori Lat DOC w. r. dr./sw. ☒ **85 86**
Soft and well-balanced wines made 30 miles south of Rome.

Cortese di Gavi See Gavi

Cortese (Oltrepò Pavese) Lomb. DOC w. dr. *→** D.Y.A.
Delicate fresh white from western Lombardy.

Corvo Sic. r. w. dr. ** **77 78 79 81 83 84 85 86**
Popular Sicilian wines. Sound dry red, pleasant soft whites.

Costanti, Emilio
Tiny estate producing top-quality BRUNELLO DI MONTALCINO.

D'Ambra
Well-known producer of ISCHIA and other wines of that island.

Dolce Sweet.

Dolceacqua See Rossese di Dolceacqua

Dolcetto
Common low-acid red grape of PIEMONTE, the everyday wine of
BAROLO and BARBARESCO-producing areas, giving its name to:

Dolcetto d'Acqui Piem. DOC r. dr. * **85 86**
Good standard table wine from s. of ASTI.

Dolcetto d'Alba Piem. DOC r. dr. ** **85 86**
Among the best Dolcetti, with a trace of bitter-almond.
Superiore after 1 yr.

Dolcetto di Diano d'Alba Piem. DOC ** **85 86**
A rival to Dolcetto d'Alba; often more potent.

Dolcetto di Ovada Piem. DOC r. dr. ** **79 80 82 83 85 86**
Reputedly the sturdiest and longest-lived of Dolcetti.

Donnaz Vd'A. DOC dr. ** **78 79 80 82 83 85 86**
A mountain NEBBIOLO, fragrant, pale and faintly bitter. Aged for
a statutory 3 yrs. Now part of the VALLE D'AOSTA regional DOC.

Donnici Cal. DOC r. dr. *
Middle-weight southern red from Cosenza.

Elba Tusc. r. w. dr. (sp.) ☒☒ **82 83 85 86**
The island's white is admirable with fish. Good dry red.

Enfer d'Arvier Vd'A. DOC r. dr. ** **79 82 83 85 86**
Alpine speciality (c.f. DONNAZ); pale, pleasantly bitter, light red.

Enoteca
Italian for "wine library", of which there are many in the
country, the most comprehensive being the Enoteca Italica
Permanente of Siena. Chianti has one at Greve.

Erbaluce di Caluso Piem. DOC w. dr. * D.Y.A.
Pleasant fresh hot-weather wine. See also CALUSO PASSITO.

Est! Est!! Est!!! Lat. DOC w. dr. or s/sw. ** D.Y.A.
Famous soft fruity white from Montefiascone, n. of Rome. The
name is more remarkable than the wine.

Etna Sic. DOC r. p. w. dr. ☒☒ **82 83 84 85 86**
Wine from the volcanic slopes. The red is warm, full, balanced
and ages well; the white is distinctly grapy. See Villagrande.

Falerio dei Colli Ascolani Mar. DOC w. dr. ☒ D.Y.A.
Made in the province of Ascoli Piceno. Pleasant, fresh, fruity; a
wine for the summer.

Falerno Camp. r. w. dr. ** **82 83 84 85 86**
One of the best-known wines of ancient times. Strong red, fruity
white, improving in quality.

Fara Piem. DOC r. dr. ☒☒ **78 79 80 82 83 85 86**
Good NEBBIOLO wine from Novara, n. PIEMONTE. Fragrant;
worth ageing. Small production.

Faro Sic. DOC r. dr. ** **83 84 85 86**
Rare strong Sicilian red, made in sight of the Straits of Messina.

Favonio Apu. r. w. dr. ☒☒☒ **80 81 82 83 84 85 86**
Revolutionary estate east of Foggia using CABERNET, CHARDON-
NAY and PINOT BIANCO.

Fazi-Battaglia Well-known producer of VERDICCHIO, etc.

Felluga
Brothers Livio and Marco have separate companies in the COLLIO and COLLI ORIENTALI zones. Both are highly esteemed.

Ferrari
Firm making one of Italy's best dry sparkling wines by the champagne method near Trento, Trentino-Alto Adige.

Fiano di Avellino Cam. w. dr. ★★→★★★ 81 82 83 84 85 86
Considered the best white of Campania.

Fiorano Lat. r. w. dr. s/sw. ★★ 75 77 78 79 80 81 82 83 85 86
Interesting Roman reds of Cabernet Sauvignon and Merlot.

Florio The major producer of Marsala, owning several brands, controlled by CINZANO.

Foianeghe Tr-Aad. r. ★★
Trentino Cabernet/Merlot red to age 7–10 years.

Folonari
Large run-of-the-mill merchant at Brescia, connected with RUFFINO.

Fontana Candida One of the biggest producers of FRASCATI.

Fontanafredda
One of the biggest producers of Piemontese wines, incl. BAROLO.

Fonterutoli
High-quality CHIANTI CLASSICO estate at Castellina.

Fracia Lomb. r. dr. ★★ 78 79 82 83 85 86
Good light but fragrant red from VALTELLINA. DOC wine made by Negri.

Franciacorta Pinot Lomb. DOC w. (p.) dr. (sp.) ★★→★★★
Agreeable soft white and good sparkling wines made of PINOT BIANCO, NERO or GRIGIO. CA' DEL BOSCO is outstanding.

Franciacorta Rosso Lomb. DOC r. dr. ★★ 82 83 85 86
Lightish red of mixed CABERNET and BARBERA from Brescia.

Franco Fiorina
Highly regarded producer of BAROLO, BARBARESCO, etc.

Frascati Lat. DOC w. dr. s/sw. sw. (sp.) ★→★★★ D.Y.A.
Best-known wine of the Roman hills: soft, ripe, golden, tasting of whole grapes. Most is disappointingly neutral today: look for dated wines from small producers (e.g. Colli di Catone). The sweet is known as Cannellino.

Frecciarossa Lomb. r. w. dr. ★→★★ 83 85 86
Sound wines from an estate nr. Casteggio in the OLTREPÒ PAVESE.

Freisa d'Asti Piem. DOC r. dr. s/sw. or sw. (sp.) ★★ D.Y.A.
Sometimes sweet, often *frizzante* red, said to taste of raspberries and roses. With enough acidity it can be highly appetizing.

Frescobaldi
Ancient noble family, leading pioneers of CHIANTI PUTTO at NIPOZZANO, e. of Florence. Also excellent white POMINO. See also Montesodi.

Friuli-Venezia Giulia
The n.-e. province on the Yugoslav border. Many wines, of which the DOCs COLLIO and COLLI ORIENTALI include most of the best.

Frizzante
Semi-sparkling or "pétillant", a word used to describe wines such as LAMBRUSCO.

Gaja
Old family firm at BARBARESCO. Top-quality Piemonte wines, esp. Barbaresco. Pioneer with carbonic maceration to make VINÓT. Now an excellent new Chardonnay (Gaia & Rey), CABERNET (Darmagi) and SAUV. BLANC.

Galestro Tusc. w. dr. ★★
Name for superior light grapey white from Chianti country.

Gambellara Ven. DOC w. dr. or s/sw. (sp.) ★ D.Y.A.
Neighbour of SOAVE. Dry wine similar. Sweet (known as RECIOTO DI GAMBELLARA), agreeably fruity. Also VINSANTO.

Gancia
    Famous ASTI SPUMANTE house from Piemonte, also produces vermouth and OLTREPÒ PAVESE wines.

Garganega   The principal white grape of SOAVE.

Gattinara   Piem. DOC r. dr. ★★→★★★ 70 74 78 79 80 82 83 85 86
    Excellent big-scale BAROLO-type red from northern PIEMONTE. Made from NEBBIOLO, locally known as Spanna.

Gavi (or Cortese di Gavi)   Piem. w. dr. ★★→ ★★★ 84 85 86 (usually D.Y.A.)
    At best almost burgundian dry white of Cortese grapes. La Scolca is best known, "Principessa Gavi" v. reliable.

Geografico, Chianti
    Chianti Classico from a major growers' co-operative near Gaiole. Recently poor quality.

Ghemme   Piem. DOC r. dr. ★★ 78 79 80 82 83 85 86
    Neighbour of GATTINARA, capable of Bordeaux-style finesse.

Ghiaie della Furba   Tusc. r. dr. ★★★ 78 79 80 81 82 83 85 86
    Bordeaux-style Cabernet blend from the admirable Tenuta di CAPEZZANA, CARMIGNANO.

Giacobazzi
    Well-known producers of Lambrusco wines with cellars in Nonantola and Sorbara, near Modena.

Most Italian wines have a simple name, in contrast to the combination village and vineyard names of France and Germany.

SOAVE CLASSICO VINO A DENOMINAZIONE DI ORIGINE CONTROLLATA IMBOTTIGLIATO DAL PRODUTTORE ALL 'ORIGINE CANTINA SOCIALE DI SOAVE	Soave is the name of this wine. It is qualified only by the word Classico, a legal term for the central (normally the best) part of many long-established wine regions. "Denominazione di Origine Controllata" is the official guarantee of authenticity. Imbottigliato . . . all 'origine means bottled by the producer. Cantina Sociale di Soave means the growers' co-operative of Soave.

Giacosa, Bruno
    Old family business making excellent BARBARESCO and other Piemonte wines at Neive (Cuneo).

Girò di Cagliari   Sard. DOC r.dr. or sw. ★ 85 86
    A formidably alcoholic red, most sympathetic when some of its sugar content is left unfermented.

Goldmuskateller
    Aromatic grape made into wonderful dry white, esp. by TIEFENBRUNNER.

Gradi   Degrees (of alcohol) i.e. percent by volume.

Grave del Friuli   Fr-VG. DOC r. w. dr. ★★ 82 83 85 86
    A DOC covering 15 different wines named after their grapes, from near the Yugoslav border. Good MERLOT and CABERNET.

Gray, Giorgio
    Merchant and consultant to top ALTO-ADIGE and other estates. Own labels incl. Bellendorf, Herrnhofer, Kehlburg.

Grechetto (or Greco)
    A traditional white grape with more spirit than the ubiquitous Trebbiano, increasingly used and referred to by name in the centre and south of Italy.

Greco di Bianco (or Greco di Gerace)   Cal. DOC w.sw. ★★ 77 78 79 81 83 85 86
    An original smooth and fragrant dessert wine from Italy's toe. See also Mantonico.

Greco di Tufo Camp. DOC w. dr. (sp.) ★★★ 83 84 85 86
> One of the best whites of the south, fruity and slightly "wild" in flavour. A character.

Grignolino d'Asti Piem. DOC r. dr. ★ D.Y.A.
> Pleasant lively standard wine of PIEMONTE.

Grumello Lomb. DOC r. dr. ★★ 78 79 80 82 83 85 86
> NEBBIOLO wine from VALTELLINA, can be delicate and fine.

Gutturnio dei Colli Piacentini Em-Ro. DOC r. dr. (s/sw.) ★★82 83 85
> Full-bodied BARBERA/BONARDA blend from the hills of Piacenza. Ages admirably. (DOC is Colli Piacentini.)

Inferno Lomb. DOC r. dr. ★★ 78 79 82 83 85 86
> Similar to GRUMELLO and like it classified as VALTELLINA Superiore.

Ischia Camp. DOC (r.) w. dr. ★ 85 86
> The wine of the island off Naples. The slightly sharp white Superiore is best; ideal with fish.

Isonzo Fr-VG. DOC r. w. dr. ★ 82 83 85 86
> DOC covering 10 varietal wines in the extreme north-east.

Kalterersee German name for Lago di CALDARO.

Lacryma Christi del Vesuvio Camp. r. p. w. (f.) dr. (sw.) ★→★★85 86
> Famous but frankly ordinary wines in great variety from the slopes of Mount Vesuvius. (DOC is Vesuvio.) MASTROBERAR-DINO makes the only good example.

Lageder, Alois
> The senior producer of the Bolzano DOC's: STA. MADDALENA, etc. Exciting wines, incl. barrel-aged CHARD. and v.g. reds.

Lago di Caldaro See Caldaro

Lagrein Tr-Aad. DOC r. p. dr. ★★ 78 79 80 82 83 85 86
> Lagrein is a Tyrolean grape with a bitter twist. Good fruity wine—at best very satisfying. The rosé is called Kretzer, the dark Dunkel.

Lamberti
> Producers of SOAVE, VALPOLICELLA and BARDOLINO at Lazise on the east shore of Lake Garda.

Lambrusco DOC (or not) r. p. (w.) s/sw. ⊡ D.Y.A.
> Bizarre but popular fizzy red, generally drunk secco (dry) in Italy but a smash hit in its sweet version in the U.S.A.

Lambrusco di Sorbara Em-Ro. DOC r. (w.) dr. or s/sw. sp. ★★★ D.Y.A.
> The best of the Lambruscos. From near Modena.

Lambrusco Grasparossa di Castelvetro Em-Ro. DOC r. dr. or s/sw. sp. ★★ D.Y.A
> Similar to above. Highly scented, pleasantly acidic; often drunk with rich food.

Lambrusco Salamino di Santa Croce Em-Ro. DOC r. dr. or s/sw. sp. ★ D.Y.A
> Similar to above. Fruity smell, high acidity and a thick "head".

Langhe The hills of central PIEMONTE.

Latisana Fr-VG. DOC r. w. dr. ★★ 83 85 86
> DOC for 7 varietal wines from some 50 miles n.e. of Venice. Particularly good TOCAI FRIULANO.

Leone de Castris
> Leading producer of Apulian wines with an estate at SALICE SALENTINO, near Lecce.

Lessona Piem. DOC r. d. ★★ 78 79 80 82 83 85 86
> Soft, dry, claret-like wine produced in the province of Vercelli from Nebbiolo, Vespolina and Bonarda grapes.

Liquoroso Strong and usually sweet (whether fortified with alcohol or not), e.g. Tuscan VINSANTO.

Locorotondo Apu. DOC w. dr. (sp.) ★ D.Y.A.
> A pleasantly fresh southern white.

Lugana Lomb. DOC w. dr. (sp.) ★★★ D.Y.A.

One of the best white wines of s. Lake Garda: fragrant, smooth, full of body and flavour. Co' de Fer is a good producer.

Lungarotti

Leading producer of TORGIANO wine, with cellars and a Wine Museum near Perugia. Recently also fine CHARDONNAY.

Maculan

The top producer of DOC BREGANZA. Also Torcolato, dessert VINO DA TAVOLA (★★★).

Malfatti

Recent go-ahead estate with modern methods, near Lecce, Apulia, producing Bianco, Rosso and SALICE SALENTINO.

Malvasia Important white or red grape for luscious wines, incl. Madeira's Malmsey. Used all over Italy for dry and sweet, still and sparkling wines.

Malvasia di Bosa Sard. DOC w. dr. sw. ★★ 83 85 86

A wine of character. Strong and aromatic with a slightly bitter after-taste.

Malvasia di Cagliari Sard. DOC w. dr. s/sw. or sw. (f. dr. s.) ★★ 83 85 86

Interesting strong Sardinian wine, fragrant and slightly bitter.

Malvasia di Casorzo d'Asti Piem. DOC r. sw. sp. ★★ D.Y.A.

Fragrant grapey sweet red, sometimes sparkling.

Malvasia di Castelnuovo Don Bosco Piem. DOC r. sw. (sp.) ★★

Peculiar method of interrupted fermentation gives very sweet aromatic red.

Malvasia delle Lipari Sic. DOC w. sw. (pa. f.) ★★★ 82 83 84 85 86

Among the very best Malvasias, aromatic and rich, produced on the Lipari or Aeolian Islands n. of Sicily. Top producer: Carlo Hauner.

Malvoisie de Nus Vd'A. w. dr. s/sw. ★★★

Rare Alpine white, with a deep bouquet of honey. Small production and high reputation. Can age remarkably well.

Mandrolisai Sard. DOC r. p. dr. ⊡ 83 85 86

CANNONAU at a lower strength and more approachable than the traditional style.

Manduria (Primitivo di) Apu. DOC r. s/sw. (f. dr. or sw.) ★★ 83 84 85 86

Heady red, naturally strong but often fortified. From nr. Taranto. Primitivo is a southern grape.

Mantonico Cal. w. dr. or sw. f. ★★ 78 79 81 83 85 86

Fruity deep amber dessert wine from Reggio Calabria. Can age remarkably well. Named from the Greek for "prophetic". See also Greco di Bianco.

Marino Lat. DOC w. dr. or s/sw. (sp.) ⊡ D.Y.A.

A neighbour of FRASCATI with similar wine, often a better buy. Look for Colle Picchioni brand.

Marsala Sic. DOC br. dr. s/sw. or sw. f. ★★★ NV

Dark sherry-type wine invented by the Woodhouse Brothers from Liverpool in 1773; excellent apéritif or for dessert. The dry ("virgin"), sometimes made by the solera system, must be 5 years old. Top producers: VECCHIO SAMPERI, Diego, Pellegrino, Ralli.

Marsala Speciali

These are Marsalas with added flavours of egg, almond, strawberry, etc.

Martina Franca Apu. DOC w. dr. (sp.) ★ D.Y.A.

Agreeable but rather neutral southern white, first cousin to LOCOROTONDO.

Martini & Rossi

Well-known vermouth and sparkling wine House, also famous for its fine wine museum in Pessione, near Turin.

Marzemino (del Trentino) Tr–Aad. DOC r. dr. ★ 85

>Pleasant local red of Trento. Fruity fragrance; slightly bitter taste. Mozart's Don Giovanni liked it.

Mascarello

>The name of two top producers of BAROLO, etc.: Cantina M. and Giuseppe M. & Figli.

Masi, Agricola

>Well-known specialist producers of VALPOLICELLA, RECIOTO, SOAVE, etc., including fine red Campo Fiorin.

Maso Lodron Tr–Aad. r. ★★★ 79 81 82 83 85 86

>One of the best Cabernet/Merlot reds, from Nogaredo.

Mastroberardino

>The leading wine-producer of Campania, incl. TAURASI and LACRYMA CHRISTI DEL VESUVIO.

Melini

>Long-established important producers of CHIANTI CLASSICO at Pontassieve. Inventors of the standard *fiasco*, or flask.

Melissa Cal. DOC r. w. dr. ★★ 82 83 84 85 86

>Mostly made from Gaglioppo grapes in the province of Catanzaro. Delicate, balanced, ages rather well.

Meranese di Collina Tr–Aad. DOC r. dr. ★ D.Y.A.

>Light red of Merano, known in German as Meraner Hügel.

Merlot

>Adaptable red Bordeaux grape widely grown in n.e. Italy and elsewhere. For example:

Merlot di Aprilia Lat. DOC r. dr. ★ 83 84 85 86

>Harsh at first, softer after 2–3 yrs.

Merlot Colli Berici Ven. DOC r. dr. ★ 79 81 82 83 85 86

>Pleasantly light and soft. Campo del Lago from Villa dal Ferro is one of Italy's best Merlots.

Merlot Colli Orientali del Friuli Fr–VG. DOC r. dr. ★★ 81 82 83 85 86

>Pleasant herby character, best at 2–3 yrs (Riserva). Some ages well; notably Vigne dal Leon.

Merlot Collio Goriziano Fr–VG. DOC r. dr. ★★ 83 85 86

>Grassy scent, slightly bitter taste. Best at 2–3 yrs.

Merlot Grave del Friuli Fr–VG. DOC r. dr. ★★ 82 83 85 86

>Pleasant light wine, usually best at 1–2 yrs, but potentially a keeper.

Merlot Isonzo Fr–VG. DOC r. dr. ★★ 83 84 85 86

>A DOC in Gorizia. Dry, herby, agreeable wine.

Merlot del Piave Ven. DOC r. dr. ★★ 82 83 85 86

>Sound tasty red, best at 2–4 yrs.

Merlot di Pramaggiore Ven. DOC r. dr. ★★ 82 83 84 85 86

>A cut above most other Merlots; improves in bottle. Riserva after 2 yrs.

Merlot (del Trentino) Tr–Aad. DOC r. dr. ★ 83 85 86

>Full flavour, slightly grassy scent, Riserva after 2 yrs. (ALTO ADIGE has better; esp. from Margreid and Siebeneich v'yds.)

Methodo classico or tradizionale

>Terms increasingly in use to identify champagne method sparkling wines.

Monica di Cagliari Sard. DOC r. dr. or sw. (f. dr. or sw.) ★★ 83 85 86

>Strong spicy red, often fortified and comparable with Spanish Malaga. Monica is a Sardinian grape.

Monica di Sardegna Sard. DOC r. dr. ★ 83 85 86

>Dry version of above, not fortified.

Monsanto

>Highly regarded CHIANTI CLASSICO estate, esp. for IL POGGIO v'yd.

Montalcino

>Village in the province of Siena, Tuscany, famous for its deep red BRUNELLO and lighter Rosso di Montalcino.

Monte Vertine

Top CHIANTI CLASSICO estate at Radda. ★★★ Vino da tavola Le Pergole Torte.

Montecarlo Tusc. DOC w. dr. r. ★★ 85 86

One of Tuscany's best whites, smooth and delicate. Now applies to a Chianti-style red too.

Montecompatri Colonna Lat. DOC w. dr. or s/sw. ★ D.Y.A.

A neighbour of FRASCATI. Similar wine.

Montefalco Umb. DOC r.dr. or sw. ☐★★☐ 82 83 85 86

The Sagrantino grape can give this deep red sweetness and bite.

Montepaldi

Well-known producers and merchants of CHIANTI CLASSICO at San Casciano Val di Pesa. Owned by the Corsini family.

Montepulciano, Vino Nobile di

See Vino Nobile di Montepulciano.

Montepulciano d'Abruzzo (or Molise) Abr & M. DOC r. p. dr. ☐★★★☐ 82 83 85 86

One of Italy's best reds, full of flavour and warmth, from the Adriatic coast round Pescara. See also Cerasuolo.

Monterosso (Val d'Arda) Em-Ro. DOC w. dr. or sw. (sp.) ★ D.Y.A.

Agreeable minor white from Piacenza. (DOC Colli Piacentini.)

Montesodi Tusc. r. ★★★ 74 78 79 80 82 83 85 86

Tip-top CHIANTI riserva from FRESCOBALDI.

Moscadello di Montalcino Tusc. DOC w. sw./sp. ★★ D.Y.A.

Light, fizzy, not oversweet muscat. A refreshing speciality of MONTALCINO, esp. VILLA BANFI.

Moscato Fruitily fragrant grape grown all over Italy.

Moscato d'Asti Piem. DOC w. sw. sp. ☐★★☐ NV

Low-strength sweet fruity sparkler normally made in bulk. ASTI SPUMANTE is the theoretically superior version.

Moscato dei Colli Euganei Ven. DOC w. sw. (sp.) ★★ D.Y.A.

Golden wine, fruity and smooth, from near Padua.

Moscato di Noto Sic. DOC w. s/sw. or sw. or sp. or f. ★ NV

Light sweet still and sparkling versions, or strong Liquoroso. Noto is near Siracusa. Perhaps extinct.

Moscato (Oltrepò Pavese) Lomb. DOC w. sw. (sp.) ★★ D.Y.A.

The Lombardy equivalent of Moscato d'Asti.

Moscato di Pantelleria Sic. DOC w. sw. (sp.) (f. pa.) ★★★

Italy's best muscat, from the island of Pantelleria close to the Tunisian coast; rich, fruity and aromatic. Ages well. Top wine: Bukkuram from De Bartoli.

Moscato di Siracusa Sic. DOC w. sw. ★★ NV

Amber dessert wine reputedly from Syracuse. Perhaps extinct.

Moscato di Sorso Sennori Sard. DOC w. sw. (f.) ☐★☐ D.Y.A.

Strong golden dessert wine from Sassari, n. Sardinia.

Moscato di Trani Apu. DOC w. sw. or f. ★ 81 82 83 84 85 86

Another strong golden dessert wine, sometimes fortified, with "bouquet of faded roses".

Müller-Thurgau

Makes wine to be reckoned with in TRENTINO-ALTO ADIGE and FRIULI, esp. TIEFENBRUNNER's 'Feldmarschall'.

Nasco di Cagliari Sard. DOC w. dr. or sw. (f. dr. or sw.) ★ 85 86

Sardinian speciality, light bitter taste, high alcoholic content.

Nebbiolo

The best red grape of PIEMONTE and Lombardy.

Nebbiolo d'Alba Piem. DOC r. dr. s/sw. (sp.) ☐★★☐ 79 82 83 85 86

Like light-weight BAROLO; often easier to appreciate than the more powerful classic wine. Roero is a new DOC for such wine from n. of ALBA.

Negroamaro

Literally "black bitter"; Apulian red grape with potential for quality. See Copertino.

Neive, Castello di

Leading producer of BARBARESCO, in castle where Louis Oudart pioneered cask-ageing of NEBBIOLO in 1850s.

Nipozzano, Castello di

The most important CHIANTI producer outside the Classico zone, to the north near Florence. Owned by FRESCOBALDI.

Nozzole Famous estate in the heart of CHIANTI CLASSICO n. of Greve.

Nuragus di Cagliari Sard. DOC w. dr. ⟨*⟩ D.Y.A.

Lively Sardinian white, not too strong.

Oliena Sard. r. dr. ★★

Interesting strong fragrant CANNONAU red; a touch bitter.

Oltrepò Pavese Lomb. DOC r. w. dr. sw. sp. ★→★★

DOC applicable to 15 wines produced in the province of Pavia, mostly named after their grapes.

Orvieto Umb. DOC w. dr. or s/sw. ★★→★★★ D.Y.A.

The classical Umbrian golden-white, smooth and substantial, though the dry version is sometimes flat and rather dull. O. Classico is superior. Only the finest examples e.g. BIGI, Decugnano dei Barbi, Barberani, age well.

Ostuni Apu. DOC r. or w. dr. ★ D.Y.A.

From the Pr. of Brindisi. Nothing to write home about.

Pagadebit Em-Ro. w.dr./s.sw. D.Y.A.

Pleasant traditional "payer of debts" from round Bertinoro.

Paradiso, Fattoria

Century-old family estate near Bertinoro (EM-RO). Excellent ALBANA, fine PAGADEBIT and unique red BARBAROSSA.

Parrina Tusc. r. or w. dr. ★★ 85 86

Light red and fresh appetizing white from s. Tuscany.

Passito Strong sweet wine from grapes dried in the sun or indoors.

Per'e Palummo Camp. r. dr. ★★ 83 84 85 **86**

Excellent red produced on the island of Ischia; delicate, slightly grassy, a bit tannic, balanced.

Petit Rouge Vd'A. ⟨★★⟩ 79 82 83 85 86

Good dark lively REFOSCO-like red. Part of VALLE D'AOSTA DOC.

Pian d'Albola

Renowned old CHIANTI CLASSICO estate owned by ZONIN.

Piave Ven. DOC r. or w. dr. ⟨★★⟩ 82 83 85 86 (w. D.Y.A.)

Flourishing DOC covering 8 wines, 4 red and 4 white, named after their grapes. CABERNET, MERLOT and RABOSO reds all need ageing.

Picolit (Colli Orientali del Friuli) Fr-VG. DOC w. s/sw. or sw. ★★★ 83 85 86

Delicate, well balanced, high alcohol dessert wine. Ages up to 6 years, but wildly overpriced.

Piemonte

The most important Italian region for quality wine. Turin is the capital, ASTI and ALBA the wine-centres. See Barolo, Barbera, Grignolino, Moscato, etc.

Pieropan Outstanding producers of SOAVE that deserves its fame.

Pighin, Fratelli

Top producers of COLLIO, GRAVE DEL FRIULI, etc.

Pinocchio Tusc. r. w. ★

Long-established brand notable for its variable nose.

Pinot Bianco

Increasingly popular in n.e., esp. good for sparkling wine.

Pinot Bianco (Alto Adige) Tr-Aad. DOC. w. dr. ⟨★★⟩ 84 85 86

Italy's best and longest-lived wine of this variety.

Pinot Bianco (dei Colli Berici) Ven. DOC w. dr. ★★ D.Y.A.

Straight satisfying dry white.

Pinot Bianco (Colli Orientali del Friuli) Fr-VG. DOC w. dr. ★★ 85 86

Good white; smooth rather than showy.

Pinot Bianco (Collio Goriziano) Fr-VG. DOC w. dr. ⋆⋆ 85 86
    Similar to the above.

Pinot Bianco (Grave del Friuli) Fr-VG. DOC w. dr. ⋆⋆ 85 86
    Same again.

Pinot Grigio Tasty, low-acid white grape popular in n.e. Italy.

Pinot Grigio (Collio Goriziano) Fr-VG. DOC w. dr. ⋆⋆ 84 85
    Fruity, soft, agreeable dry white. The best age well.

Pinot Grigio (Grave del Friuli) Fr-VG. DOC w. dr. ⋆⋆ 84 85
    Hardly distinguishable from the above.

Pinot Grigio (Oltrepò Pavese) Lomb. DOC w. dr. (sp.) ⌐⋆⋆⌐ 85
    Lombardy's P.G. is among the best.

Pinot Nero Tr-Aad. DOC r. dr. ⌐⋆⋆⌐ 80 82 83 85 86
    Pinot Nero (Noir) gives lively burgundy-scented light wine in
    much of n.e. Italy, incl. Trentino. Riserva after 2 yrs.

Pio Cesare
    A producer of top-quality red wines of PIEMONTE, incl. BAROLO.

Poggio al Sole
    CHIANTI CLASSICO estate. Both young and Riserva wines
    excellent.

Poggione, Tenuta Il
    Perhaps the most consistent top estate for BRUNELLO and ROSSO
    DI MONTALCINO.

Pomino Tusc. DOC (r.) w. dr. (br.) ⋆⋆⋆
    Fine white, partly Chardonnay ("Il Benefizio" is 100%) and a
    Sangiovese/Cabernet blend. Also Vinsanto. From FRES-
    COBALDI.

Polyphemo
    Monster monocular Sicilian overfond of Greek red.

Predicato
    Name for four new kinds of VINI DA TAVOLA from central
    Tuscany. P. del Muschio is CHARD., P.BIANCO, P. del Selvante is
    SAUV.BL., P. di Biturica is CAB.S. with SANGIOVESE, P. di
    Cardisco is SANGIOVESE straight. RUFFINO's Cabreo brand are
    examples.

Primitivo di Apulia Apu. r. dr. ⌐⋆⋆⌐ 83 84 85 86
    Southern red. Fruity when young, soft and full-flavoured with
    age (see also MANDURIA). Best is Rosso di Sava.

Prosecco di Conegliano Ven. DOC w. dr. or s/sw. (sp.) ⋆⋆⋆ D.Y.A.
    Popular sparkling wine of the n.e. Slight fruity bouquet, the dry
    pleasantly bitter, the sweet fruity; the best are known as
    Superiore di Cartizze. Best producer: Carpene-Malvolti.

Prunotto, Alfredo
    Very serious Alba company with v.g. BAROLO, BARBARESCO,
    NEBBIOLO, etc.

Raboso del Piave (now DOC) Ven. r. dr. ⋆⋆ 79 82 83 85 86
    Powerful, sharp, interesting country red; needs age.

Ramandolo See Verduzzo Colli Orientali del Friuli

Rampolla, Castello dei
    Top CHIANTI CLASSICO estate at Panzano; also excellent
    Cabernet-based Sammarco.

Rapitalà See Alcamo

Ratti, Renato
    Maker of v.g. BAROLO and other ALBA wines; also author and
    industry leader.

Ravello Camp. r. p. w. dr. ⋆⋆ 83 84 85 86
    Among the best wines of Campania: full dry red, fresh clean
    white. Caruso is the best-known brand.

Recioto Wine made partly of half-dried grapes. Speciality of Veneto.
    R. Amandorlato is ½ sweet, ½ dry.

Recioto di Gambellara Ven. DOC w. s/sw. sp. ⋆ 83 85 86
    Sweetish golden wine, often half-sparkling.

Recioto di Soave   Ven. DOC w. s/sw. (sp.) ★★ 83 85 86
Soave made from selected half-dried grapes; sweet, fruity, fresh, slightly almondy: high alcohol.

Recioto della Valpolicella   Ven. DOC r. s/sw. sp. ★★78 80 81 83 85 86
Strong late-harvested red, sometimes sparkling. "Amabile" is fully sweet.

Recioto Amarone della Valpolicella   Ven. DOC r. dr. ★★★★ 77 78 79 80 81 83 85 86
Dry version of the above; strong concentrated flavour, rather bitter. Impressive and expensive.

Refosco (Colli Orientali del Friuli)   Fr-VG. DOC r. dr. ★★82 83 85 86
Full-bodied dry red; Riserva after 2 yrs. Refosco is said to be the same grape as the MONDEUSE of Savoie (France).

Refosco (Grave del Friuli)   Fr-VG. DOC r. dr. ★★ 81 82 83 85 86
Similar to above but slightly lighter.

Regaleali   Sic. w. r. p.   ★★ 79 80 81 83 84 85 86
Among the best Sicilian table wines, produced between Caltanissetta and Palermo.

Ribolla (Colli Orientali del Friuli)   Fr-VG. DOC w. dr. ★ D.Y.A.
Clean and fruity north-eastern white.

Ricasoli
Famous Tuscan family, "inventors" of CHIANTI, whose Chianti is named after their BROLIO estate and castle.

Riecine   Tusc.   ★★★
First-class CHIANTI CLASSICO estate at Gaiole started by an Englishman, John Dunkley. First wine 1975.

Riesling
Formerly referred to Italian Riesling (R. Italico or "Welschriesling"). German Riesling, now ascendant, is R. Renano.

Riesling Alto Adige   DOC w. dr. ★★ 84 85 86
Can often be Italy's best Riesling.

Riesling (Oltrepò Pavese)   Lomb. DOC w. dr. (sp.) ★★
The Lombardy version, quite light and fresh. Occasionally sparkling. Keeps well. Made of both types of Riesling.

Riesling (Trentino)   Tr-Aad. DOC w. dr. ★★ D.Y.A.
Delicate, slightly acid, very fruity.

Riserva   Wine aged for a statutory period, usually in barrels.

Riunite   One of the world's largest coop cellars near Reggio Emilia producing huge quantities of LAMBRUSCO and other wines.

Rivera   Important and reliable winemakers at Andria, near Bari, with good red Il Falcone and CASTEL DEL MONTE rosé.

Riviera del Garda Chiaretto   Ven. and Lom. DOC p. dr. ★★ D.Y.A.
Charming cherry-pink, fresh and slightly bitter, from s.w. Garda, especially round Moniga del Garda.

Riviera del Garda Rosso   Ven. DOC r. dr. ★★ 82 83 85 86
Red version of the above; ages surprisingly well.

Rosa del Golfo   Apu. p.dr.   ★★   D.Y.A.
An outstanding example of ALEZIO rosato.

Rosato   Rosé.

Rosato del Salento   Apu. p. dr. ★→★★ D.Y.A.
Strong but refreshing southern rosé from round Brindisi.

Rossese di Dolceacqua   Lig. DOC r. dr. ★★ 83 85 86
Well-known fragrant light red of the Riviera, as clean as claret. Superiore is stronger.

Rosso   Red.

Rosso Cònero   Mar. DOC r. dr. ★★ 80 82 83 85 86
Substantial CHIANTI-style wine from the Adriatic coast.

Rosso delle Colline Lucchesi   Tusc. DOC r. dr. ★★ 82 83 85
Produced round Lucca but not greatly different from CHIANTI.

Rosso di Montalcino   Tusc. DOC r. dr.   ★★→★★★
Recent DOC for younger wines from BRUNELLO grapes. Still variable but potentially a winner.

Rosso Piceno Mar. DOC r. dr. *→ ⬜****** 79 81 82 83 85 86
   Adriatic red with a touch of style. Can be Superiore.

Rubesco The excellent popular red of TORGIANO.

Rubino di Cantavenna Piem. DOC r. dr. **** 85 86**
   Lively red, principally BARBERA, from a well-known co-operative s.e. of Turin.

Rufina A sub-region of CHIANTI in the hills east of Florence.

Ruffino
   The biggest and best known of all CHIANTI merchants. Riserva Ducale is the top wine. N.B. New PREDICATO wines.

Salice Salentino Apu. DOC r. **** 79 80 81 83** 85 86
   Strong red from Negroamaro grapes, Riserva after 2 yrs., ages to smooth full wine. Leading maker: LEONE DE CASTRIS.

Sangiovese Principal red grape of ITALY, used alone for:

Sangiovese d'Aprilia Lat. DOC r. or p. dr. ***** D.Y.A.
   Strong dry rosé from south of Rome.

Sangiovese di Romagna Em-Ro. DOC r. dr. **** 82 83 85** 86
   Pleasant standard red; gains character with a little age.

Sangue di Giuda (Oltrepò Pavese) Lomb. DOC r. dr. or s/sw. **** 85 86**
   "Judas' blood". Strong soft red of w. Lombardy.

San Severo Apu. DOC r. p. w. dr. ***** 85 86
   Sound neutral southern wine; not particularly strong.

Santa Maddalena Tr-Aad. DOC r. dr. ⬜****** 85 86
   Perhaps the best Tyrolean red. Round and warm, slightly almondy. From Bolzano.

Santa Margherita
   The Veneto winery that popularized Pinot Grigio, now on a broad base with many good wines.

Sassella (Valtellina) Lomb. DOC r. dr. ***** 78 79 80 82 83** 85 86
   Considerable NEBBIOLO wine, tough when young. Known since Roman times, mentioned by Leonardo da Vinci.

Sassicaia Tusc. r. dr. ⬜******** 72 75 76 77 78 79 80 81 82 83 85 86
   Outstanding pioneer CABERNET from the Tenuta San Guido of the Incisa family, at Bolgheri near Livorno, since 1968. Distributed by ANTINORI. Limited production.

Sauvignon
   The Sauvignon Blanc: excellent white grape used in n.e., perhaps best at TERLANO, ALTO ADIGE.

Sauvignon (Colli Berici) Ven. DOC w. dr. ****** D.Y.A.
   Delicate, slightly aromatic, fresh white from near Vicenza.

Sauvignon (Colli Orientali del Friuli) Fr-VG. DOC w. dr. **** 84 85 86**
   Full, smooth, freshly aromatic n.e. white.

Sauvignon (Collio Goriziano) Fr-VG. DOC w. dr. **** 84 85 86**
   Very similar to the last; slightly higher alcohol.

Savuto Cal. DOC r. p. dr. **** 83 85** 86
   The ancient Savuto produced in the provinces of Cosenza and Catanzaro. Fragrant juicy wine.

Schiava
   Good red grape of TRENTINO-ALTO ADIGE with characteristic bitter after-taste, used for SANTA MADDALENA, etc.

Sciacchetrà See Cinqueterre

Secco Dry.

Secentenario Tusc. r. ********
   Perhaps ANTINORI's best-ever red, bottled (in magnums) for the firm's 600th anniversary in 1985.

Sella & Mosca
   Major Sardinian growers and merchants at Alghero. Their port-like Alghelu Ruju is good.

Settesoli
   Sicilian growers' co-operative with range of adequate table wines.

Sforzato (Valtellina) Lomb. DOC r. dr. ★★★ 78 79 80 82 83 85 86
Valtellina equivalent of RECIOTO AMARONE made with partly dried grapes. Velvety, strong, ages remarkably well. Also called Sfursat.

Sfursat See SFORZATO.

Sizzano Piem. DOC r. dr. ★★ 78 79 80 82 83 85 86
Attractive full-bodied red produced at Sizzano in the Pr. of Novara, mostly from NEBBIOLO. Ages up to 10 years.

Soave Ven. DOC w. dr. ★★★ D.Y.A.
Famous, if not very characterful, Veronese white. Fresh and attractive texture. S. Classico is more restricted and better.

Solaia Tusc. r. ★★★ 79 82
Very fine Bordeaux-style wine of CAB.SAUV. and now 25% SANGIOVESE from ANTINORI, first made in 1979.

A new top category, DOCG, Denominazione Controllata e Garantita, is gradually being added to the Italian wine classification. It is awarded only to certain wines from top-quality zones which have been bottled and sealed with a government seal by the producer. The first five areas to be "guaranteed" are Barolo, Barbaresco, Brunello di Montalcino, Chianti and Vino Nobile di Montepulciano. The sixth (and first white) was Albana di Romagna, for no very good reason. But it should be remembered that many of Italy's best wines are not covered by the DOC system. Examples are Sassicaia, Tignanello, Venegazzù, Bricco Manzoni.

Solopaca Camp. DOC r. w. dr. ★ 83 85 86
Comes from near Benevento, rather sharp when young, the white soft and fruity.

Sorni Tr-Aad. r. w. dr. ★★ 85 86
Made in the Pr. of Trento. Light, fresh and soft. Drink young.

Spanna See GATTINARA.

Spumante Sparkling, as in sweet Asti or many good dry wines, incl. both METHODO CLASSICO and tank-made cheapos.

Squinzano Apu. DOC r. p. dr. ★ 79 80 81 82 83 84 85
Strong southern red from Lecce. Riserva after 2 yrs.

Stravecchio Very old.

Sylvaner
German white grape successful in ALTO ADIGE and elsewhere.

Taurasi Camp. DOC r. dr. ★★★ 75 77 78 79 80 81 82 83 85 86
The best Campanian red, from Avellino. Bouquet of cherries. Harsh when young, improves with age. Riserva after 4 yrs.

Terlano Tr-Aad. DOC w. dr. ★★ 84 85 86
A DOC applicable to 7 white wines from the Pr. of Bolzano, named after their grapes, esp. outstanding SAUVIGNON. Terlaner in German.

Teroldego Rotaliano Tr-Aad. DOC r. p. dr. ★★ 83 85 86
The attractive local red of Trento. Blackberry-scented, slight bitter after-taste, ages moderately.

Terre Rosse
Distinguished small estate near Bologna. CABERNET, CHARDONNAY, SAUV.BL., PIONOT GRIGIO, etc., are the best of the region.

Tiefenbrunner
Distinguished grower of some of the very best ALTO ADIGE white and red wines at Schloss Turmhof, Kurtatsch (Cortaccio).

Tignanello Tusc. r. dr. ★★★ 75 78 79 80 81 82 83 85 86
One of the leaders of the new style of Bordeaux-inspired Tuscan reds, made by ANTINORI. Small production.

Tocai Friulano (Collio). ★★ 85 86
North-east Italian white grape; no relation of Hungarian or Alsace Tokay. Light dry wine. The Tocais of the Colli Orientale del Friuli and Collio Goriziano are best.

Tocai di Lison Ven. DOC w. dr. ★★ D.Y.A.

From e. Veneto, delicate smoky/fruity scent, fruity taste. Classico is better.

Tocai (Colli Berici) Ven. DOC w. dr. ★

Less character than the last.

Tocai (Grave del Friuli) Fr-VG. DOC w. dr. ★★ D.Y.A.

Similar to TOCAI DI LISON, generally rather milder.

Tocai di S. Martino della Battaglia Lomb. DOC w. dr. ★★ D.Y.A.

Small production s. of Lake Garda. Light, slightly bitter.

Torbato di Alghero Sard. w. dr. (Pa.) ★★ D.Y.A.

Good n. Sardinian table wine. Also PASSITO of high quality.

Torgiano (Rubesco di) Umb. DOC r. w. dr. ★★★ 75 77 78 79 80 81 82 83 85 86

The creation of the LUNGAROTTI family. Excellent red from near Perugia comparable with CHIANTI CLASSICO. RUBESCO is the standard quality. Riserva Monticchio is superb. Keep 10 years. White Torre di Giano is good, but not as outstanding as the reds.

Torricella Tusc. w. dr. ★★★ 81

Remarkable aged, soft, buttery MALVASIA dry white from BROLIO.

Traminer Aromatico Tr-Aad. DOC w. dr. ★★ D.Y.A.

Delicate, aromatic, rather soft Gewürztraminer.

Trebbiano

The principal white grape of Tuscany, found all over Italy. Ugni Blanc in French. Rarely remarkable unless blended.

Trebbiano d'Abruzzo Abr & M. DOC w. dr. ★ D.Y.A.

Gentle, rather neutral, slightly tannic. From round Pescara. Valentini is much the best producer.

Trebbiano d'Aprilia Lat. DOC w. dr. ★ D.Y.A.

Heady, mild-flavoured, rather yellow. From south of Rome.

Trebbiano di Romagna Em-Ro. DOC w. dr. or s/sw. (sp.) ★ D.Y.A.

Clean, pleasant white from near Bologna.

Trentino Tr-Aad. DOC r. w. dr. or sw. ★→★★

DOC applicable to as many as 20 different wines, mostly named after their grapes.

Umani Ronchi A leading producer of quality wines of the Marches; notably VERDICCHIO and ROSSO CÒNERO.

Uzzano, Castello di

Fine old CHIANTI CLASSICO estate at Greve. Watch for innovations.

Valcalepio Lomb. DOC r. w. dr. ★ 83 85 86

From nr. Bergamo. Pleasant red; lightly scented, fresh white.

Valdadige Tr-Aad. DOC r. w. dr. or s/sw. ★

Name for the ordinary table wines of the Adige valley—in German Etschtal.

Valle d'Aosta/Valleé d'Aosta V.d'A DOC

New regional DOC for 15 wines including DONNAZ etc. A very mixed bag.

Val d'Arbia Tusc. DOC w. dr. ★ D.Y.A.

Another new DOC for a pleasant white from Chianti country.

Valgella (Valtellina) Lomb. DOC r. dr. ★★ 78 79 80 82 83 85 86

One of the VALTELLINA NEBBIOLOS: good dry red, growing nutty with age. Riserva at 4 yrs.

Vallana, Antonio & Figlio

The protagonist of the "SPANNA" (Nebbiolo) near Novara, Piem. Uses the DOC name BOCA. Rich-flavoured reds.

Valle Isarco Tr-Aad. DOC w. dr. ★→★★ 84 85 86

A DOC applicable to 5 varietal wines made n.e. of Bolzano.

Valpolicella Ven. DOC r. dr. ★★→ ★★★ 83 85 86

Attractive light red from nr. Verona; most attractive when young. Delicate nutty scent, slightly bitter taste. (None of this is true of Valpolicella sold in litre and bigger bottles.) Classico more restricted; Superiore has 12% alcohol and 1 yr. of age.

Valtellina Lomb. DOC r. dr. ★★→★★★ 78 79 80 82 83 85 86

A DOC applicable to wines made principally from Chiavennasca (NEBBIOLO) grapes in the province of Sondrio, n. Lombardy. V. Superiore is GRUMELLO, INFERNO, SASSELLA or VALGELLA.

Vecchio Samperi Sic. des. ★★★

The outstanding wine of MARSALA today, although not DOC. A dry aperitif not unlike Amontillado sherry.

Velletri Lat. DOC r. w. dr. or s/sw. ★★ (r.) 83 85 86

Agreeable Roman dry red and smooth white. Drink young.

Vendemmia Harvest or vintage.

Venegazù Ven. r. w. dr. sp. ★★★ 78 79 82 83 85 86

Remarkable rustic Bordeaux-style red produced from CABER-NET grapes nr. Treviso. Rich bouquet, soft, warm taste, "della Casa" is best quality. Also sparkling white.

Verdicchio dei Castelli di Jesi Mar. DOC w. dr. (sp.) ★→★★★ D.Y.A.

Ancient, famous and very pleasant fresh pale white from nr. Ancona. Goes back to the Etruscans. Classico is more restricted. Comes in amphora-shaped bottles.

Verdicchio di Matelica Mar. DOC w. dr. (sp.) ★★ D.Y.A.

Similar to the last, though less well known.

Verdiso Native white grape of n.e. Italy, used with PROSECCO.

Verduzzo (Colli Orientali del Friuli) Fr-VG. DOC w. dr. s/sw. or sw. ★★ 85 86

Full-bodied white from a native grape. The best sweet is called Ramandolo.

Verduzzo (Del Piave) Ven. DOC w. dr. ★★ D.Y.A.

Similar to the last but fresh and dry.

Vermentino Lig. w. dr. DOC ☐★★☐ D.Y.A.

The best dry white of the Riviera: good seafood wine made at Pietra Ligure and San Remo. DOC is Rivera Ligure del Ponente.

Vermentino di Gallura Sard. DOC w. dr. ★★ D.Y.A.

Soft, dry, rather strong white from northern Sardinia.

Vernaccia di Oristano Sard. DOC w. dr. (sw.) (f.) ☐★★★☐ 77 79 81 82 83 84 85 86

Sardinian speciality, like light sherry, a touch bitter, full-bodied and interesting. Superiore with 15.5% alcohol and 3 yrs. of age.

Vernaccia di San Gimignano Tusc. DOC w. dr. (f.) ★★ 85 86

Should be a distinctive strong high-flavoured wine from near Siena. Michelangelo's favourite. Much today is light and bland. Try Teruzzi & Puthod, Falchini or (old-style) Pietrafitta. Riserva after 1 yr.

Vernaccia di Serrapetrona Mar. DOC r. dr. s/sw. sp. ★★ D.Y.A.

Comes from the province of Macerata; aromatic bouquet, pleasantly bitter after-taste.

Vernatsch German for SCHIAVA.

Vicchiomaggio

Important CHIANTI CLASSICO estate near Greve.

Vietti Excellent small producer of some of Piedmont's most character-ful wines, incl. BAROLO. At Castiglione Falletto, Prov. Cuneo.

V.I.D.E.

An association of better-class Italian producers for marketing their estate wines.

Vignamaggio

Historic and beautiful CHIANTI CLASSICO estate near Greve.

Villa Banfi

The production department of the biggest U.S. importer of Italian wine. Huge new plantings at MONTALCINO, incl. MOS-CADELLO, CABERNET, CHARDONNAY, are part of a drive for quality plus quantity. BRUNELLO is proving excellent. Santa Costanza is v. fruity VINO NOVELLO. In PIEMONTE Banfi produces sp. Banfi Brut, Principessa GAVI, BRACCHETTO D'ACQUI, Pinot Grigio.

Villagrande
　　Imposing old estate on the slopes of Mt. Etna, Sicily, ETNA DOC.

Vino da arrosto
　　"Wine for roast meat", i.e. good robust dry red.

Vino da pasto
　　"Mealtime" wine: i.e. nothing special.

Vino da tavola
　　"Table wine" – but the only appellation open to many of Italy's best new-coined wines (see box on page 93).

Vino Nobile di Montepulciano Tusc. DOCG r. dr. ★★★ 77 78 79 81 82 83 85 86
　　Impressive traditional Chianti-like red with bouquet and style. Aged for 3 yrs. Riserva; for 4 yrs. Riserva Speciale. Best estates incl. BOSCARELLI, AVIGNONESI, Fognano, Poliziano.

Vino novello
　　Italy's equivalent of France's "primeurs", (as in BEAUJOLAIS).

Vinòt Italy's first "VINO NOVELLO", inspired by Beaujolais Nouveau. From GAJA.

Vinsanto or **Vin Santo**
　　Term for certain strong sweet wines esp. in Tuscany: usually PASSITI.

Vinsanto di Gambellara Ven. DOC w. sw. ★★
　　Powerful, velvety, golden: made near Vicenza and Verona.

Vinsanto Toscano Tusc. w. s/sw. ★★→★★★
　　Aromatic bouquet, rich and smooth. Aged in very small barrels known as Carratelli. Can be astonishing.

Vintage Tunina Fr.-VG. w. dr. ★★★ 82 83 84 85 86
　　The trade name of a notable blended COLLIO white from the Jermann estate.

Volpaia, Castello di
　　First-class CHIANTI CLASSICO estate at Radda (Siena). See also Coltassala.

VQPRD
　　Often found on the labels of DOC wines to signify "Vini di Qualita Prodotti in Regioni Delimitate", or quality wines from restricted areas in accordance with E.E.C. regulations.

Zagarolo Lat. DOC w. dr. or s/sw. ★★ D.Y.A.
　　Neighbour of FRASCATI, similar wine.

Zonin
　　One of Italy's biggest privately owned estates and wineries, based at GAMBELLARA, with DOC VALPOLICELLA, etc. Other large estates are at ASTI and in CHIANTI, San Gimignano and FRIULI. Now also at Barboursville, Virginia, U.S.A.

Germany

German wine is suffering a crisis of confidence. To the regret of
those who admire and respect the many fine examples of her
unique style of wine that truly reflect her traditions and her soil,
Germany is considered to have betrayed herself in recent years
by offering the world a mass of low-grade watery wine at bucket-
shop prices.

Some of it is imported wine dressed up to look German. Alas,
much of it is genuinely German, but made to the minimum
standards allowed by a too-liberal wine law. The minimum
requirements for the status of Qualitätswein b.A. (see below)
are such as to allow the most dreary commodity to benefit from
this apparently elevated denomination.

Active debate has started about overhauling the wine law of
1971, which is largely to blame for this and other problems in the
German wine industry. In 1987 morale was low, especially
among the best and most honourable producers. A number in
certain areas have formed themselves into associations (such as
"Charta" in the Rheingau) pledged to uphold high standards of
their own definition, and to ignore as irrelevant the minimum
standards set up by the Government.

Meanwhile young wine-drinkers very reasonably call for a
revision of the labelling system that they find over-com-
plicated: long on logic but short on practical help for the
consumer. "Like a Greek telex" is one newcomer's view of the
stately nomenclature in Gothic script typical not just of classic
wines of high quality, but unfortunately also of some very basic
blends.

This is not the place to debate a reform of national legislation:
only to point out that German labels need very close scrutiny,
and that the differences between the fine long-lived Riesling
wines of conscientious growers and the bulk of Liebfraumilch
and the like are far greater than their labels, and even their
official denominations, suggest.

Meanwhile German taste is changing. The role of wine in
Germany up to very recent times has been as refreshment
between meals, as an aperitif before or a succulent throatful
after. To the grower delicacy and balance have been ends in
themselves, with sweetness and fruity acidity counterpoised;
the wine a drink to be enjoyed and contemplated alone.

The new fashion is for dry wines made specifically for
drinking with meals. More than half the production of most
good growers is now in the "trocken" (dry) category. This
change is beneficial: drinkers rapidly realize that a poor-quality
wine without even a veil of sugar to hide its nakedness is a
miserable drink. The move to dry wines is therefore likely to
raise wine-making standards.

Consumers familiar with the old pattern, in which, for
example, a Spätlese was expected to be a moderately sweet wine,
now need to understand the concept of a dry Spätlese, in which
all the sugar of a ripe grape is converted to alcohol with an effect
closer to (though still not quite as strong as) a wine from Alsace
on the French side of the Rhine.

The Labels and the Law

German wine law is based on the ripeness of the grapes at
harvest time. Vintages vary, but most German wine needs

sugar added to make up for the missing warmth and sunshine of the world's northernmost vineyards.

The exceptional wine, from grapes ripe enough not to need sugar, is kept apart as Qualitätswein mit Prädikat or QmP. Within this top category its natural sugar content is expressed by traditional terms — in ascending order of ripeness: Kabinett, Spätlese, Auslese, Beerenauslese, Trockenbeerenauslese.

But reasonably good wine is also made in good vineyards from grapes that fail to reach the natural sugar content required for a QmP label. The authorities unfortunately allow this to be called Qualitätswein as well, but with the different qualification of bestimmter Anbaugebiete (i.e. QbA) instead of mit Prädikat. In other words Prädikat is the key word to look for on a bottle.

The third level, Tafelwein, has no pretensions to quality and is not allowed to give itself airs beyond the name of the general region or sub-region it comes from. (But see LANDWEIN).

Though there is very much more detail in the laws this is the gist of the quality grading. Where it differs completely from the French system is in ignoring geographical difference. There are no Grands Crus, no VDQS. In theory all any German vineyard has to do to make the best wine is to grow the ripest grapes.

The law distinguishes only between degrees of geographical exactness. In labelling quality wine the grower or merchant is given a choice. He can (and always will) label the relatively small quantities of his best wine with the name of the precise vineyard or Einzellage where it was grown. Germany has about 3,000 Einzellage names. Obviously only particularly good ones are famous enough to help sell the wine. Therefore the law has created a second class of vineyard name: the Grosslage. A Grosslage is a group of neighbouring Einzellages of supposedly similar character and standing. Because there are fewer Grosslage names, and far more wine from each, Grosslagen have a better chance of building reputations, brand-name fashion.*

Thirdly the grower or merchant (more likely the latter) may choose to sell his wine under a regional name: the word is Bereich. To cope with the vast demand for "Bernkasteler" or "Niersteiner" or "Johannisberger" these world-famous names have been made legal for considerable districts. "Bereich Johannisberg" is the whole of the Rheingau; "Bereich Bernkastel" the whole of the Mittelmosel. By the same logic the whole of the Médoc could be called Margaux.

As with all wine names, in fact, the better the wine the more precise the labelling. The trick with German labels is to be able to recognize which is the most precise. Finally, though, and above all, it is to recognize the grower and his vineyard.

The basic German label

The order of wording on German quality wine labels follows a standard pattern.

MOSEL-SAAR-RUWER
TRIERER
ABSTBERG
RIESLING AUSLESE
Qualitätswein mit Prädikat
A.P. NR. 12345678
ERZEUGERABFÜLLUNG
WINZERVEREIN TRIER

The first mention is the Gebiet or wine region. The second is the town or parish, with the suffix -er. The third is the vineyard (either Einzellage or Grosslage—see introduction). The fourth (optional) is the grape variety. The fifth is the quality in terms of ripeness. For Qualitätswein mit Prädikat see page 111. For A.P. Nr. see page 102. Erzeugerabfüllung means bottled by the grower, in this case the grower's co-operative of Trier. For other words appearing on German labels see the Germany A–Z.

---

*Where the law is less than candid, however, is in pretending to believe that the general public will know a Grosslage name from an Einzellage name, when the two are indistinguishably similar (see any entry on the following pages). It is actually against the law to indicate on the label whether the name in question is that of a particular plot or a wider grouping. The names of all relevant Grosslagen are given in this book. Note that Grosslage wines are only rarely of the quality of Einzellage wines.

N.B. on the vintage notes

Vintage notes after entries in the German section are given in a different form from those elsewhere, to show the style of the vintage as well as its quality. Three styles are indicated:
The classic, super-ripe vintage with a high proportion of natural (QmP) wines, including Spätleses and Ausleses.
Example: 83
The "normal" successful vintage with plenty of good wine but no great preponderance of sweeter wines. Example: 79
The cool vintage with generally poor ripeness but a fair proportion of reasonably successful wines, tending to be over-acid. Few or no QmP wines,

but correspondingly more selection in the QbA category. Such wines sometimes mature better than expected. Example: *84*
Where no mention is made the vintage is generally not recommended, or most of its wines have passed maturity.

Recent Vintages

Mosel/Saar/Ruwer

Mosels (including Saar and Ruwer wines) are so attractive young that their keeping qualities are not often enough explored, and wines older than seven years or so are unusual. But well-made wines of Kabinett class gain from three or more in bottle, Spätleses by longer, and Ausleses and Beerenausleses by anything from 10 to 20 years.

As a rule, in poor years the Saar and Ruwer make sharp, thin wines, but in the best years they can surpass the whole of Germany for elegance and "breed".

1986	Fair Riesling year despite autumn rain: 13% QmP wines, mostly Kabinett.
1985	A modest summer but beautiful autumn. 40% of the harvest is QmP. Highly promising Riesling vintage from best v'yds, incl. Eiswein.
1984	A late and rainy year. Two-thirds QbA, one-third Tafel- or Landwein. Almost no QmP. But good acidity means some wines (esp. Ruwers) will keep well.
1983	The best since 1976; much good QbA, a little Kabinett, 31% Spätlese, Ausleses few but some fine, others have serious sulphur problems.
1982	A huge ripe vintage marred by rain which considerably diluted the wines. Most is plain QbA but good sites made Kabinett, Spätlese and a little Auslese. Drink up.
1981	A wet vintage but some good middle Mosels up to Spätlese. Also Eiswein. Drink up.
1980	A terrible summer. Some pleasant wines but little more. Avoid.
1979	A patchy vintage after bad winter damage. But several excellent Kabinetts and better. Light but well-balanced wines should be drunk up.
1978	A similar vintage to '77, though very late and rather small. Very few sweet wines but many with good balance. Drink up.
1977	Big vintage of serviceable quality, mostly QbA. Drink up.
1976	Very good small vintage, with some superlative sweet wines and almost no dry. Most wines now ready; the best will keep 2–3 years.
1975	Very good; many Spätleses and Ausleses. Most now ready.
1971	Superb, with perfect balance. Some top wines will still improve.

Older fine vintages: '69, '67, '64, '59, '53, '49, '45.

Rhine/Nahe/Palatinate

Even the best wines can be drunk with pleasure after two or three years, but Kabinett, Spätlese and Auslese gain enormously in character by keeping for longer. Rheingau wines tend to be longest-lived, improving for 10 years or more, but wines from the Nahe and Palatinate can last nearly as long. Rheinhessen wines usually mature sooner, and dry Franconian wines are best young.

1986	Well-balanced Rieslings, mostly QbA but some Kabinett and Spätlese, esp. in Rheinhessen and Nahe.
1985	Frost, hail and drought led to sadly small crops, but good quality, esp. Riesling. Average 65% QmP. Comparable quality to 1983.
1984	Poor flowering and ripening. Three-quarters QbA, with QmP only in Rheinhessen, Rheinpfalz, Baden and Nahe. But flavour can be good.
1983	Very good Rieslings, esp. in the Rheingau and central Nahe. Generally about half QbA, but plenty of Spätleses.
1982	A colossal vintage gathered in torrential rain. Spätleses and even Kabinett are rare, but QbA wines are good drinking now.
1981	Poor conditions in the Rheingau but better in Nahe and Rheinhessen and very good in Palatinate.
1980	Bad weather from spring to autumn. Only passable wines.
1979	Uneven and reduced in size. Few great wines but many typical and good, esp. in Palatinate. Drink up.
1978	Satisfactory vintage saved by late autumn. 25% QmP, but very few Spätleses. Some excellent wines in the south. Drink soon.
1977	Big and useful; few Kabinett wines or better. Drink up.
1976	The richest vintage since 1921 in places. Very few dry wines. Balance less consistent than 1975. Generally mature.
1975	A splendid Riesling year, a high percentage of Kabinetts and Spätleses. Should be drunk fairly soon.
1971	A superlative vintage. The finest are still improving.

Older fine vintages: '69, '67, '66, '64, '59, '57, '53, '49, '45.

Achkarren Bad. (r.) w. ★★
    Well-known wine village of the KAISERSTUHL, esp. for SILVANER, RULÄNDER. Best site: Schlossberg.

Adelmann, Graf
    Famous grower with 37 acres at Kleinbottwar, WÜRTTEMBERG. Uses the name Brussele. Light reds; good RIESLINGS.

Affental
    An area, not a village, just s. of Baden-Baden, producing a popular red Affentaler SPÄTBURGUNDER in a bottle moulded with a monkey ("Affe") climbing it.

Ahr Ahr r. ★→★★ 75 76 82 83 84 85 86
    Germany's best-known red-wine area, s. of Bonn. Very light pale SPÄTBURGUNDERS.

Amtliche Prüfungsnummer See PRÜFUNGSNUMMER

Anheuser
    Name of two distinguished growers of the NAHE.

Annaberg Rhpf. w. ★★★ 75 76 79 82 83 84 85 86
    Eighteen-acre estate at DÜRKHEIM famous for sweet and pungent wines, esp. SCHEUREBE, with prodigious keeping qualities.

A.P.Nr. Abbreviation of AMTLICHE PRÜFUNGSNUMMER.

Assmannshausen Rhg. r. ★→★★★ 71 75 76 82 83 84 85 86
    RHEINGAU village known for its pale, sometimes sweet, reds. Top v'yd.: Höllenberg. Grosslagen: Steil and Burgweg.

The German Wine Academy runs regular courses of wine-instruction at all levels for both amateurs and professionals, in German and English. The Academy is based at the glorious 12th-century Cistercian monastery of Kloster Eberbach in the Rheingau. The course normally includes tasting-tours of Germany's wine regions. Particulars can be obtained from the Academy, P. O. Box 1705, D-6500 Mainz, West Germany.

Auslese
    Specially selected wine with high natural sugar content, often affected by 'noble rot' and correspondingly unctuous in flavour.

Avelsbach M-S-R (Ruwer) w. ★★★ 71 75 76 79 82 83 84 85 86
    Village near TRIÉR. Supremely delicate wines. Growers: Staatliche Weinbaudomäne (see STAATSWEINGUT), BISCHÖFLICHE WEINGÜTER. Grosslage: Römerlay.

Ayl M-S-R (Saar) w. ★★★ 71 75 76 79 82 83 84 85 86
    One of the best villages of the SAAR. Top v'yds.: Kupp, Herrenberger. Grosslage: Scharzberg.

Bacchus Modern highly perfumed grape variety.

Bacharach (Bereich) ★→★★
    District name for the s. Mittelrhein v'yds. downstream from the RHEINGAU. Steely, racy wines, some v. pleasant. Bacharach is a romantic old town, the tourist centre of the Mittelrhein.

Baden Huge area of scattered wine-growing. The style is substantial, relatively low in acid, well adapted for mealtimes. Best areas are KAISERSTUHL and ORTENAU.

Badische Bergstrasse/Kraichgau (Bereich)
    Widespread district of n. BADEN. RIESLING and RULÄNDER are best.

Bad Dürkheim See DÜRKHEIM, BAD

Badisches Frankenland (Bereich)
    Minor district name of n. BADEN; Franconian-style wines.

Bad Kreuznach Na. w. ★★→★★★ 75 76 79 82 83 84 85 86
    Main town of the NAHE with some of its best wines. Many fine v'yds., incl. Brückes, Kahlenberg, Steinweg, Krötenpfuhl. Grosslage: Kronenberg.

Balbach Erben, Bürgermeister

One of the best NIERSTEIN growers. 44 acres, 80% Riesling. Best v'yds: Pettenthal, Ölberg.

Basserman-Jordan

117-acre MITTELHAARDT family estate with many of the best v'yds. in DEIDESHEIM, FORST, RUPPERTSBERG, etc.

Becker, J.B.

Excellent family estate and brokerage house at WALLUF, Rheingau.

Beerenauslese

Extremely sweet and luscious wine from exceptionally ripe selected individual bunches.

Bereich

District within an Anbaugebiet (region). See under Bereich names, e.g. Bernkastel (Bereich).

Bergweiler-Prüm Erben (Dr Pauly-Bergweiler), Zach., Weingut

Fine 24-acre estate based at BERNKASTEL. V'yds there and in WEHLEN etc. Also Nicolay wines from ÜRZIG and ERDEN.

Bergzabern, Bad Rhpf. (r.) w. ★→★★ 75 76 79 82 83 *84* 85 86

Town of SÜDLICHE-WEINSTRASSE. Pleasant sweetish wines. Grosslage: Liebfrauenberg.

Bernkastel M-M w. ★★→★★★★ 71 75 76 79 82 83 *84* 85 86

Top wine-town of the Mosel; the epitome of RIESLING. Best v'yds.: Doctor (8 acres), Graben, Bratenhöfchen, etc. Grosslagen: Badstube (★★★) and Kurfürstlay (★★).

Bernkastel (Bereich)

Wide area of mixed quality but decided flowery character. Includes all the Mittelmosel.

Bingen Rhh. w. ★★→★★★ 71 75 76 79 82 83 *84* 85 86

Town on Rhine and Nahe with fine v'yds., incl. Scharlachberg. Grosslage: Sankt Rochuskapelle.

Bingen (Bereich) District name for w. Rheinhessen.

Bischöfliche Weinguter Verwaltung

Outstanding M-S-R estate at TRIER, a union of the Cathedral properties with two other famous charities, the Bischöfliches Priesterseminar and the Bischöfliches Konvikt. 230 acres of top v'yds. in AVELSBACH, WILTINGEN, SCHARZHOFBERG, AYL, KASEL, EITELSBACH, PIESPORT, TRITTENHEIM, ÜRZIG, etc.

Blankenhornsberg

Outstanding KAISERSTUHL estate; 62 acres based at IHRINGEN.

Blue Nun The best-selling brand of LIEBFRAUMILCH, from SICHEL.

Bodenheim Rhh. w. ★★

Village nr. NIERSTEIN with delicate wines, esp. from Silberberg.

Bodensee (Bereich)

Minor district of s. BADEN, on Lake Constance.

Bocksbeutel Flask-shaped bottle used for FRANKEN wines.

Brauneberg M-M w. ★★★ 71 75 76 79 82 83 *84* 85 86

Village near BERNKASTEL with 750 acres. Excellent full-flavoured Rieslings. Best v'yd.: Juffer. Grosslage: Kurfürstlay.

Breisach Baden

Frontier town on Rhine nr. KAISERSTUHL. Seat of the largest German cooperative, the ZBW.

Breisgau (Bereich)

Minor district of BADEN, just n. of KAISERSTUHL. Best known for very pale pink WEISSHERBST.

Brentano, von

25-acre old family estate in WINKEL, Rheingau.

Buhl, von, Geheimrat

Great RHEINPFALZ family estate. 250+ acres in DEIDESHEIM, FORST, RUPPERTSBERG, etc. In the very top class.

Bullay M-S-R ★→ ★★ 75 76 83 *84* 85 86

Lower Mosel village. Good light wines.

Bundesweinprämierung

> The German state Wine Award: a gold, silver or bronze medal on bottles of a sufficiently high standard.

Bürgerspital zum Heiligen Geist

> Ancient charitable estate at WÜRZBURG. 333 acres in WÜRZBURG, RANDERSACKER, etc., make rich dry wines.

Bürklin-Wolf, Dr

> Great RHEINPFALZ family estate. 247 acres in WACHENHEIM, FORST, DEIDESHEIM and RUPPERTSBERG, with rarely a dull, let alone poor, wine.

Castell'sches, Fürstlich Domänenamt

> 142-acre princely estate in STEIGERWALD. Good typical FRANKEN wines: SILVANER, RIESLANER. Also SEKT.

Charta Organization of top RHEINGAU estates concentrating on TROCKEN and HALBTROCKEN RIESLINGS. Members must observe higher standards then the legal minima.

Crown of Crowns

> Popular brand of LIEBFRAUMILCH from LANGENBACH & CO.

Crusius

> 30-acre family estate at TRAISEN, Na. Excellently-made, fresh RIESLINGS from Bastei and Rotenfels v'yds age v. well. Also SEKT of high quality.

Deidesheim Rhpf. w. (r.) ★★→★★★★ 71 75 76 79 82 83 *84* 85 86

> Biggest top-quality wine-village of RHEINPFALZ with 1,000 acres. Rich, high-flavoured, lively wines. V'yds. incl. Grainhübel, Herrgottsacker, Leinhöhle, Hohenmorgen, Kieselberg, Paradiesgarten, etc. Grosslagen: Hofstück (★★), Mariengarten (★★★).

Deinhard

> Famous old Koblenz merchants and growers of top-quality wines in RHEINGAU, MITTELMOSEL and RHEINPFALZ (see WEGELER-DEINHARD), also makers of v.g. SEKT.

Deinhard, Dr

> 62-acre family estate in DEIDESHEIM with many of the best v'yds.

Deutscher Tafelwein

> TAFELWEIN from Germany (only). See also Tafelwein.

Deutsches Weinsiegel

> A quality "seal" (i.e. neck label) for wines which have passed a statutory tasting test.

DLG (Deutsche Landwirtschaft Gesellschaft)

> The German Agricultural Society. The body that awards national medals for quality.

Dhron See Neumagen-Dhron

Diabetiker Wein

> Wine with minimal residual sugar (less than 4gms/litre); thus suitable for diabetics—or those who like very dry wine.

Dienheim Rhh. w. ★★ 76 83 *84* 85 86

> Southern neighbour of OPPENHEIM. Mainly run-of-the-mill wines. Best v'yds.: Kreuz, Herrenberg, Schloss. Grosslagen: Güldenmorgen, Krötenbrunnen.

Dom German for Cathedral. Wines from the famous TRIER Cathedral properties have "Dom" before the v'yd. name.

Domäne

> German for "domain" or "estate". Sometimes used alone to mean the "State domain" (Staatliche Weinbaudomäne).

Durbach Baden w. (r.) ★★→ ★★★ 76 83 *84* 85 86

> 775 acres of the best v'yds. of BADEN. Top growers: Schloss Staufenberg, Wolf-Metternich, von Neveu. Choose their KLINGELBERGERS and KLEVNERS. Grosslage: Fürsteneck.

Dürkheim, Bad Rhpf. w. or (r.) ★★→★★★ 76 79 82 83 *84* 85 86

> Main town of the MITTELHAARDT. Top v'yds.: Hochbenn, Michelsberg. Grosslagen: Feuerberg, Schenkenböhl.

Edel Means "noble". Edelfäule means "noble rot": the condition which gives the greatest sweet wines (see p. 46).

Edenkoben Rhpf. w.(r.) ★→ ★★ 76 79 83 *84* 85 86
Important village of n. SÜDLICHE WEINSTRASSE. Grosslage: Ludwigshöhe. The best wines have plenty of flavour.

Egon Müller zu Scharzhof
Top Saar estate of 32 acres at WILTINGEN. His delicate, racy SCHARZHOFBERGER Rieslings are supreme in vintages that produce AUSLESES.

Eiswein
Wine made from frozen grapes with the ice (e.g. water content) rejected, thus very concentrated in flavour and sugar, of Beerenauslese ripeness or more. Rare and expensive. Sometimes produced as late as the January or February following the vintage. Alcohol content can be as low as 5.5 percent.

Eitelsbach Ruwer w. ★★→★★★ 71 75 76 82 83 *84* 85 86
RUWER village now part of TRIER, incl. superb Karthäuserhofberg estate. Grosslage: Römerlay.

Elbling
Generally inferior grape widely grown on upper Mosel but capable of great freshness and vitality in the best conditions (e.g. at MENNIG).

Eltville Rhg. w. ★★ →★★★ 71 75 76 79 83 *84* 85 86
Major wine-town with cellars of the Rheingau State domain, FISCHER and VON SIMMERN estates. Excellent wines. Top v'yds.: Sonnenberg, Taubenberg. Grosslage: Steinmächer.

Enkirch M-M w. ★★→ ★★★★ 71 76 83 *84* 85 86
Minor middle-Mosel village, often overlooked but with lovely light tasty wine. Grosslage: Schwarzlay.

Erbach Rhg. w. ★★★→★★★★ 71 76 79 83 *84* 85 86
One of the best parts of the Rheingau with powerful, perfumed wines, incl. the great MARCOBRUNN; other top v'yds.: Schlossberg, Siegelsberg, Honigberg, Michelmark. Grosslage: Deutelsberg. Major estates: SCHLOSS REINHARTSHAUSEN, von SCHÖNBORN.

Erden M-M w. ★★→★★★ 71 75 76 82 83 *84* 85 86
Village between Urzig and Kröv with full-flavoured vigorous wine. Top v'yds.: Prälat, Treppchen. Leading grower: BISCHÖFLICHE WEINGÜTER, BERGWEILER-PRÜM, Nicolay. Grosslage: Schwarzlay.

Erzeugerabfüllung
Estate-bottled; bottled by the grower.

Escherndorf Franc. w. ★★→★★★ 76 82 83 *84* 86
Important wine-town near WÜRZBURG. Similar tasty dry wine. Top v'yds.: Lump, Berg. Grosslage: Kirchberg.

Remember that vintage information about German wines is given in a different form from the ready/not ready distinction applying to other countries. Read the explanation on page 98.

Forst Rhpf. w. ★★→★★★★ 71 75 76 79 82 83 *84* 85 86
MITTELHAARDT village with 500 acres of Germany's best v'yds. Ripe, richly fragrant but subtle wines. Top v'yds.: Kirchenstück, Jesuitengarten, Ungeheuer, etc. Grosslagen: Mariengarten, Schnepfenflüg.

Franken
Franconia: region of excellent distinctive dry wines, esp. SILVANER. The centre is WÜRZBURG. BEREICH names: MAINVIERECK, MAINDREIECK, STEIGERWALD.

Freiburg Baden w. (r.) ★→★★ D.Y.A.
Centre of MARKGRÄFLERLAND. Good GUTEDEL. Look for NOBLING.

Friedrich Wilhelm Gymnasium

  Superb 111-acre charitable estate based in TRIER with v'yds. in
  BERNKASTEL, ZELTINGEN, GRAACH, TRITTENHEIM, OCKFEN,
  etc., all M-S-R.

Geisenheim   Rhg. w. ★★→★★★ 71 75 76 83 *84* 85 86

  Village famous for Germany's leading wine-school. Best v'yds.
  incl. Rothenberg, Kläuserweg. Grosslagen: Burgweg and Erntebringer.

Gemeinde   A commune or parish.

Gewürztraminer

  Spicy grape, speciality of Alsace, used a little in s. Germany, esp.
  RHEINPFALZ and BADEN. See Traminer.

Gimmeldingen   Rhpf. w. ★→★★ 76 82 83 *84* 85 86

  Village just s. of MITTELHAARDT. At their best, similar wines.
  Grosslage: Meerspinne.

Goldener Oktober

  Popular brand of Rhine and Mosel blends from ST. URSULA.

Graach   M-M w. ★★→ [★★★] 71 75 76 83 *84* 85 86

  Small village between BERNKASTEL and WEHLEN. Top v'yds.:
  Himmelreich, Domprobst, Abstberg, Josephshöfer. Grosslage:
  Münzlay.

Green Label

  Germany's best-selling MOSEL (BEREICH BERNKASTEL). Brand-
  name of DEINHARD.

Grosslage   See Introduction, p. 99

Guntersblum   Rhh. w. ★→★★ 76 83 *84* 85 86

  Big wine-town s. of OPPENHEIM. Grosslagen: Krötenbrunnen,
  Vogelsgarten.

Guntrum, Louis

  Fine 164-acre family estate in NIERSTEIN, OPPENHEIM, etc., and
  merchant house with high and reliable standards.

Gutedel   German for the Chasselas grape, used in s. BADEN.

Gutsverwaltung   Estate administration.

Halbtrocken

  "Semi-dry". Containing less than 18 but more than 9 grams per
  litre unfermented sugar. An increasingly popular category of
  wine intended for meal-times, often better-balanced than
  TROCKEN.

Hallgarten   Rhg. w. ★★→★★★ 71 76 82 83 *84* 85 86

  Important little wine-town behind HATTENHEIM. Robust full-
  bodied wines. Top v'yds. incl. Schönhell, Jungfer. Grosslage:
  Mehrhölzchen.

Hallgarten, House of

  Well-known London-based wine-merchant.

Hanns Christof

  Estimable Rhine-wine brand from DEINHARD'S.

Hattenheim   Rhg. w. ★★→★★★★ 71 75 76 83 *84* 85 86

  Superlative 500-acre wine-town. V'yds. incl. STEINBERG,
  NUSSBRUNNEN, MANNBERG, HASSEL ETC. GROSSLAGE: Deutelsberg. MARCOBRUNN lies on the ERBACH boundary.

Heilbronn   Württ. w. r. ★→★★ 76 83 *84* 85 86

  Wine-town with many small growers and a big coop. Seat of DLG
  competition.

Hessische Bergstrasse   w. ★★→★★★ 76 83 84 85 86

  Germany's smallest wine-region (1000 acres) n. of Heidelberg.
  Pleasant Riesling from State domain v'yds. in Heppenheim and
  Bensheim.

Hessische Forschungsanstalt für Wein-Obst-& Gartenbau. . . . .

  Germany's top wine-school and research establishment, at
  GEISENHEIM, Rheingau.

Heyl zu Herrnsheim

  Fine 72-acre estate at NIERSTEIN, 55% Riesling.

Hochheim Rhg. w. ★★→★★★ 71 75 76 79 82 83 *84* 85 86
600-acre wine-town 15 miles e. of RHEINGAU. Similar fine wines. Top v'yds.: Domdechaney, Kirchenstück, Hölle, Königin Viktoria Berg. Grosslage: Daubhaus.

Hock English term for Rhine-wine, derived from ̇HOCHHEIM.

Huesgen, Adolph Important merchant house at TRABEN-TRARBACH.

Huxelrebe
Modern very aromatic grape variety.

Ihringen Bad. r. w. ★→★★★ 81 82 83 *84* 85 86
One of the best villages of the KAISERSTUHL, BADEN. Proud of its SPÄTBURGUNDER red, WEISSHERBST and v.g. SILVANER.

Ilbesheim Rhpf. w. ★→★★ 83 *84* 85 86
Base of important growers' cooperative of SÜDLICHE WEIN-STRASSE. See also SCHWEIGEN.

Ingelheim Rhh. r. or w. ★ 76 82 83 *84* 85 86
Town opposite the Rheingau historically known for red wine.

Iphofen Franc. w. ★★ 75 76 81 82 *83 84* 85
Village e. of WÜRZBURG. Superb top v'yd.: Julius-Echter-Berg. Grosslage: Burgweg.

Jesuitengarten
15-acre vineyard in FORST. One of Germany's best.

Johannisberg Rhg. w. ★★→★★★★ 71 75 76 79 82 83 *84* 85 86
260-acre vilage with superlative subtle RIESLINGS. Top v'yds. incl. SCHLOSS JOHANNISBERG, Hölle, Klaus, etc. Grosslage: Erntebringer.

Johannisberg (Bereich) District name of the entire RHEINGAU.

Josephshöfer
Fine v'yd. at GRAACH, the property of von KESSELSTATT.

Juliusspital
Ancient charity at WÜRZBURG with 374 acres of top FRANKEN v'yds. Look for SILVANERS.

Kabinett
The term for the lightest category of natural unsugared (QmP) wines. Low in alcohol (average 7–9%).

Kaiserstuhl-Tuniberg (Bereich)
Best v'yd. area of BADEN. Vilages incl. IHRINGEN, ACHKARREN.

Kallstadt Rhpf. w. (r.) ★★→★★★ 75 76 82 83 *84* 85 86
Village of n. MITTELHAARDT. Fine rich wines. Top v'yd.: ANNABERG. Grosslagen: Saumagen (★★★), Kobnert (★★).

Kammerpreismünze See Landespreismünze.

Kanzem M-S-R (Saar) w. ★★→★★★ 71 75 76 83 *84* 85 86
Small but excellent neighbour of WILTINGEN. Top v'yds.: Sonnenberg, Altenberg. Grosslage: Scharzberg.

Kasel M-S-R (Ruwer) w. ★★→★★★ 71 75 76 83 *84* 85 86
Village with wonderfully attractive light wines. Best v'yd.: Nies'chen. Grosslage: Römerlay.

Keller Wine-cellar. Kellerei: winery.

Kerner Modern grape variety, earlier-ripening than Riesling, of good quality but without the lingering flavour of Riesling.

Kesselstatt, von
The biggest private Mosel estate, 600 years old. Over 200 acres in GRAACH (Josephshöfer), PIESPORT, KASEL, MENNIG, WILTIN-GEN, etc., plus substantial rented or managed estates, making light and fruity typical Mosels. Now belongs to Gunther Reh of Leiwen.

Kesten M-M-M w. ★→★★★ 71 75 76 79 83 *84* 85 86
Neighbour of BRAUNEBERG. Best wines (from Paulinshofberg v'yd.) similar. Grosslage: Kurfürstlay.

Kiedrich Rhg. w. ★★→★★★★ 71 75 76 79 82 83 *84* 85 86
Neighbour of RAUENTHAL; almost as splendid and high-flavoured. Top v'yds.: Gräfenberg, Wasseros, Sandgrub. Grosslage: Heiligenstock.

Klevner (or Clevner)
  Red Klevner (synonym, Blauer Frühburgunder) is supposedly either Pinot Noir or Italian Chiavenna, an early-ripening black Pinot. Also an ORTENAU (BADEN) synonym for TRAMINER.

Klingelberger
  BADEN term for the RIESLING, esp. at DURBACH.

Kloster Eberbach
  Glorious 12th-century Abbey at HATTENHEIM, Rheingau, now State domain property and H.Q. of the German Wine Academy. See panel, p. 101.

Klüsserath M-M w. ★★→ ⎡★★★⎤ 71 76 83 *84* 85 86
  Minor Mosel village worth trying in good vintages. Best v'yds.: Bruderschaft, Königsberg. Grosslage: St. Michael.

Kraichgau
  Small BADEN region s. of Heidelberg. Best-known wines are from Neckarzimmern and Wiesloch.

Kreuznach (Bereich)
  District name for the entire northern NAHE. See also BAD KREUZNACH.

Kröv M-M w. ★→★★★ 76 83 *84* 85 86
  Popular tourist resort famous for its Grosslage name: Nacktarsch, meaning "bare bottom".

Landespreismünze
  Prizes for quality at state, rather than national, level. Considered by some more discriminating than DLG medals.

Landgräflich Hessisches Weingut
  Wide-ranging 75-acre estate in JOHANNISBERG, WINKEL, KIEDRICH and ELTVILLE.

Landwein
  A new (1982) category of better quality TAFELWEIN (the grapes must be slightly riper) from 15 designated regions. It must be TROCKEN or HALBTROCKEN. Similar in intention to France's *vins de pays*.

Lauerburg
  One of the four owners of the famous Doctor v'yd. in BERNKASTEL, with THANISCH, DEINHARD and Heilig-Geist-Armenspende.

Liebfrauenstift
  26-acre v'yd. in the city of WORMS, said to be the origin of the name LIEBFRAUMILCH.

Liebfraumilch
  Legally defined as a QbA "of pleasant character" from RHEIN-HESSEN, RHEINPFALZ, NAHE or RHEINGAU, of a blend with at least 51% of RIESLING, SILVANER, KERNER or MÜLLER-THUR-GAU. Most is mild semi-sweet wine from RHEINHESSEN and RHEINPFALZ. The rules now say it must have more than 18 gms. per litre unfermented sugar. Nowadays sometimes very cheap and of inferior quality, depending on brand/shipper.

Lieser M-M w. ★→ ⎡★★⎤ 71 76 83 *84* 85 86
  Little-known neighbour of BERNKASTEL. Grosslage: Beerenlay, Kurfürstlay.

Lorch Rhg. w. (r.) ★→★★ 71 76 83 *84* 85 86
  At extreme w. end of Rheingau. Some fine light RIESLINGS more like MITTELRHEIN wines. Best grower: von Kanitz.

Löwenstein, Fürst
  66-acre FRANKEN estate: classic dry powerful wines.

Maikammer Rhpf. w. (r.) ★→ ⎡★★⎤ 83 *84* 85 86
  Village of n. SÜDLICHE WEINSTRASSE. Very pleasant wines incl. those from coop at Rietburg. Grosslage: Mandelhöhe.

Maindreieck (Bereich)
  District name for central part of FRANKEN, incl. WÜRZBURG.

Marcobrunn
>Historic RHEINGAU vineyard; one of Germany's best. See ERBACH.

Markgräflerland (Bereich)
>Minor district s. of Freiburg (BADEN). GUTEDEL wine is delicious refreshment when drunk very young.

Martinsthal Rhg. w. **→ ★★★** 71 75 76 82 83 84 85 86
>Little-known neighbour of RAUENTHAL. Top v'yds.: Langenberg, Wildsau. Grosslage: Steinmächer.

Matuschka-Greiffenclau, Graf Erwein
>Owner of the ancient SCHLOSS VOLLRADS estate. President of the VdP and CHARTA associations.

Maximin Grünhaus M-S-R (Ruwer) w. ★★★★ 71 75 76 79 82 83 84 85 86
>Supreme RUWER estate of 80 acres at Mertesdorf.

Mennig M-S-R (Saar) w. **★★** 71 75 76 79 82 83 84 85 86
>Village between TRIER and the SAAR. Its Falkensteiner v'yd. is more famous than the village (Nieder-Obermennig).

Mertesdorf See MAXIMIN GRÜNHAUS

Mittelheim Rhg. w. **→ ★★★** 71 75 76 79 82 83 84 85 86
>Minor village between WINKEL and OESTRICH. Top grower: WEGELER-DEINHARD. Grosslage: Honigberg.

Mittelhaardt
>The north-central and best part of RHEINPFALZ, incl. FORST, DEIDESHEIM, RUPPERTSBERG, WACHENHEIM, etc., largely planted with RIESLING.

Mittelmosel
>The central and best part of the Mosel, incl. BERNKASTEL, PIESPORT, etc. Its best sites are entirely RIESLING.

Mittelrhein
>Northern Rhine area of secondary importance, incl. BACHARACH. Some attractive RIESLINGS, esp. in 1983, 1985.

Morio Muskat
>Stridently aromatic grape variety popular in RHEINPFALZ.

Moselblümchen
>The "LIEBFRAUMILCH" of the Mosel, but on a lower quality level: mostly TAFELWEIN, seldom QbA.

Mosel-Saar-Ruwer
>31,000-acre region between TRIER and KOBLENZ. Includes MITTELMOSEL, SAAR, RUWER and lesser areas.

Müller, Felix
>Fine small SAAR estate with delicate SCHARZHOFBERGER, now run by VON KESSELSTATT.

Müller zu Scharzhof, Egon See Egon Müller

Müller-Thurgau
>Fruity, usually low-acid grape variety; the commonest in RHEINPFALZ and RHEINHESSEN, the NAHE, BADEN and FRANKEN, and increasingly planted in all areas, including the Mosel; there generally to the detriment of quality.

Mumm, von
>173-acre estate in JOHANNISBERG, RUDESHEIM, etc. Under the same control as SCHLOSS JOHANNISBERG.

Munster Nahe w. **★→★★★** 71 75 76 83 84 85 86
>Best village of northern NAHE, with fine delicate wines. Top grower: State Domain. Grosslage: Schlosskapelle.

Nackenheim Rhh. w. **★→** **★★★** 75 76 79 82 83 85 86
>Neighbour of NIERSTEIN; best wines (Engelsberg, Rothenberg) similar. Grosslagen: Spiegelberg (★★★), Gutes Domtal (★).

Nahe
>Tributary of the Rhine and high quality wine region. Balanced, fresh and clean but full-flavoured wines, the best are RIESLING. Two Bereiche: KREUZNACH and SCHLOSS BÖCKELHEIM.

Neef M-S-R w. ★→ ⭐⭐ 71 76 83 *84* 85 86
    Village of lower Mosel with one fine v'yd.: Frauenberg.

Neipperg, Graf
    71-acre top WÜRTTEMBERG estate at Schwaigern, esp. known for
    red wines and TRAMINER.

Nell, von (Weingut Thiergarten)
    40-acre family estate at TRIER and AYL, etc.

Neumagen-Dhron M-M w. ★★→★★★ 71 75 76 83 *84* 85 86
    Neighbours of PIESPORT. Top v'yd.: Hofberger. Grosslage:
    Michelsberg.

Neustadt
    Central city of RHEINPFALZ, with a famous wine school.

Niederhausen Na. w. ★★→★★★★ 71 75 76 79 82 83 *84* 85 86
    Neighbour of SCHLOSS BÖCKELHEIM and H.Q. of the Nahe State
    Domain. Wines of grace and power. Top v'yds. incl. Hermanns-
    höhle, Steinberg. Grosslage: Burgweg.

Niedermennig See MENNIG

Niederwalluf See WALLUF

Nierstein (Bereich)
    Large e. RHEINHESSEN district of very mixed quality.

Nierstein Rhh. w. ★→★★★ 71 75 76 82 83 *84* 85 86
    Famous but treacherous name. 1,300 acres incl. superb v'yds.:
    Hipping, Ölberg, Pettenthal, etc., and their Grosslagen Reh-
    bach, Spiegelberg, Auflangen: ripe, racy wines. But beware
    Grosslage Gutes Domtal: no guarantee of anything (except
    boredom).

GERMANY'S QUALITY LEVELS
The range of qualities in ascending order is
1) Deutscher Tafelwein; sweetish light wine of no special character.
2) Landwein: dryish Tafelwein with some regional style.
3) Qualitätswein: dry or sweetish wine with sugar added to increase the strength but
   tested for quality and with distinct local and grape character.
4) Kabinettwein: dry or dryish natural (unsugared wine) of distinct personality and
   distinguishing lightness – can be very fine.
5) Spätlese: stronger, often sweeter than Kabinett. Full bodied.
6) Auslese: sweeter, sometimes stronger than Spätlese, often with honey-like
   flavours, intense and long.
7) Beerenauslese: very sweet and usually strong, intense, can be superb.
8) Trockenbeerenauslese: intensely sweet and aromatic.
9) Eiswein: (Beeren- or Trockenbeerenauslese) concentrated, sharpish and very
   sweet. Extraordinary and everlasting.

Nobling
    New white grape variety giving light fresh wine in BADEN, esp.
    Markgräflerland.

Norheim Nahe w. ★→★★★ 71 75 76 79 82 83 *84* 85 86
    Neighbour of NIEDERHAUSEN. Top v'yds.: Klosterberg, Kafels,
    Kirschheck. Grosslage: Burgweg.

Oberemmel M-S-R (Saar) w. ★★→★★★ 71 75 76 83 *84* 85 86
    Next village to WILTINGEN. Very fine wines from Rosenberg,
    Hütte, etc. Grosslage: Scharzberg.

Obermosel (Bereich)
    District name for the upper Mosel above TRIER. Generally
    uninspiring wines from the Elbling grape.

Ockfen M-S-R (Saar) w. ★★→★★★ 71 75 76 82 83 *84* 85 86
    200-acre village with superb fragrant austere wines. Top v'yds.:
    Bockstein, Herrenberg. Grosslage: Scharzberg.

Oechsle
    Scale for sugar-content of grape-juice (see page 19).

Oestrich Rhg. w. ★★→★★★ 71 75 76 82 83 *84* 85 86
    Big village; variable but capable of splendid Riesling Ausleses.
    V'yds. incl. Doosberg, Lenchen, Klosterberg. Grosslage: Gottes-
    thal.

Oppenheim Rhh. w. *→★★★ 71 75 76 79 82 83 *84* 85 86

Town s. of NIERSTEIN with a 13th-century cathedral. Best wines (Kreuz, Sackträger) similar. Grosslagen: Guldenmorgen (★★★) Krötenbrunnen (*).

Ortenau (Bereich)

District just s. of Baden-Baden. Good KLINGELBERGER and RULÄNDER. SPÄTBURGUNDER (not so good) is a speciality. Best village DURBACH.

Palatinate English for RHEINPFALZ.

Perlwein Semi-sparkling wine.

Pfalz See RHEINPFALZ

Pieroth

Major wine-sales company; also has vineyard holdings.

Piesport M-M w. ★★→★★★★ 71 75 76 83 *84* 85 86

Tiny village with famous amphitheatre of vines giving (at best) glorious gentle fruity RIESLINGS. Top v'yds.: Goldtröpfchen, Falkenberg. Treppchen is on flatter land and inferior. Grosslage: Michelsberg (much planted with MÜLLER-THURGAU).

Plettenberg, von

Fine 100-acre Nahe estate at BAD KREUZNACH.

Pokalwein

Wine by the glass. A pokal is a big glass.

Portugieser

Second-rate red-wine grape now often used for WEISSHERBST.

Prädikat

Special attributes or qualities. See QmP.

Prüfungsnummer

The official identifying test-number of a quality wine.

Prüm, J. J.

Superlative 34-acre Mosel estate in WEHLEN, GRAACH, BERN-KASTEL. Delicate, long-lived wines, esp. in Wehlener Sonnenuhr.

Prüm, S. A., Erben

Small separate part of the Prüm family estate making fine Wehleners, etc.

Qualitätswein bestimmter Anbaugebiete (QbA)

The middle quality of German wine, with added sugar but strictly controlled as to grape areas, etc.

Qualitätswein mit Prädikat (QmP)

Top category, incl. all wines ripe enough to be unsugared, from KABINETT to TROCKENBEERENAUSLESE.

Randersacker Franc. w. ★★→ ★★★ 76 79 82 *83 84* 86

Leading village for distinctive dry wine. Top v'yds. incl. Teufelskeller. Grosslage: Ewig Leben.

Rauenthal Rhg. w. ★★★ →★★★★ 71 75 76 79 82 83 *84* 85 86

Supreme village for spicy complex wine. Top v'yds. incl. Baiken, Gehrn, Wulfen. Grosslage: Steinmacher. The State Domain is an important grower.

Rautenstrauch Erben

Owners of the Karthäuserhof, EITELSBACH.

Reh, Franz & Sohn

Thriving wine-merchant at Leiwen (Mosel) with two small estates.

Ress, Balthasar

RHEINGAU grower with 50 acres of good land, cellars in HATTENHEIM. Also runs SCHLOSS REICHARTSHAUSEN. Fine fresh wines; highly original artists' labels.

Reverchon, Eddie

Substantial SAAR estate in Filzen, WITTINGEN, etc.

Rheinart Erben

26-acre SAAR estate known for its OCKFENER BOCKSTEIN. Owned by H. SCHMITT SÖHNE.

Rheinburgengau (Bereich)
> District name for the v'yds. of the MITTELRHEIN round the famous Rhine gorge. Moderate quality only.

Rheingau
> The best v'yd. region of the Rhine, near Wiesbaden. 7,000 acres. Classic, substantial but subtle RIESLING. Bereich name, for the whole region, JOHANNISBERG.

Rheinhessen
> Vast region (62,000 acres of v'yds.) between Mainz and Worms, bordered by the river NAHE, most second-rate, but incl. top wines from NIERSTEIN, OPPENHEIM, etc.

Rheinpfalz
> Almost as vast 56,000-acre v'yd. region s. of Rheinhessen. (See MITTELHAARDT and SÜDLICHE WEINSTRASSE.) This and the last are the chief sources of LIEBFRAUMILCH. Grapes ripen to relatively high degrees. The great classics are rich wines but TROCKEN and HALBTROCKEN are increasingly fashionable.

Rhodt
> Village of SÜDLICHE WEINSTRASSE with well-known co-operative. Agreeable fruity wines. Grosslage: Ordensgut.

Richter, Max Ferd, Weingut
> 37-acre MITTELMOSEL family estate based at Müllheim. Fine barrel-aged RIESLINGS from WEHLEN, GRAACH, BRAUNEBERG (Juffer), Mülheim (Helenenkloster).

Rieslaner
> Cross between SILVANER and RIESLING; has made fine Auslesen in FRANKEN.

Riesling
> The best German grape: fine, fragrant, fruity, long-lived.

Roseewein
> Rosé wine made of red grapes fermented without their skins.

Rotwein   Red wine.

Rüdesheim   Rhg. w. ★★→★★★★ **71 75 76** 79 *81* 82 **83** *84* 85 86
> Rhine resort with 650 acres of excellent v'yds.; the three best called Rüdesheimer Berg ... Full-bodied wines, fine-flavoured, often remarkable in 'off' vintages. Grosslage: Burgweg.

Rüdesheimer Rosengarten .
> Rüdesheim is also the name of a NAHE village near BAD KREUZNACH. Do not be misled by the ubiquitous blend going by this name. It has nothing to do with Rheingau RÜDESHEIM.

Ruländer
> The PINOT GRIS: grape giving soft, full-bodied wine, alias Grauburgunder. Best in BADEN.

Ruppertsberg   Rhpf. w. ★★→★★★   **75 76** 79 82 **83** 84 85 86
> Southern village of MITTELHAARDT. Top v'yds. incl. Hoheburg. Reiterpfad, Linsenbusch. Grosslage: Hofstück.

Ruwer
> Tributary of Mosel near TRIER. Very fine delicate wines. Villages incl. EITELSBACH, MERTESDORF, KASEL.

Saar   Tributary of Mosel s. of RUWER. Brilliant austere "steely" RIESLINGS. Villages incl. WILTINGEN (SCHARZHOFBERG) AYL, OCKFEN, SERRIG. Grosslage: Scharzberg.

Saar-Ruwer (Bereich)
> District incl. the two above.

Salem, Schloss
> 190-acre estate of Margrave of Baden on L. Constance in s. Germany. MÜLLER-THURGAU and WEISSHERBST.

St. Ursula
> Well-known merchants at BINGEN; owners of VILLA SACHSEN.

Scharzberg
> Grosslage name of WILTINGEN and neighbours.

Scharzhofberg Saar w. ★★★★ 71 75 76 79 82 83 *84* 85 86

Superlative 30-acre SAAR v'yd.: austerely beautiful wines, the perfection of RIESLING. Do not confuse with the last entry. Top estate: EGON MÜLLER.

Schaumwein Sparkling wine.

Scheurebe Fruity aromatic grape of good quality used in RHEINHESSEN and RHEINPFALZ.

Schillerwein

Light red or rosé QbA, speciality of WÜRTTEMBERG (only).

Scholl & Hillebrand

RÜDESHEIM merchants with fine Breuer estate wines.

Schlossböckelheim Nahe w. ★★→★★★★ 71 75 76 79 82 83 *84* 85 86

Village with the best NAHE v'yds., incl. Kupfergrube, Felsenberg. Firm yet delicate wine. Grosslage: Burgweg.

Schloss Böckelheim (Bereich)

District name for the whole southern NAHE.

Schloss Groenesteyn

Fine Rheingau estate (80 acres) in KIEDRICH and RÜDESHEIM, owned by Baron von Ritter zu Groenesteyn. Top-grade wines.

Schloss Johannisberg Rhg. w. ★★★→★★★★ 76 79 82 83 *84* 85 86

Famous RHEINGAU estate of 86 acres owned by Prince Metternich and the Oetker family, and now run in conjunction with VON MUMM. Polished elegant wines incl. fine SPÄTLESE and KABINETT TROCKEN.

Schloss Reichartshausen

10-acre formerly Cistercian HATTENHEIM v'yd run by RESS.

Schloss Reinhartshausen

Fine 165-acre estate in ERBACH, HATTENHEIM, etc. much improved since 1976.

Schloss Vollrads Rhg. w. ★★★→★★★★ 71 75 76 82 83 85 86

Great estate at WINKEL, since 1300. 116 acres producing classical RHEINGAU RIESLING, esp. since 1977. TROCKEN and HALB-TROCKEN wines a speciality. The owner, Graf MATUSCHKA-GREIFFENCLAU, leads the "German wine with food" campaign.

Schmitt, Gustav Adolf

Merchant house with fine old 250-acre family estate at NIERSTEIN.

Schmitt, Franz Karl Even older 74-acre ditto.

Schmitt H., Söhne

One of the largest merchant-houses of the Mosel, at LONGUICH, also with three small estates.

Schönborn, Schloss

One of the biggest and best Rheingau estates, based at HATTENHEIM. Full-flavoured wines, at best excellent. Also very good SEKT.

Schoppenwein Café wine: i.e. wine by the glass.

Schorlemer, Freiherr von

Historically important MOSEL estate of 116 acres in 5 parts, now in divided ownership.

Schubert, von Owner of MAXIMIN GRÜNHAUS.

Schweigen Rhpf. w. ★→ ★★ 83 *84* 85 86

Southernmost Rheinpfalz village with important cooperative, Deutsches WEINTOR. Grosslage: Guttenberg.

Sekt German (QbA) sparkling wine, best when RIESLING is on the label.

Senfter, Reinhold

One of the best growers in NIERSTEIN, with 32 acres. Best v'yds: Niersteiner Hipping and Oppenheimer Sackträger.

·**Serrig** M-S-R (Saar) w. ★★→★★★★ 71 75 76 79 83 *84* 85 86

Village known for "steely" wine, excellent in hot years. Top growers: VEREINIGTE HOSPITIEN and State Domain. Grosslage: Scharzberg.

Sichel H., Söhne

Famous wine-merchants of London and Mainz with new KELLEREI in Alzey, Rhh. Owners of 'Blue Nun' LIEBFRAUMILCH.

Silvaner

The third most-planted German white grape, best in FRANKEN and the KAISERSTUHL.

Simmern, Langwerth von

Top 120-acre family estate at ELTVILLE. Famous v'yds: Mannberg, MARCOBRUNN, Baiken etc. Some of the very best, most typical RHEINGAU RIESLINGS.

Sonnenuhr

"Sun-dial." Name of several v'yds., esp. the famous one at WEHLEN.

Spätburgunder

PINOT NOIR: the best red-wine grape in Germany esp. in BADEN and WÜRTEMBERG.

Spätlese

"Late gathered." One better (stronger/sweeter) than KABINETT. Wines to age *at least* three years. Dry spätleses can be v. fine.

Spindler, Wilhelm

Fine 33-acre family estate at FORST, Rheinpfalz.

Staatlicher Hofkeller

The Bavarian State Domain. 287 acres of finest FRANKEN v'yds with spectacular cellars under the great baroque Residenz at WÜRZBURG.

Staatsweingut (or Staatliche Weinbaudomäne)

The State wine estate or domain.

Staufenberg, Schloss

69-acre DURBACH estate of the Margrave of Baden. Fine "Klingelberger" (RIESLING).

Steigerwald (Bereich)

District name for eastern part of FRANKEN.

Steinberg   Rhg. w. ★★★→★★★★ 71 75 76 79 83 *84* 85 86

Famous 79-acre v'yd. at HATTENHEIM walled by Cistercians 700 yrs. ago. Now property of the State Domain, ELTVILLE.

Steinwein

Wine from WÜRZBURG's best v'yd., Stein. In the past the term was loosely used for all Franconian wine.

Stuttgart

Chief city of WÜRTTEMBERG, producer of some pleasant wines (esp. Riesling), recently beginning to be exported.

Südliche Weinstrasse (Bereich)

District name for the s. RHEINPFALZ. Quality has improved tremendously in the last 25 years.

Tafelwein

"Table wine." The vin ordinaire of Germany. Mostly blended with other EEC wines. But DEUTSCHER TAFELWEIN must come from Germany alone. (See also LANDWEIN.)

Thanisch, Weingut Wwe. Dr. H

32-acre BERNKASTEL family estate of top quality, incl. part of Doctor v'yd.

Traben-Trarbach   M-M w. ★★ 76 83 *84* 85 86

Secondary wine-town, some good light wines. Top v'yds. incl. Würzgarten, Schlossberg. Grosslage: Schwarzlay.

Traisen   Na. w. ★★★ 71 75 76 79 82 83 *84* 85 86

Small village incl. superlative Bastei and Rotenfels v'yds, making RIESLINGS of great concentration and class.

Traminer   See GEWÜRZTRAMINER

Trier   M-S-R w. ★★→★★★

Important wine city of Roman origin, on the Mosel, adjacent to RUWER, now incl. AVELSBACH and EITELSBACH. Grosslage: Römerlay.

Trittenheim M-M w. **★★** 71 75 76 *83 84* 85 86

Attractive light wines. Top v'yds. Apotheke, Altärchen, Grosslage: Michelsberg.

Trocken

Dry. On labels Trocken *alone* means with a statutory maximum of unfermented sugar (9 grams per litre). But see next entry. See also HALBTROCKEN.

Trockenbeerenauslese

The sweetest and most expensive category of wine, extremely rare, made from selected withered grapes. See also EDELFÄULE.

Trollinger

Common red grape of WÜRTTEMBERG: locally very popular.

Ungstein Rhpf. w. **★★→** **★★★** 71 75 76 79 82 83 *84* 85 86

MITTELHAARDT village with fine harmonious wines. Top v'yd. Herrenberg. Top growers Fuhrmann (Weingut Pfeffingen), Fitz-Ritter, BASSERMANN-JORDAN. Grosslage: Honigsäckel.

Ürzig M-M w. **★★★** 71 75 76 79 82 83 *84* 85 86

Village famous for lively spicy wine. Top v'yd.: Würzgarten. Grosslage: Schwarzlay.

VdP

The Deutscher Prädikats – und Qualitätsweinguter, an association of premium growers.

Vereinigte Hospitien

"United Hospitals." Ancient charity at Trier with large holdings in SERRIG, WILTINGEN, TRIER, PIESPORT, etc.

Verwaltung Administration (of property/estate etc).

Villa Sachsen

67-acre BINGEN estate belonging to ST. URSULA Weingut.

Wachenheim Rhpf. w. **★★★**→**★★★★** 71 75 76 79 81 82 *83* *84* 85 86

840 acres, incl. exceptionally fine Rieslings. V'yds. incl. Gerümpel, Böhlig, Rechbächel. Top grower: BÜRKLIN-WOLF. Grosslagen: Schenkenböhl, Schnepfenflug, Mariengarten.

Waldrach M-S-R (Ruwer) w. **★★** 75 76 79 *81* 82 *83* *84* 85

Some charming light wines. Grosslage: Römerlay.

Walluf Rhg. w. **★★** 75 76 79 *81* 82 83 *84* 85

Neighbour of ELTVILLE; formerly Nieder- and Ober-Walluf. Underrated wines. Grosslage: Steinmächer.

Walporzheim Ahrtal (Bereich)

District name for the whole AHR valley.

Walthari-Hof

Much-discussed estate at Edenkoben, Rheinpfalz, making wine without recourse to sulphur dioxide.

Wawern M-S-R (Saar) w. **★★→★★★** 71 75 76 83 *84* 85 86

Small village with fine RIESLINGS. Grosslage: Scharzberg.

Wegeler-Deinhard

136-acre RHEINGAU estate. V'yds. in OESTRICH, MITTELHEIM, WINKEL, GEISENHEIM, RÜDESHEIM, etc. Consistent quality; classic AUSLESES, finest EISWEIN. Also 67 acres in MITTELMOSEL, incl. major part of BERNKASTELER DOCTOR (GRAACH, WEHLEN etc.) and 46 acres in MITTELHAARDT (FORST, DEIDESHEIM, RUPPERTSBERG).

Wehlen M-M w. **★★★**→**★★★★** 71 75 76 79 82 83 *84* 85 86

Neighbour of BERNKASTEL with equally fine, somewhat richer, wine. Best v'yd.: Sonnenuhr. Top growers: Prüm family. Grosslage: Münzlay.

Weil, Dr.

Fine 46-acre estate at KIEDRICH. Currently below top form.

Weinbaugebiet Viticultural region, whether for QbA wines, TAFELWEIN or LANDWEIN.

Weingut Wine estate. Can only be used on the label by estates that grow all their own grapes, make their wines from these grapes and bottle these same wines.

Weinkellerei Wine cellars or winery. See Keller.

Weinstrasse

"Wine road." Scenic route through v'yds. Germany has several, the most famous the Deutsche Weinstrasse in RHEINPFALZ.

Weintor, Deutsches See SCHWEIGEN

Weissherbst

Very pale pink or 'blush' wine of QbA standard or above, even occasionally BEERENAUSLESE, the speciality of BADEN, WÜRTTEMBERG, and RHEINPFALZ. Currently v. popular in Germany.

Werner, Domdechant

Fine 33-acre family estate on the best slopes of HOCHHEIM.

Wiltingen Saar w. ★★→★★★★ 71 75 76 79 82 83 85 86

The centre of the Saar. 790 acres. Beautiful subtle austere wine. Top v'yds. incl. SCHARZHOFBERG, Braune Kupp, Braunfels, Klosterberg. Grosslage (for the whole Saar): Scharzberg.

Winkel Rhg. w. ★★★→★★★★ 71 75 76 79 82 83 84 85 86

Village famous for fragrant wine, incl. SCH. VOLLRADS. V'yds. incl. Hasensprung, Jesuitengarten. Grosslagen: Honigberg and Erntebringer.

Winningen M-S-R. w. ★★

Village of lower Mosel near Koblenz with some fine delicate RIESLING. Best v'yds: Uhlen, Röttgen.

Wintrich M-M w. ★★→★★★ 71 75 76 83 84 85 86

Neighbour of PIESPORT; similar wines. Top v'yds.: Grosser Herrgott, Ohligsberg, Sonnenseite. Grosslage: Kurfürstlay.

Winzergenossenschaft

Wine-growers' cooperative, usually making good and reasonably priced wine.

Winzerverein The same as the last.

Wirsching, Hans

Well-known estate in IPHOFEN, FRANKEN. Robust, full-bodied wines. 100 acres in top v'yds: Julius-Echter-Berg, Kalb etc.

Wonnegau (Bereich) District name for s. RHEINHESSEN.

Worms Rhh. w. ★★

City with the famous LIEBFRAUENSTIFT v'yd.

Württemberg

Vast s. area little known for wine outside Germany. Some good RIESLINGS, esp. from Neckar valley. Also TROLLINGER.

Würzburg Frank. ★★→★★★★ 71 76 81 82 83 84 85 86

Great baroque city on the Main, centre of Franconian (FRANKEN) wine: fine, full-bodied and dry. Top v'yds.: Stein, Leiste, Schlossberg. No Grosslage. See also MAINDREIECK.

ZBW (Zentralkellerei Badischer Winzergenossenschaften)

Germany's (and Europe's) biggest ultra-modern co-operative, at Breisach, BADEN, with 25,000 grower-members with 12,000 acres, producing 80 percent of Baden's wine at all quality levels.

Zell M-S-R w. ★→★★ 76 83 84 85 86

The best-known lower Mosel village, esp. for its Grosslage name Schwarze Katz ("Black Cat"). RIESLING on steep slate gives aromatic light wines.

Zell (Bereich)

District name for the whole lower Mosel from Zell to Koblenz.

Zeltingen-Rachtig M-M w. ★★ →★★★★ 71 75 76 79 83 84 85 86

Important Mosel village next to WEHLEN. Typically lively crisp RIESLING. Top v'yds.: Sonnenuhr, Schlossberg. Grosslage: Münzlay.

Zentralkellerei Mosel-Saar-Ruwer

The biggest coop of the MOSEL, incl. Saar-Winzer-Verein at Wiltingen. Its 5,200 members produces 25% of all M-S-R wines.

Zwierlein, Freiherr von

55-acre family estate in Geisenheim. 100% Riesling. Best v'yds: Rothenberg, Kläuserweg.

Spain & Portugal

The following addition abbreviations are used in the Spanish section (see box p. 122):

R'a.A. Rioja Alta
R'a.Al. Rioja Alavesa
Res. Reserva
g. see Vino generoso

Abbreviations of regional names shown in bold type are used in the text.

In 1986 Spain and Portugal joined the European Common Market, a move which symbolized (and indeed provoked) a new wave of interest in the growing scope and quality of their wine industries.

Modern ideas have arrived to enrich (or replace) their traditions. The state of ferment is highly productive, and splendid new wines are appearing, both in their few traditional quality areas, and in former bulk-wine regions.

Currently in Spain (apart from sherry country), Catalonia, Rioja, Rueda and Ribera del Duero hold most interest; in Portugal (apart from port and madeira) Bairrada, the Douro, the Tagus regions of Ribatejo and Estremadura, and the Minho. New delimited ("V.Q.P.R.D.") areas are tending to overshadow the old-fashioned appellations.

The listing here includes the best and most interesting types and regions of each country, whether legally delimited or not. Geographical references (see map) are to the traditional division of Spain into the old kingdoms, and the major provinces of Portugal.

Sherry, port and Madeira are listed separately on pages 129 to 133.

Spain

A.G.E., Bodegas Unidas R'a.A. r. (p.) w. dr. or sw. res. ∗→∗∗73 74 75 78 80 81 82

    Large bodega making a wide range of wines, of which the best are the red Siglo Saco and Marqués de Romeral.

Alavesas, Bodegas R'a. Al. r. (w. dr.) res. ∗∗→∗∗∗74 75 76 78 80 81 83

    The pale orange-red SOLAR DE SAMANIEGO is one of the most delicate of the soft, fast-maturing Alavesa wines.

Albariño del Palacio Gal. w. dr. ∗∗

    Flowery and pétillant young wine from FEFIÑANES near Cambados, made with the Albariño grape, the best of the region.

Alella Cat. r. (p.) w. dr. or sw. ∗∗

    Small demarcated region just n. of Barcelona. Makes pleasantly fresh and fruity wines. (See MARFIL and MARQUÉS DE ALELLA.)

Alicante Lev. r. (w.) ∗

    Demarcated region: wines tend to be "earthy" and high in alcohol.

Almansa Lev. r. ∗

    Demarcated region w. of ALICANTE, with similar wines.

Aloque N. Cas. r. ⋆ D.Y.A.

    A light (though not in alcohol) variety of VALDEPEÑAS, made by fermenting together red and white grapes.

Almendralejo Ext. r. w. ∗

    Commercial wine centre of the Extremadura. Much of its produce is distilled to make the spirit for fortifying sherry.

Alvear, S.A. And. g. ⋆⋆⋆

    The largest producer of excellent sherry-like apéritif and dessert wines from MONTILLA-MORILES.

Ampurdán See PERELADA

Año 4° Año (or Años) means 4 years old when bottled.

Bach, Masía Cat. r. p. w. dr. or sw. res. ⋆⋆ →∗∗∗ 70 74 78 80 81

    Excellent villa-winery nr. SAN SADURNÍ DE NOYA, now owned by CODORNIU. Best known for luscious oaky white Extrísimo Bach. Now also good red reserva.

Banda Azul R'a.A. r. ∗∗75 76 80 81

    Big-selling wine from BODEGAS PATERNINA, S.A..

Barceló S.A. And. br. ∗∗→∗∗∗

    One of the best-known makers of dessert Málaga.

Berberana, Bodegas R'a.A. r. (w. dr.) res. ∗→∗∗∗73 74 75 76 78 79 80 82 83

    Best are the fruity, full-bodied reds: the 3° año Carta de Plata, the 5° año Carta de Oro and the smooth velvety reservas.

Beronia, Bodegas R'a.A. r. w. dr. res. ∗∗→∗∗∗73 75 77 78 80 81 82 83

    A small modern bodega making excellent reds in the traditional oaky style. Their light unaged "Beron" is very attractive.

Bilbainas, Bodegas R'a.A. r. (p.) w. dr. sw. or sp. res. ⋆⋆ →∗∗∗ 66 69 70 72 73 75 76 78 79 81 82

    Large bodega in HARO, making a wide range of reliable wines, including the dark Viña Pomal, Pomal Junior, the lighter Viña Zaco, Vendimia Especial Reservas and "Royal Carlton" by the champagne method.

Blanco White.

Bodega

    Spanish for 1. a wineshop; 2. a concern occupied in the making, blending and/or shipping of wine.

Campanas, Las See VINICOLA NAVARRA.

Campo Nuevo Nav. r. p. w. dr. ∗

    Worthwhile bodega for NAVARRA wines.

Campo Viejo, Bodegas R'a.A. r. (w. dr.) res. ⋆ →∗∗∗ 64 70 71 73 75 76 78 79 80 81 82 83

    Branch of Savin S.A., one of Spain's largest wine companies. Makes the popular 2° año San Asensio and some big, fruity red reservas, esp. Marqués de Villamagna.

Can Rafols de Caus   Cat. r. w. dr. ★★ 85
>New small PENEDÈS bodega, growing its own fruity CAB. SAUV. and pleasant CHARD.

Cañamero   Ext. w. ★
>Remote village near Guadalupe whose wines grow FLOR and acquire a sherry-like taste.

Caralt, Cavas Conde de   Cat. sp. r. w. res. ★★ 78 80 81 82 83
>"CAVA" sparkling wines from SAN SADURNÍ DE NOYA; also pleasant still wines.

Carbonell   And. br. ★★
>Producer of good Montilla ("Sombra") and olive oil, at Cordoba.

Cariñena   Ara. r. (p.w.) ★
>Demarcated region and large-scale supplier of strong wine for everyday drinking, now being invigorated (and its wines lightened) by modern technology.

Casar de Valdaigo   O.Cas. r. w. dr. ★★
>Producer in El Bierzo, n. of LEÓN, with a light, very dry clarete of fair quality.

Castellblanch   Cat. sp. ★★
>PENEDÈS CAVA firm, owned by FREIXENET. Recently much praised for Brut Zero and slightly sweeter Cristal Seco.

Castillo Ygay   See MARQUÉS DE MURRIETA.

Cava   Spanish sparkling wine made by the champagne method. Also the bodega making it.

Cenalsa   Nav. r. w. dr. ★★
>A marketing organization shipping a range of Navarra wines, inc. a flowery new-style white and a fruity red "Agramont".

Cenicero   Wine township in the RIOJA ALTA.

Cepa   Wine or grape variety.

Chacolí   Gui. (r.) w. ★ D.Y.A.
>Alarmingly sharp pétillant wine from the Basque coast. It contains only 9% to 11% alcohol.

Chaves, Bodegas   Gal. w. dr. ★★→★★★ 81 82 84 (D.Y.A.)
>Small family firm making a good and fragrant, though slightly acidic, ALBARIÑO; perhaps the best Galician wine exported.

Chivite, Bodegas Julián   Nav. r. (p.) w. dr. or sw. res. ★★ 82 83
>Largest of the firms in Navarra, producing full-bodied, fruity red wines and a flowery, well-balanced white.

Clarete   Term frowned upon by the EEC describing light red wine (occasionally dark rosé).

Codorníu, S.A.   Cat. sp. ★★→★★★
>One of the two largest and best known of the firms in SAN SADURNÍ DE NOYA making good wines by the champagne method. Non Plus Ultra is matured, Ana de Codorníu a fresher style.

Compañía Vinícola del Norte de España (C.V.N.E.)   R'a.A. r. (p.) w. dr. or sw. res. ★★→★★★ 66 70 73 74 75 76 78 80 81 82 83
>The 3° año is among the best of young red Riojas and Monopole one of the best slightly oaky whites. Excellent red Imperial and Viña Real reservas. C.V.N.E. is pronounced "Coonay."

Consejo Regulador
>Official organization for the defence, control and promotion of a DENOMINACIÓN DE ORIGEN.

Contino   R'a. Al. r. res. ★★★ 74 75 76 78 80 82
>Superior single-vineyard red wine made by a subsidiary of COMPAÑIA VINICOLA DEL NORTE DE ESPAÑA.

Cosecha   Crop or vintage.

Criado y embotellado por . . .
>Grown and bottled by . . .

Crianza   Literally, "nursing", the ageing of wine. New or unaged wine is "sin crianza". Crianza wines are at least 2 years old, with one year in oak.

Cumbrero   See MONTECILLO, BODEGAS

De Muller Cat. (r. w. dr.) br. ★★→★★★

Old TARRAGONA firm famous for altar wines, making a good PRIORATO and superb v. old solera-aged dessert wines, incl. Priorato Dulce and Paxarete.

Denominación de origen

Officially regulated wine region. (See introduction, p. 116.)

Domecq, S.A. R'a Al. r. (w. dr.) res. ★★→★★★ 73 74 76 78 80 82

Best of the wines from this Riojan outpost of Pedro Domecq is the fruity red Domecq Domain, exceptional in '76, and Marqués de Arienzo RESERVAS.

Dulce Sweet.

Elaborado y añejado por ... Made and aged by ...

El Coto, Bodegas R'a. Al. r. (w. dr.) res. ★★→★★★ 73 76 78 80 81 82

Best-known for light, soft red El Coto and Coto de Imaz.

Espumoso Sparkling (but see CAVA.)

Faustino Martinez, S.A. R'a. Al. r. w. dr. (p.) res. ★★ →★★★ 64 70 72 73 74 75 76 78 80 81

Good red wines and the dry, light, fruity new-style white Faustino V. Gran Reserva is Faustino I. Do not be put off by the repellent bottles.

Ferrer, José L. Mallorca r. res. ★★

His wines, made in Binisalem, are still the only ones of any distinction from Mallorca.

Flor A wine yeast peculiar to sherry and certain other wines that oxidize slowly and tastily under its influence.

Franco-Españolas, Bodegas R'a.A. r. w. dr. or sw. res. ★→★★ 64 68 70 73 74 75 76 78 79 82 83

Reliable wines from LOGROÑO. Bordón is a fruity red. The semi-sweet white Diamante is a favourite in Spain.

Freixenet, S.A., Cavas Cat. sp. ★★→★★★

CAVA, rivalling Codorníu in size through new acquisitions, making a range of good sparkling wines by the champagne method. It has recently acquired vineyards (GLORIA FERRER) in California and the Champagne house of Henri Abelé in Reims. Paul Cheneau is a low-price brand.

Gaseoso

A cheap sparkler made by pumping carbon dioxide into wine.

Gonzalez y Dubosc, S.A., Cavas Cat. sp. ★★

A branch of the sherry giant Gonzales Byass. Pleasant sparkling wines exported as "Jean Perico".

Gran Vas

Pressurized tanks (*cuves closes*) for making inexpensive sparkling wines; also used to describe this type of wine.

Green Wines

There are objections from the EEC and the Portuguese to the use of this harmless English translation of VINHOS VERDES.

Gurpegui, Bodegas R'a. B. r. (p. w. dr.) res. ★→★★70 73 75 78 80 81 82

Large family firm making some of the best wines from the RIOJA BAJA, labelled as Berceo. They incl. a fresh rosé.

Haro The wine centre of the RIOJA ALTA.

Huelva And. r. w. br. ★→★★

Demarcated region w. of Cadiz. White table wines and sherry-like *generosos*, formerly sent to JEREZ for blending.

Irache, S.L. Nav. r. p. (w. dr.) res. ★★ 64 70 73 78 81 82

Well-known bodega with substantial exports.

Jean Perico See GONZALEZ Y DUBOSC

Jerez de la Frontera

The capital city of sherry. (See p. 129).

Jumilla Lev. r. ★ (w. dr. p.) ★

Demarcated region in the mountains north of MURCIA. Its overstrong wines (sometimes 18% alcohol) are now being lightened by earlier harvesting and better wine-making.

Juvé y Camps Cat. sp. ★★➔★★★
    Family CAVA firm aiming for top quality.

Labastida, Cooperativa Vinícola de R'a.Al. r. res. ★★➔   ★★★ 66
70 75 78 82
    Very drinkable Manuel Quintano; fruity, well-balanced Montebuena, Gastrijo and Castillo Labastida reservas and gran reservas, and a fresh dry white of real character.

La Granja Remelluri R'a. Al. r. res. ★★★ 74 76 79 **80** 81 83
    Small firm (founded 1970), making good red Riojas by traditional methods.

Laguardia
    Picturesque walled town at the centre of LA RIOJA ALAVESA.

Lagunilla, Bodegas R'a.A. r. ★★ **73 75 78** 81
    Modern firm owned by the British Grand Met. Co. Easy oaky light reds incl. Viña Herminia and Gran Reserva.

Lan, Bodegas R'a.A. r. (p.w.) res. ★★➔★★★ 73 75 78 82
    Huge modern bodega, lavishly equipped and making aromatic red Riojas, incl. the good Lancorta and fresh white Lan Blanco.

La Rioja Alta, Bodegas R'a.A. r. (p.) w. dr. (or sw.) res. ⟨★★➔★★★⟩
64 68 70 73 76 78 80 81 83
    Excellent wines, esp. the red 3° año Viña Alberdi, the velvety 5° año Ardanza, the lighter 6° año Araña, the splendid Reserva 904 and dry white Metropol Extra *(not* D.Y.A.).

León O.Cas. r. p. w. ★➔★★ 78
    Northern region becoming better known. Its wines, particularly those from the unfortunately named V.I.L.E. (e.g. the young Coyanza and Don Suero reserva), are fruity, dry and refreshing.

León, S.A., Jean Cat. r. w. dr. res ★★★ 77 78 79 80
    Small firm owned by a Los Angeles restaurateur and making a good oaky CHARDONNAY and deep, full-bodied CABERNET that repays long bottle-ageing.

Logroño Principal town of the RIOJA region.

López de Heredia, S.A. R'a.A. r. (p.) w. dr. or sw. res. ★★➔ ⟨★★★★⟩
68 70 73 75 76 77 78 79 80 81
    Old established bodega in HARO with typical and good dry red Viña Tondonia of 6° año or more. Its wines are exceptionally long-lasting, and the Tondonia whites are also impressive.

RIOJA VINTAGES

Thanks to a more consistent climate and the blending of a proportion of wine from better vintages in poor years, Riojas do not vary to the same extent as the red wines from Bordeaux and Burgundy. With few exceptions the '72 and '77 vintages were a disaster, owing to high rainfall and the onset of rot and oidium. Of other recent years, the best were: 52 55 58 64 66 68 70 73 76 78 80 81 82 83 and 85. (Those in bold type were outstanding.)

Riojas are put on the market when they are ready to drink. The best reservas of the best vintages, however, have very long lives and improve with more bottle age. Certain '64s, for example, are still improving.

Los Llanos N.Cas. r. (p. w. dr.) res. ⟨★★⟩ 75 78
    One of the few VALDEPEÑAS bodegas to age wine in oak. Señorio de Los Llanos Gran Reserva is remarkably scented and silky.

Majorca No wine of interest except from José FERRER.

Málaga And. br. sw. ★★➔★★★
    Demarcated region around the city of Málaga. At their best, its dessert wines yield nothing to tawny port.

Mancha N.Cas. r. w. ★
    Large demarcated region n. and n.e. of VALDEPEÑAS. Mainly white wines, lacking the lively freshness of the best Valdepeñas, but showing signs of improvement.

Marfi Cat. r. (p.) w. ★★

Brand name of Alella Vinicola (Bodegas Cooperativas), best known of the producers in ALELLA. Means "ivory".

Marqués de Alella Cat. w. dr. (sp.) ★★→★★★ 83 84 85 (D.Y.A.)

Small bodega making light and fragrant white Alella wines by modern methods. Also a little CAVA.

Marqués de Cáceres, Bodegas R'a.A. r. p. w. dr. res. ★★→★★★ 70 71 73 75 76 78 80 81 82

Good red Riojas of various ages made by French methods from Cenicero (R'a.A.) grapes and also a surprisingly light and fragrant white (D.Y.A.).

Marqués de Griñon O. Cas. (r.) w. dr. ★★★ (r.) 82 83

Enterprising nobleman making very fine CABERNET nr. Toledo, not a recognized wine region. Also refreshing white from Verdejo grapes in RUEDA.

Marqués de Monistrol, Bodegas Cat. w. r. (dr. or sw.) sp. res. ★★→★★★ 75 77 78 80 82

Old bodega now owned by Martini & Rossi. Refreshing whites, esp. the Vin Nature, a good red reserva and an odd sweet red wine.

Marqués de Murrieta, S.A. R'a.A. r. p. w. dr. res. ★★→ ★★★★ 34 42 60 62 64 68 70 73 74 75 76 78 79 80 81 82

Highly reputed bodega near LOGROÑO making some of the best of all Riojas. Makes 4° año Etiqueta Blanca, superb red Castillo Ygay and an "old-style" oaky white, dry, fruity, and worth bottle-ageing.

Marqués de Riscal, S.A. R'a.Al. r. (p. and w. dr.) res. ★★→★★★★ 64 65 68 71 73 75 76 78 80 81 82

The best-known bodega of the RIOJA ALAVESA. Its red wines are relatively light and dry. Old vintages are very fine; recent ones disappointing.

Marqués de Romeral R'a.A. r. w. dr. ★★ 76 78

Everyday Romeral and Gran Reserva are both v.g. values.

Martinez-Bujanda R'a.Al. r. w. dr. res ★★★ 73 75 80 82 83

Refounded (1985) family-run RIOJA bodega, remarkably equipped. Excellent wines, incl. fruity SIN CRIANZA as well as reservas.

Mascaró, Cavas Cat. sp. (w. dr. r.) ★★→ ★★★

Maker of some of the best Spanish brandy, good sparkling wine and a refreshing dry white Viña Franca.

Mauro, Bodegas O. Cas. r. ★★→★★★ 81

New bodega in Tudela del Duero making round and fruity Tinta fina red.

Méntrida N.Cas. r. w. ★

Demarcated region w. of Madrid, supplying everyday red wine.

Monopole See COMPANIA VINICOLA DEL NORTE DE ESPAÑA.

Montánchez Ext. r. g. ★

Village near Mérida, interesting because its red wines grow FLOR yeast like FINO sherry.

Montecillo, Bodegas R'a.A. r. w. (p.) res. ★★ 73 75 76 78 80 81 82

"State of the art" Rioja bodega owned by Osborne (see Sherry). Red and fresh, dry white Cumbrero are currently among the best of the 3° año wines. Viña Monty is the worthy Reserva.

Montecristo, Bodegas ★★

Well-known brand of MONTILLA-MORILES wines.

Monterrey Gal. r. ★

Region near the n. border of Portugal, making strong wines like those of VERIN.

Montilla-Moriles And. g. ★★★

Demarcated region near Cordoba. Its crisp, sherry-like FINO and AMONTILLADO contain 14% to 17.5% natural alcohol and remain unfortified and singularly toothsome.

Morenito, Bodegas N.Cas. r. (p. w. dr.) res. ★★ 78 79

Old Valdepeñas bodega ageing its best reds in oak.

Muga, Bodegas R'a.A. r. (w.) res. (sp.) ⬜ ★★★ 70 73 75 76 78 80 81
Small family firm in HARO, making some of the best red Rioja now available by strictly traditional methods in oak. Its wines are light but intensely aromatic, with long complex finish. The best is Prado Enea. Whites not so good.

Navarra Nav. r. p. (w.) ★→ ★★
Demarcated region; mainly fresh and fruity rosés and sturdy red wines, but some reservas up to Rioja standards. See CENALSA, CHIVITE, etc.

Nuestro Padre Jésus del Perdón, Coop. de N. Cas. r. w. dr ★
Inexpensive Yuntero, Casa la Teja and fresh white Lazarillo (D.Y.A.).

Olarra, Bodegas R'a.A. r. (w. p.) res. ★★→★★★ 73 75 76 78 80 81 82
Vast modern bodega near LOGROÑO, one of the show-pieces of RIOJA, making good red and white wines and excellent Cerro Añon reservas. Since '81, Añares is the top reserva.

Palacio de Arganza O. Cas. r. p. w. dr. res. ★★→★★★ 65 70 74 76 79
Best-known bodega in El Bierzo between LEÓN and GALICIA. White Vega Burbia; red Almeña del Bierzo.

Palacio de Fefiñanes Gal. w. res. ★★★
Best of all the ALBARIÑO wines, though without pétillance, since it is aged in oak for 2–6 yrs.

RIOJA'S CHARACTERISTIC STYLE

To the Spanish palate the taste of luxury in wine is essentially the taste of oak. Oak contains vanillin, the taste of vanilla. Hence the characteristic vanilla flavour of all mature Spanish table wines of high quality — exemplified by the reservas of Rioja (red and white).

Historically the reason for long oak-ageing was to stabilize the best wines while their simple fruity flavours developed into something more complex and characteristically winey. Fashion has swung (perhaps too far) against the oaky flavour of old Rioja whites. But the marriage of ripe fruit and oak in red Rioja is still highly appreciated.

Paternina, S.A., Bodegas R'a.A. r. (p.) w. dr. or sw. res. ★→★★★ 28 59 67 68 71 73 75 76 78 79 80 81 82 83
Bodega at Ollauri and a household name esp. for Banda Azul red (currently 81) and Banda Dorada white. Its best wines are the red Viña Vial (now 80) and the magnificent older reservas.

Pazo Gal. r. p. w. dr. ★ D.Y.A.
Brand name of the co-operative at RIBEIRO, making wines akin to Portuguese VINHOS VERDES. The rasping red is the local favourite. The pleasant slightly fizzy white is safer.

Peñafiel O.Cas. r. and w. dr. res. ★★ 76
Village on the R. Duero near Valladolid. Best wines are fruity reds from the Cooperativa de RIBERO DEL DUERO, including the notably tasty 5° año PROTOS.

Penedès Cat. r. w. dr. sp. ★→★★★
Demarcated region including Vilafranca del Penedès, SAN SADURNÍ DE NOYA and SITGES. See also TORRES.

Perelada Cat. (r. p.) w. sp. ★★
In the demarcated region of Ampurdán on the Costa Brava. Best known for sparkling wines made both by the champagne and tank or *cuve close* system.

Priorato Cat. br. dr. r. ★★
Demarcated region, an enclave in that of TARRAGONA, known for its alcoholic "rancio" wines and also for almost black full-bodied reds, often used for blending. Lighter blended Priorato is a good carafe wine in Barcelona restaurants.

Protos See PEÑAFIEL

Raimat Cat. r. w. p. sp. ★→★★ 76 82 83

Intriguing, well-made wines from old v'yds. near Lérida, recently replanted by CODORNÍU with CABERNET, CHARDONNAY and other foreign vines. Also a 100% CHARD CAVA.

Remelluri, Bodegas R'a Al. r. ★★ 82

Modern bodega with trad. methods at Labastida.

René Barbier Cat. r. w. dr. res. ★★ 73 80

Part of the FREXINET group known for fresh white Kraliner and red R.B. Reservas.

Reserva

Good-quality wine matured for long periods. Red reservas must spend at least 1 year in cask and 2 in bottle; Gran Reservas 2 in cask and 3 in bottle.

Ribeiro Gal. r. (p.) w. dr. ★→★★

Demarcated region on the n. border of Portugal making wines similar to Portuguese VINHO VERDE – and others.

Ribera del Duero

Demarcated region e. of Valladolid, potentially excellent for Tinta fina (TEMPRANILLO) reds. See VEGA SICILIA, PEÑAFIEL, MAURO, TORREMILANOS, TINTA PESQUERA.

Rioja O.Cas. r. p. w. sp. esp. 64 66 68 70 73 75 76 78 80 81 82 83 85

This upland region along the R. Ebro in the n. of Spain produces most of the country's best table wines in some 50 BODEGAS DE EXPORTACIÓN. It is sub-divided into:

Rioja Alavesa

North of the R. Ebro, the R'a.Al. produces fine red wines, mostly light in body and colour.

Rioja Alta

South of the R. Ebro and w. of LOGROÑO, the R'a.A. grows most of the finest red and white wines; also some rosé.

Rioja Baja

Stretching e. from LOGROÑO, the Rioja Baja makes coarser red wines, high in alcohol and often used for blending.

Riojanas, Bodegas R'a.A. r. (w. p.) res. ★★→★★★ 34 42 56 64 66 68 70 73 74 75 76 78 80 81 82

One of the older bodegas, making a good traditional Viña Albina. Monte Real reservas are big, mellow, above average.

Rioja Santiago, S.A. R'a.A. r. (w. dr. or sw. p.) res. ★→★★★ 78 82

Bodega at HARO with well-known wines. The flavour sometimes suffers from pasteurization, and appropriately, as it now belongs to Pepsi-Cola, it makes the biggest-selling bottled SANGRÍA. Top reds: Condal and Gran Enologica.

Rosado Rosé.

Rueda O.Cas. br. w. dr. ★→★★

Small demarcated area w. of Valladolid. Traditional producer of flor-growing sherry-like wines up to 17° of alcohol, now making fresh young whites including that of the MARQUÉS DE RISCAL.

Salceda, S.A., Bodegas Viña R'a.Al. r. res. ★★→★★★ 73 75 78 80 81 82

Makes fruity, well-balanced red wines.

Sangre de Toro

Brand name for a rich-flavoured red wine from TORRES S.A.

Sangría Cold red wine cup with citrus fruit, fizzy lemonade, ice and brandy.

Sanlúcar de Barrameda

Centre of the Manzanilla district. (See Sherry p. 129.)

San Sadurní de Noya Cat. sp. ★★→★★★

Town s. of Barcelona, hollow with cellars where dozens of firms produce sparkling wine ("CAVA") by the champagne method. Standards are high, even if the ultimate finesse is lacking.

San Valero, Bodega Cooperative Ara. r. p. (w.) res. ★

Large CARIÑENA coop with some modern wines. Good red reserva Villalta; fresh Percebal rosé.

Sarría, Señorio de Nav. r. (p.w.dr.) res. **☆☆→★★★** 74 75 76 78 82 84
The vineyards and model winery near Pamplona produces wines up to (high) RIOJA standards.

Scholtz, Hermanos, S.A. And. br. **★★→** **★★★**
Makers of the best MÁLAGA, including a good, dry 10-year-old amontillado. Best is the dessert Solera Scholtz 1885.

Seco Dry.

Segura Viudas, Cavas Cat. sp. **★★→★★★**
CAVA of PENEDÈS. Buy the N.V.

Siglo Popular sack-wrapped RIOJA brand of Bodegas A.G.E.

Sin Crianza See Crianza.

Sitges Cat. w. sw. **★★**
Coastal resort s. of Barcelona noted formerly for sweet dessert wine made from Moscatel and MALVASIA grapes.

Tarragona Cat. r. w. dr. or sw. br. **★→★★★**
1. Table wines from the demarcated region; of little note. 2. Dessert wines from the firm of DE MULLER. 3. The town makes vermouth and Chartreuse and exports cheap blended wine.

Tierra de Medina O.Cas. w. **★→★★**
Area w. of Valladolid. Includes La Nava and RUEDA.

Tinta Pesquera O. Cas. r. **★★**
RIBERA DEL DUERO red of good quality from Alejandro Fernandez.

Tinto Red.

Toro O.Cas. r. **★→★★**
Town, 150 miles n.w. of Madrid, and its powerful (to 16°) wine. Leading producer Bodegas Mateos. His 3° año is good.

Torremilanos O. Cas. r. res. **★★** 76 79 81 82 83
Label of Bodegas López Peñalba, a small family firm near Aranda de Duero making good red wines from the Tinta Fina (TEMPRANILLO) grape. Also labelled "Peñalba".

Torres, Bodegas Cat. r. w. dr. or semi-sw. p. res. **★★→★★★★** 70 71 73 74 75 76 77 78 79 80 81 82 83 84
Distinguished family firm making the best wines of PENEDÈS, esp. flowery white Viña Sol and Gran Viña Sol, semi-dry aromatic Esmeralda, Waltraud RIESLING, red Tres Torres and Gran Sangredetoro, superlative Gran Coronas (Cabernet) reservas, and Santa Digna (alias Viña Magdala) from Pinot Noir. The family now also has vineyards in Chile and California.

Utiel-Requeña Lev. r. (w.) p.
Demarcated region w. of Valencia. Apart from sturdy reds and chewy vino de doble pasta for blending, it makes some deliciously light and fragrant rosé.

Valbuena O.Cas. r. **★★★** 75 76 77 78 79 80 82
Made with the same grapes as VEGA SICILIA but sold as 3° año or 5° año. Some prefer it to its elder brother.

Valdeorras Gal. r. w. dr. **★→★★**
Demarcated region e. of Orense. Dry and refreshing wines.

Valdepeñas N.Cas. r. (w.) **★→** **★★**
Demarcated region near the border of Andalucia. Its mainly red wines, though high in alcohol, are sometimes surprisingly light in flavour. Some superior wine is now being matured in oak.

Valencia Lev. r. w. **★**
Demarcated region producing earthy high-strength wine.

Vega Sicilia O.Cas. r. res. **★★★★** 41 48 53 59 61 64 66 67 69 72 73
One of the very best Spanish wines, full-bodied, fruity and almost impossible to find. Contains up to 16% alcohol. VALBUENA is the same wine with less time in oak (78 79 80 82).

Vendimia Vintage.

Verín Gal. r. **★**
Town near n. border of Portugal. Its wines are the strongest from Galicia, without a bubble, and up to 14% alcohol.

Vicente, Suso y Pérez, S.A. Ara. r. ★★
    A bodega s. of Saragossa producing superior CARIÑENA.

Viña Literally, a vineyard. But wines such as Tondonia (LOPEZ DE HEREDIA) or Zaco (BILBAINAS) are not necessarily made with grapes exclusively from the vineyard named.

Vinícola de Castilla N.Cas. r. p. w. dr. ★
    One of the largest firms in LA MANCHA, marketing its wines under the labels of "Castillo de Manza" and Gran Verdad.

Vino Blanco White wine.

Vino comun/corriente Ordinary wine.
    clarete Light red wine.
    dulce Sweet wine.
    espumoso Sparkling wine.
    generoso Apéritif or dessert wine rich in alcohol.
    rancio Maderized (brown) white wine.
    rosado Rosé wine.
    seco Dry wine.
    tinto Red wine.
    verde Wine akin to Portuguese VINHO VERDE.

Yecla Lev. r. w. ★
    Demarcated region n. of Murcia. Its cooperative, "La Purisima", is said to be Spain's biggest. Its wines, once heavy-weight bruisers, have been lightened for export.

Ygay See MARQUÉS DE MURRIETA

Portugal

For Port and Madeira see pages 129 to 133.

Adega A cellar or winery.

Alentejo Alen. r. ★→★★
    Vast and long-neglected area s. of the R. Tagus, now being developed as a wine region, chiefly for red wine.

Algarve Alg. r. w. ★
    Newly demarcated region in the holiday area. It wines are nothing to write home about.

Aliança, Caves r. w. dr. sp. res. ★★→★★★
    Large Bairrada-based firm, making champagne-method sparkling wines. Reds and whites include good Bairrada wines and mature DÃOS. Tinta Velha is the best-selling red in Portugal.

Amarante
    Sub-region in the VINHOS VERDES area. Rather heavier and stronger wines than those from farther n.

Arruda, Adega Cooperative de B'a. al. r. res. ★
    Vinho Tinto Arruda is a best buy. Avoid the Reserva.

Aveleda Douro dr. ★★ D.Y.A.
    A first-class VINHO VERDE made on the Aveleda estate of the Guedes family. Sold dry in Portugal but sweetened for export.

Bacalhoa, Quinta de Est'a. r. res. ★★★ 81 82 83
    American-owned estate near Setúbal, whose excellent CABERNET SAUVIGNON wine is vinified by JOÃO PIRES.

Bairrada Bei. Lit. r. w. dr. and sp. ★→ ★★ 66 70 75 76 77 82
    Recently demarcated region supplying much of Oporto's carafe wine and some excellent red GARRAFEIRAS. Also good-quality sparkling wines by the champagne method.

Barca Velha ("Ferreirinha") Trás-os-m. r. res. ★★★★ 57 64 65 66 78
    Perhaps Portugal's best red, made in very limited quantity by the port firm of FERREIRA. Powerful and fine with deep bouquet.

Barrocão, Cavas do Bei. Lit. r. w. dr. res. ★→ ★★★
    Based in the BAIRRADA, the firm blends good red DÃOS and makes first-rate old BAIRRADA garrafeiras, such as **60** and **64**.

Basto A sub-region of the VINHOS VERDES area on the R. Tamego, producing more astringent red wine than white.

Borba Alen. r. ★
Small V.Q.P.R.D. area near Evora, making some of the best wine from the ALENTEJO.

Borges & Irmão
Merchants of port and table wines at Vila Nova de Gaia. Brands incl. Gatão and (better) Gamba VINHOS VERDES. Also Fita Azul sp.

Braga Sub-region of the VINHOS VERDES area, good red and white.

Buçaco B'a.Al. r. (p.) w. res. ★★★★ r. 51 53 57 58 60 63 67 70 72 75 77; w. 56 65 66 70 72 75
The legendary speciality of the luxury Buçaco hotel near Coimbra, not seen elsewhere. Incredible quality.

Bucelas Est'a. w. dr. ★★★ 79
Tiny demarcated region just n. of Lisbon. CAVES VELHAS make delicate, perfumed wines with 11% to 12% alcohol.

Camarate Est'a. r. ★★ 74 78 80
Notable CLARETE from FONSECA at Azeitão, s. of Lisbon, incl. detectable CABERNET SAUVIGNON.

Carcavelos Est'a. br. sw. ★★★
Minute demarcated region w. of Lisbon. Its excellent sweet aperitif or dessert wines average 19% alcohol and are drunk cold.

Cartaxo Ribatejo r. w. ★
A district in the Ribatejo n. of Lisbon, now a V.Q.P.R.D. area making everyday wines popular in the capital.

Carvalho, Ribeiro & Ferreira B'a. al. r. w. des. ★★→★★★
Large merchants bottling CONDE DE SANTAR Dão and blending SERRADAYRES and other excellent RIBATEJO GARRAFEIRAS.

Casal García Douro w. dr. ★★ D.Y.A.
One of the biggest-selling VINHOS VERDES in Portugal, made by SOGRAPE.

Casal Mendes M'o. w. dr. ★★ D.Y.A.
The VINHOS VERDES from CAVES ALIANÇA.

Casaleiro Trademark of Caves Dom Teodosio-Joao T. Barbosa, who make a variety of reliable wines: DÃO, VINHOS VERDES, etc.

Caves Velhas Bei. Lit. r.w. dr. res ★★→★★★
Only maker of BUCELAS; also good DÃO and Romeira GARRAFEIRAS.

Cepa Velha M'o. (r.) w. dr. ★★★
Brand name of Vinhos de Monção, Lda. Their Alvarinho, from the grape of that name, is one of the best VINHOS VERDES.

Clarete Light red wine.

Colares Est'a. r. ★★★
Small demarcated region on the coast w. of Lisbon. Its classical dark red wines, rich in tannin, are from vines which survived the phylloxera epidemic. Drink the oldest available.

Conde de Santar B'a.al. r. (w. dr.) res. ★★→★★★ 70 73 78
The only estate-grown DÃO, later matured and sold by CARVALHO, RIBEIRO & FERREIRA. The reservas are fruity, full-bodied and exceptionally smooth.

Dão B'a.al. r. w. res. ★→ ★★★ 66 67 69 70 71 74 75 80
Demarcated region round Viseu on the R. Mondego. Produces some of Portugal's best table wines: solid reds of some subtlety with age: substantial dry whites. All are sold under brand names.

Douro The northern river whose valley produces port and more than adequate demarcated table wines.

Evelita Trás-os-m. r. ★→★★ 75
Reliable middle-weight red made near VILA REAL by Real Companhia Vinícola do Norte de Portugal. Ages well.

Faisca Est'a. p. ★
Sweet carbonated rosé from FONSECA INTERNACIONAL.

Fonseca, J. M. da Est'a. r. w. dr. br. res. `*→★★★`

Large, old-established family firm in Azeitão making a wide range of good wines, incl. the red PERIQUITA, PASMADOS and CAMARATE (formerly known as Palmela) and Terras Altas DÃO, as well as the famous MOSCATEL DE SETÚBAL.

Fonseca Internacional J.M. da Est'a p. ★

Formerly part of the last, now owned by Heublein Inc. Produces LANCERS rosé and FAISCA for the mass market.

Gaeiras Est'a. r. ★★

Dry, full-bodied and well-balanced red made near Óbidos.

Garrafeira The "private reserve" aged wine of a merchant; usually his best, though often of indeterminate origin.

Gatão M'o. w. dr. ★★ D.Y.A.

Reliable "GREEN WINE" from the firm of Borges & Irmão, fragrant but sometimes a little sweetened.

Gazala M'o. w. dr. ★★ D.Y.A.

A new VINHO VERDE made at Barcelos by SOGRAPE since the AVELEDA estate went to a different branch of the Guedes family.

Grão Vasco B'a.al. r. w. res. `*★★→★★★` `70 73 75 78` 80 81

One of the best brands of DÃO, blended and matured at Viseu by SOGRAPE. Fine red reservas; fresh young white (D.Y.A.).

Lagoa See ALGARVE.

Lagosta M'o. w. dr. ★★ D.Y.A.

Well-known VINHO VERDE from the Real Companhia Vinícola do Norte de Portugal.

Lancers Est'a. p. ★

Sweet carbonated rosé extensively shipped to the USA by FONSECA INTERNACIONAL.

Lima Sub-region in the n. of the VINHOS VERDES area making mainly astringent red wines.

Madeira Island br. dr./sw. ★★→★★★★

Source of famous aperitif and dessert wines. See pp. 129 to 132.

Magrico M'o. w. dr. `★★` D.Y.A.

Many VINHOS VERDES are slightly sweetened for export. This is a genuinely dry one.

Mateus Rosé Trás-os-m. p. (w.) ★

World's biggest-selling medium-sweet carbonated rosé, made by SOGRAPE at VILA REAL and Anadia in the BAIRRADA.

Monção

Sub-region of the VINHOS VERDES area on R. Minho, producing the best of them from the ALVARINHO grape.

Palacio de Brejoeira M'o. (r.) w. dr. ★★★

Outstanding estate-made VINHOS VERDE from MONÇÃO, with astonishing fragrant nose and full, fruity flavour.

Penafiel Sub-region in the s. of the VINHOS VERDES area.

Periquita Est'a. r. `★★` `71 74 77 78` 80

One of Portugal's most enjoyable robust reds, made by J. M. DA FONSECA at Azeitão s. of Lisbon from a grape of that name.

Pinhel B'a.al. (r.). w. sp. ★

V.Q.P.R.D. region e. of the DÃO, making similar white wine, mostly processed into sparkling.

Planalto Duoro w. dr. ★★

Good white wine from SOGRAPE.

Pires, João Est'a r. w. dr./sw. res. `*★★→★★★`

Producers of red Tinto de Anfora, white dry Moscato, Catarina CHARDONNAY and CAB. SAUV. (See Bacalhoa, Quinta de.)

Ponte de Lima, cooperativa de M'o. r. ★★

Maker of one of the best bone dry *red* VINHOS VERDES.

Quinta de S. Claudio M'o. w. dr. ★★★ D.Y.A.

Estate at Esposende and maker of some of the best VINHO VERDE outside MONÇÃO.

Quinta do Côtta Tras-os-M. r. w. dr. res. ★★ 82

>Red Grande Escolha and Q. du Côtta are dense, fruity, tannic wines that will repay long keeping. Also port.

Quinta do Corval Trás-os-m. r. ★★

>Estate near Pinhão making good light CLARETES.

Raposeira B'a.al. sp. ★★

>One of the best-known Portuguese sparkling wines, made by the champagne method at Lamego. Ask for the *Bruto*.

Ribalonga, Vinícola B'a.al. r. res. ★★ 71 74 76 78 80

>Makers of a sound and very reasonably priced red DÃO.

Ribatejo

>Region on the R. Tagus n. of Lisbon. Source of several good GARRAFEIRAS etc.

Rosado Fernandes, Viuva Alen. r. res. ★★ 71 75 79

>Small private firm, producing the most sophisticated of the full-bodied wines from the Alentejo and ageing them in oak.

Santola B'a.al. w. dr. ★★ D.Y.A.

>A refreshing dry VINHO VERDE from Vinhos Messias.

São João, Caves Bei. Lit. r. w. dr. sp. res. ★★→ ★★★ 70 75 76 78 80

>One of the best firms in the BAIRRADA, known for its fruity and full-bodied reds and Porto dos Cavaleiros DÃOS. Also fizz.

Serradayres Est'a. r. (w.) res. ★★ 78

>Blended RIBATEJO table wines from CARVALHO, RIBEIRO & FERREIRA, Lda. Sound and very drinkable.

Setúbal Est'a. br. ★★★

>Small demarcated region s. of the R. Tagus, where J.M. DA FONSECA make an aromatic dessert muscat, 6 and 25 years old.

Sogrape

>Sociedad Comercial dos Vinhos de Mesa de Portugal. Largest wine concern in the country, making VINHOS VERDES, DÃO, MATEUS ROSÉ, VILA REAL red, etc.

Terras Altas B'a.al. r. w. res. ★★ 75 76 78 79 80 81

>Good DÃO wines made by J. M. DA FONSECA.

Vila Real Trás-os-m. r. ★→ ★★

>Town in the newly demarcated DOURO region, now making some good red table wine.

Vinho branco White wine.

>**consumo** Ordinary wine.

>**doce** Sweet wine.

>**espumante** Sparkling wine.

>**garrafeira** A reserve with long bottle age.

>**generoso** Apéritif or dessert wine rich in alcohol.

>**maduro** A mature table wine — as opposed to a VINHO VERDE.

>**rosado** Rosé wine.

>**seco** Dry wine.

>**tinto** Red wine.

>**verde** See under Vinhos Verdes.

Vinhos Verdes M'o. and Douro. r. ★ w. dr. ★→★★★

>Demarcated region between R. Douro and n. frontier with Spain, producing "green wines": wine made from barely ripe grapes and undergoing a special secondary fermentation which leaves it with a slight sparkle. Ready for drinking in the spring after the harvest. It may be white or red. "Green wine" is not an official term.

Remember that vintage years generally ready for drinking in 1988 are printed in **bold type.** *Those in light type will benefit from being kept.*

Sherry, Port & Madeira

The original, classical sherries of Spain, ports of Portugal and madeiras of Madeira are listed below. References to their many imitators in South Africa, California, Australia, Cyprus, Argentina will be found under their respective countries.

The map on page 116 locates the port and sherry districts. Madeira is an island 400 miles out in the Atlantic from the coast of Morocco, a port of call for west-bound ships: hence its historical market in North America.

In this section most of the entries are shippers' names followed by a brief account of their wines. The names of wine-types are included in the alphabetical listing.

Almacenista
Individual old unblended sherry; high-quality, usually dark dry wines for connoisseurs. Often superb quality and value.

Amontillado
In general use means medium sherry; technically means a FINO which has been aged to become more powerful and pungent.

Amoroso
Type of sw. sherry, not much different from a sweet OLOROSO.

Barbadillo, Antonio
The largest SANLUCAR firm, with a range of 50-odd MANZANILLAS and sherries, incl. Sanlucar Fina, Solera Manzanilla Pasada, Eva Cream, etc. Also fresh young Castillo de San Diego table wines.

Barbeito
Shippers of good-quality Madeira, including one of the driest and best aperitif Madeiras "Island Dry".

Bertola Sherry shippers, best known for their Bertola Cream Sherry.

Blandy Old family firm of Madeira shippers. Duke of Clarence Malmsey is their most famous wine. 10-y-o Malmsey v. popular.

Blazquez
Sherry bodega at JEREZ with outstanding FINO, "Carta Blanca", and "Carta Oro" amontillado "al natural" (unsweetened).

Brown sherry British term for a style of dark sweet sherry.

Bual One of the best grapes of Madeira, making a soft smoky sweet wine, not as sweet as Malmsey.

Caballero
Sherry shippers best known for Gran Señor Choice Old Cream. Their best FINO is Don Guisa.

Calem Old Portuguese house with a good reputation, owning the excellent Quinta da Foz. Vintages: **50** 58 **60 63** 70 **75** 77 78 83. Adequate light tawny.

Cockburn
British-owned port shippers with a range of good wines incl. 20-y-o "Directors' Reserve". Fine vintage port from very high v'yds. can look deceptively light when young, but has great lasting power. Vintages: **55 60 63 67** 70 **75** 83 85.

Cossart Gordon
Leading firm of Madeira shippers founded 1745, best known for their "Good Company" range of wines but also producing old vintages (latest, 1952) and soleras (esp. v.g. Sercial Duo Centenary).

Cream sherry
A style of amber sweet sherry made by sweetening a blend of well-aged OLOROSOS.

Crofts One of the oldest firms shipping vintage port: 300 years old in 1978. Bought early this century by Gilbey's. Well-balanced vintage wines last as long as any. Vintages: **55 60 63 66** 70 **75** 77, and lighter vintage wines under the name of their Quinta da Roeda in several other years ('80). Also now in the sherry business with Croft Original (PALE CREAM), Delicado (FINO).

Crusted

Term for a vintage-style port, but blended from several vintages not one, bottled young and aged in bottle, so forming a "crust" in the bottle. Needs decanting.

Cuvillo

Sherry bodega at Puerto de Santa Maria best known for their Cream, dry Oloroso Sangre y Trabajadero and Fino "C" and a fine PALO CORTADO.

Delaforce

Port shippers owned by I.D.V., particularly well known in Germany. "His Eminence" is an excellent tawny. "Vintage Character" is also good. Vintage wines are very fine, among the lighter kind: **55 58 60 63 66** 70 75 77. "Quinta da Corte" in 1980.

Diez-Merito S.A.

Fast-growing JEREZ firm specializing in "own-brand" sherries. Latest acquisition is Zoilo Ruiz Mateus, formerly part of the ill-fated Rumasa empire. Its own Fino Imperial and Oloroso Victoria Regina are excellent. DON ZOILO wines are outstanding.

Domecq

Giant family-owned sherry bodegas at JEREZ. Double Century Original Oloroso is their biggest brand, La Ina their excellent FINO, Guitar a new pale cream. Other famous wines incl. Celebration Cream, Botaina (old amontillado) and Rio Viejo (dry oloroso). Now also in Rioja (p. 123).

Don Zoilo

Luxury sherries, incl. deep velvety FINO, sold by DIEZ-MERITO.

Dow

Old name used on the British market by the port shippers Silva & Cosens, well known for their relatively dry vintage wines, said to have a faint "cedarwood" character. Also v.g. "Vintage Character". Vintages: **55 58 60 63 66** 70 **75** 77 80 83. Dow, WARRE, GRAHAM, GOULD CAMPBELL, QUARLES HARRIS and SMITH WOODHOUSE all belong to the Symington family.

Dry Sack See Williams & Humbert

Duff Gordon

Sherry shippers best known for their El Cid AMONTILLADO. Owned by the big Spanish firm Bodegas Osborne.

Duke of Wellington

Luxury range of sherries from Bodegas Internacionales.

Eira Velha, Quinta da

Small port estate with old-style vintage wines shipped by HARVEY's of Bristol. Vintages: **72** 78 80 82.

Ferreira

The biggest Portuguese-owned port growers and shippers (since 1751); well-known for old tawnies and good, relatively light, vintages: **60 63 66 70 75** 77 80 83. Also Special Reserve, Donna Antonia and sublime tawny Duque de Braganza.

Findlater's

Old established London wine merchant shipping his own very successful brand of medium sherry: Dry Fly amontillado.

Fino

Term for the lightest and finest of sherries, completely dry, very pale and with great delicacy. Fino should always be drunk cool and fresh: it deteriorates rapidly once opened. TIO PEPE is the classic example.

Flor The characteristic natural yeast which gives FINO sherry its unique flavour.

Fonseca

British-owned port shipper of high reputation, connected with TAYLOR. Robust, deeply coloured vintage wine, sometimes said to have a slight "burnt" flavour. Vintages: **55 60 63 66** 70 75 77 83. Also popular Vintage Character "Bin 27".

Garvey's

Famous old sherry shippers at JEREZ. Their finest wines are Fino San Patricio, Tio Guillermo Dry Amontillado and Ochavico Dry Oloroso. San Angelo Medium Amontillado is their most popular. Also Bicentenary Pale Cream.

Gonzalez Byass

Enormous concern shipping the world's most famous and one of the best sherries: Tio Pepe. Other brands incl. La Concha Medium Amontillado, Elegante Dry Fino, San Domingo Pale Cream, Nectar Cream and Alfonso Dry Oloroso.

Gould Campbell   See Smith Woodhouse.

Graham

Port shippers famous for one of the richest and sweetest of vintage ports, largely from their own Quinta Malvedos, also excellent brands, incl. Ruby, Late Bottled 10- and 20-year-old Tawny. Vintages: **55 58 60 63 66** 70 **75** 77 80.

Harvey's

Probably the largest sherry firm, having recently bought PALOMINO and DE TERRY. World-famous Bristol shippers of Bristol Cream and Bristol Milk sweet sherries, Club Amontillado and Bristol Dry, which are medium. Luncheon Dry and Bristol Fino, which are dry, and excellent Palo Cortado. Also a sound new range: "1796".

Henriques & Henriques

Well-known Madeira shippers of Funchal. Their wide range includes a good dry apéritif wine: Ribeiro Seco.

Jerez de la Frontera

Centre of the sherry industry, between Cadiz and Seville in s. Spain. The word sherry is a corruption of the name, pronounced in Spanish "Hereth". In French, Xérés.

Late-bottled vintage

Port of a single vintage kept in wood for twice as long as vintage port (about 5 years). Therefore lighter when bottled and ageing quicker. A real "L.B.V." will "throw a crust" like vintage port.

Leacock

One of the oldest Madeira shippers. Most famous wine is "Penny Black" Malmsey. 10-y-o Malmsey and 13-y-o Bual are excellent.

Lustau

The largest independent family-owned sherry bodega in JEREZ, making many wines for other shippers, but with a very good "Dry Lustau" range (particularly the OLOROSO) and "Jerez Lustau" PALO CORTADO. Also shippers of excellent ALMACENISTA wines.

Macharnudo

One of the best parts of the sherry v'yds., n. of Jerez, famous for wines of the highest quality, both FINO and OLOROSO.

Malmsey

The sweetest form of Madeira; dark amber, rich and honeyed yet with Madeira's unique sharp tang.

Manzanilla

Sherry, normally FINO, which has acquired a peculiar bracing salty character from being kept in bodegas at Sanlucar de Barrameda, on the Guadalquivir estuary near JEREZ.

Morgan   A subsidiary of Croft port, best known in France.

Offley Forester

Port shippers and owners of the famous Quinta Boa Vista. Their vintage wines tend to be round, "fat" and sweet, good for relatively early drinking. Vintages: **60 62 63 66 67 70 72 75** 77 83.

Oloroso

Style of sherry, heavier and less brilliant than FINO when young, but maturing to greater richness and roundness. Naturally dry, but generally sweetened for sale, as CREAM.

Osborne

Brandy well known, but good sherries include Fino Quinta, Coquinero, dry AMONTILLADO, 10 R.S. Oloroso.

Pale Cream

Increasingly popular style of sherry made by sweetening FINO, pioneered by CROFTS.

Palo Cortado

A style of sherry close to OLOROSO but with some of the character of an AMONTILLADO. Dry but rich and soft. Not often seen.

Palomino & Vergara

Sherry shippers of JEREZ bought in 1986 by HARVEYS, best known for Palomino Cream, Medium and Dry. Best FINO: Tio Mateo.

Puerto de Santa Maria

Second city of the sherry area, with important bodegas.

P.X. Short for Pedro Ximenez, the grape part-dried in the sun used in JEREZ for sweetening blends.

Quarles Harris

One of the oldest port houses, since 1680, now owned by the Symingtons (see DOW). Vintages: **60 63** 66 70 **75** 77 80 83.

Quinta Portuguese for "estate".

Quinta do Noval

Great Portuguese port house making splendidly dark, rich and full-bodied vintage port; a few pre-phylloxera vines still at the Quinta make a small quantity of "Nacional"—very dark, full and slow-maturing wine. Vintages: **55 58 60 63 66** 70 **75** 78 82.

Rainwater A fairly light, not very sweet blend of Madeira—in fact of VERDELHO wine—traditionally popular in N. America.

Real Tesoro, Marques de

One of the smaller family firms of JEREZ, with excellent MANZANILLA La Bailadora and a range of good sherries, esp. their AMONTILLADO.

Rebello Valente

Name used for the vintage port of ROBERTSON. Their vintage wines are light but elegant and well-balanced, maturing rather early. Vintages: **55 60 63 66 67** 70 **75** 77.

La Riva

Distinguished firm of sherry shippers making one of the best FINOS, Tres Palmas, among many good wines.

Robertson

Subsidiary of SANDEMAN'S, shipping REBELLO VALENTE vintage port and Gamebird Tawny and Ruby.

Rozes Port shippers controlled by Moët-Hennessy. Tawny very popular in France; also Ruby and **77**.

Ruby The youngest (and cheapest) style of port: very sweet and red. The best are vigorous and full of flavour. Others can be merely strong and rather thin.

Rutherford & Miles

Madeira shippers with one of the best known of all Bual wines: Old Trinity House.

Sanchez Romate

Family firm since 1781. Best known in Spanish-speaking world esp. for their brandy, Cardinal Mendoza. Makes good sherry—Fino Cristal, Oloroso Dona Juana, Amontillado N.P.U.

Sandeman

Giant of the port trade and a major figure in the sherry one owned by Seagrams. Founder's Reserve is their best-known tawny port; their vintage wines are robust—some of the old vintages were superlative [**55 58 60 63 66 67** 70 **75** 77 80 82 83]. Of the sherries, Medium Dry Amontillado is best-seller, Don Fino is v.g. and a new range of wonderful luxury sherries incl. Royal Ambrosante, Imperial Corregidor, Character Amoroso, etc.

Sanlucar Seaside sherry-town (see MANZANILLA).

Sercial Grape (reputedly a RIESLING) grown in Madeira to make the driest of the island's wines—a good apéritif.

Smith Woodhouse

Port firm founded in 1784, now owned by the Symington family (see DOW). GOULD CAMPBELL is a subsidiary. Wines incl. Old Priory Vintage Character, Old Lodge Tawny, 70 **75** 77 80 83.

Solera System used in making both sherry and Madeira, also some port. It consists of topping up progressively more mature barrels with slightly younger wine of the same sort: the object to attain continuity in the final wine. Most commercial sherries are blends of several solera wines.

Tarquinio Lomelino

Madeira shippers famous for their collection of antique wines. Standard range is Dom Henriques; top range, "Lomelino".

Tawny A style of port aged for many years in wood (in contrast to vintage port, which is aged in bottle) until tawny in colour.

Taylor Perhaps the best port shippers, particularly for their full, rich, long-lived vintage wine and tawnies of stated age (40-year-old, 20-year-old, etc.). Their Quinta de Vargellas is said to give Taylor's its distinctive scent of violets. Vintages: **55 60** 63 66 70 75 77 80 83. Vargellas is shipped unblended in certain (lesser) vintages (**67 72 74**). Their L.B.V. is also better than most.

De Terry, Carlos y Javier

Bodega at PUERTO DE SANTA MARIA with a good range of sherries, bought in 1986 by HARVEYS.

Tio Pepe The most famous of FINO sherries (see GONZALEZ BYASS).

Valdespino

Famous family-owned bodega at JEREZ, owner of the Inocente v'yd., making the excellent FINO of the same name. Tio Diego is their splendid dry AMONTILLADO, Solera 1842 a ditto oloroso, Matador the name of their popular range.

Varela Sherry shippers best known for their Medium and Cream.

Verdelho Madeira grape making fairly dry wine without the distinction of SERCIAL. A pleasant aperitif. Some fine old vintage wines.

Vintage Port

The best port of exceptional vintages is bottled after only 2 years in wood and matures very slowly, for up to 20 years or even more, in its bottle. It always leaves a heavy deposit and therefore needs decanting.

Vintage Character

Somewhat misleading term used for a good-quality full and meaty port like a first-class RUBY made by the solera system. Lacks the splendid "nose" of vintage port.

Warre Probably the oldest of all port shippers (since 1670), now owned by the Symington family (see DOW). Fine long-maturing vintage wines, Nimrod and Vintage Character Warrior. Vintages: **55 58 60** 63 **66** 70 75 77 80 83.

White Port

Port made of white grapes, golden in colour. Formerly made sweet, now more often dry: a good apéritif but a heavy one.

Williams & Humbert

Famous and first-class sherry bodega. Dry Sack (medium AMONTILLADO) is their best-selling wine. Pando is an excellent FINO. Canasta Cream and Walnut Brown are good in their class. Dos Cortados is their famous PALO CORTADO.

An excellent 1985 vintage for port was declared by many shippers in summer 1987.

Asia & North Africa

Algeria The massive v'yds. of Algeria have dwindled in the last ten years from 860,000 acres to under 500,000. Red, rosé and white wines of some quality are made in the coastal hills of Tlemcen, Mascara, Haut-Dahra, Zaccar and Ain-Bessem. Most goes for blending.

China Germans and Russians started making wine on the Shantung (now Shandong) peninsula in the early 1900s. Since 1980 a modern industry, initiated by Rémy Martin, has produced the adequate white Dynasty and Tsingtao wines, and plantings in Shandong and Tianjin, further north, promise more interest.

India In 1985 a Franco-Indian firm launched a sparkling wine, Royal Mousseux, made at Narayangaon, s.e. of Bombay. Plans are to export up to 2m. bottles.

Israel Israeli wine, since the industry was re-established by a Rothschild in the 1880s, has been primarily of Kosher interest until recently, when CABERNET, SAUVIGNON BLANC, SEMILLON, PETITE SIRAH and GRENACHE of fair quality have been introduced. Carmel is the principal brand. Galilee and Samson are two areas producing superior reds.

Japan Japan has a small wine industry in Yamanashi Prefecture, w. of Tokyo. Wines are here blended with imports from Argentina, E. Europe, etc. Premium wines of SEMILLON, CABERNET and the local white grape, Koshu, are light but can be good, though expensive. The main producers are Suntory, Mercian, Mann's. In 1985 tainted Austrian wine was discovered being sold as Japanese by a major company. Regrettably, Japanese labelling laws are so lax that misrepresentation of imported wines as "Japanese" is the rule rather than the exception.

Lebanon The small Lebanese wine industry, based on Ksara in the Bekaa valley n.e. of Beirut, has made red wine of real vigour and quality. Château Musar (★★★) produces splendid matured reds, largely of CABERNET SAUVIGNON.

Morocco Morocco today makes North Africa's best wine from v'yds. along the Atlantic coast and round Meknes. In ten years the v'yds. have declined from 190,000 to 54,000 acres. Chante Bled and Tarik are the best reds, Gris de Guerrouane a very pale dry rosé. In Morocco they sell as Les Trois Domaines.

Tunisia Tunisia now has 75,000 acres compared with 120,000 ten years ago. Her speciality is sweet muscat, but reasonable reds and rosés come from Carthage, Mornag and Cap Bon.

Turkey Most of Turkey's huge v'yds. produce table grapes. But her wines, from Thrace, Anatolia and the Aegean, are remarkably good. Trakya (Thrace) white and Buzbag (Anatolian) red are the well-known standards of the State wineries. Doluca and Kavaklidere are private firms of good quality. Villa Doluca red from Thrace is very well made. Buzbag is a bargain.

USSR With over 3 million acres of v'yds. the USSR is the world's fourth-biggest wine-producer — almost entirely for home consumption. Ukraine (incl. the Crimea) is the biggest v'yd. republic, followed by Moldavia, the Russian Republic and Georgia. The Soviet consumer has a sweet tooth, for both table and dessert wines. Of the latter the best come from the Crimea (esp. Massandra). Moldavia and Ukraine use the same grapes as Romania, plus CABERNET, RIESLING, PINOT GRIS, etc. The Russian Republic makes the best Rieslings (Arbau, Beshtau, Anapa) and sweet sparkling Tsimlanskoye "Champanski". Georgia uses mainly traditional grapes (esp. white Tsinandali and red Mukuzani) for the best table wines of the USSR.

Central & South-east Europe

Weinviertel
Langenlois
Wachau • Vienna
Mátraa
Somló
Sopron • Buda
Burgenland
AUSTRIA Graz • Balaton HUNGARY
Styria
Lutomer
Vilanyi-Pecs
Ljubljana • Slavonia
Slovenia Vojvod
Trieste Zagreb
Croatia
Bosnia-Herzegovina
Dalmatia YUGOSLAVIA
Split • Sarajevo
Monte
Dubrovnik

Co

The countries covered by this map, on both sides of the Iron
Curtain, offer some very good value for money, complete with
off-the-beaten-track characters which true wine-lovers will
enjoy exploring. Quality is moderate to high, tending to
improve, and pretty consistent, if rarely exciting.

The references are arranged country by country, with all
geographical references back to the map on this page.

Labelling in all the countries involved except Greece and
Cyprus is broadly based on the German, now international,
pattern of place-name plus grape-variety. The main grape-
varieties are therefore included alongside areas and other terms
in the alphabetical listings. Quality ratings in this section are
given where experience justifies more than a single, everyday,
star.

Austria

In 1986-7 the Austrian wine industry has been struggling to recover from its scandal of 1985, when diethylene glycol was found in wines claiming high natural sweetness, particularly from the Burgenland. Although nobody was poisoned, enormous damage was done to many innocent and well-run businesses. New legislation should now ensure that nothing of the kind happens again. Meanwhile, Austria offers (as it did before) very good value in fresh, fruity dry wines and succulent sweet ones.

Recent vintages:
1986	An outstanding vintage in most cases.
1985	A small but excellent-quality harvest.
1984	Good wines for early drinking.
1983	Outstandingly ripe; many sweet wines though some are low in acidity.
1982	Early harvest of record size, fewer sweet wines.
1981	Small crop, quality high, esp. sweet wines.

Apetlon Burgenland w. s./sw. or sw. ★→ **★★**
> Village of the SEEWINKEL making tasty whites on sandy soil, incl. very good sweet wines, esp. from LENZ MOSER.

Ausbruch
> Term used for very sweet wines between Beerenauslese and Trockenbeerenauslese (see Germany) in richness.

Baden Vienna (r.) w. dr. or sw. ★→★★★
> Town and area s. of VIENNA incl. GUMPOLDSKIRCHEN. Some good lively high-flavoured wines, whites best from ROTGIPFLER and ZIERFÄNDLER grapes.

Blaufränkisch
> Reputedly the GAMAY grape; gives adequate reds. Kékfrankos in Hungary.

Blue Danube
> Popular GEWÜRZ/WÄLSCHRIESLING blend from LENZ MOSER.

Bouvier Native Austrian grape giving soft but aromatic wine.

Burgenland Burgenland r. w. dr. sw. ★→ **★★★**
> Region on the Hungarian border with ideal conditions for sweet wines. "Noble rot" occurs regularly and AUSBRUCH, Beerenausleses, etc., are abundant. (See Oggau, Rust, etc.)

Dürnstein w. dr. sw. ★★→★★★
> Wine centre of the WACHAU with a famous ruined castle and important WINZERGENOSSENSCHAFT. Some of Austria's best whites, esp. Rheinriesling and GRÜNER VELTLINER.

Eisenstadt Burgenland (r.) w. dr. or sw. ★★→★★★
> Town in BURGENLAND and historic seat of the ESTERHAZYS.

Esterhazy
> Noble and historic family (patrons of Haydn) whose AUSBRUCH and other BURGENLAND wines are often of superlative quality.

Falkenstein See Weinviertel.

Grinzing Vienna w. ★★ D.Y.A.
> Suburb of VIENNA with delicious lively HEURIGE wines.

Grüner Veltliner
> Austria's most characteristic white grape (32% of her white v'yds.) making short-lived but marvellously spicy and flowery, racy and vital wine—ideal HEURIGE, in fact.

Gumpoldskirchen Vienna (r.) w. dr. or sw. ★★→★★★
> Pretty resort s. of VIENNA with wines of great character from ROTGIPFLER and ZIERFÄNDLER grapes.

Heiligenkreuz, Stift
> Cistercian Monastery at THALLERN making some of Austria's best wine, particularly RIESLING from a fine steep v'yd.: Wiege.

Heurige Means both new wine and the tavern where it is drunk.

Kahlenberg Vienna w. ★★
Village and v'yd. hill n. of VIENNA, famous for HEURIGEN.

Kamp Langenlois (r.) w. dr. or sw. ★→★★
Tributary of the Danube (Donau) giving its name to wines from its valley, n. and e. of the WACHAU, incl. pleasant Veltliner (see Grüner Veltliner) and RIESLING.

Klöch Steiermark (r.) p. w. ★→★★
The chief wine town of Styria, the s.e. province. No famous wines, but several agreeable ones, esp. Traminer.

Klosterneuburg Danube r. w. ★→★★★
District just n. of VIENNA, with a famous monastery, which is a major producer, a wine college and a research station.

Krems Danube w. ★→★★★
Town and district just e. of the WACHAU with good GRÜNER VELTLINER and Rheinriesling (see Riesling) esp. from Austria's biggest WINZERGENOSSENSCHAFT.

Langenlois Langenlois r. w. ★→★★
Chief town of the KAMP valley with many modest and some good wines, esp. peppery GRÜNER VELTLINER and Rheinriesling (see Riesling) from its loess soil. Reds less interesting.

Lenz Moser
Austria's best known and most progressive grower, invented a high vine system and makes good to excellent wine at Röhrendorf near KREMS, APETLON, MAILBERG and elsewhere.

Mailberg Weinviertel w. ★★
Town of the WEINVIERTEL known for lively light wine, esp. LENZ MOSER's Malteser.

Morandell, Alois
Big-scale Viennese wine-merchant.

Mörbisch Burgenland r. w. dr. or sw. ★→ ★★★
Leading wine-village of BURGENLAND. Good sweet wines. Reds and dry whites not inspiring.

Müller-Thurgau
Far less interesting than GRÜNER VELTLINER, but nonetheless 10% of all Austria's vines.

Muskat-Ottonel
The strain of muscat grape grown in e. Europe, incl. Austria.

Niederösterreich
Lower Austria: i.e. all the n.e. corner of the country.

Neuberger
Popular white grape: pleasant wine in KREMS/LANGENLOIS but soft and coarse in BURGENLAND.

Neusiedlersee
A broad shallow lake in flat sandy country on the Hungarian border, creating autumn mists and giving character to the sweet wines of BURGENLAND.

Nussdorf Vienna w. ★★
Suburb of VIENNA with well-known HEURIGEN.

Oggau Burgenland w. sw. ★→ ★★★
One of the wine-centres of BURGENLAND, famous for Beerenausleses (see Germany) and AUSBRUCH.

Portugieser
With BLAUFRÄNKISCH, one of the two main red-wine grapes of Austria, giving dark but rather characterless wine.

Retz Weinviertel (r.) w. ★
Leading wine-centre of the WEINVIERTEL, known for pleasant GRÜNER VELTLINER, etc.

Ried Vineyard: when named on the label it is usually a good one.

Riesling
German Riesling is always called Rheinriesling. "Riesling" is Wälschriesling, and always inferior.

Rotgipfler

Good and high-flavoured grape peculiar to BADEN and GUMPOLDSKIRCHEN. Used with ZIERFÄNDLER to make powerful but lively whites. Very heavy/sweet on its own.

Rust Burgenland (r.) w. dr. or sw. ★→★★★

Most famous wine centre of BURGENLAND, long and justly famous for its AUSBRUCH, often made of mixed grapes.

St. Laurent

Traditional Austrian red grape, faintly muscat-flavoured.

Schilcher

Pleasant sharp rosé, a speciality of STYRIA.

Schloss Grafenegg

Famous castle and estate of the Metternich family near KREMS. Good standard whites and excellent Ausleses.

Schluck

Name for the common white wine of the WACHAU, good when drunk very young. Also a good brand of GRÜNER VELTLINER from LENZ MOSER.

Seewinkel

"Sea corner": the sandy district around the NEUSIEDLERSEE.

Sepp Hold

Well-known BURGENLAND grower and merchant.

Siegendorf, Klosterkeller

First-class private BURGENLAND wine estate.

Sievering Vienna w. ★★

Picturesque suburb of VIENNA with notable HEURIGEN.

Spätrot Another name for the ZIERFÄNDLER grape.

Spitzenwein

Top wines—as opposed to TISCHWEIN: ordinary table wines.

Steiermark (Styria)

Province in the s.e., not remarkable for wine but well-supplied with it. See KLÖCH.

Stift The word for a monastery. Monasteries have been, and still are, very important in Austria's wine-making, combining tradition and high standards with modern resources.

Thallern Vienna (r.) w. dr. or sw. ★★→★★★

Village near GUMPOLDSKIRCHEN and trade-name of wines from Stift HEILIGENKREUZ.

Tischwein

Everyday wine, as opposed to SPITZENWEIN.

Traiskirchen Vienna (r.) w. ★★

Village near GUMPOLDSKIRCHEN with similar wine.

Veltliner See Grüner Veltliner

Vöslau Baden r. (w.) ★

Spa town s. of BADEN (and WIEN) known for its reds made of PORTUGIESER and BLAUFRÄNKISCH: refreshing but no more.

Wachau

District on the n. bank of the Danube round DÜRNSTEIN with cliff-like slopes giving some of Austria's best whites, esp. Rheinriesling (see Riesling) and GRÜNER VELTLINER.

Weinviertel

"The wine quarter": name given to the huge and productive district between VIENNA and the Czech border. Mainly light white wines. Now officially divided into Falkenstein – Matzen (east) and Retz (west).

Wien (Vienna)

The capital city, with 1,800 acres of v'yds. in its suburbs to supply its cafés and HEURIGEN.

Winzergenossenschaft Growers' cooperative.

Zierfändler

White grape of high flavour peculiar to the BADEN area. Used in a blend with ROTGIPFLER.

Hungary

The traditional and characteristic firmness and strength of character which can make Hungarian wine the most exciting of Eastern Europe have been modified by modern ideas. Average quality is still high; whites are lively and reds made to last, but much of the drama has gone—at least from the standard exported lines. Foreign buyers seem frightened of real character. Visitors to the country will find plenty of excellent wines in the old style. They are distinguished by numbered bottles – and higher prices.

Alföld

Hungary's Great Plain, producer of much everyday wine. See also HAJÓS.

Aszu

Word meaning "syrupy" applied to very sweet wines, esp. Tokay (TOKAJI), where the "aszu" is late-picked and "nobly rotten" as in Sauternes. (See p. 46.)

Aszu Eszencia Tokaji br. sw. ★★★★

The highest quality of Tokay commercially available: superb amber wine of Yquem-like quality.

Badacsony Balaton br. dr. sw. │★★→★★★│

Famous 1,400 ft. hill on the n. shore of L. BALATON whose basalt soil can give rich high-flavoured wines, among Hungary's best.

Balatonfüred Balaton (r.) w. dr. sw. ★★

Town on the n. shore of L. BALATON centre of the Balatonfüred-Csopak district. Good but softer, less fiery wines.

Balaton Balaton r. w. dr. sw. │★│ →★★★

Hungary's inland sea and Europe's largest lake. Many wines take its name and most are good. The ending "i" (e.g. Balatoni, Egri) is the equivalent of -er in Londoner.

Bikavér Eger r. ★

"Bull's Blood"—or words to that effect. The historic name of the best-selling red wine of EGER: formerly full-bodied and well-balanced, but much less impressive in its export version today.

Chardonnay

Experiments with Chardonnay at BALATON show promise.

Csopak

Village next to BALATONFÜRED, with similar wines.

Debrö Mátraalya w. sw. ★★

Important centre of the MÁTRAALYA famous for its pale, aromatic and sweet HÁRSLEVELÜ.

Eger Eger district r. w. dr. sw. ★★

Best-known red wine centre of n. Hungary; fine baroque city of cellars full of BIKAVÉR. Also delicate white LEANYKA (perhaps its best product today) and dark sweetish MÉDOC NOIR.

Eszencia

The fabulous quintessence of Tokay (TOKAJI): intensely sweet grape-juice of very low, if any, alcoholic strength, reputed to have miraculous properties. Now almost unobtainable.

Ezerjó The grape grown at MÖR to make one of Hungary's best dry white wines: potentially distinguished, fragrant and fine.

Furmint

The classic grape of Tokay (TOKAJI), with great flavour and fire, also grown for table wine on L. BALATON, sometimes with excellent results.

Hajós Alföld r. │★│

Village in s. Hungary becoming known as a centre for good lively CABERNET SAUVIGNON reds of medium body.

Hárslevelü

The "lime-leaved" grape used at DEBRÖ and as the second main grape of TOKAJI. Gentle sweet wine.

Kadarka

The commonest red grape of Hungary, grown in vast quantities for everyday wine on the plains in the s.; capable (e.g. at SZEKSZÁRDI and VILÁNY) of ample flavour and interesting maturity.

Kékfrankos

Hungarian for Blaufränkisch; reputedly Gamay. Makes good light red at SOPRON on the Austrian border but poor "Bull's Blood" at EGER.

Kéknyelü

High-flavoured white grape making the best and "stiffest" wine of Mt. BADACSONY. It should be fiery and spicy stuff.

Leanyka

Old Hungarian white grape also grown in Transylvania. Makes admirable pale soft wine at EGER.

Mátraalya

Wine-district in the foothills of the Matra range in n. Hungary, incl. DEBRÖ, GYÖNGYÖS and NAGYREDE.

Mecsekalja

District in the foothills of the Mecsek range in s. Hungary, known for the good whites of PÉCS.

Médoc Noir

Grape apparently similar to MERLOT, used to make sweet red and in the blend of BIKAVER, at EGER.

Monimpex

The main Hungarian export company, with great cellars at Budafok, near Budapest.

Mór North Hungary w. dr. ★★★

Town in n. Hungary famous for its fresh dry EZERJÓ.

Muskotály

Hungarian muscat, used to add aroma to Tokay (TOKAJI) and occasionally alone at EGER, where its wine is long-lived and worth tasting.

Nagyburgundi

Literally "black burgundy" — the PINOT NOIR makes sound solid wine in s. Hungary, esp. round VILÁNY and SZEKSZÁRDI.

Olaszriesling

The Hungarian name for the Italian, or Wälschriesling.

Pécs Mecsek (r.) w. dr. ★ → ★★

Town in the Mecsek hills known in the West for its agreeable well-balanced (if rather sweet) Riesling.

Puttonyos

The measure of sweetness in Tokay (TOKAJI). A 7-gal. container from which ASZU is added to SZAMORODNI. One "putt" makes it sweetish; 6 (the maximum) very sweet indeed.

Sauvignon Blanc

Recent results at BALATON have been impressive — with plenty of Hungarian vigour.

Siklos Southern district known for its white wines.

Siller Pale red or rosé. Usually made from KADARKA grapes.

Somló North Hungary w. dr. ★★

Isolated small v'yd. district n. of BALATON making white wines formerly of high repute from FURMINT and RIESLING.

Sopron West Hungary r. ★★

Little Hungarian enclave in Burgenland s. of the Neusiedlersee (see Austria) specializing in light KÉKFRANKOS red.

Szamorodni

Word meaning "as it comes"; used to describe (TOKAJI) without ASZU grapes. Can be dry or (fairly) sweet.

Szürkebarát
> Literally means "grey friar": Hungarian for PINOT GRIS, which makes rich heavy wine in the BALATON v'yds.

Szekszárdi Mecsek r. **★★**
> District in south-central Hungary. Dark strong KADARKA red wine which needs age.

Tokaji (Tokay) Tokaji w. dr. sw. **★★** →**★★★★**
> Hungary's famous strong sweet wine, comparable to an oxidized Sauternes, from hills in the n.e. close to the Soviet Union. See Aszu, Eszencia, Furmint, Puttonyos, Szamorodni.

Tramini The TRAMINER grape; increasingly grown in Hungary.

Vilány Siklos r. p. (w.) **★★**
> Southernmost town of Hungary and well-known centre of red wine production. Vilányi Burgundi is largely KÉKFRANKOS and rather good. See also NAGYBURGUNDI.

Wälschriesling
> Austrian name sometimes used for Olasz (Italian) Riesling.

Zöldszilváni
> "Green Sylvaner" —i.e. Sylvaner. Grown round L. BALATON.

Romania

The wine industry is orientated towards Russia as its biggest customer, and consequently specializes in the sweet wines that Russians like. Recent Soviet moves to discourage drinking threaten this trade. The need for foreign currency makes export to the West highly desirable, so the best qualities are available at subsidized prices. They include sound and cheap reds and whites, including dry ones, but at present nothing memorable.

Alba Iulia
> Town in the TIRNAVE area in Transylvania, known for off-dry whites blended from Italian Riesling, FETEASCA and MUSKAT-OTTONEL.

Aligoté The junior white burgundy grape makes pleasantly fresh white wine in Romania.

Babeasca
> Traditional red grape of the FOCSANI area: agreeably sharp wine tasting slightly of cloves.

Banat The plain on the border with Serbia. Workaday Riesling and light red CADARCA.

Cabernet
> Increasingly grown in Romania, particularly at DEALUL MARE, to make dark intense wines, though generally too sweet for Western palates.

Cadarca
> Romanian spelling of the Hungarian Kadarka.

Chardonnay
> The great white burgundy grape is used at MURFATLAR to make honey-sweet dessert wine.

Cotesti
> Part of the FOCSANI area making reds of PINOT NOIR, MERLOT, etc., and dry whites claimed to resemble Alsace wines.

Cotnari
> Romania's most famous historical wine: light dessert wine from MOLDAVIA. Rather like very delicate Tokay.

Dealul Mare
> Important up-to-date v'yd. area in the s.e. Carpathian foothills. Red wines from CABERNET, MERLOT, PINOT NOIR, etc.

Dobruja

>Black Sea region round the port of Constanta. MURFATLAR is the main v'yd. area.

Dragasani

>Region on the River Olt south of the Carpathians, growing both traditional and "modern" grapes. Good MUSKAT-OTTONEL.

Feteasca

>Romanian white grape of mild character, the same as Hungary's Leanyka (and some say Switzerland's Chasselas).

Focsani

>Important eastern wine region including those of COTESTI, ODOBESTI and NICORESTI.

Grasa A form of the Hungarian Furmint grape grown in Romania and used in, among other wines, COTNARI.

Mehana Branded wines shipped to Britain, tending to sweetness.

Moldavia The n.e. province, now largely within the USSR.

Murfatlar

>Big modern v'yds. near the Black Sea specializing in sweet wines, incl. CHARDONNAY. Now also dry reds and whites.

Muskat-Ottonel

>The e. European muscat, at its best in Romania.

Nicoresti

>Eastern area of FOCSANI best known for its red BABEASCA.

Odobesti

>The central part of FOCSANI; mainly white wines of FETEASCA, RIESLING, etc.

Perla The speciality of TÎRNAVE: a pleasant blended semi-sweet white of RIESLING, FETEASCA and MUSKAT-OTTONEL.

Pitesti Principal town of the Arges region south of the Carpathians. Traditionally whites from FETEASCA, TAMÎIOASA, RIESLING.

Premiat Reliable range of higher-quality wines for export.

Riesling

>Italian Riesling. Very widely planted. No exceptional wines.

Sadova Town in the SEGARCEA area exporting a rosé.

Segarcea

>S. wine area near the Danube. Exports rather sweet CAB.

Tamîioasa A traditional white-wine grape variety of no very distinct character.

Tîrnave

>Important Transylvanian wine region, known for its PERLA and MUSKAT-OTTONEL.

Trakia

>Branded wines that are shipped to U.S.A. Better judged for Western palates than other Romanian wines.

Valea Calugareasca

>"The Valley of the Monks", part of the DEALUL MARE v'yd. with a well-known research station. CABERNET, MERLOT and PINOT NOIR are generally made into heavy sweetish wines.

Yugoslavia

A well-established supplier of wines of international calibre if not generally exciting quality. Yugoslav "Riesling" was the pioneer, now followed by Cabernet, Pinot Blanc and Traminer, as well as such worthwhile specialities as Zilavka, Plavać and Prokupac. All parts of the country except the central highlands make wine, almost entirely in giant cooperatives. Tourists on the Dalmatian coast and in Macedonia will find more original products—all well worth trying. 1985 was a very good vintage.

Amselfelder
>   German marketing name for the Red Burgundac (Spätburgunder or PINOT NOIR) wine of KOSOVO. Disagreeably sweet.

Babic Agreeable standard red of the Dalmatian coast, ages better than ordinary PLAVAĆ.

Banat Sandy north-eastern area, partly in Romania, with up-to-date wineries making adequate RIESLING.

Beli Pinot The PINOT BLANC, a popular grape in SLOVENIA.

Bijelo White.

Blatina
>   The red grape and wine of MOSTAR. Not in the same class as the white ZILAVKA.

Bogdanusa
>   Local white grape of the Dalmatian islands, esp. Hvar and Brac. Pleasant refreshing faintly fragrant wine.

Burgundac Bijeli
>   The CHARDONNAY, grown a little in SLAVONIA and VOJVODINA.

Cabernet
>   See Grapes for red wine. Now introduced in many places with usually pleasant, occasionally exciting, results. See KOSOVO.

Crno Black—i.e. red wine.

Ćviček
>   Traditional pale red or dark rosé of the Sava valley, SLOVENIA.

Dalmacijavino
>   Important co-operative based at Split and selling a full range of Dalmation coastal and island wines.

Dalmatia
>   The middle coast of Yugoslavia from Rijeka to Dubrovnik. Has a remarkable variety of wines of character.

Dingac
>   Heavy sweetish red from the local PLAVAĆ grape, speciality of the mid-Dalmatian coast.

Faros Substantial age-worthy PLAVAĆ red from the island of Hvar.

Fruska Gora
>   Hills in VOJVODINA, on the Danube n.w. of Belgrade, with a growing modern v'yd. and a wide range of wines, incl. good Traminer and Sauvignon Blanc.

Grasevina
>   Slovenian for Italian Riesling (also called Wälschriesling, LASKI RIZLING, etc.). The normal Riesling of Yugoslavia.

Grk White grape, speciality of the island of Korcula, giving strong sherry-like wine (and also a lighter pale one).

Istria Peninsula in the n. Adriatic, Porec its centre, with a variety of pleasant wines, the MERLOT as good as any.

Jerusalem
>   Yugoslavia's most famous v'yd., at LJUTOMER. Its best wines are late-picked RAJNSKI RIZLING, LASKI RIZLING and more aromatic whites.

Kadarka
>   The major red grape of Hungary, widely grown in SERBIA.

Kosovo (or Kosmet)
>   Region in the s., between SERBIA and Macedonia, with modern v'yds. The source of AMSELFELDER and some well-balanced, lively CABERNET.

Kraski
>   Grown on the coastal limestone "karst" of SLOVENIA.

Laski Rizling
>   Yet another name for Italian Riesling.

Ljutomer (or Lutomer)-Ormoz
>   Yugoslavia's best known and probably best white-wine district, in n.e. SLOVENIA, famous for its Wälschriesling: full-flavoured, full-strength and at its best rich and satisfying wine.

Malvasia
> White grape giving luscious heavy wine, used in w. SLOVENIA.

Maraština
> Strong dry white of the Dalmatian islands, best from Čara Smokvica.

Maribor
> Important wine-centre of n. SLOVENIA. White wines, mainly from VINAG, incl. LASKI RIZLING, RIESLING, SAUV BLANC, PINOT BLANC, TRAMINER.

Merlot Grown in SLOVENIA and ISTRIA with reasonable results.

Mostar
> Islamic-looking little city inland from DALMATIA, making admirable dry white from the ZILAVKA grape. Also BLATINA.

Muskat–Ottonel
> The East European muscat, grown in VOJVODINA.

Navip The big growers' co-operative of SERBIA, with its headquarters at Belgrade.

Opol Pleasantly light pale red made of PLAVAĆ grapes round Split and Sibenik in DALMATIA.

Plavać Mali
> Native red grape of SLOVENIA and DALMATIA; capable of great body and strength and ageing well. DINGAC, POSTUP, OPOL, etc. Ordinary reds are often called "Plavać". There is also a white Plavać Beli.

Plavina Light red of the DALMATIAN coast round Zadar.

Plovdina
> Native red grape of Macedonia in the s., giving mild wine. Grown and generally blended with PROKUPAC.

Portugizac Austria's Portugieser: plain red wine.

Pošip Pleasant, not-too-heavy white wine of the Dalmatian islands, notably Korcula.

Postup
> Sweet and heavy DALMATIAN red from the Peljesać peninsula near Korcula. Highly esteemed locally.

Prokupać
> Principal native red grape of s. SERBIA and Macedonia: 85% of the production. Makes good dark rosé (RUZIĆA) and full-bodied red of character. Some of the best comes from ZUPA. PLOVDINA is often added for smoothness.

Prošek
> The dessert wine of DALMATIA, of stupefying natural strength and variable quality. The best is excellent, but hard to find.

Radgonska Ranina
> Ranina is Austria's BOUVIER grape (see Austria). Radgona is near MARIBOR. The wine is sweet and carries the trade name TIGROVO MLJEKO (Tiger's Milk).

Rajnski Rizling
> The Rhine Riesling, rare in Yugoslavia but grown a little in LJUTOMER-ORMOZ.

Refosco
> Italian grape grown in e. SLOVENIA and ISTRIA under the name TERAN.

Renski Rizling Alternative spelling for Rhine Riesling.

Riesling Used without qualification formerly meant Italian Riesling. Now limited to real Rhine Riesling.

Ruzića
> Rosé, usually from PROKUPAĆ. Darker than most; and better.

Serbia The e. state of Yugoslavia, with nearly half the country's v'yds., stretching from VOJVODINA to Macedonia.

Sipon Yugoslav name for the FURMINT grape of Hungary, also grown in SLOVENIA.

Slamnak A good late-harvest LJUTOMER estate Riesling.

Slavonia

Northern Croatia, on the Hungarian border between SLOVENIA and SERBIA. A big producer of standard wines, mainly white, including most "Yugoslav Riesling".

Slovenia

The n.w. state, incl. Yugoslavia's most European-style v'yds. and wines: LJUTOMER, etc. Slovenija-vino, the sales organization, is Yugoslavia's biggest.

Smederevka

Important white grape of SERBIA and KOSOVO. Fresh dry wines.

Teran Stout dark red of ISTRIA. See REFOSCO.

Tigrovo Mljeko See Radgonska Ranina

Tocai The PINOT GRIS, making rather heavy white wine in SLOVENIA.

Traminac

The TRAMINER. Grown in SLOVENIA and VOJVODINA. Particularly successful in the latter.

Vinag Huge production cellars at MARIBOR.

Vojvodina

An autonomous province of n. SERBIA with substantial, growing and improving v'yds. Wide range of grapes, both European and Balkan.

Vranać

Red grape making attractive vigorous wine in Montenegro.

Vugava

Rare white variety of Vis in DALAMATIA. Linked in legend with France's VIÒGNIER.

Zilavka

The white wine of MOSTAR in Hercegovina. Can be one of Yugoslavia's best: dry, pungent and memorably fruity, with a faint flavour of apricots. Exported samples are disappointing.

Zupa Central SERBIAN district giving its name to above-average red and rosé (or dark and light red) of PROKUPAC and PLOVDINA: respectively Zupsko Crno and Zupsko Ruzića.

Bulgaria

A dramatic entry into the world's wine-diet in the late 1970s. State-run and state-subsidized wineries have learned a great deal from the New World and offer Cabernet and Chardonnay at bargain prices and in rapidly improving quality and variety. Controlled appellation ("Controliran") wines, recently introduced in 1985, have marked an important new step in quality.

Asenovgrad

Main MAVRUD-producing cellar on the outskirts of Plovdiv, Bulgaria's second city.

Cabernet

The Bordeaux grape is highly successful in n. Bulgaria. Dark, vigorous, fruity and well-balanced wine, needs ageing.

Chardonnay

The white burgundy grape is scarcely less successful. Very dry but full-flavoured wine improves with a year in bottle. Recent oak-aged examples show distinct promise.

Controliran See introductory note.

Dimiat

The common native white grape, grown in the east towards the coast. Agreeable dry white without memorable character.

Euxinograd (Chateau)

Ageing cellar on the coast, part of the ex-King's palace. Wines reserved for State functions and top restaurants.

Fetiaska

The same grape as Romania's Feteasca and Hungary's Leanyka. Pleasant pale wine, best a trifle sweet, sold as Donau Perle.

Gamza

Good red grape, Hungary's Kadarka. Aged examples, esp. from PAVLIKENI, can be fine.

Han Krum

Bulgaria's most modern white-wine plant, near Varna in the east.

Iskra The national brand of sparkling wine, normally sweet but of fair quality. Red, white or rosé.

Kadarka Popular brand of GAMZA red from n. Bulgaria.

Karlovo

Town in central Bulgaria famous for the "Valley of Roses" and its very pleasant white MISKET.

Lositza

"Controliran" CABERNET from the north; perhaps Bulgaria's most elegant red wine yet.

Mavrud

Darkly plummy red from s. Bulgaria, esp. ASENOVGRAD. Improves with age. Traditionally considered the country's best.

Melnik

City of the extreme s.e. and its highly prized grape. Such concentrated red wine that locals say it can be carried in a handkerchief. Needs at least 5 years.

Merlot

Soft red grape variety grown mainly in Haskovo in the s.

Misket Muscat-flavoured local grape used for sweet whites.

Muscat Ottonel

Normal muscat grape, grown in eastern Bulgaria for medium-sweet, fruity whites.

Novi Pazar

Controlled appellation CHARDONNAY winery near VARNA. Finer wines than VARNA.

Novo Selo

"Controliran" red MISKET from the north.

Orjahoviza

Major s. area for "Controliran" CABERNET/MERLOT. Rich savoury red best at 4–5 years.

Pamid

The light soft everyday red of the south-west and north-west.

Pavlikeni

Northern wine town with a prestigious estate specializing in GAMZA and CABERNET of high quality.

Pleven

Northern cellar important for PAMID, GAMZA and CABERNET. Also Bulgaria's wine research station.

Provadya

East of SHUMEN, near the coast, another centre for good white wines, especially dry CHARDONNAY.

Rcatzitelli

One of Russia's favourite white grapes for strong, sweet wine. Grown in north-east Bulgaria to produce bulk dry or medium white wines.

Riesling

Normally refers to Italian Riesling. Some Rhine Riesling is grown and is now made into Germanic-style whites.

Sauvignon Blanc

Grown in eastern Bulgaria, just being released as dry white wine on export markets.

Shumen

Eastern Bulgaria's largest white wine-producing cellar specializing in dry wines. Also makes good brandy.

Sonnenkuste

Brand of medium-sweet white sold in Germany.

Suhindol

PAVLIKENI'S neighbour, site of Bulgaria's first cooperative (1909). Good cellar for GAMZA, CABERNET and PAMID.

Sungarlare

Eastern town giving its name to a dry "controliran" MISKET.

Svishtov

CABERNET-producing winery by the Danube in the n. The frontrunner in Bulgaria's controlled appellation wines.

Sylvaner

Some pleasant dry Sylvaner is exported as "Klosterkeller".

Tamianka Sweet white; sweeter than HEMUS.

Targovichte

Independent (non-VINPROM) white wine cellar near SHUMEN that concentrates on medium and sweet wines.

Tirnovo Strong sweet dessert red wine.

Trakia "Thrace". Brand name of a good export range.

Varna Major coastal appellation for CHARDONNAY.

Vinimpex

The "State Commercial Enterprise for Export and Import of Wines and Spirits".

Vinprom

State body controlling all 145 cooperative cellars and responsible for dramatic quality improvements over last 7 years. Owns 10% of the country's vineyards and 3 research institutes.

Greece

Entry into the EEC gives Greece the challenge of modernizing and internationalizing a wine industry that has been up a backwater for two thousand years, concentrating on resin-flavoured white Retsina. (The resin is that of the Aleppo pine.) A new EEC-style system of 29 appellations is now in place and much is spoken of the hopeful future for Greek wines.

Achaia-Clauss

The best-known Greek wine-merchant, with cellars at Patras, n. PELOPONNESE, makers of DEMESTICA, etc.

Agioritikos

Mount Athos, the monastic peninsula in Chalkidiki. Source of CABERNET and other grapes for TSANTALI wines. Brand name of a good dry rosé.

Aminteion (Appellation)

Crisp red or rosé from the mountains of Macedonia.

Attica Region round Athens, the chief source of RETSINA.

Boutari

Merchants and makers with high standards in Macedonian and other wines, esp. good NAOUSSA. Grand Réserve is the best wine.

Calliga

Modern winery with 800 acres on CEPHALONIA. ROBOLA white and reds from indigenous grapes are adequately made but grossly over-dressed.

Cambas, Andrew

Important Athenian wine-growers and merchants.

Carras, John

Hotelier at Sithonia, Chalkidiki, n. Greece, producing interesting new red and white wines under the names Château Carras, Porto Carras and CÔTES DU MELITON. Ch. Carras is a Bordeaux-style barrel-aged red, particularly good in **79 80 81** 82.

Castel Danielis

One of the best brands of dry red wine, from ACHAIA-CLAUSS.

Cephalonia (Kephalonia)

Ionian (western) island with good white ROBOLA and red Thymiatiko. Also MAVRODAPHNE. See also GENTILINI, CALLIGA.

Corfu Adriatic island with wines scarcely worthy of it. Ropa is the traditional red.

Côtes du Meliton (Appellation)

Thracian red, white and rosé of fair quality, made by CARRAS.

Courtakis, D.

Athenian merchant with good dark NEMEAN red.

Crete Island with the home for some of Greece's better (red) wine. Appellations are: Archanes, Daphnes, Peza and Sitia.

Demestica

A reliable standard brand of dry red and white from ACHAIA-CLAUSS.

Gentilini New ('84) up-market white from CEPHALONIA, a Robola blend. To watch.

Goumenissa (Appellation)

Good-quality, oak-aged mid-weight red from BOUTARI.

Hymettus

Standard brand of red and dry white without resin.

Kokkineli

The rosé version of RETSINA: like the white. Drink very cold.

Lac des Roches

Sound, blended Dodecanese white from BOUTARI.

Lindos Name for the higher quality of RHODES wine, whether from Lindos itself or not. Acceptable; no more.

Malvasia

The famous grape is said to originate from Monemvasia in the s. PELOPONNESE.

Mantinia (Appellation)

A fresh white from the PELOPONNESE, offered by CAMBAS.

Mavro "Black"— the word for dark (usually sweet) red wine.

Mavrodaphne

Literally "black laurel": dark sweet concentrated red; a speciality of the Patras region, n. PELOPONNESE.

Mavroudi (Appellation)

The red wine of Delphi and the n. shore of the Gulf of Corinth: dark and plummy.

Metsovo (Appellation)

CABERNET red from Epirus in the north.

Minos Popular Cretan brand; the Castello red is best.

Naoussa (Appellation)

Above-average strong dry red from Macedonia in the n., esp. from BOUTARI and TSANTALI.

Nemea (Appellation)

Town in the e. PELOPONNESE famous for its lion (a victim of Hercules) and its fittingly forceful MAVRO.

Patras (Appellation)

Important wine town at the mouth of the Gulf of Corinth.

Peloponnese

The s. landmass of mainland Greece, with a half of the whole country's vineyards.

Pendeli

Reliable brand of dry red from ATTICA, grown and bottled by Andrew CAMBAS.

Retsina
> White wine with pine resin added, tasting of turpentine and oddly appropriate with Greek food. The speciality of ATTICA. Drink it very cold.

Rhodes
> Easternmost Greek island. Its sweet MALVASIAS are its best wines. LINDOS is the brand name for tolerable table wines.

Robola (or Rombola) (Appellation)
> The fashionable dry white of Cephalonia; island off the Gulf of Corinth. Can be a pleasant soft wine of some character.

Samos (Appellation)
> Island off the Turkish coast with a reputation for its sweet pale-golden muscat. The normal commercial quality is nothing much.

Santorin
> Island north of Crete, making sweet Vinsanto from sun-dried grapes, and dry white Thira.

Tsantali
> Producers at Agios Pavlos with a wide range of table wines, including Macedonian Cabernet, wine from the monks of Mt. Athos, NAOUSSA and Muscat from PATRAS. "Cava" is a good blend.

Verdea The dry white of Zakinthos, the island just w. of the
> PELOPONNESE. The red is Byzantis.

Xynomavro
> The best Greek red grape, basis for NAOUSSA and other northern wines.

Cyprus

A well-established exporter of strong wines of reasonable quality, best known for very passable Cyprus sherry, though old Commandaria, a treacly dessert wine, is the island's finest product. Until recently only traditional grape varieties of limited potential were available; now better kinds are beginning to improve standards, but regrettably slowly.

Afames
> Village at the foot of Mt. Olympus, giving its name to one of the better red (MAVRON) wines from SODAP.

Aphrodite
> Full-bodied medium-dry white from KEO, named after the Greek goddess of love.

Arsinöe
> Dry white wine from SODAP, named after an unfortunate female whom Aphrodite turned to stone.

Bellapais
> Fizzy medium-sweet white from KEO named after the famous abbey near Kyrenia. Essential refreshment for holidaymakers.

Commandaria
> Good-quality br. dessert wine made since ancient times in the hills n. of LIMASSOL, named after a crusading order of knights. The best (sold as "100 yrs old") is superb, of incredible sweetness.

Domaine d'Ahera
> Modern-style lighter red from KEO.

Emva Cream
> Best-selling sw. sherry from Etko, a HAGGIPAVLU subsidiary.

Etko See Haggipavlu

Haggipavlu
> Well-known wine-merchant at LIMASSOL. Trades as Etko.

Hirondelle
>The sweet white and some of the other wines of this popular brand are produced by Etko (see Emva).

Keo One of the biggest and most go-ahead firms in the wine trade at LIMASSOL.

Khalokhorio
>Principal COMMANDARIA village, growing only XYNISTERI.

Kokkineli
>Rosé: the name is related to "cochineal".

Kolossi
>Red and white table wines from SODAP.

Limassol
>"The Bordeaux of Cyprus". The wine-port in the south.

Loel Major producer. Amathus and Kykko brands, Command Cyprus sherry and good Negro red.

Mavron
>The black grape of Cyprus (and Greece) and its dark wine.

Mosaic
>KEO's brand of Cyprus sherries. Includes a fine dry wine.

Othello
>A good standard dry red: solid, satisfying wine from KEO.

Palomino
>Soft dry white made of this (sherry) grape by LOEL. Very drinkable ice-cold.

Pitsilia
>Region south of Mt. Olympus producing the best white and COMMANDARIA wines.

Rosella
>Brand of strong medium-sweet rosé.

St Panteleimon
>Brand of strong sweet white from Keo.

Semeli
>Good traditional red from HAGGIPAVLU.

Sherry
>Cyprus makes a full range of sherry-style wines, the best (particularly the dry) of very good quality.

SODAP
>Major wine cooperative at LIMASSOL.

Xynisteri
>The native white grape of Cyprus.

Zoopiyi
>Principal COMMANDARIA village, growing MAVRON grapes.

California

California has made wine for 150 years, but her modern wine industry has grown from scratch in scarcely more than 25. Today it challenges the world with good-quality cheap wines and a growing number of luxury wines of brilliant quality. In the last 12 years the industry has expanded and altered at a frenzied pace. Many of the wineries listed here have a history shorter than ten years. Quality ratings must therefore be tentative.

Grape varieties combined with brand-names are the key to California wine. Since grapes in California play many new roles they are separately listed on pages 154 to 155.

Vineyard areas

Amador
> County in the Sierra foothills e. of Sacramento. Grows very good Zinfandel, esp. in Shenandoah Valley.

Central Coast
> A long sweep of coast with increasing though scattered wine activity, from San Francisco Bay s. to Santa Barbara.

Central Coast/Santa Barbara
> Some of the most promising vineyard land (esp. for white wines) in the state is in the Santa Ynez Valley n. of Santa Barbara, where coastal fog gives particularly cool conditions.

Central Coast/Santa Cruz Mts.
> Wineries are scattered round the Santa Cruz Mts. s. of San Francisco Bay, from Saratoga down to the HECKER PASS.

Central Coast/Hecker Pass
> Pass through the Santa Cruz Mts. s. of San Francisco Bay with a cluster of small old-style wineries.

Central Coast/Salinas Valley/Monterey
> The Salinas Valley runs inland s.e. from Monterey. After frenzied expansion in the '70s, many vines were removed. What are left make wines of great character.

Central Coast/San Luis Obispo
> Edna Valley just s. of San Luis Obispo and new more scattered v'yds. nr. Paso Robles.

Livermore
> Valley e. of San Francisco Bay long famous for white wines but now largely built over.

Lodi Town and district at the n. end of the San Joaquin Valley, its hot climate modified by a westerly air-stream.

Mendocino
> Northernmost coastal wine country; a varied climate coolest in Anderson Valley nr. the coast, warm around Ukiah inland.

Napa The Napa Valley, n. of San Francisco Bay, long established as a top-quality wine area. Coolest at southern end (Los Carneros).

San Joaquin Valley
> The great central valley of California, fertile and hot, the source of most of the jug wines and dessert wines in the State.

Sonoma
> County n. of San Francisco Bay, between Napa and the sea. Most v'yds. are in the north (see below). A few, historically important, are in the Valley of the Moon in the south. Vineyards extend south into Los Carneros. (See also Napa.)

Sonoma/Alexander Valley/Russian River
> Top-quality area from Alexander Valley (n. of Napa Valley) towards the sea (Russian River). Incl. Dry Creek Valley.

Temecula (Rancho California)
> New small area in s. California, 25 miles inland, halfway between San Diego and Riverside.

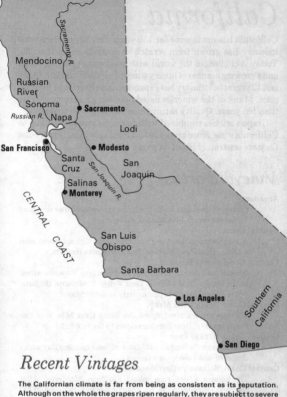

Recent Vintages

The Californian climate is far from being as consistent as its reputation. Although on the whole the grapes ripen regularly, they are subject to severe spring frosts in many areas, sometimes a wet harvest-time, and such occasional calamities as the two-year drought of 1975–7.

Wines from the San Joaquin Valley tend to be most consistent year by year. The vintage date on these, where there is one, is more important for telling the age of the wine than its character.

Vineyards in the Central Coast are widely scattered; there is little pattern.

The Napa and Sonoma valleys are the area where comment can be made on the last dozen vintages of the top varietal wines: Cabernet Sauvignon and Chardonnay. All Chardonnays can be considered "ready" at 2 years, though the best may improve.

	Chardonnay	Cabernet Sauvignon
1986	Cool season; fine promise.	Early reactions very favourable.
1985	Big crop, good acidity, excellent.	Coolish ripening season, elegant wines with great promise.
1984	Wonderfully perfumed when young, now fulfilling promise.	Exceptional; very ripe and fragrant. Will improve for years.
1983	Drink soon.	Similar to '80 but will mature faster.
1982	Sound, agreeable; drink up.	Many outstanding.
1981	Good if not too strong. Drink.	
1980	Small crop; high alcohol. The best well-balanced.	Outstanding for current drinking.
1979	Excellent; drink up.	Rain; generally light.
1978	Very good if not too heady.	Excellent. Generally ready.
1977	Generally excellent.	Attractive: ageing well.
1976	Difficult: variable.	Small crop but splendid.
1975	Very good; drink up.	Delicate: charming; drink soon.
1974	Should have been drunk.	Difficult: but many superb.
1973	Very good, but drink up.	Big and good; drink up.
1970	Good all round: not great: mature.	One of the best ever.

California has adopted the world's repertoire of 'classic' grapes: for notes on these see pages 6–10. Grapes specific to California include: **Emerald Riesling** an original in the German manner. Clean, flowery/fruity and a touch tart. **Flora** mildy flowery white, best made sweet and/or sparkling (e.g. by SHRAMSBERG. **Gamay Beaujolais** not true Gamay but a Pinot Noir clone. **Gray Riesling** not a Riesling, makes full-bodied but scarcely notable white. **Johannisberg Riesling** real (also called Rhine) Riesling. **Petite Sirah** no relation to Syrah, a synonym for the obscure French Durif. **Ruby Cabernet** California-bred cross between Carignan and Cabernet Sauvignon, with enough of the latter's character to be interesting. Good in hot conditions. **Zinfandel** California's own red, open to many interpretations from light-weight and fruity to galumphing. The current fad is for white or "blush" Zin. The red is capable of ageing to high quality.

California wineries

Acacia Napa. ★★★★ CH 80 81 82 83 84 85 PN 80 81 82 83 84
> Carneros winery, now owned by CHALONE, specializing in CHARDONNAY and PINOT NOIR. Both are fulfilling marvellous promise.

Alderbrook Sonoma. ⟨★★⟩ CH 84 85
> New ('82) winery using owner-grown and other grapes to make full-flavoured whites. CHARD, SAUVIGNON BLANC and SEMILLON all good.

Alexander Valley Vineyards Alexander Valley. ⟨★★→★★★⟩ CH 80 81 82 83 84 85 CS 81 82 83
> Small winery best known for well-balanced CHARD., and J.R. CABERNET also v. well made.

Almaden Central Coast. ★→★★ CS 79 80 81 82
> Famous pioneer name bought in '87 by Heublein to be dismantled and downgraded.

S. Anderson Vineyard Napa. ★★★ CH 80 81 82 83 84
> Young winery with extensive caves. Good CHARDONNAY and recently good sparkling wine.

Balverne Sonoma/Russian River. ★★ CH 80 81 83
> Mid-sized winery near Windsor, started in '80 with fine CHARDONNAY, SAUVIGNON BLANC, and blended "Healdsburger". C.S. and ZIN are above average.

Beaulieu Napa. ★★★ CS 74 76 77 78 79 80 81 82 83
> Justly famous medium-size growers and makers of esp. CABERNET. Top wine: De Latour Private Reserve Cabernet. Crackerjack SAUV. BLANC. Now owned by Grand Metropolitan.

Bel Arbres A second label of FETZER.

Belvedere Wine Co. Sonoma. ★★
> Born-1980 winery featuring single-v'yd. wines. incl. Robert Young CAB. from Alex Valley, York Mtn. Napa CAB. Bacigalupi Russian River CHARD. They go down well.

Beringer Napa. ⟨★★→★★★★⟩ CH 80 81 82 83 84 85
> Century-old winery recently restored to the front rank. Increasingly fine wines incl. esp. CHARD (excellent Private Reserve), CABERNET (ditto) and "Nightingale", the eponymous winemaker's induced-botrytis dessert wine.

Boeger Amador. ★★ CS 79 80 81 82
> Small winery in Sierra foothills. Good ZIN.

Bonny Doon Vineyard C. Coast/Santa Cruz Mtns. ★★
> Small winery (since '81) with original ideas about Rhône grapes, incl. Syrah, Grenache, and even Roussanne and Marsanne.

Brander Central Coast/Santa Barbara. ★★★ CS 83
> Small new winery specializes in excellent SAUVIGNON BLANC of Santa Ynez valley grapes.

Bruce, David Central Coast. ★★ CH 80 81 82 83 84
> Small luxury winery with heavy-weight wines. Improving.

Buena Vista Sonoma. |★★→★★★| CH 80 81 82 83 84 85
> Historic pioneer winery with German owners and very sound recent record esp. in whites (RIESLING, FUMÉ BLANC).

Burgess Cellars Napa. ★★★ CH 80 81 82 83 84 CS 80 81 82 Z 81 82 83
> Small hillside winery, in former Souverain cellars, making good CHARDONNAY, CABERNET, and very good ZIN.

Bynum, Davis Sonoma. ★→★★ CH 83 84 CS 82
> Well-established maker of standard varieties, w. of Healdsburg.

B.V. Abbreviation of BEAULIEU VINEYARDS used on their labels.

Cakebread Napa. ★★★ CH 80 81 82 83 84 85
> Started 1973. Increasing reputation, esp. for SAUVIGNON BLANC and CABERNET (79 esp.); also CHARDONNAY.

Calera Monterey-San Benito. ★★★ PN 80 81 82 83
> 1975 winery ambitious with PINOT NOIR; also high-alcohol ZIN and now CHARDONNAY.

Callaway S. California. ★★ CH 83 84 85
> Small winery in new territory at TEMECULA. Sound whites.

Carmenet Sonoma. ★★→★★★
> Where CHALONE emulates Burgundy, the same owners have chased Bordeaux here since '82 with SAUV.BL. from EDNA VALLEY, CAB/MERLOT from high above Sonoma town. Also "Gavilan" FRENCH COLOMBARD from Napa.

Carneros Creek Napa. ★★★ CH 80 81 82 83 CS 74 77 80 81 82
> The first winery in the cool Carneros area between Napa and San Francisco Bay. Good P.N., CHARDONNAY and CABERNET. Good value MERLOT.

Cassayre-Forni Napa. ★★→★★★ CH 81 82 83 CS 79 80 81
> Small new Rutherford winery. Good CABERNET, ZIN, dry CHENIN BLANC and CHARDONNAY.

Caymus Napa. |★★★→★★★★| CS 74 75 76 77 78 79 80 81 82 83
> Outwardly modest small winery at Rutherford with v. high standards, esp. for notably complex CAB and ZIN; also white P.NOIR, CHARDS, SAUV. BLANC. Second label: Liberty School. (Value.)

Chalone Central Coast/Salinas. |★★★★| CH 80 81 82 83 84 85 PN 80 81 82
> Unique small hilltop v.'yd./winery at the Pinnacles. French-style CHARDONNAY and PINOT NOIR of superb quality. Also excellent PINOT BLANC. See also Acacia, Carmenet.

Chappellet Napa. ★★★★ CH 80 81 82 83 84 CS 74 75 76 78 79 80 81 82 83
> Luxury winery and beautiful amphitheatrical hillside v'yd. Excellent long-lived CABERNET, CHARDONNAY and RIESLING: very good dry CHENIN BLANC.

Château Bouchaine Napa/Carneros. ★★★ CH 83 84
> New firm in old Carneros barn started with Acacia-style oaky PINOT NOIR. Now similar CHARDONNAY and SAUV. BLANC.

Château Montelena Napa. ★★★ CH 80 81 82 83 84 CS 75 77 78 79 80 81 82
> Small 1969 winery making very good distinctive CHARDONNAY and very tannic CABERNET SAUVIGNON.

Château St Jean Sonoma. ★★★ CH 80 81 82 83 84 85
> Impressive winery specializing in whites from individual v'yds., incl. CHARD, P.BL. and esp. late harvest RIES.. Now also fine sparkling wine and bargain "Vin Blanc". Owned by Suntory.

Chateau Souverain Alexander Valley. ★★ CH 81 82 83 84 CS 78 79 80 81 82 83
> Luxurious mid-sized winery with a record of competent wines, bought by BERINGER in 1986.

Christian Brothers Napa and San Joaquin. `*→*★★`
　The biggest Napa winery, run by a religious order. Sound CABERNET, useful FUMÉ BLANC, sweet white Ch. La Salle, very good brandy and ZIN "port".

Clos du Bois Sonoma. `**` →★★★ CH 80 81 82 83 84 85 CS 78 79 80 81 82 83
　Healdsburg winery of big grower in Dry Creek and Alexander Valleys. V.g. GEWÜRZ, P.NOIR, MERLOT, CHARD, SAUV. BLANC.

Clos du Val Napa. ★★★→★★★★ CH 80 81 82 83 84 CS 77 78 79 80 81 82
　French-run. V.g. bold ZIN, fine delicate CAB, CHARD and SEM.

Concannon Livermore. Table. ★★→★★★ CH 83 84
　Substantial winery first famous for whites, reds now prominent. Now owned by Distillers' Company. A name to follow.

Congress Springs Santa Clara/Santa Cruz. ★★→★★★ CH 84 85
　Tiny winery above Saratoga. Well-made whites, esp. SAUVIGNON BLANC, SEMILLON.

Conn Creek Napa. ★★→★★★ CH 80 81 82 83 84 CS 78 79 80 81 82
　Winery built on Silverado Trail in 1979 has a growing reputation. Best known for CABERNET.

Corbett Canyon Central Coast/San Luis Obispo. `**` CH 84 85
　New ('83) Edna Valley winery to make sizeable amounts of varietal and generic ("Coastal Classic") wines. (Value.) Also Shadow Creek sparkling.

Cresta Blanca Mendocino. ★★
　Old name from Livermore revived on the n. coast by GUILD in 1975. Husky ZIN and PETITE SYRAH. Mild whites.

Cuvaison Napa. ★★→★★★ CH 80 81 82 83 CS 78 79 80 81
　Small winery with expert new direction. Formerly austere CABERNET and CHARDONNAY have become more approachable.

Culbertson San Diego. ★★★
　Young sparkling-wine specialist using local grapes of an improbable region with gold-medal results.

Dehlinger Sonoma. ★★→ `★★★` CH 80 81 82 83 84 CS 78 80 81 82
　Small winery and v'yd. w. of Santa Rosa. Since 1976 CHARDONNAY, CABERNET and since '81 P.NOIR all extremely well made.

DeLoach Vineyards Sonoma. ★★★ CH 80 81 82 83 84 85 PN 80 81 82 83
　Russian River winery founded 1975 for CHARDONNAY, GEWÜRZ, P. NOIR. Also good ZIN. (v.g. white ZIN), C.S. and SAUV. BLANC.

Diamond Creek Napa. ★★★ CS 74 75 76 77 78 79 80 81 82 83 84
　Small winery since the 60s with austere, long-ageing CABERNET from hills w. of Calistoga, e.g. "Volcanic Hill", "Gravelly Meadow".

Domaine Chandon Napa. `★★★`
　Californian outpost of Moët & Chandon Champagne. Launched 1976. Promise is being fulfilled. First Reserve wine (released in 1985) was a showstopper.

Domaine Laurier Sonoma. `★★★` CH 80 81 82 83 84 CS 78 79 80 81
　Small new winery with beautifully structured wines, esp. CABERNET and SAUVIGNON BLANC, using the new appellation Green Valley. A classic in the making.

Domaine Mumm Napa. ★★ (?)
　Seagram-owned. Sparkling-wine house on STERLING property. First wine looked good in '86.

Dominus Napa. ★★★★ 83
　First fruits (1983 vintage released '87) of partnership ("John Daniel Society") between inheritor of ex-Inglenook v'yd. n. of Yountville and Christian Moueix of Pomerol. B'x-style Cabernets-Merlot blend shows immense promise.

Donna Maria Sonoma/Russian River. ★★ CH 84 85 CS 83 84
　Considerable vineyards in Chalk Hill near Windsor. Encouraging early wines.

Dry Creek Sonoma. ★★★ CH 80 81 82 83 84 85 CS 79 80 81 82 83 84
Small winery with high ideals, making old-fashioned dry wines, esp. whites, incl. CHARDONNAY, CHENIN BLANC and FUMÉ BLANC and outstanding CAB. SAUV. (Best California Wine award 1985).

Duckhorn Vineyards Napa. ★★★ M 79 80 81 82 83 84 CS 79 80 81 82 83
Small winery on Silverado Trail best known for reds, esp. v.g. MERLOT. Also SAUVIGNON BLANC and now "Robert Hunter" Sparkling Brut de Noirs from Sonoma grapes.

Durney Vineyard Central Coast/Monterey. ★★→★★★ CS 79 80 81 82
Well-established source of splendid rich and robust CABERNET. Also CHENIN BL., RIESLING.

Eberle Winery C. Coast/San Luis Obispo. ★★
Most stylish and consistent CAB. producer in Paso Robles area since '79. Also CHARD.

Edmeades Mendocino. ★★ CH 81 82 83 84 CS 78 79 80 81 82
Tiny winery in Anderson Valley near Pacific. CABERNET and now good CHARD and ZIN (esp. '82).

Edna Valley Vineyard Cen. Coast/San Luis Obispo. ★★→★★★ CH 84 85
Joint venture of grape-grower with CHALONE winemakers. Fat, CHARDONNAY full of character, and PINOT NOIR to keep.

Estrella River San Luis Obispo/Santa Barbara. ★★ CH 79 80 81 82 83 84
Impressive new winery with 700 acres. CHARDONNAY, RIESLING, MUSCAT, SYRAH are promising.

Far Niente Napa. ★★★ CH 80 81 82 83 84 85
Founded 1885; reactivated in 1979. Full-flavoured CHARDONNAY first; now promising CABERNET.

Felton–Empire Vineyards Cent. Coast/Santa Cruz Mts. ★★★
The famous old Hallcrest property revived. Excellent RIESLING; good GEWÜRZ. Reds still rather shaky.

Fetzer Mendocino. ★★→★★★ CH 81 82 83 84 85 CS 79 80 81 82
Rapidly expanding winery with interesting reliable wines, esp. CHARD and CAB. Also SAUV. BLANC, RIES and strong dark ZIN. A byword for value.

Ficklin San Joaquin. ★★★
Family firm making California's best "port" and minute quantities of table wine.

Field Stone Sonoma (Alexander Valley). ★★
Small subterranean winery founded by mechanical harvester maker. Good wines incl. delicious CABERNET rosé.

Firestone Central Coast/Santa Barbara. ★★★ CH 80 81 82 83 84 CS 81 82 83
Ambitious 1973 winery n. of Santa Barbara. Cool conditions are producing full spectrum of unusual wines of gentle savour.

Flora Springs Wine Co. Napa. ★★★ CH 80 81 82 83 84 CS 80 81 82 83
Old stone cellar in St. Helena reopened 1979. CHARDONNAY and SAUV. BLANC are v. successful, CABERNET less certain.

Folie à Deux Napa. ★★
Tiny producer of impeccable Chardonnays, v. good CHENIN BL., CAB., from bought-in grapes.

Foppiano Sonoma. ★★
Old winery at Healdsburg refurbished with estate varieties incl. CHENIN BLANC, FUMÉ BLANC, CAB, ZIN, PETITE SYRAH.

Franciscan Vineyard Napa. ★★ CH 81 82 83 84 CS 80 81 82 83
Rapidly growing enterprise with a meet-the-folks approach. Good ZIN., CAB., CHARD. and RIES.; also "Harvest Nouveau".

Franzia San Joaquin. ★
Large old winery with well-distributed brands. Various labels, but all say "made and bottled in Ripon".

Freemark Abbey Napa. ★★★★ CH 80 81 82 83 84 CS 74 75 76 77 78 79 80 81 82
Small connoisseur's winery with high reputation for CABERNET, CHARDONNAY and RIESLING (esp. late-harvest "Edelwein").

Frog's Leap Napa. ★★
> Little St Helena winery as charming as its name. Now CAB.S. and CHARD. outclass the original SAUV.BL. and ZIN.

Gallo, E. & J. San Joaquin. `┌→→★★┐` CS 78 80
> The world's biggest winery, pioneer in both quantity and quality. Family owned. Hearty Burgundy and Chablis Blanc set national standards. Varietals incl. (esp.) SAUV. BLANC, GEWÜRZ, RIES., CHARD, CABERNET. Vintage-dated CAB. has won wide approval. Also "André" fizz and many others.

Geyser Peak Sonoma. ★★
> Old winery revived by Schlitz Brewery then sold to local grower Henry Trione. Best wines bear his name.

Giumarra San Joaquin. `★★`
> Modern installation in hottest part of San Joaquin Valley with broad range from valley and Central Coast grapes.

Glen Ellen Sonoma. ★★→★★★ CH 84 CS 83
> Father-and-son team making restrained elegant wines from own-grown and other Sonoma grapes. SAUV. BLANC, CHARD and CABERNET. "Proprietor's Reserve" indicates bought-in wines.

Gloria Ferrer. Sonoma ★★★ (?)
> Big new sparkling winery launched in '85 by FREIXENET of Spain. An impressive start.

Grand Cru Sonoma. ★★→★★★ CS 78 79 80 81 82 83
> Small 1971 winery making good GEWÜRZ and increasingly CABERNET, CHENIN and SAUVIGNON BLANC.

Green and Red Napa ★★
> Tiny Pope Valley winery with freshly fruity ZIN.

Grgich Hills Cellars Napa. ★★★★ CH 80 81 82 83 84 Z 77 78 79 80 81 82
> Grgich (formerly of Ch. Montelena) is winemaker, Hills grows the grapes—esp. CHARDONNAY and RIESLING. Delicate, lively wines include ZINFANDEL and (esp.) CABERNET.

Guenoc Vineyards Lake County. `★★` CH 84
> Ambitious new vineyard/winery venture just beyond the Napa county line. CHENIN BLANC and PETITE SIRAH are esp. appealing.

Guild San Joaquin. ★
> Big growers' cooperative famous for Vino da Tavola semi-sweet red and B. Cribari label.

Gundlach-Bundschu Sonoma. `★★★` CH 81 82 83 84 CS 79 80 81 82
> Very old small family winery revived by the new generation. Excellent CABERNET, MERLOT, ZIN and good whites: CHARDONNAY, GEWÜRZ, RIESLING.

Hacienda Sonoma. ★★→★★★ CH 82 83 84 CS 79 80 81 82
> Small winery at Sonoma specializing in high-quality CHARDONNAY and GEWÜRZ. Recently good CABERNET.

Hanzell Sonoma. ★★★ CH 80 81 82 83 84 PN 80 81
> Small winery whose (late) founder revolutionized Californian CHARDONNAYS in the '50s. CHARD and P. NOIR are both huge wines. CABERNET first released in 1986.

Haywood Vineyard Sonoma. ★★→★★★ CH 81 83 84 CS 83
> Small new estate on hills above SEBASTIANI. First wines were lovely fruity CHARDONNAY and RIESLING. Now CABERNET.

Heitz Napa. ★★★★ CH 80 81 82 83 84 CS 76 77 78 79 80 81 82
> An inspired individual winemaker who has set standards for the whole industry. His CABERNETS (esp. "Martha's Vineyard" and "Bella Oaks") are dark, deep and emphatic, his best CHARDONNAYS potent and long-lived. But Chard and other wines can be eccentric. Added substantial new v'yds. in 1984.

Hill, William Winery Napa. ★★→★★★ CH 81 82 83 84 CS 80 81 82 83
> Huge new plantings in the Mayacamas mts. and a new winery have yielded very emphatic (but well-received) early wines.

Hop Kiln Sonoma/Russian River. ★★ CH 83
> Small winery. Individual, tasty PETITE SYRAH, ZIN, GEWÜRZ.

Husch Vineyards Mendocino. ******
>Reliable CHARD. and P. NOIR from Anderson Valley; CAB. and SAUV. BLANC from Ukiah.

Inglenook Napa and San Joaquin. ***** →*** CS 76 77 78 79 80 81 82 83
>One of the great old Napa wineries much changed by current owners: Heublein Corp (now Grand Metropolitan). Inglenook Napa Valley is Napa label, with three qualities: Reserve, Estate, Cabinet. Reserve CAB is best wine. CHARD and S. BLANC now v.well made. Petite Syrah is tasty. Inglenook Navalle are good-value Central Valley wines.

Iron Horse Vineyards Sonoma. *** CH 80 81 82 83 84 CS 79 80 81 82
>Stylish Russian River property with CHARDONNAY, CABERNET, P. NOIR and SAUV. BLANC of vivid flavours. Sparkling I.H. is v. dry and fine. Tin Pony is second label.

(Italian Swiss) Colony San Joaquin and Sonoma. *→**
>Honourable old name from Sonoma recently re-acquired by Allied Growers. Policy steering upwards.

Jekel Vineyards Central Coast/Monterey. **→*** CH 80 81 82 83 CS 78 79 81 82
>Well-made RIESLING, CHARDONNAY, and CABERNET have rich resounding flavours. Wines (esp. whites) mature fast but tastily.

J. Lohr Central Coast. **
>Substantial winery in San José with its own v'yds. in SALINAS. Reliable RIESLING, CABERNET rosé. and CHENIN BLANC.

Johnson-Turnbull Napa. **→*** CS 80 81 82
>Very small new estate producing balanced and distinguished, not overweight, CABERNETS from next-door to MONDAVI.

Johnsons of Alexander Valley Sonoma. ** CS 79 80
>Small winery with good v'yd. land. CABERNET best.

Jordan Sonoma. **** CH 80 81 82 83 84 CS 76 77 78 79 80 81 82
>Extravagant winery. CABERNET modelled on Bordeaux, smooth CHARDONNAY. Polished wines to please sophisticates.

Keenan, Robert Napa. *** CH 80 81 82 83 84 CS 83
>V'yds. on Spring Mountain started with over-strong and tannic wines. Style growing more polite.

Kendall–Jackson Lake County. **→*** CH 84 85
>Young (1980) and growing maker of good uncomplicated CHARD. RIES., SAUV. BLANC., CABERNET and ZIN show real promise. White House favourites.

Kenwood Vineyards Sonoma. ****→***** CH 80 81 82 83 84 85 CS 78 79 80 81 82 83
>Small producer of steadily stylish reds, esp. CABERNET and ZIN. also v.g. SAUV. BLANC, good CHARD and CHENIN.

Kistler Vineyards Sonoma. ** CH 80 81 82 83 84 85 CS 80 81 82
>Young small winery in hills. First CHARDONNAY (79) was overwhelming; recent wines show more restraint. Now also CAB and P. NOIR.

Konocti Cellars Lake County ******
>Mid-sized cooperative winery in remote north, half-owned by John PARDUCCI. RIESLING, Fumé Blanc, CAB.S. is consistently attractive.

Korbel Sonoma. ******
>Long-established sparkling wine specialists. "Natural" and "Brut" are among California's best standard "champagnes".

Kornell, Hanns Napa. ******
>Independent-minded sparkling wine house making full-flavoured dry wines: Brut and Sehr Trocken.

Krug, Charles Napa. *→** CS 74 77 78 79 80 81
>Historic old winery with generally sound wines. Good CABERNET (incl. releases of mature vintages), sweet CHENIN BLANC and very sweet Muscat Canelli. C.K. is the jug-wine brand.

La Crema Vinera   Sonoma. **→***CH 80 81 82 83 84 85 PN 79 80 81 82
> Founded 1979 at Petaluma. CHARD. is huge; P. NOIR impressive.

Lakespring Winery   Napa. **
> Steady small winery for well-made MERLOT, CAB. S. Also powerful whites.

Lambert Bridge   Sonoma. ** CS 80 81 82
> Small 1975 winery nr. Healdsburg. CHARD less oaky in '82, '83 than formerly; CABERNET austere, needs ageing.

Landmark   Sonoma.   ** CH 80 81 82 83 84 85 CS 78 79 80 81
> Young winery nr. Windsor; sound CHARD. and CAB. Signs of class.

Laurel Glen Sonoma. ** CS 81 82
> Splendid '81 CABERNET was first wine of tiny Glen Ellen winery.

Laurent Perrier   Central Coast/San Jose.   *** CH 81 82
> Almaden-linked branch of the French Champagne firm started 1981 with excellent dry still CHARDONNAY. Future uncertain.

Leeward Winery   Central Coast/Ventura. *** CH 80 81 82 83 84 CS 80 81
> CHARDONNAY from Monterey and San Luis Obispo grapes started this new venture near Santa Barbara well in 1980.

Long Vineyards   Napa. **→*** CH 80 81 82 83 84 CS 79 80 81
> Small winery in eastern hills nr. CHAPPELLET. First good CHARDONNAY and late-harvest RIESLING, now CABERNET.

Lyeth Vineyard   Sonoma. **
> New estate winery with ambitions for Bordeaux-style red and white.

Lytton Springs   Sonoma. ** Z 83
> Small specialist in Russian River ZIN; thick, heady, tannic.

Maison Deutz   Sonoma. ** (?)
> New sparkling winery with Champagne parentage. Promising first wines.

Mark West   Sonoma **→*** CH 80 81 82 83 84 85 PN 79 80 81 82 83 84
> New winery in cool sub-region. Very satisfactory GEWÜRZ, CHARDONNAY. Now P. NOIR and sparkling Blanc de Noirs.

Markham   Napa. *** CS 79 80 81 82
> 1979 winery with 300 acres. CABERNET very sound, not thrilling. Good bone dry CHENIN BLANC. Chard. gaining a reputation.

Martin Bros   C. Coast/San Luis Obispo. **
> Excellently crisp SAUV. BL., CHENIN BL. and CHARD. The small family winery aims to justify Nebbiolo in Paso Robles.

Martin Ray   Central Coast/S. Cruz Mts. *** CH 81 82 83 CS 81
> Small winery long famous for high prices. "On hold" since 1986.

Martini, Louis   Napa. **→ *** CS 78 79 80 81 82 83 Z 78 79 80 81 82 83 84
> Large but individual winery with very high standards, from standard "Mountain" wines up. CABERNET "Vineyard Selection" one of California's best. BARBERA, MERLOT, PETITE SIRAH, P. NOIR, ZIN, GEWÜRZ, FOLLE BLANCHE and Moscato Amabile are all well made.

Masson, Paul   Central Coast. *→**
> Famous old name sold by Seagram's in '87, moved to Monterey. Future uncertain.

Matanzas Creek   Sonoma. *** CH 80 81 82 83 84 CS 79 80 81 82 83
> Young winery now settled in with well-balanced CHARD, SAUV. BL., CAB. and MERLOT.

Mayacamas   Napa. **** CH 80 81 82 83 CS 76 77 78 79 80 81 82
> First-rate very small v'yd. and winery offering CABERNET, CHARDONNAY, SAUV. BLANC and ZINFANDEL (sometimes).

McDowell Valley Vineyards   Mendocino. ** CS 80 81 82 83
> Big new development using old-established v'yd. to make wide range. To watch, esp. for ZIN and real SYRAH.

Milano Winery   Mendocino. ** CH 80 81 82 83 84 CS 79 80 81
> Very small winery worth noting for CHARD. CAB is overweight.

Mill Creek Sonoma. ★★ CH 84
1974 winery near Healdsburg with pleasant, easy-going CHARDONNAY, MERLOT, CABERNET.

Mirassou Central Coast. ★★→★★★
Dynamic mid-sized growers and makers, the fifth generation of the family. Pioneers in SALINAS v'yds. Notable GAMAY BEAUJOLAIS, GEWÜRZ and very pleasant sparkling.

Mondavi, Robert Napa. ★★→★★★★ CH 80 81 82 83 84 CS 74 75 76 77 78 79 80 81 82
Twenty-two-year-old winery with a brilliant record of innovation in styles, equipment and technique. Solid successes incl. CABERNET, SAUV. BLANC (sold as Fumé Blanc), CHARDONNAY, PINOT NOIR. "Reserves" are marvellous – regularly among California's best. Also useful table wines. See also Opus One.

Monterey Peninsula Central Coast/Salinas. ★★→★★★ CH 80 81 82 83 CS 78 80 81 82
Very small winery near Carmel making chunky chewable ZINFANDEL and CABERNET from SALINAS and other grapes.

Monterey Vineyard Central Coast/Salinas. ★★
The first big modern winery of SALINAS, opened 1974. Now owned by Seagrams. Good ZIN, GEWÜRZ and SYLVANER and fruity feather-weight GAMAY BEAUJOLAIS. "Classic Red" is value.

Monteviña Amador. ★★ CS 79 80 81 82 83 Z 80 81 82 83
Pioneer small winery in revitalizing area: the Shenandoah Valley, Amador County, in the Sierra foothills. ZINFANDEL, BARBERA and SAUVIGNON BLANC are achieving balance.

Monticello Cellars Napa. ★★★ CH 81 82 83 84 CS 80 81 82 83
Ultra-modern new winery near TREFETHEN. Outstanding GEWÜRZ and SAUVIGNON BLANC first caught the eye. Now very good CHARDONNAY, fine tannic CABERNET, and SEMILLON.

De Moor Napa. ★★ CH 80 81 82 83 84 CS 80 81 82
Small Yountville winery (formerly Napa Cellars) with steady record, esp. for CAB. and ZIN. New (European) owners.

J. W. Morris Sonoma. ★★★
Small former specialist in high-quality port-types from SONOMA grapes. Now in Healdsburg, with table wines too.

Mount Eden Vineyards Central Coast. ★★★ CH 80 81 82 83 84
Company owning a major share of what were MARTIN RAY Vineyards. Expensive wines. M.E.V. is a second-line label.

Mount Veeder Napa. ★★★ CS 74 75 77 78 79 80 81
Ambitious little 1973 winery. High prices but good CABERNET.

Navarro Vineyards Mendocino. ★★
Grower of sound CHARD, P. NOIR, outstanding GEWÜRZ in cool Anderson Valley.

Newton Vineyards Napa. ★★★
Luxurious estate. Big oak-scented CAB.S., MERLOT, CHARD., SAUV. BL..

Opus One Napa. ★★★★ CS 79 80 81 82
Not a winery but a wine; the joint venture of Robert Mondavi and Baron Philippe de Rothschild. So far, in effect, a Mondavi Reserve of Reserves at a far-fetched price, however good.

Papagni, Angelo San Joaquin. ★★
Long-established grower with a technically outstanding modern winery at Madera. Dry coastal-style varietals incl. ZIN, CHARD, light "Moscato d'Angelo" and enjoyable Alicante Bouschet.

Parducci Mendocino. ★★→★★★ CH 80 81 83 84 CS 78 79 80 81 82
Well-established mid-sized winery with v'yds. in several locations. Good sturdy reds: CABERNET (and an excellent Cab./Merlot blend), PETITE SYRAH, ZIN, "Burgundy". Also pleasant CHENIN BLANC and FRENCH COLOMBARD.

Pat Paulsen Vineyards Sonoma. ★★★
Property of T.V. comedian offers thoroughly well-made range, esp. SAUV. BLANC and incl. a near-dry Muscat.

Pecota, Robert Napa. ⟦******⟧ CH **82 83 84 85**

Small cellar of ex-BERINGER man with high standards. Wines are CABERNET, SAUV. BLANC, CHARD, good light GAMAY.

Pedroncelli Sonoma/Russian River. ⟦****→*****⟧ CH **80 81 82 83 84** CS **78 79 80 81 82**

Long-established family business with recent reputation for well-above-average ZIN and CHARDONNAY, all growing more stylish with practice.

Pepi, Robert Napa. ****** CH **83 84** CS **82**

Young stone hilltop winery between Oakville and Yountville has launched well as a SAUVIGNON BLANC specialist.

Phelps, Joseph Napa. ⟦*******⟧ →******** CH **80 81 82 83** CS **74 75 76 77 78 79 80 81 82**

De luxe mid-size winery and v'yd. Late harvest RIESLING exceptional. Very good CHARDONNAY, CABERNET, SYRAH. The "Reserve" wine, "Insignia", can be monstrously tannic.

Pine Ridge Napa. ****→***** CH **80 81 82 83 84 85** CS **79 80 81 82 83**

Small winery near STAG'S LEAP has made constantly stylish CHARD, MERLOT and CAB. Also mild but fresh off-dry CH. BLANC.

Piper-Sonoma Sonoma. *******

A joint venture between Piper-Heidsieck of Champagne and Sonoma Vineyards released its first (very good) sparkling cuvée in 1980. The '81 needed until '85 to round out.

Preston Sonoma. ******* CS **83**

Tiny winery with very high standards in Dry Creek Valley, Healdsburg. Esp. for SAUV. BLANC, and ZIN.

Quady Winery Central Valley. *******

Imaginative dessert wines from Madera since '75. Celebrated orangey "Essencia"; "Elysium" from Black Muscat.

Quail Ridge Napa. ****** CH **84 85**

Small specialist in barrel-fermented CHARD. Good, if pricey.

Rafanelli, J. Sonoma. ⟦******⟧

Tiny cellar specializing in outstanding ZIN; also Gamay.

Raymond Vineyards Napa. ⟦*****→******⟧ CH **80 81 82 83 84 85** CS **77 78 79 80 81 82 83**

Small 1974 winery near St. Helena with experienced owners. CHARD, RIESLING and CABERNET all excellent.

Ridge Central Coast S. CRUZ. ******** CS **77 78 79 80 81 82 83**

Small winery of high repute among connoisseurs for concentrated reds needing long maturing in bottle. Notable CAB and ZIN from named v'yds; esp. Montebello and York Creek, Napa.

River Oaks Sonoma. ***→****

Sound commercial wines from same winery as CLOS DU BOIS, but different vineyards.

Rombauer Vineyards Napa. ******

Young ('80) small winery buying Napa grapes for impressive CHARD and CAB. SAUV.

Roudon-Smith Santa Clara/Santa Cruz. ****→** ⟦*******⟧ CH **80 81 82 83 84** CS **78 79 81 82**

Small winery offering really stylish CHARDONNAY.

Round Hill Napa. ⟦****→*****⟧ CH **80 81 82 83 84 85** CS **80 81 82 83**

Consistent good value, esp. GEWÜRZ and FUMÉ BLANC, from St. Helena. Rutherford Ranch is label for best wines. Big new winery under construction.

Rutherford Hill Napa. ⟦*******⟧ CH **80 81 82 83** CS **79 80 81 82**

Larger stable-mate of FREEMARK ABBEY. Good GEWÜRZ. Excellent CHARD, MERLOT and CABERNET.

Rutherford Ranch See Round Hill.

Rutherford Vintners, Inc. Napa. ⟦****→*****⟧ CH **80 81 82 83 84** CS **77 78 79 80 81 82**

Small winery started in 1977 by Bernard Skoda. "Chateau Rutherford" is "Reserve" label.

St. Andrews Napa. ★★★ CH 81 82 83 84 85 CS 83
Small CHARDONNAY estate on Silverado Trail near Napa city. Steadily excellent wine.

St. Clement Napa. ★★★ CH 80 81 82 83 84 CS 78 79 80 81 82 83
Small production. Good CABERNET, powerful CHARD and delicious SAUVIGNON BLANC.

St. Francis Sonoma. ★★ CH 80 81 82 83 84 85
New small winery is using excellent CHARD, CABERNET, GEWÜRZ grapes from older v'yd. Wines have been disappointing.

Saintsbury Napa. ★★★ CH 81 82 83 84 PN 81 82 83
Young winery using Carneros grapes to make perhaps the best P. NOIR and CHARD of this region.

Sanford Santa Barbara. ★★★ CH 84 85
New winery started with striking 1982 SAUV. BLANC and CHARDONNAY in the toast and oak school. '83 P. NOIR is outstanding; also P. Noir Blanc.

San Martin Central Coast. ★★ CS 78 80 81
Restructured old company using SALINAS and SAN LUIS OBISPO grapes to make clean, correct varietals. "Select Vintage" is top label. Also pioneers in "soft" (low-alcohol) wines.

Santa Cruz Mountain V'yd. C. Coast. ★★→★★★ CS 78 79 80 81 82 PN 79 80 81
Small winery in the hills with hopes for fine PINOT NOIR, but problems with overbearing alcohol. Now CABERNET too.

Santa Ynez Valley Winery Santa Barbara. ★★★ CH 80 81 82
Established producer of very good SAUV. BLANC and CHARD.

Sausal Sonoma. ★★
Small specialist in stylish ZIN, etc.

Schramsberg Napa. ★★★★
A dedicated specialist using historic old cellars to make California's best "champagne", incl. splendid "Reserves". "Blanc de Noirs" is outstanding, deserves 2-3 years' ageing.

Schug Winery Napa. ★★★ CH 82 83 PN 80 81 82 83
New (1982) enterprise of PHELPS' ex-winemaker. Very tough PINOT NOIR.

Sebastiani Sonoma. ★→★★★ CS 78 79 80 81 82
Substantial and distinguished old family firm with robust appetizing wines, incl. BARBERA. Top wines have SONOMA appellation. Family problems in '86. To watch.

Sequoia Grove Napa. ★★★ CH 83 84 CS 83
Small winery nr. Oakville. CHARD since '79 has been well-balanced. CAB. SAUV. (Napa and Alexander Valleys) is tannic and meant to age.

Shadow Creek see Corbett Canyon.

Shafer Vineyards Napa. ★★→★★★ CH 80 81 82 83 CS 80 81 82 83
Young winery and vineyard near STAG'S LEAP is making polished CHARDONNAY and very stylish CABERNET and MERLOT.

Shaw, Charles F., Vineyards and Winery Napa. ★★ CH 83 84
St. Helena specialist in GAMAY light red, has added CHARD, CABERNET, SAUVIGNON BLANC (N.B. 83).

Silver Oak Napa. ★★→★★★ CS 78 79 80 81 82
Small 1972 winery succeeding with oaky CABERNETS, incl. v. expensive "Bonny's Vineyard".

Silverado Cellars Napa. ★★★ CH 84 85 CS 83
A showy new winery east of Yountville. Early CHARD and SAUV. BLANC made news. Now CAB is even better. The owner is Mrs. Walt Disney, which suggests adequate capital.

Simi Alexander Valley. ★★★ CH 80 81 82 83 84 CS 78 79 80 81 82 83
Restored historic winery with expert direction of Zelma Long. Some of America's best, most lively CHARDONNAY, delicate CABERNET and (since '82) splendid SAUV. BLANC. Also good Chenin.Bl., irresistible rosé.

Smith–Madrone Napa. ★★→★★★ CH 81 82 83 84 CS 79 80 81 82
New v'yd. high on Spring Mountain made first good RIESLING in '77. CHARD is now eye-catching. Also P.N. and CAB.

Smothers Santa Clara/Santa Cruz. ★★ CS 82
Tiny winery owned by T.V. comic made promising first wines, esp. late-harvest GEWÜRZ. Still more smoke than fire.

Sonoma–Cutrer Vineyards, Inc. Sonoma. ★★★★ CH 81 82 83 84 85
Perhaps the ultimate (so far) in specialist estates, using new techniques to display the characters individual v'yds give to CHARDs (as in Burgundy). So far Les Pierres v'yd is No. 1.

Spring Mountain Napa. ★★★ CH 80 81 82 83 CS 75 77 78 79 81
Renovated small 19th-century property with winery noted for good CHARDONNAY, SAUVIGNON BLANC and CABERNET.

Stag's Leap Wine Cellars Napa. ★★★→★★★★ CH 80 81 82 83 84 CS 74 75 76 77 78 79 80 81 82
Celebrated small v'yd. and cellar with the highest standards. Excellent CABERNET and MERLOT, fresh GAMAY, fine CHARD.

Sterling Napa. ★★★ CH 80 81 82 83 84 CS 82 83
Extremely proficient (also scenic) winery owned by Seagrams. Strong, tart SAUVIGNON BLANC and CHARDONNAY; fruity CABERNET and MERLOT. See also Domaine Mumm.

Stonegate Napa. ★★→★★★ CH 80 81 82 83 84 CS 78 79 80 81 82 83
Small privately owned winery and v'yd. making CABERNET, CHARDONNAY and better and better SAUV. BLANC.

Stony Hill Napa. ★★★★ CH 74 75 76 77 78 79 80 81 82 83 84
Many of California's very best whites have come from this minute winery over 30 years. Owner Fred McCrea died in 1977; his widow Eleanor carries on. Stony Hill CHARDONNAY, GEWÜRZ and RIESLING are all delicate and fine.

Stratford Napa. ★★ CH 84 CS 83
First wine ('82) was an impressive blended CHARD. New winery nr. Rutherford provides more; also good SAUV. BL. (from '85).

Strong, Rodney, Vineyards Sonoma/Russian River. ★★ →★★★ CS 78 79 80
Formerly called Sonoma Vineyards. Well regarded, esp. for CHARD. Range includes single-v'yd. wines, esp. Alexander's Crown CABERNET. See also Piper-Sonoma.

Sutter Home Napa. ★★ Z 77 78 79 80 81 82 83 84
Small winery revived and hugely expanded on the success of its invention: white ZINFANDEL. (1m. cases a year.)

Swan, J. Sonoma. ★★ Z 74 76 77 78 80 81 82 83
Young one-man winery with a name for rich ZIN, CHARD, P.N.

Trefethen Napa. ★★★→★★★★ CH 80 81 82 83 84 CS 74 75 76 77 78 79 80 81 82
Growing family-owned winery in Napa's finest old wooden building. Very good dry RIESLING, CABERNET, P. NOIR. Tense CHARDONNAY for ageing and a notable low-price blend, Eshcol.

Tulocay Napa. ★★ CS 80 81
Tiny new winery at Napa City. First wines are good PINOT NOIR and CABERNET.

Ventana Central Coast/Monterey. ★★ CH 78 79 80 81 82 83
New in '78 with flavoury PINOT BLANC and CHARDONNAY.

Vichon Winery Napa. ★★→★★★ CH 80 81 82 83 CS 77 78 79 80 81
Founded 1980; original and ambitious. Fine CHARDONNAY and blended (50/50) SAUVIGNON/SEMILLON "Chevrignon Blanc". Now promising CABs. Bought (1985) by ROBERT MONDAVI.

Villa Mount Eden Napa. ★★★ CH 80 81 82 83 CS 77 78 79 80 81 82
Small Oakville estate with excellent dry CH. BLANC, good CHARD, outstanding CAB. Bought (1986) by CH. STE. MICHELLE. (p. 166).

Weibel Central Coast and Mendocino. ★→★★
Veteran mid-sized winery giving value in its class. Specialist in own-label sparkling wines.

Wente Livermore and Central Coast. ★→★★★ CH 84
> Important and historic specialists in Bordeaux-style whites. Fourth-generation Wentes are as dynamic as ever. CHARD, SAUV. BLANC and RIESLING are all successful. Arroyo Secco Chard is v.g. Now also sparkling.

William Wheeler Winery Sonoma. ★★
> Young Dry Creek Valley family firm. Big CAB., good SAUV.BL., rather dull CHARD.

Zaca Mesa Central Coast/Santa Barbara. ★★ CH 81 82 83 84 85 CS 79 80 81 82 83
> Santa Ynez Valley pioneer with good CHARD. and RIESLING now scaling the heights with P.N.

Z D Wines Napa. ★★ CH 80 81 82 83 84 CS 79 80 81 82
> Very small winery (moved from Sonoma to Rutherford) with a name for powerful PINOT NOIR and CHARDONNAY.

The Pacific North-West

There are now over 15,000 acres of vines and about 100 wineries in the States of Washington, Oregon and Idaho.

Oregon's vines lie mainly in the cool-temperate Willamette and warmer Umpqua valleys between the Coast and Cascades ranges. Those of Washington and Idaho are mainly east of the Cascades in the semi-arid Yakima Valley and Columbia basin areas, with very hot days and cold nights. Most Oregon-grown wines are consequently more delicate, Washington's more intensive in flavour. Some wineries use both. Whites are in the majority, though Oregon does very well with Pinot Noir and Washington with Merlot. The principal producers are:

Adelsheim Vineyard Willamette, Oregon
> Small winery: promising P. NOIR, oaky CHARDONNAY.

Amity Vineyards Willamette, Oregon
> 1976 70-acre winery; variable quality: PINOT NOIR best.

Arbor Crest Spokane, Washington
> Expanding and encouraging newcomer. Early CHARD and SAUV. BLANC v.g. Reds also promising. To watch.

Chateau Benoit Oregon
> Sound producer of M.THÜRGAU, CHARD. and P. NOIR has acquired a winemaker from Chablis and is launching sparkling.

Champs de Brionne George, Washington
> New winery. Fast start in whites but ? direction.

Château Ste. Michelle Seattle, Columbia and Yakima valleys, Washington
> The largest north-west winery, with some 5,000 acres, ultra-modern equipment and a wide range of labels. Best wines are CABERNET, SEMILLON, CHARDONNAY, MERLOT. Sparkling wines also good. Jug wines: Farron Ridge.

Columbia (formerly Associated Vintners) Washington
> A Washington pioneer and still a leader, nr. Seattle. CABERNET, RIESLING, dry spicy GEWÜRZ and esp. SEMILLON have all been successful. Good value. Now good CHARDONNAY.

Covey Run (formerly Quail Run) Yakima, Washington
> Admirable whites incl. ALIGOTÉ; reds are over strength in alcohol and flavour.

Elk Cove Vineyards Willamette, Oregon
> Very small 1977 winery. Good CHARDONNAY and RIESLING from named v'yds. PINOT NOIR inconsistent.

The Eyrie Vineyards Willamette, Oregon
> Early (1965) winery with Burgundian ideas. Oregon's most consistently good P. NOIR, and v. oaky CHARD. Also Pinots Gris and Meunier and dry Muscat.

Hillcrest Vineyard Umpqua Valley, Oregon
>Early (1961) winery in warmer area. Inconsistent; CAB best.

Hogue Cellars Yakima, Washington
>Big young winery noted for off-dry whites, esp. RIESLING, CHENIN BLANC, SAUV. BLANC. And bold CHARD. Since '83 really stylish CAB, MERLOT.

Knudsen Erath Willamette, Oregon
>Oregon's second-biggest winery with reliable good-value PINOT NOIR, esp. Vintage Select. Austere CHARDONNAY.

F. W. Langguth Winery Yakima, Washington
>German Mosel-maker succeeded with German-style RIESLINGS, esp. late harvest, now sold to SNOQUALMIE. Second label: Saddle Mountain.

Latah Creek Spokane, Washington
>Recent source of fruity, off-dry young whites, esp. CHENIN BL., RIES., SAUV.BL.

Oak Knoll Willamette, Oregon
>Fruit-winemaker also making fair-value red wines, esp. P. NOIR (red and white).

Preston Wine Cellars Yakima Valley, Washington
>Early winery with broad range of sound wines.

Rex Hill Yamhill City, Oregon
>Well-financed assault on top levels of P.NOIR from individual v'yds, incl. Reserve wines. Also Riesling. Fine new winery.

Château Ste. Chapelle Caldwell, Idaho
>The first Idaho winery, near Boise. Early CHARD and RIESLING had intense flavours but beautiful balance. Can Mimi Mook (new winemaker) keep it up?

Shafer Vineyard Cellars Willamette, Oregon
>Small meticulous P. NOIR specialist. White P. Noir may be Oregon's best; CHARD almost certainly is.

Snoqualmie Snoqualmie, Washington
>Ex-Ch. Ste. Michelle winemaker has bought LANGGUTH as winery – must be watched. So far SEMILLON is best wine.

Sokol Blosser Vineyards Willamette, Oregon
>Largest Oregon winery with wide range, incl. CHARD (esp. "Yamhill County"), SAUV. BLANC, MERLOT and (slightly sweet) RIESLING. P. NOIR is best regular effort.

Stewart Vineyards Yakima, Washington
>New estate nr. LANGGUTH. First whites v. impressive.

Tualatin Vineyards Willamette, Oregon
>Third-largest Oregon winery. Mainly whites with emphasis on CHARD, P. NOIR (red and white). Both Washington and home-grown grapes. Mixed reports.

Woodward Canyon Walla Walla, Washington
>New district, small cellar but first SEM, CAB.S. v. stylish.

Texas

In the past five years a brand-new Texan wine-industry has sprung noisily to life. It already seems past the experimental stage, with some very passable wines, though such a short track-record offers little to judge by.

The biggest winery, Ste Genevieve, at Fort Stockton, involved a French investor. Wines include Sauv. Bl., Chenin Blanc, French Colombard. But there have been money problems. Llano Estacado, at 3,000 feet near Lubbock, is a substantial enterprise with 220 acres. Nearby and much smaller is Pheasant Ridge, which has made good Chardonnay and Semillon. Cypress Valley, near Round Mountain, also on the high western plateau, has some 60 acres.

The North and East

New York State and its neighbours Ohio and Ontario have traditionally made their own style of wine from grapes of native American ancestry. American grapes have a flavour known as "foxy"; a taste acquired by many easterners. Fashion is moving in favour of hybrids between these and European grapes with less, or no, foxiness, and now increasingly towards true European varieties. Recent examples of European-style wines both from old vineyards and new areas such as Long Island show a bright future for the industry. Chardonnays and Rieslings can both be excellent. The entries below include both wineries and grape varieties.

Andres Canada's second-largest wine-producer, with wineries in Ontario and British Columbia.

Aurora One of the best white French-American hybrid grapes, the most widely planted in New York. Good for sparkling wine.

Baco Noir

One of the better red French-American hybrid grapes. High acidity but good clean dark wine.

Banfi

55-acre CHARD v'yd at Old Brookville, Long Island, released its first wine in 1986. To watch.

Benmarl

Highly regarded and expanding v'yd. and winery at Marlboro on the Hudson River. Wines are mainly from French-American hybrids (e.g. Seyval Blanc), but CHARD can be splendid.

Bridgehampton Wine Co.

Tiny property on Long Island. RIESLING and CHARD.

Brights

Canada's biggest winery, in Ontario, now tending towards French-American hybrids and experiments with European vines. Their BACO NOIR is a sound red, CHARDONNAY is steely, ALIGOTÉ pleasant. Now also in British Columbia.

Bully Hill

FINGER LAKES winery founded 1970, using both American and hybrid grapes to make varietal wines.

Canandaigua Wine Co.

Major traditional eastern winemaker with interests in WIDMERS, also in California.

Château des Charmes

Smaller Ontario winery, doing well with CHARD, P. NOIR, GAMAY, RIESLING.

Château Gai

Big Canadian (Ontario) winery making European and hybrid wines, incl. v. light CHARD, GAMAY, MERLOT.

Catawba One of the first American wine-grapes, still the second most widely grown. Pale red and foxy flavoured.

Chautauqua

The biggest grape-growing district in the east, along the s. shore of Lake Erie from New York to Ohio.

Chelois Popular red hybrid. Dry wine with some richness, slightly foxy.

Delaware

Old American white-wine grape making pleasant, slightly foxy dry wines. Used in "Champagne" and for still wine.

De Chaunac

A good red French-American hybrid grape, popular in Canada as well as New York. Full-bodied dark wine.

Finger Lakes

Century-old wine district in upper New York State, best-known for its "Champagne". The centre is Hammondsport.

Finger Lakes Wine Cellars

Young winery making good CHARD., and (esp.) RIES.

Glenora Wine Cellars
Recent FINGER LAKES winery. Very successful RIES and CHARD.

Gold Seal
One of New York's biggest and best wineries, makers of Charles Fournier "Champagne" and the HENRI MARCHANT range. Recent CHARDONNAY has been excellent, winning major prizes.

Great Western
The brand name of the PLEASANT VALLEY WINE CO'S "Champagne", one of New York's sound traditional wines.

Hargrave Vineyard
Trend-setting winery planting extensively on North Fork of Long Island, N.Y. Very promising CHARDONNAY, PINOT NOIR.

Henri Marchant
GOLD SEAL'S range of mainly traditional American wines.

Heron Hill Vineyards
Small FINGER LAKES estate with good RIES, CHARD, etc.

Inniskillin
Leading quality Canadian winery at Niagara. European and hybrid wines, incl. good MARÉCHAL FOCH, also CHARDONNAY.

Phylloxera is an insect that lives on the roots of the vine. Its arrival in Europe from North America in the 1860s was an international catastrophe. It destroyed almost every vineyard on the continent before it was discovered that the native American vine is immune to its attacks. The remedy was (and still is) to graft European vines on to American rootstocks. Virtually all Europe's vineyards are so grafted today. Whether their produce is just as good as the wine of pre-phylloxera days is a favourite debate among old-school wine-lovers.

Maréchal Foch
Useful red French hybrid between PINOT NOIR and GAMAY.

Niagara   Old American white grape used for sweet wine. Very foxy.

Pindar Vineyards
Substantial new company on North Fork, Long Island. RIESLING has been successful.

Pleasant Valley Wine Co.
Winery at Hammondsport, FINGER LAKES, owned by TAYLOR'S, producing GREAT WESTERN wines.

Seibel   Famous French grape hybridist. Many successful French-American crosses originally known by numbers, since christened as AURORA, DE CHAUNAC, CHELOIS.

Seyve-Villard
Another well-known French hybridist. His best-known cross, no. 5276, is known as Seyval Blanc.

Taylor's
The biggest wine-company of the E. States, based in the FINGER LAKES. Brands incl. GREAT WESTERN and LAKE COUNTRY. Most vines are American. Also in California. Changed hands in 1987.

Vinifera Wines
Small but influential winery of Dr Konstantin Frank, pioneer in growing European vines, incl. RIESLING, CHARDONNAY and PINOT NOIR, in the FINGER LAKES area. Some excellent wines.

Wagner Vineyards
Excellent CHARD., also GEWÜRZ, AURORA from Finger Lakes.

Widmers
Major FINGER LAKES winery selling native American varietal wines: DELAWARE, NIAGARA, etc. Now also good RIESLING.

Wiemer, Herman J.
Creative and daring German FINGER LAKES winemaker. Fine RIESLINGS; ferments v.g. CHARDONNAY in oak.

The flourishing vineyards of Argentina (the world's fifth largest) and Chile are known to the world chiefly as a source of cheap wine of sometimes remarkable quality. Most of it is drunk within South America. Recently Chile has been gaining in international reputation with some striking show successes. Argentina meanwhile continues to raise her standards. Brazil also has an expanding wine industry in the Rio Grande do Sul area, but as yet no exports.

ARGENTINA

The quality vineyards are concentrated in Mendoza province in the Andean foothills at about 2,000 feet. They are all irrigated. San Raphael, 140 miles s. of Mendoza city, is centre of a slightly cooler area. San Juan, to the north, is hotter and specializes in sherry and brandy. Salta, in the north, and Rio Negro, to the south, also produce interesting wines.

Bianchi, Bodegas

> Well-known premium wine producer at San Rafael owned by Seagrams. "Don Valentin" CABERNET and Bianchi Borgoña are best-sellers. "Particular" is their top CABERNET.

Canale, Bodegas

> Restored winery in Rio Negro makes promising SEM.

Crillon, Bodegas

> 1972-built winery owned by Seagram's, only for tank-method sparkling wines.

Esmeralda   Producers of a good CABERNET, St Felician, at Mendoza.

Flichman, Bodegas

> Old Mendoza firm now owned by a bank. Top "Caballero de la Cepa" white and red, plus SYRAH, MERLOT and sparkling.

Giol   The enormous State cooperative of Maipu province. Mainly bulk wines. Premium range called "Canciller" is good.

Gonzales Videla, Bodegas

> Old-established family firm re-equipped for modern methods. Brands include "Tromel" and "Panquehue".

Goyenechea, Bodegas

> Basque family firm in San Rafael making old-style wines, including Aberdeen Angus red.

La Rural, Bodegas ("San Filipe")

> Family-run winery at Coquimbito (Mendoza) making some of Argentina's best RIESLING and GEWÜRZ whites and some good reds. Also a charming wine museum.

Lopez, Bodegas

> Family firm best known for their "Château Montchenot" red and white and "Château Vieux" CABERNET.

Norton, Bodegas

> Old firm, originally English. Reds (esp. Malbec) are best. "Perdriel" is their premium brand. Also good sparkling wines.

Orfila, José   Long-established bodega at St. Martin, Mendoza. Top wines: Cautivo CAB. and white Extra Dry (P. BLANC).

Peñaflor   Argentina's biggest wine company, reputedly the world's third-largest. Bulk wines, but also some of Argentina's finest premium wines incl. Trapiche (esp. "Medalla"), Andean Vineyards and Fond de Cave CHARDONNAY and CABERNET. A respectable sherry, Tio Quinto, is exported.

Proviar, Bodega   Producers of "Baron B" and "M. Chandon" sparkling wine under MOËT ET CHANDON supervision. Also still reds and whites including v.g. Castel Chandon, less exciting Kleinburg, Wunderwein (whites), smooth easy Comte de Valmont, Beltour and Clos du Moulin reds.

Santa Ana, Bodegas

> Small, old-established family firm at Guaymallen, Mendoza. Wide range of wines include good Syrah Val Semina.

San Telmo   Modern winery with an almost Californian air and outstanding fresh, full-flavoured CHARD, MERLOT, CAB and esp. MALBEC.

Suter, Bodegas

Swiss-founded firm owned by Seagram's, making best-selling "Etiquetta Marron" white and good "Etiquetta Blanca" red.

Toso, Pascual Old Mendoza winery at San José, making one of Argentina's best reds, Cabernet Toso. Also RIES and sparkling wines.

Trapiche See PEÑAFLOR

Weinert, Bodegas

Small winery. Tough old-fashioned reds and promising SAUV. BLANC.

CHILE

Natural conditions are ideal for wine-growing in central Chile, just south of Santiago. But political conditions have been very difficult, and the country's full potential still has to be explored. Chilean Cabernets lead the way with resounding flavours that will one day lead to world-wide renown. New oak barrels are starting to revolutionize standards. The principal bodegas exporting wine from Chile are:

Canepa, José

Chile's most modern big bodega, handling wine from several areas. Very good frank and fruity CABERNET from Lontüé, Talca, 100 miles south; dry SAUV and SEMILLON, sweet Moscatel.

Concha y Toro

The biggest and most outward-looking wine firm, with several bodegas and 2,500 acres in the Maipo valley. Remarkable dark and deep CABERNET, MERLOT, Verdot. Brands are St. Emiliana, Marques de Casa Concha, Cassillero del Diablo. 300 acres of new white varieties have recently been established.

Cousiño Macul

Distinguished and beautiful old estate near Santiago. Very dry SEMILLON and CHARDONNAY. Don Luis light red, Don Matias dark and tannic, are good CABERNETS. Some old vintages are notable.

Errazuriz Panquehue

Historic firm in Aconcagua Valley, n. of Santiago, making very rich full-bodied wines.

Los Vascos New family estate in Colchagua Prov. 400 acres starting to make really stylish SAUV/SEM "Chevrier" and some of Chile's best CAB ('84, '85) influenced by B'x and California.

Santa Carolina

Splendid old Santiago bodega with old-style "Reserva de Familia" and better "Ochagavia" wines.

San Pedro Long established at Lontüé, Talca. The second-biggest exports, with a range of good wines sold all over S. America, esp. Bordeaux-like CABERNET Llave de Oro.

Santa Rita

Long-established bodega in the Maipo valley s. of Santiago. "120" brand CABERNET ('84) has recently gained fame at a Paris tasting. Standard CAB also v.g.

Torres, Miguel

New enterprise of Catalan family firm (see Spain) at Lontüé. Good SAUV ("Bellaterra" is oak-aged) and CHARD, v.g. RIESLING. CAB is made more "elegantly" than others in Chile.

Undurraga Famous family business; one of the first to export to the U.S.A. Wines in both old and modern styles: good clean SAUVIGNON BLANC and oaky yellow "Viejo Roble". "Gran Vino Tinto" is one of the best buys in Chile.

Viña Linderos

Small family winery in the Maipo valley exports good full-bodied CABERNET which gains from bottle-age.

PERU

Tacama, Viña

Amazing SAUV. BLANC and sparkling from Ica Prov. Also CAB.

England

The English wine industry started again in earnest in the late 1960s after a pause of some 400 years. More than a million bottles a year are now being made from over 1,000 acres; almost all white and generally Germanic in style, many from new German and French grape varieties designed to ripen well in cool weather. The annual Gore-Brown Trophy is awarded for the best English wine. N.B. Beware "British Wine", which is neither British nor wine, and has nothing to do with the following

Adgestone nr. Sandown, Isle of Wight. K. C. Barlow
Prize-winning 9½-acre v'yd. on chalky hill site. Vines are MÜLLER-THURGAU, Reichensteiner, SEYVAL BLANC. First vintage 1970. Light, fragrant, dryish wines age surprisingly well.

Barnsgate Manor nr. Uckfield, Sussex. Pieroth Co.
A showpiece 21 acres of MÜLLER-THURGAU, Reichensteiner, Kerner, Seyval, P. NOIR, CHARD.

Barton Manor East Cowes, Isle of Wight. A. Goddard
5½-acre v'yd producing an aromatic medium dry blend, winner of the '84 Gore-Brown Trophy. Consistently good.

Beaulieu nr. Lymington, Hampshire. The Hon. Ralph Montagu
6-acre v'yd, principally of MÜLLER-THURGAU, established in 1960 by the Gore-Brown family on an old monastic site.

Biddenden nr. Tenterden, Kent. R. A. Barnes
18-acre mixed v'yd. planted in 1970, making crisp medium-dry white of MÜLLER-THURGAU and Ortega; also a rosé with PINOT NOIR. First vintage 1973. Also makes wine for other growers. Gold medal winner in 1983.

Bosmere nr. Chippenham, Wiltshire. G. H. Walton
16 acres of MÜLLER-THURGAU and SEYVAL BLANC; some GAMAY and PINOT NOIR.

Breaky Bottom nr. Lewes, Sussex P. Hall
Good dry wines from 4-acre vineyard.

Bruisyard nr. Saxmundham, Suffolk. I. H. Berwick
10 acres of MÜLLER-THURGAU making medium-dry wines since 1976. Well distributed.

Carr Taylor Vineyards nr. Hastings, Sussex. D. Carr-Taylor
21 acres, planted 1974. Gutenborner, Huxelrebe, KERNER and Reichensteiner. Exports to France.

Cavendish Manor nr. Sudbury, Suffolk. B. T. Ambrose
10½-acre v'yd. of MÜLLER-THURGAU planted on a farm. Fruity dry wine has won several awards at home and abroad since 1974.

Chilford Hundred Linton, nr. Cambridge. S. Alper
20 acres of MÜLLER-THURGAU, Schönburger, Huxelrebe, Siegerrebe and Ortega making fairly dry wines since 1974.

Chilsdown nr. Chichester, Sussex. Paget Brothers
10 acres of MÜLLER-THURGAU, Reichensteiner and SEYVAL BLANC making full dry French-style white since 1974.

Ditchling nr. Hassocks, Sussex. D. & A. Mills
5-acres v'yd well-reputed for consistency.

Downers Vineyard Henfield, Sussex, E.G. Downer
6 acres of MÜLLER-THURGAU, planted 1976.

Elmham Park nr. East Dereham, Norfolk. R. Don
7½-acre v'yd. of a wine-merchant/fruit farmer, planted with MÜLLER-THURGAU, Madeleine-Angevine, etc. "Mosel-style" light dry flowery wines. First vintage 1974. Also a fine dry cider.

Felsted (formerly Felstar) Felsted, Essex. K. Dawson, winemaker
A pioneer 8-acre v'yd planted 1966. MÜLLER-THURGAU, Seyval, P. NOIR, Madeleine Angevine. New owners in 1985.

Gamlingay nr. Sandy, Bedfordshire. G. P. and N. Reece
8½ acres of MÜLLER-THURGAU, Reichensteiner and SCHEUREBE making wine since 1970.

Hambledon nr. Petersfield, Hampshire. Hambledon Vineyards Ltd
The first modern English v'yd., planted in 1951 on a chalk slope
with advice from Champagne. Grapes are CHARDONNAY, PINOT
NOIR and SEYVAL BLANC. Now 7½ acres. Fairly dry wines.

Highwaymans nr. Bury St. Edmunds, Suffolk. Macrae Farms
25 acres, planted 1974. MÜLLER-THURGAU and PINOT NOIR.

Lamberhurst Priory nr. Tunbridge Wells, Kent. K. McAlpine
England's biggest v'yd. with 48 acres, planted 1972. Largely
MÜLLER-THURGAU, SEYVAL BLANC, also Reichensteiner, Schön-
burger. Production capacity approx. half a million bottles a year
including winemaking for other small v'yds. Also makes Horam
Manor, 8 acres at Heathfield, Sussex. A regular prize-winner.

Lexham Hall nr. King's Lynn, Norfolk. N. W. D. Foster
8 acres, planted 1975. MÜLLER-THURGAU, SCHEUREBE, Reichensteiner and Madeleine-Angevine.

New Hall nr. Maldon, Essex. S. W. Greenwood
24 acres of a mixed farm planted with Huxelrebe, MÜLLER-
THURGAU and PINOT NOIR. Makes award-winning whites.
Experimental reds.

Penshurst nr. Tunbridge Wells, Kent. D. E. Westphal
12 acres of the usual varieties in production since 1976.

Pilton Manor nr. Shepton Mallet, Somerset. N. Godden
6½-acre hillside v'yd., chiefly of MÜLLER-THURGAU and SEYVAL
BLANC, planted 1966. Also a méthode champenoise sparkling.

Pulham nr. Norwich, Norfolk. P. W. Cook
6-acre v'yd. planted 1973; principally MÜLLER-THURGAU,
Auxerrois and experimental Bacchus.

Rock Lodge nr. Haywards Heath, Sussex. N. D. Cowderoy
3½-acre v'yd. of MÜLLER-THURGAU and Reichensteiner making
dry white since 1970.

St. Etheldreda nr. Ely, Cambridgeshire. N. Sneesby
2-acre mixed v'yd. making a MÜLLER-THURGAU and a CHAR-
DONNAY since 1974.

St. George's Waldron, Heathfield, E. Sussex. P. & G. Biddlecombe
5 acres planted 1979. MÜLLER-THURGAU etc. and some GEWÜRZ.
Well-publicized young venture has sold wine to Japan, etc.

Staple nr. Canterbury, Kent. W. T. Ash
7 acres, mainly MÜLLER-THURGAU. Some Huxelrebe and
Reichensteiner. Dry and fruity wines.

Stocks nr. Suckley, Worcestershire. R. M. O. Capper
Successful 11-acre v'yd. All MÜLLER-THURGAU.

Tenterden nr. Tenterden, Kent. S. P. Skelton
10 acres of a 100-acre fruit farm. Planted 1977. Six wines from
very dry to sweet, incl. MÜLLER-THURGAU, Gutenborner, SEYVAL
BLANC and rosé.

Three Choirs nr. Newent, Gloucestershire. T. W. Day.
17½ acres of MÜLLER-THURGAU and Reichensteiner.

Westbury nr. Reading, Berkshire. B. H. Theobald
12½ acres of a mixed farm. 11 varieties in commercial quantities
since 1975, incl. England's only real PINOT NOIR red.

Wootton nr. Wells, Somerset. Major C. L. B. Gillespie
6-acre v'yd. of Schönburger, MÜLLER-THURGAU, SEYVAL BLANC,
etc., making award-winning fresh and fruity wines since 1973.

Wraxall nr. Shepton Mallet, Somerset. A. S. Holmes
6 acres of MÜLLER-THURGAU and SEYVAL BLANC. Planted 1974.

Australia

It is only 20 years since new technology revolutionized Australia's 150-year-old wine industry, ending the dominance of fortified wines and making table wines of top quality possible. Old-style Australian wines were thick-set and burly Shiraz reds or Semillon or Riesling whites grown in warm to hot regions. A progressive shift to cooler areas, to new wood fermentation and maturation, to noble varieties (with Cabernet, Merlot, Pinot Noir, Chardonnay and Sauvignon Blanc at the forefront) has seen a radical change in style which has by no means run its course. Nonetheless, extract and alcohol levels continue to be high and the best wines still have great character and the ability to age splendidly.

Parallels with California abound. The most obvious is a suddenly-developed need to find new markets. At last Australia's best wines are to be found in London and New York. But it is not easy to keep tabs on them. There are now almost 500 wineries in commercial production. Labels are becoming less garrulous (but less informative) as Australian consumers become more sophisticated. Such information as they give can be relied on, while prizes in shows (which are highly competitive) mean a great deal. In a country lacking any formal grades of quality the buyer needs all the help he can get.

Wine areas

The vintages here are those rated as good or excellent for the reds of the areas in question. Excellent recent vintages are marked with an accent.

Adelaide Hills (Sth Aust)   84′ 85′ 86′
> Spearheaded by PETALUMA: numerous new v'yds at very cool 1500′ sites in Mt Lofty ranges coming into production.

Adelaide Plains (Sth Aust)   79 80 82 84′ 86′
> Small area immediately n. of Adelaide formerly known as Angle Vale. Wineries incl. Anglesey, Normans, PRIMO ESTATE.

Barossa (Sth Aust)   66 73 75 76 79 80 81 82′ 84′ 85 86′
> Australia's most important winery (though not v'yd) area, processing grapes from diverse sources (local, to MURRAY VALLEY, through to high quality cool regions from adjacent hills to far-distant COONAWARRA) to make equally diverse styles.

Bendigo/Ballarat (Vic) 73 75 76 78 79 80' 82 84' 85
> Widespread small v'yds some of extreme quality, re-creating the glories of the last century. 14 wineries incl. CH. LE AMON, BALGOWNIE, Heathcote Winery and Passing Clouds.

Canberra District (ACT)
> 10 wineries now sell cellar door to local and tourist trade. Quality is variable, as is style.

Clare Watervale (Sth Aust) 66' 70' 71' 73' 76' 79' **80' 82'** 84' **85'** 86'
> Small high-quality area 90 miles n. of Adelaide best known for RIESLING; also planted with SHIRAZ and CABERNET. 17 wineries spill over into new adjacent sub-district of Polish Hill River.

Coonawarra (Sth Aust) 66 70 71 72 73 76 77 79 80' 82' 84 85 86'
> Southernmost and greatest v'yd. of state, long famous for well-balanced reds, recently successful with RIESLING, CHARDONNAY. Numerous recent arrivals incl. Hollicks, Haselgrove, Koppamurra, Ladbroke Grove, Zema Estates.

Geelong (Vic) 78 80' 82 84' 85
> Once famous area destroyed by phylloxera, re-established mid 60s. Very cool, dry climate produces firm table wines from premium varieties. Names incl. IDYLL, HICKINBOTHAM.

Goulburn Valley (Vic) 68 71 76 79 80' 82 84'
> A mixture of old (e.g. CH. TAHBILK) and new (e.g. MITCHELTON) wineries in temperate region; full flavoured table wines.

Great Western/Avoca (Vic) 78 80' 82' 84 85
> Adjacent cool to temperate regions in central w. of state; Avoca also known as Pyrenees area. High quality table and sparkling wines. Now 8 wineries, 6 of recent origin.

Hunter Valley (N.S.W.) 66 67 70 72 73 75 76 77 79 80' 82 84 85' 86
> The great name in N.S.W. Broad soft earthy SHIRAZ reds and SEMILLON whites with a style of their own. Now also CABERNET and CHARDONNAY. Many changes in identity.

Keppoch/Padthaway (Sth Aust) 75 76 79 80 81 82' 84 85
> Large new v'yd. area (no wineries) developed by big companies as an overspill of adjacent COONAWARRA. Cool climate; good commercial reds and whites and CHARD/PINOT NOIR sp. wines.

N.E. Victoria 66' 70' 71' 73' 75' 76' **80' 82'** 84' 86'
> Historic area incl. Rutherglen, Corowa, Wangaratta. Heavy reds and magnificent sweet dessert wines.

Margaret River (W. Aust) 75' 76' 79' **81'** 82' 83' **85**
> New cool coastal area producing superbly elegant wines, 280 kms s. of Perth. 15 operating wineries; others planned.

Mornington Peninsula (Vic.) 84' 86'
> Five commercial wineries on dolls-house scale making exciting wines in new cool coastal area 40km s. of Melbourne. 20 growers, wineries incl. Elgee Park, Merricks.

Mount Barker/Franklin River (W. Aust) 76 80 81' 82 83
> Promising new far-flung cool area in extreme south of state.

Mudgee (N.S.W.) 72 74 75 78 79 80 82' 84'
> Small isolated area 270 kms n.w. of Sydney. Big r. of colour and flavour and full coarse w., recently being refined.

Murray Valley (Sth Aust, Vic & N.S.W.) NV
> Important irrigated v'yds. near Swan Hill, Mildura (N.S.W. and Vic), Renmark, Berri, Loxton, Waikerie and Morgan (S.A.). Principally "cask" table wines. 40% of total wine production.

Pyrenees (Vic) **82'** 84' 85'
> Central Vic. region with seven wineries producing rich minty reds and one or two interesting whites, esp. FUMÉ BLANC.

Riverina (N.S.W.) NV
> Large volume producer centred around Griffith; good quality cask wines esp. whites.

Southern Vales (Sth Aust) 67′ 71′ 75′ 76′ 80′ 81′ 82′ 84′ 85′ **86′**
> Covers energetic McLaren Vale/Reynella regions on s. outskirts of Adelaide. Big styles now being rapidly refined and improved; promising CHARDONNAY.

Swan Valley (W. Aust) 75′ 78′ 81′ **82′ 84′** 85′
> The birthplace of wine in the west, on the n. outskirts of Perth. Hot climate makes strong low-acid table, good dessert wines. Declining in importance viticulturally.

Tasmania 82′ 84′ 85′
> 13 vineyards now offer wine for commercial sale, producing over 200,000 litres in all. Has great potential particularly for CHARDONNAY and P. NOIR.

Upper Hunter (N.S.W.) 75′ 79′ 80′ 81′ 83′ 85′ 86′
> Est. early 60s; with irrigated vines produce mainly w. wines, lighter and quicker-developing than Hunter w. Often good value.

Yarra Valley ("Lilydale") 76′ 78′ **80′** 81′ 82′ **84′** 85′ 86′
> Historic wine area near Melbourne fallen into disuse, now being redeveloped by enthusiasts with small wineries. A superb viticultural area with noble varieties only.

Wineries

Allandale Hunter Valley. Table ★→★★★
> Small winery without v′yds. buying selected local grapes. Quality variable; can be outstanding: esp. CHARD.

All Saints N.E. Vic. Full range ★
> Once famous old family winery with faltering quality.

Angove's Riverland. Table and dessert ★→★★
> Family business in Adelaide and Renmark in the Murray Valley. Notable value in CAB and esp. CHARD and other whites.

Arrowfield Upper Hunter. Table ★★
> Substantial vineyard, on irrigated land. Light CABERNET, succulent "Show Reserve" CHARD; also "wooded" SEM.

Bailey's N.E. Vic. Table and dessert ★★→★★★★
> Rich old-fashioned reds of great character, esp. Bundarra Hermitage, and magnificent dessert MUSCAT and TOKAY.

Balgownie Bendigo/Ballarat. Table ★★★
> Specialist in fine reds, particularly straight CABERNET and P. NOIR. Also exceptional CHARDONNAY. Now owned by MILDARA.

Basedow Barossa Valley. Table ★★
> Small winery buying grapes for reliably good range of r. and w.

Berri-Renmano Coop. Riverland. Full range ★→★★
> By far Aust's largest winery following recent merger with Renmano, selling mostly to other companies. Now developing own brands on local and export markets. (See RENMANO.)

Best's Great Western. Full range ★→★★
> Conservative old family winery at Great Western with good mid-weight reds and original tasty whites, incl. sparkling.

Blass, Wolf (Bilyara) Barossa V. Table and sp. ★★★
> Wolf Blass is the ebullient German winemaker. Dazzling labels and extraordinary wine-show successes, with mastery of blending varieties, areas and lashings of new oak. Not to be missed.

Bowen Estate Coonawarra. Table ★★★
> Small Coonawarra winery; intense but not heavy CABERNET, good RIESLING. Sparkling CHARDONNAY on the way.

Brand Coonawarra. Table ★★→★★★
> Family estate. Fine, bold and stylish CABERNET and SHIRAZ under the Laira label. A few quality blemishes in late 70's/early 80's, now rectified.

Brokenwood Hunter Valley. Table ★★★
> Exciting quality of (partly COONAWARRA) CAB and SHIRAZ since 1973; new winery 1983 added high quality CHARD and SEM.

Brown Brothers Milawa. Full range ★→★★★
> Old family firm with new ideas, wide range of rather delicate varietal wines, many from cool mountain districts. CHARD and dry white MUSCAT outstanding in a reliable range.

Buring, Leo Barossa. Full range ★★→ ★★★
> "Château Leonay", old white-wine specialists, now owned by LINDEMAN. Steady "Reserve Bin" Rhine Riesling.

Campbells of Rutherglen N.E. Vic. Full range ★★
> Impressive lively whites, smooth reds plus good dessert wines.

Cape Mentelle Margaret River. Table ★★→★★★★
> Idiosyncratic robust CABERNET departs from district style and can be magnificent; also ZINFANDEL and v. popular Semillon.

Capel Vale S.W. Western Aust. ★★
> Outstanding range of whites, incl. GEWÜRZ. New v.g. CAB.

Chambers' Rosewood N.E. Vic. Full range ★★→★★★
> Good cheap table and great dessert wines, esp. TOKAY.

Chateau Le Amon Bendigo. Table ★★★
> Very stylish minty CAB and peppery SHIRAZ.

Château Hornsby Alice Springs, N. Territory. ★→★★
> A charming aberration. Full-flavoured clean reds from the Bush.

Château Remy Great Western/Avoca. Sp. and Table ★★→★★★
> Owned by Remy Martin, run by French-trained champagne maker and winemaker wife. Trebbiano CHARD blend surprisingly successful. Also good "Blue Pyrenees" reds.

Château Tahbilk Goulburn Valley. Table ★★→★★★
> Beautiful and historic family-owned estate making long-lived CAB, SHIRAZ, Rhine Riesling and Marsanne. "Private Bins" are outstanding.

Conti, Paul, Wines Swan Valley. Table ★★
> Elegant Hermitage, also fine CHARD and other estate whites.

Craigmoor Mudgee. Table and Port ★★→★★★
> Oldest district winery now part of MONTROSE group and making very good CHARD and SEM, the two blended, and CAB/SHIRAZ.

Cullens Willyabrup Margaret River. Table ★★★
> Butch and kindly CABERNET/MERLOT, pungent SAUV. BLANC and bold "wooded" CHARDONNAY are all real characters.

d'Arenberg Southern Vales. Table and dessert ★→★★
> Old-style family outfit with strapping rustic reds and RIESLING.

De Bortoli Griffith, N.S.W. ★→★★★
> Irrigation-area winery. Standard reds and whites but magnificent sweet "botrytized" Beerenausleses of SEMILLON, TRAMINER, RIESLING.

Drayton's Bellevue Hunter Valley, N.S.W. Table ★
> Traditional Hermitage and SEMILLON; occasionally good CHARD; recent quality disappointing.

Enterprise Wines Clare Valley. Table ★★★
> Tim Knappstein, an exceptionally gifted winemaker, produces Rhine Riesling, FUMÉ BLANC, GEWÜRZ and CABERNET.

Evans and Tate Swan Valley. Table ★★→★★★
> Fine elegant reds from the Margaret River Redbrook and Swan Valley Gnangara v'yds. Good SEMILLON too.

Evans Family Hunter Valley N.S.W. ★★★
> Excellent CHARD, fermented in new oak, from small v'yd. owned by family of Len Evans.

Hardy's Southern Vales, Barossa, Keppoch, etc. Full range ★→★★★
> Famous family-run company using and blending wines from several areas. St. Thomas Burgundy, Old Castle Riesling are standards. Top wines are "Collection" series and Australia's greatest vintage Ports. Hardy's recently bought HOUGHTON and REYNELLA; the latter's beautifully restored buildings are now group headquarters.

Heemskerk Tasmania. Table ★★★
> Most successful commercial operation in Tasmania. Herby CAB; promising CHARD. Also P.N. and RIESLING. Recent partnership with Louis Roederer plans high class sp. wine in years to come.

Henschke Barossa. Table ★★★
> Family business known for sterling SHIRAZ and good CAB. New high-country v'yds on Adelaide Hills add excitement.

Hickinbotham Winemakers Geelong. Table ★★→★★★
> Innovative winemaking by Hickinbotham family (since 1980) has produced some fascinating styles incl. carbonic maceration CABERNET ("Cab Mac"), dry ausleses, etc.

Hollick Coonawarra. Table ★★★
> Ian and Wendy Hollick won instant stardom with trophy-winning '84 CAB; also v.g. CHARD and RIES from small winery.

Houghton Swan Valley, W.A. Full range. ★→★★★
> The most famous old winery of W.A. Soft, ripe White Burgundy is top wine; also excellent CAB, VERDELHO etc. See Hardy's.

Hungerford Hill Hunter Valley and Coonawarra. Table ★★→★★★
> Medium-sized winery producing high class varietals esp. RIESLING and CABERNET from COONAWARRA.

Huntington Estate Mudgee. Table ★★→★★★
> New small winery; the best in Mudgee. Fine CABERNETS and clean SEMILLON and CHARDONNAY. Invariably under-priced.

Idyll Geelong. Vic. ★★★
> Small winery with CAB and GEWÜRZ of highest quality.

Jeffrey Grosset Clare. Table ★★→★★★
> Exceedingly elegant RIESLING and CABERNET made in consistent style by fastidious young winemaker.

Kaiser Stuhl Barossa. Full range ★→★★★
> Now part of Penfolds; a huge winery processes fruit from diverse sources. "Individual v'yd." RIESLINGS can be excellent. So can Red Ribbon reds.

Katnook Estate Coonawarra. Table ★★★
> Excellent pricey CAB and CHARD; also SAUV.BL., P.NOIR, RIÉS.

Lillydale Vineyards Yarra Valley. Table ★★★
> Foremost producer of CHARD using sophisticated techniques; also scented GEWÜRZTRAMINER and crisp RIESLING.

Krondorf Wines Barossa Valley. Table ★★→ ★★★
> Acquired by MILDARA in 1986, but quality and brand image will be preserved. "Burge and Wilson" wines are best.

Lake's Folly Hunter Valley. Table ★★★★
> The work of an inspired surgeon from Sydney. CABERNET and new barrels make fine complex reds. Also exciting CHARD.

Leeuwin Estate Margaret River. Table ★★→★★★★
> Lavishly equipped estate leading W. Australia with superb (and very expensive) CHARD; developing fine P.N., RIES., and CAB.

Lehmann Wines, Peter Barossa. Table ★★→★★★
> Defender of the Barossa faith, Lehmann makes vast quantities of wine, mostly sold in bulk, and special cuvees under his own label.

Leconfield Coonawarra. Table ★→★★★
> Coonawarra CABERNET of great style. RIESLING improving.

Lindeman Orig. Hunter, now everywhere. Full range ★→★★★
> One of the oldest firms, now a giant owned by Phillip Morris. Its Ben Ean "Moselle" is market leader. Owns BURINGS in Barossa and Rouge Homme in COONAWARRA, and important v'yds at Padthaway: outstanding CHARD. Many inter-state blends. Pioneered new styles, yet still make fat old-style "Hunters".

McWilliams Hunter Valley and Riverina. Full range ★→★★
> Famous family of Hunter winemakers at Mount Pleasant (HERMITAGE and SEMILLON). Pioneers in RIVERINA with noble varieties, incl. CABERNET and sweet white "Lexia".

Mildara Coonawarra. Murray Valley. Full range ★→★★★
Sherry and brandy specialists at Mildura on the Murray river also making fine CABERNET and RIESLING at COONAWARRA. Now own BALGOWNIE and YELLOWGLEN.

Mitchells Clare Valley. Table ★★★
Small family winery, excellent RIESLING and CABERNET.

Mitchelton Goulburn Valley. Table ★★★
Big modern winery. A wide range incl. v.g. wood-matured Marsanne, CAB and botrytised RIESLING from COONAWARRA.

Montrose Mudgee. Table ★★ →★★★
Recent winemaking and marketing initiatives have had much success; superb CHARD, interesting BARBERA and NEBBIOLO.

Moorilla Estate Tasmania. Table ★★★
Senior winery on outskirts of Hobart on Derwent River producing superb P.N., v.g. CHARD and CAB in tiny quantities.

Morris N.E. Vic. Table and dessert ★★ →★★★★
Old winery at Rutherglen making Australia's greatest dessert muscats and tokays; recently v.g. cheap table wines.

Moss Wood Margaret River. Table ★★★★
Best Margaret River winery (with only 29 acres). CABERNET SAUVIGNON, PINOT NOIR, CHARDONNAY all with rich fruit flavours not unlike the best Californians.

Mount Mary Yarra Valley. Table ★★★
Dr. John Middleton is a perfectionist with tiny amounts of CHARD, P. NOIR and (best of all) CAB/CAB. FRANC/MERLOT.

Orlando (Gramp's) Barossa Valley. Full range ★★→ ★★★
Great pioneering company, now owned by Reckitt & Colman. Full range from good standard Jacob's Creek Claret to excellent COONAWARRA CABERNET; CHARDONNAY and great Steingarten RIESLING. William Jacob is a low-price line.

Penfold's Orig. Adelaide, now everywhere. Full range ★→★★★★
Ubiquitous and excellent company: in BAROSSA, RIVERINA, COONAWARRA, CLARE VALLEY, etc. Grange Hermitage (75', 76', 78) is ★★★★, St. Henri Claret some way behind. Bin-numbered wines are usually outstanding. "Grandfather Port" is sensational. New: "Magill Estate" from old Grange v'yd.

Petaluma Adelaide Hills. ★★★★
A recent rocket-like success with CAB, CHARD and RIESLING, now centred around new winery in ADELAIDE HILLS using COONAWARRA and CLARE grapes. Bollinger now part owner, with ambitious sparkling wine v'yds and facilities in ADELAIDE HILLS.

Piper's Brook Tasmania. Table ★★★
Cool-area pioneer with very good RIESLING, P. NOIR, superb CHARD from Tamar Valley near Launceston. Lovely labels.

Pirramimma S. Vales, S.A. Full range ★→★★
Big supply of good standard; reds best.

Plantaganet Mt. Barker. Full range ★★→★★★
The region's largest producer with a wide range of varieties esp. rich CHARD, SHIRAZ and vibrant, potent CAB.

Quelltaler Clare Watervale. Full range ★→★★
Old winery known for good "Granfiesta" sherry. Recently good Rhine Riesling and SEMILLON. Owned by Rémy Martin.

Redman Coonawarra. Red Table ★→★★
The most famous old name in COONAWARRA makes two wines (Claret, CABERNET). Recent quality disappointing.

Renmano Murray Valley. S.A. Full range ★→ ★★
Huge coop (see Berri-Renmano). "Chairman's Selections" are v.g. value.

Reynella S. Vales. S.A. Full range ★★→★★★
Historic red wine specialists s. of Adelaide. Rich CAB (partly COONAWARRA), Claret and excellent "port". See Hardy's.

The Robson Vineyard Hunter Valley. Table ★★→★★★
> Fastidious winery. Wide range of varietals; CHARDONNAY CABERNET and Hermitage consistently show winners.

Rosemount Upper Hunter and Coonawarra. Table ★→★★★
> Rich, unctuous HUNTER "Show" CHARD is an international smash. This and COONAWARRA CAB lead the wide range.

Rothbury Estate Hunter Valley. Table ★★→ ★★★
> Important syndicate-owned estate. Traditional HUNTER: "Hermitage" and long-lived SEMILLON: "Black Label" best. New CHARDONNAY (from Cowra) and PINOT NOIR are promising.

St. Huberts Yarra Valley. Vic. Table ★→★★★
> Small, erratic, much sought-after CABERNET.

St. Leonards N.E. Vic. Full range ★★
> Excellent varieties sold only at cellar door and mailing list, incl. exotics, e.g. Fetyaska and Orange Muscat.

Saltram Barossa. Full range ★→★★★
> Seagram-owned winery making wines of variable quality. "Pinnacle Selection" best wines; also Mamre Brook.

Sandalford Swan Valley. Table ★→★★
> Fine old winery with contrasting styles of red and white varietals from Swan and Margaret rivers. Excellent VERDELHO.

Saxonvale Hunter Valley. Table ★★
> Medium-sized operation now making good early-maturing SEMILLON and CHARDONNAY. Also good soft CABERNET, SHIRAZ. Acquired by WYNDHAM ESTATE, in 1986.

Seppelt Barossa, Great Western, Keppoch, etc. Full range ★→★★★
> Far-flung producers of Australia's most popular "champagne" (Gt. Western Brut), good dessert wines, the reliable Moyston claret and some very good private bin wines, incl. CHARD., from Gt. Western and Drumborg in Victoria, and Keppoch and Barossa in South Australia.

Seville Estate Yarra Valley. Table ★★→★★★
> Tiny Yarra Valley winery with well-made CHARDONNAY, very late-picked RIESLING, SHIRAZ, PINOT NOIR, etc.

Stanley Clare Valley. Full range ★→ ★★★
> Important medium-size quality winery owned by Heinz. Good RHINE RIESLING, CHARD and CABERNET and complex Cabernet-Shiraz-Malbec blends under Leasingham label.

Stanton & Killeen N.E. Vic. Table and dessert ★★
> Small old family firm. Rich muscats; also strong Moodemere reds.

Taltarni Great Western/Avoca. Table ★★★
> Dominique Portet, brother of Bernard (Clos du Val, Napa), son of André (Ch Lafite), produces huge but balanced reds, good SAUV. BLANC and fine sparkling wines.

Taylors Wines Clare Valley. Table ★→★★
> Large new red wine-producing unit (CABERNET and HERMITAGE) turning to whites (RHINE RIESLING, generics).

Tisdall Wines Goulburn Valley. Table ★★→★★★
> Exciting young winery in the Echuca river area, making local ("Rosbercon") wines plus finer material from central ranges (Mount Helen CABERNET, CHARDONNAY, RHINE RIESLING).

Tollana Barossa, S.A. Full range ★→★★
> Old company famous for brandy, has latterly made some quite fine CABERNET and RHINE RIESLING.

Tulloch Hunter Valley, N.S.W. Table ★→★★
> An old name at Pokolbin, with good dry reds "RIESLING" and VERDELHO, now part of PENFOLD's group.

Tyrrell Hunter Valley, N.S.W. Table ★★→ ★★★
> Some of the best traditional Hunter wines, Hermitage and SEMILLON, are "Vat 47". Also big rich CHARDONNAY, delicate PINOT NOIR and v.g. sparkling.

Vasse Felix Margaret River. Table ★★→★★★
> The pioneer of the Margaret River. Elegant CABERNETS notable for mid-weight balance.

Virgin Hills Bendigo/Ballarat. Table ★★★★
> Tiny supplies of one blended (CAB/SHIRAZ/MALBEC) red of legendary style and balance.

Westfield Swan Valley. Table ★→ ★★
> John Kosovich's CABERNETS and VERDELHOS show particular finesse in a hot climate. Also good "port".

Wirra Wirra Southern Vales. S.A. Table ★★→★★★
> Under PETALUMA influence high quality, beautifully packaged whites and reds have made a big impact recently.

Woodleys Barossa, S.A. Table ★
> Well-known for low-price Queen Adelaide label. "Reference" CAB is best wine. Acquired by SEPPELT's in late 1985.

Wyndham Estate Branxton, N.S.W. Full range ★ →★★
> Aggressive large new Hunter group with Richmond Grove, Hunter Estate, Hollydene and Saxonvale as its brands.

Wynns Coonawarra, Southern Vales. Table ★ →★★★
> Large inter-state company, originators of flagon wines, with largest winery and vineyards at COONAWARRA, making good CAB (esp. "John Riddoch"). Acquired by PENFOLD's in 1985.

Yalumba (S. Smith & Sons) Barossa. Full range ★→ ★★★
> Big old family firm with considerable verve, using computers, juice evaluation, etc., to produce full spectrum of high quality wines, incl. "Hill-Smith Estate". "Heggies V'yd" is best.

Yarra Yering Yarra Valley. Table ★★★
> The largest (30 acre) Lilydale boutique winery and one of the best. Esp. racy powerful PINOT and deep CABERNET.

Yellowglen Bendigo/Ballarat. Sparkling ★★→★★★
> High-flying sparkling winemaker acquired by MILDARA but run autonomously by French-trained Dominique Landragin.

Yeringberg Yarra Valley. Table ★★★
> Historic estate now again producing v. high-quality CHARD., CAB., P.N. in minute quantities.

New Zealand

In the past 10 years New Zealand has made an international impact with table wines of startling quality, particularly whites, well able to compete with those of Australia or California. Progress has accelerated since new vineyard areas were planted in the early '70s on both North and South Islands. There are now well over 10,000 acres. White grapes predominate. Müller-Thurgau is the most planted variety, but it is Sauvignon Blanc and Chardonnay that point to a starry future.

The general style of wine is relatively light with fairly high acidity. The distinctive flavours of grape varieties are well marked; barrel-ageing is adding to the impact and interest of their wines. The principal producers are:

Babich
> Old Dalmatian family firm nr. Auckland. Standard "Riesling-Sylvaner"; good GEWÜRZ, CHARD, SAUV.BL. and reds.

Cape Mentelle
> Offshoot of W. Australia winery making excellent "Cloudy Bay" SAUV.BL. at MARLBOROUGH.

Collard

Small winery using grapes from several areas for good CHARD, SAUV.BL., CHENIN BL. and CAB/MERLOT.

Cooks

Progressive company based at Te Kauwhata nr. Auckland. 1,000 acres +, mainly in Gisborne and Hawkes Bay, produce fine light CABERNET, CHARDONNAY and GEWÜRZ: also late-picked MÜLLER-THURGAU. Now incorporates McWilliams.

Cooper's Creek

New Auckland winery exporting good CHARD, SAUV.BL. and GEWÜRZ.

Corbans

Old-established firm at Henderson, nr. Auckland. New v'yds at MARLBOROUGH produce v.g. SAUV.BL., RIESLING and CHARD.

De Redcliffe

Estate with "Hotel du Vin" nr. Auckland. Wines are CAB/MERLOT, CHARD and SEMILLON.

Delegat's Impressive Gisborne whites, esp. CHARD and M-T Auslese.

Esk Valley

Hawkes Bay winery (formerly Glenvale). Both reds and whites are well made.

Gisborne Major white-grape district in n.e. of North Island.

Goldwater

Small winery on island in Auckland gulf with CAB/MERLOT and oaky SAUV.BL.

Hawkes Bay

The biggest vineyard area on the east coast of North Island.

Hunter Estate

New producer at MARLBOROUGH and Christchurch. Stunning early CHARD and SAUV. BLANC both straight and oak-aged ("Fumé").

Marlborough

Vineyard area at n. end of South Island, now with over 2,000 acres mostly in white grapes. Potential quality is remarkable.

Matawhero

Small GISBORNE producer with high-quality GEWÜRZ-TRAMINER, CHARDONNAY, SAUV and CHENIN BLANC.

Montana

The largest wine company, now incorporating Penfold's, originally at GISBORNE, pioneer with fine wines and in planting at MARLBOROUGH. Range incl. CHARDs (Marlborough and Gisborne), SAUV.BL., RIESLING and CAB.SAUV. (Marlborough). Also Lindauer *méthode champenoise* sp.

Ngatarawa

Boutique winery in old stables at Hastings, Hawkes Bay. CHARD, SAUV.BL. and CAB/MERLOT under "Glazebrook" label.

Nobilo's

Yugoslav family firm, making deep-flavoured, ageable reds at Huapai, n. of Auckland.

Selak's

Successful little winery exporting CHARD, SAUV.BL. and oak-aged SAUV.BL./SEMILLON blend.

Te Mata Estate

Old HAWKES BAY property restored, making excellent CABERNET/MERLOT. Also CHARDONNAY, SAUV.BL.

Vidal's

Highly proficient and atmospheric Hawkes Bay winery. Trophy-winning CHARD and fine CABERNET. P.NOIR Fumé Bl. and GEWÜRZ.

Villa Maria

Yugoslav family winery nr. Auckland airport. GEWÜRZ, CHARD, SAUV. BLANC, CAB all well made from various N. Island sources.

South Africa

South Africa has made excellent sherry and port for many years, but has taken table wine seriously only in the past 15 or so. In 1972 a new system of Wines of Origin and registered "estates" started a new era of competitive modern wine-making. Cabernet Sauvignon reds of high quality are well established. Chardonnay, Sauvignon Blanc and other superior grapes now being introduced are already showing great promise.

Allesverloren ★★
> Estate in MALMESBURY with 395 acres of v'yds., well known for "port", and now also specializing in powerful, almost roasted, reds, incl. ripe, soft CABERNET, and Tinta Barocca.

Alphen ★
> Winery at Somerset West. Name is used as a brand by Gilbeys.

Alto ★★
> STELLENBOSCH estate of 247 acres high on a hill, best known for massive-bodied CAB and a good SHIRAZ blend: Alto Rouge.

Backsberg ★★ →★★★
> A prize-winning 395-acre estate at PAARL with notably good white wines (incl. CHARD.) and med. body CABERNET and SHIRAZ.

Bellingham ★→★★★
> Top brand name of Union Wine Co. Reliable reds and whites, esp. CABERNET. The GRAND CRU is well known.

Bergkelder
> Big wine concern at STELLENBOSCH, member of the OUDE MEESTER group, making and distributing many brands (FLEUR DU CAP, GRÜNBERGER) and estate wines. Now combined with STELLENBOSCH FARMERS' WINERY.

Bertrams ★★
> Gilbeys' brand with a wide range, good CAB and SHIRAZ.

Blaauwklippen ★★→★★★
> Estate s. of STELLENBOSCH producing top reds, CAB, P. NOIR and ZIN, and good RHINE RIES, and SAUV BLANC.

Boberg Controlled region of origin for fortified wines consisting of the districts of PAARL and TULBAGH.

Boschendal ★★
> Vast (617 acre) estate in PAARL area on an old fruit farm. Emphasis on white wines and sparkling "Brut", but CABERNET improving. Also a charming restaurant.

Breede River Valley
> Fortified wine region east of Drakenstein Mtns.

Buitenverwachting
> Revived part of 17thC Constantia estate. First vintages creditable.

Bukettraube
> White-wine grape with high acidity and muscat aroma, most popular as a blend component.

Cabernet The great Bordeaux grape, particularly successful in the COASTAL REGION. Sturdy, long-ageing wines.

Cavendish Cape ★★
> Range of remarkably good sherries from the K.W.V.

Chardonnay
> Classic white variety, very rare in S.A. due to official restrictions. Most S.A. bottles carrying Chardonnay labels, vintaged 1985 and earlier, contain Auxerrois, a minor white var., due to widespread smuggling by growers and subsequent confusion.

Chenin Blanc
> Workhorse grape of the Cape; one vine in four. Adaptable and sometimes very good. Alias STEEN. K.W.V. makes a very good example at a bargain price.

Cinsaut

The principal bulk-producing French red grape in S. Africa; formerly known as Hermitage. Often blended with CABERNET, but can make reasonable wine on its own.

Coastal Region

Demarcated wine region, includes PAARL, STELLENBOSCH, Durbanville, SWARTLAND, TULBAGH.

Colombard

The "FRENCH COLOMBARD" of California. Prized in S. Africa for its high acidity and fruity flavour.

Constantia

Once the world's most famous muscat wine, from the Cape. Now the southernmost district of origin.

Delheim ★★→★★★

Winery at Driesprong in one of the highest areas of STELLEN-BOSCH, known for delicate STEEN and GEWÜRZ whites and also light reds: PINOTAGE, SHIRAZ. The CABERNET is more gripping. Grande Reserve (presently pure CAB.) is top class.

Drostdy ★★

Range of sherries from BERGKELDER.

Edelkeur ★★★★

Excellent intensely sweet white made with nobly rotten (p. 46) grapes by NEDERBURG.

Estate wine

Strictly controlled term applying only to registered estates making wines made of grapes grown on the same property.

Fleur du Cap ★★

Popular and well-made range of wines from the BERGKELDER. Good CAB; interesting SAUV.BL.

Gewürztraminer

The famous spicy grape of Alsace, best at SIMONSIG. Naturally low acidity makes wine-making difficult at the Cape.

Grand Cru (or Premier Grand Cru)

Term for a totally dry white, with no quality implications. Generally to be avoided.

Groot Constantia ★★

Historic estate, now government-owned, near Cape Town. Source of superlative muscat wine in the early 19th century. Now making wide range of wines, esp. good RHINE RIESLING.

Grünberger ★

Brand of not-quite-dry STEEN white from the BERGKELDER.

Hamilton-Russell ★★

Young estate in cool coastal valley. Very promising P.NOIR, also Bordeaux-style red, CHARDONNAY and SAUVIGNON BLANC.

Hanepoot

Local name for the sweet Muscat of Alexandria grape.

Hartenberg ★★

Previously known as Montagne, this Stellenbosch estate still produces fine CABERNET and SHIRAZ. Whites less good.

Hazendal ★★

Family estate in w. STELLENBOSCH specializing in semi-sweet STEEN, marketed by the BERGKELDER.

Kanonkop ★★★

Outstanding estate in n. STELLENBOSCH. Full-bodied CAB and PINOTAGE. Paul Sauer Fleur is a Bordeaux-style blend.

Klein Constantia

Sophisticated new estate. No expense spared in plan to create wines of equivalent quality to original CONSTANTIA muscats.

Koopmanskloof ★

STELLENBOSCH estate making good dry Chenin Blanc-based blend "Blanc de Marbonne".

K.W.V. The Kooperatieve Wijnbouwers Vereniging, S. Africa's national wine co-operative, originally organized by the State to absorb embarrassing surpluses. Vast premises in PAARL making a range of good wines, particularly sherries.

Laborie ★

New K.W.V.-owned showpiece estate on Paarl Mtn. CABERNET and PINOTAGE-based Blanc de Noirs sparkling.

Landgoed

South African for Estate; a word which appears on all estate-wine labels and official seals.

Landskroon ★

Family estate owned by Paul and Hugo de Villiers. Mainly port-type wines for K.W.V. but recently some good dry reds – PINOT NOIR, TINTA BAROCCA and CABERNETS Sauv. and Franc.

Late Harvest Term for a mildly sweet wine. "Special Late Harvest" must be naturally sweet. "Noble Late Harvest" is the highest quality level of all.

Le Bonheur ★★★

Stellenbosch estate producing Cape's finest white, Blanc Fumé, a non-wooded SAUVIGNON BLANC.

J.C. Le Roux ★

Old Cape brand revived as BERGKELDER'S sparkling wine house. SAUV. BLANC (Charmat) and P.NOIR (Méthode Champenoise).

Malmesbury

Centre of the SWARTLAND wine district, on the w. coast n. of Cape Town, specializing in dry whites and distilling wine.

Meerendal ★★

Estate near Durbanville producing robust reds (esp. SHIRAZ and PINOTAGE) marketed by the BERGKELDER.

Meerlust ★★★

Beautiful old family estate s. of STELLENBOSCH making outstanding CABERNET and Rubicon (Médoc-style blend).

Monis ★→★★

Well-known wine concern of PAARL, with fine "Vintage Port".

Montpellier ★

Pioneering TULBAGH estate with 370 acres of v'yds. specializing in white wine. Recent wines have been distinctly dull.

Muratie ★

Ancient estate in STELLENBOSCH, best known for its port.

Nederburg ★★→★★★

The most famous wine farm in modern S. Africa, operated by the STELLENBOSCH FARMERS' WINERY. Its annual auction is a major event. Pioneer in modern cellar practice and with fine CABERNET, "Private Bin" blends, EDELKEUR and GEWÜRZ. Also good sparkling wines and Paarl RIESLINGS.

Neethlingshof ★

Estate in development. Full-bodied Colombard and CAB best.

Overberg

Demarcated wine district in the Caledon area, COASTAL REGION, with some of the coolest Cape vineyards.

Overgaauw ★→★★★

Estate w. of STELLENBOSCH making good STEEN, very good CABERNET, and Tria Corda, a CABERNET/MERLOT blend.

Paarl South Africa's wine capital, 30 miles n.e. of Cape Town, and the surrounding demarcated district, among the best in the country, particularly for white wine and sherry.

Paarlsack ★

Well-known range of sherries made at PAARL by the K.W.V.

Pinot Noir

Like counterparts in California and Australia, Cape producers struggle to get complexity of flavour. Best are HAMILTON RUSSELL, BLAAUWKLIPPEN, MEERLUST.

Pinotage

South African red grape, a cross between PINOT NOIR and CINSAUT, useful for high yields and hardiness. Its wine is lush and fruity but never first-class.

Premier Grand Cru   See GRAND CRU

Rhine Riesling

Produces full-flavoured dry and off-dry wines. Generally needs two years or more of bottle age. See WEISSER RIESLING.

Riesling

South African Riesling (actually Crouchen Blanc) is very different from RHINE RIESLING, which has only recently been planted in any quantity in S. Africa.

Rietvallei ★★

New ROBERTSON estate. Excellent fortified Muscadel.

Robertson

Small demarcated district e. of the Cape and inland. Mainly dessert wines (notably Muscat), but red and white table wines are on the increase. Includes Bonnievale. Irrigated vineyards.

Roodeberg ★★

High-quality brand of blended red wine from the K.W.V. Has good colour, body and flavour and ages well in bottle.

Rustenberg ★★★

Effectively, if not officially, an estate red wine from just n.e. of STELLENBOSCH. Rustenberg Dry Red is a good CAB/CINSAUT blend. The straight CAB is outstanding.

Sauvignon Blanc

Adapting well to warm conditions. Widely grown and marketed in both "wooded" and "unwooded" styles.

Schoongezicht ★

Partner of RUSTENBERG, one of S. Africa's most beautiful old farms and producer of agreeable white wine from STEEN, RIESLING and Clairette Blanche. Now registered as an estate.

Shiraz

Gaining in popularity in S. Africa for rich deep-coloured wine.

Simonsig ★★

Estate owned by F.J. Malan, pioneering estate producer. Produces a wide range, incl. GEWÜRZ, Vin Fumé, wood-matured dry white and a "Méthode Champenoise".

Simonsvlei

One of S. Africa's best-known co-operative cellars, just outside PAARL. A prize-winner with PINOTAGE.

Spier ★→★★

Estate of five farms w. of STELLENBOSCH producing reds and whites. COLOMBARD and PINOTAGE are best.

Steen South Africa's commonest white grape, said to be a clone of the CHENIN BLANC. It gives strong, tasty and lively wine, sweet or dry, normally better than S. African Riesling.

Stein Name used for any medium dry white wine.

Stellenbosch

Town and demarcated district 30 miles e. of Cape Town, extending to the ocean at False Bay. Most of the best estates, esp. for red wine, are in the mountain foothills of the region.

Stellenbosch Farmers' Winery (S.F.W.)

South Africa's biggest winery (after the K.W.V.) with several ranges of wines, incl. NEDERBURG and ZONNEBLOEM. Wide range of mid- and low-priced wines. See CAPE WINE AND DISTILLERS.

Stellenryck ★★★

Top-quality BERGKELDER range, RHINE RIESLING, Fumé Blanc and CABERNET.

Superior

An official designation of quality for WINES OF ORIGIN. The wine must meet standards set by the Wine & Spirit Board.

Swartland

Demarcated district around MALMESBURY. ALLESVERLOREN is the best estate.

Tassenberg ★

Popular and good-value red known to thousands as Tassie.

Theuniskraal ★★

Well-known TULBAGH estate specializing in white wines, esp. RIESLING, GEWÜRZTRAMINER and Sémillon.

Tulbagh

Demarcated district n. of PAARL best known for the white wines of MONTPELLIER, THEUNISKRAAL and TWEE JONGEGEZELLEN, and the dessert wines from Drostdy. See also BOBERG.

Twee Jongegezellen ★★

Estate at TULBAGH. One of the great pioneers which revolutionized S. African wine in the 1950s, still in the family of its 18th-century founder. Mainly white wine, incl. RIESLING, STEEN and SAUVIGNON BLANC. Best wines: "Schanderl" and "T.J.39".

Uiterwyk ★★

Old estate w. of STELLENBOSCH making a good CABERNET SAUVIGNON and pleasant whites.

Uitkyk ★★

Old estate (400 acres) at STELLENBOSCH famous for Carlonet (big gutsy CAB) and Carlsheim (chiefly SAUV BLANC) white.

Van Riebeck

Co-operative at Riebeck Kasteel, MALMESBURY, known for pioneering work in white wine technology.

Vergenoegd ★★→★★★

Old family estate in s. STELLENBOSCH supplying high-quality sherry to the K.W.V. but recently offering deeply flavoured CABERNET and excellent SHIRAZ under an estate label.

Villiera ★★→★★★

Paarl estate with Tradition top class Méthode Champenoise, good SAUVIGNON BLANC and RHINE RIESLING.

Vriesenhof ★★★

Small-scale winery with vines high on Stellenbosch mountain slope. Highly rated CABERNET.

Weisser Riesling

Alias Rhine Riesling. Gradually replacing S.A. RIESLING.

Welgemeend ★★★

Boutique PAARL estate producing delicate CABERNET and Amadé, a Grenache, SHIRAZ and PINOTAGE blend.

Weltevrede ★→★★

Progressive ROBERTSON estate. Blended white and fortified wines.

De Wetshof ★★

Pioneering estate in ROBERTSON district. CHARDONNAY, SAUVIGNON BLANC and a sweet noble-rot white, Edeloes.

Wine of Origin

The S. African equivalent of Appellation Contrôlée. Demarcated regions are described on these pages.

Worcester

Demarcated wine district round the Breede and Hex river valleys, e. of PAARL. Many co-operative cellars make mainly dessert wines, brandy and dry whites.

Zandvliet ★★

Estate in the ROBERTSON area making a light SHIRAZ.

Zonnebloem ★★

Good-quality brand of CABERNET, RIESLING, PINOTAGE and SHIRAZ from the STELLENBOSCH FARMERS' WINERY.

A few words about words

In the shorthand essential for this little book (and sometimes in bigger books as well) wines are often described by adjectives that can seem irrelevant, inane – or just silly. What do "fat", "round", "full", "lean" and so on mean, when used about wine? Some of the more irritatingly vague are expanded in this list:

Attack The first impression of the wine in your mouth. It should "strike" positively, if not necessarily with force. Without attack it is feeble.

Attractive Means "I like it, anyway". A slight put-down for expensive wines; encouragement for juniors. At least a refreshing drink.

Big Concerns the whole flavour, including the alcohol content. Sometimes implies clumsiness, the opposite of elegance. Generally positive, but big is easy in California and less usual in, say, Bordeaux. So the context matters.

Charming Rather patronizing when said of wines that should have more impressive qualities. Implies lightness, possibly slight sweetness. A standard comment on Loire wines.

Crisp With pronounced but pleasing acidity; fresh and eager.

Deep/ depth This wine is worth tasting with attention. There is more to it than the first impression; it fills your mouth with developing flavours as though it had an extra dimension. (Deep colour simply means hard to see through.) All really fine wines have depth.

Easy Used in the sense of "easy come, easy go". An easy wine makes no demand on your palate (or intellect). The implication is that it drinks smoothly, doesn't need maturing, and all you will remember was a pleasant drink.

Elegant A professional taster's favourite term when he is stuck to describe a wine whose proportions (of strength, flavour, aroma), whose attack, middle and finish, whose texture and all its qualities call for comparison with other forms of natural beauty, as in the movement of horses, the forms and attitudes of women . . . .

Fat With flavour and texture that fills your mouth, but without aggression. Obviously inappropriate in e.g. a light Moselle, but what you pay your money for in Sauternes.

Finish See Length

Firm Flavour that strikes the palate fairly hard, with fairly high acidity or tannic astringency giving the impression that the wine is in youthful vigour and will age to gentler things. An excellent quality with high-flavoured foods, and almost always positive.

Flesh   Refers to both substance and texture. A fleshy wine is fatter than a "meaty" wine, more unctuous if less vigorous. The term is often used of good Pomerols, whose texture is notably smooth.

Flowery   Often used as though synonymous with fruity, but really means floral, like the fragrance of flowers. Roses, violets, etc., are sometimes specified.

Fresh   Implies a good degree of fruity acidity, even a little nip of sharpness, as well as the zip and zing of youth. All young whites should be fresh: the alternative is flatness, staleness . . . ugh.

Fruity   Used for almost any quality, but really refers to the body and richness of wine made from good ripe grapes. A fruity aroma is not the same as a flavoury one. Fruitiness usually implies at least a slight degree of sweetness.

Full   Interchangeable with full-bodied. Lots of "vinosity" or wineyness: the mouth-filling flavours of alcohol and "extract" (all the flavouring components) combined.

Hollow   Lacking a satisfying middle flavour. Something seems to be missing between first flavour and last. A characteristic of wines from greedy proprietors who let their vines produce too many grapes. An extremely hollow wine is "empty".

Lean   A bit more flesh would be an improvement. Lack of mouth-filling flavours: often astringent as well. But occasionally a term of appreciation of a distinct and enjoyable style.

Length   The flavours and aromas that linger after swallowing. In principle the greater the length the better the wine. One second of flavour after swallowing = one "caudalie". Ten caudalies is good; 20 terrific.

Light   With relatively little alcohol and body, as in most German wines. A very desirable quality in the right wines.

Meaty   Savoury in effect with enough substance to chew. The inference is lean meat; leaner than in "fleshy".

Oaky   Smelling or tasting (or both) of fresh-sawn oak; e.g. a new barrel.

Plump   The diminutive of fat, implying a degree of charm as well.

Rich   Not necessarily sweet, but giving an opulent impression.

Robust   In good heart, vigorous, and on a fairly big scale.

Rough   Flavour and texture give no pleasure. Acidity and/or tannin are dominant and coarse.

Round   Almost the same as fat, but with more approval.

Stylish   Style is bold and definite; wears its cap on its ear.

Supple   Often used of young red wines which might be expected to be more aggressive. More lively than an "easy" wine, with implications of good quality.

Well-balanced Contains all the desirable elements (acid, alcohol, flavours, etc) in appropriate and pleasing proportions.

What to drink in an ideal world

Wines at their peak in 1988

Red Bordeaux:
Top growths of 1980, 1979, 1976, 1975, 1970, 1966, 1961
Other Crus Classés of 1981, 1980, 1979, 1978, 1976, 1975, 1970,
   1966, 1961
Petits châteaux of 1984, 1983, 1982, 1981, 1979, 1978 . . .
Red Burgundy
Top growths of 1982, 1980, 1979, 1978, 1976, 1973, 1971, 1969,
   1966, 1964
Premiers Crus of 1984, 1983, 1982, 1980, 1979, 1978, 1976,
   1971 . . .
Village wines of 1985, 1984, 1983 . . .
White Burgundy
Top growths of 1984, 1983, 1982, 1981, 1979, 1978 . . .
Premiers Crus of 1985, 1984, 1983, 1982, 1981, 1978 . . .
Village wines of 1986, 1985, 1983
Sauternes
Top growths of 1982, 1981, 1980, 1979, 1978, 1976, 1975, 1971,
   1970, 1967 . . .
Other wines of 1983, 1982, 1981, 1980, 1979, 1978, 1976, 1975 . . .
Sweet Loire wines
Top growths of (Anjou/Vouvray) 1982, 1981, 1980, 1979, 1978,
   1976, 1975, 1973, 1971, 1969, 1964 . . .
Alsace
Grands Crus and late-harvest wines of 1984, 1983, 1981, 1979,
   1978, 1976 . . .
Standard wines of 1986, 1985, 1983 . . .
Rhône
Hermitage/top Northern Rhône reds of 1981, 1980, 1979, 1978,
   1976, 1973, 1971, 1969
Châteauneuf-du-Pape of 1984, 1982, 1980, 1979, 1978 . . .

German wines
Great sweet wines of 1976, 1975, 1971 . . .
Ausleses of 1983, 1981, 1979, 1976 . . .
Spätleses of 1985, 1983, 1981, 1979, 1976 . . .
Kabinett and QbA wines of 1986, 1985, 1984, 1983 . . .

Californian
Top Cabernets, Pinot Noirs, Zinfandels of 1983, 1981, 1980, 1979,
   1978 . . .
Most Cabernets etc. of 1984, 1983, 1982, 1981, 1980, 1978 . . .
Top Chardonnays of 1983, 1982, 1981 . . .
Most Chardonnays of 1985, 1984, 1983 . . .

Vintage Port 1975, 1970, 1967, 1966, 1963, 1960 . . .

===

The 1986 vintage

Abundance – in some cases embarrassing abundance – was
the keynote of the 1986 vintage in much of Europe. It is
not an easy year to sum up in generalities, beyond the
comforting thought that it was scarcely anywhere a
disaster.

Bordeaux dominated the news by making an enormous
quantity of good wine, with the debate immediately
starting on whether it would turn out to be as good as '85,
or better. Early indications are that the wines are rather
better structured with more depth of flavour and will
probably mature more slowly. Sauternes had excellent
harvest conditions. Burgundy suffered from rain at the
start of the vintage. Patient and optimistic growers sat it
out, to be rewarded by hot sunshine in October. Their
wines are very promising; others made watery wine. There

will be more reasonably priced burgundies of good quality to be had – especially from Chablis. The Rhône, the Loire, Champagne and Alsace are all happy with a large harvest which should be well balanced without really striking ripeness. (This will be a relief for those who have found Alsace wines of '83 and '85 too potent for their liking.) Germany is still waiting for a great late-picking vintage. It is 10 years since the super-ripe '76s. But 1986 made a great deal of the sort of wine fashion now requires: sound QbA and Kabinett suitable for bottling as "trocken". Italy had a poor spring but an excellent summer leading to another very good vintage overall. Spain and Portugal were less lucky: rain interfered with the harvest. California enjoyed lower than usual temperatures during the summer and looks forward to particularly well-balanced reds and whites. Australia continued a run of favourable conditions that have produced an enviable supply of the sort of cleanly fruity wine that everybody wants.

What remains in 1987 is to strike sensible bargains over the price of all this delectable drinking.

Quick reference vintage charts for France and Germany

These charts give a picture of the range of qualities made in the principal areas (every year has its relative successes and failures) and a guide to whether the wine is ready to drink or should be kept.

♦ drink now — needs keeping ✓ can be drunk with pleasure now, but the better wines will continue to improve

0 no good   10 the best

(There are often wines in several categories.)

FRANCE

	Médoc/Graves		Pom/St-Em.		Sauternes & sw.		Graves & dry	
	Red Bordeaux				**White Bordeaux**			
86	6–9	—	6–8	—	7–10	—	7–9	✓
85	6–8	—	7–9	—	6–8	—	5–8	✓
84	4–7	✓	2–5	—	4–7	—	5–7	✓
83	6–9	✓	6–9	✓	6–10	✓	7–9	✓
82	8–10	✓	7–9	✓	3–7	♦	7–8	♦
81	5–8	✓	6–9	✓	5–8	✓	7–8	✓
80	4–7	♦	3–5	✓	5–9	♦	5–7	✓
79	5–8	✓	5–9	✓	6–8	✓	4–6	✓
78	6–9	✓	6–8	✓	4–6	✓	7–9	✓
77	3–5	♦	2–5	♦	2–4	♦	6–7	♦
76	6–8	✓	7–8	✓	7–9	✓	4–8	✓
75	7–9	✓	8–9	✓	8–10	✓	8–10	♦
74	4–6	♦	3–5	♦	0		4–6	♦
73	5–7	♦	5–7	♦	0–4	♦	7–8	♦
72	2–5	♦	2–4	♦	2–4	♦	4–5	♦
71	5–8	♦	6–8	✓	8–9	♦	8–9	♦
70	9–10	✓	9–10	✓	9–10	♦	9–10	♦

	Côte d'Or		Côte d'Or		Chablis		Alsace	
	Red Burgundy		**White Burgundy**					
86	5–8	✓	6–8	✓	7–9	✓	7–8	✓
85	7–10	✓	5–8	✓	6–9	✓	7–10	✓
84	3–6	✓	4–7	✓	4–7	♦	4–6	✓
83	5–9	✓	6–9	✓	7–9	✓	8–10	✓
82	4–7	✓	6–8	✓	6–7	✓	6–8	✓
81	3–6	♦	4–8	✓	6–9	✓	7–8	✓
80	4–7	♦	4–6	✓	5–7	✓	3–5	♦
79	5–6	♦	6–8	✓	6–8	✓	7–8	♦
78	8–10	✓	7–9	✓	7–10	✓	6–8	♦
77	2–4	♦	4–6	♦	5		3–5	♦
76	7–10	✓	7–8	♦	8		10	♦
75	0–5	♦	4–8	♦	6–9	♦	9	♦

Beaujolais: 86 was good, 85 excellent. **Mâcon-Villages** (white): 86, 85, 84, 83 are good now. **Loire:** Sweet Anjou and Touraine. Best recent vintages; 85, 84, 83, 82, 79, 78, 76. **Upper Loire:** Sancerre and Pouilly-Fumé 86, 85 are good now. **Muscadet:** D.Y.A.

GERMANY

	Rhône			Rhine		Moselle	
86	5–8	✓	86	4–8	✓	5–8	✓
85	6–8	✓	85	6–8	✓	6–9	✓
84	5–7	✓	84	4–6	✓	4–6	✓
83	6–9	✓	83	6–9	✓	7–10	✓
82	6–8	✓	82	4–6	✓	4–7	♦
81	5–7	✓	81	5–8	✓	4–8	♦
80	6–8	—	80	4–7	✓	3–7	♦
79	6–7	✓	79	6–8	✓	6–8	♦
78	8–10	✓	78	5–7	✓	4–7	♦
77	4–6	♦	77	5–7	♦	4–6	♦
76	6–9	♦	76	9–10	♦	9–10	♦
75	0–5	♦	75	7–9	♦	8–10	♦
74	4–7	♦	74	3–6	♦	2–4	♦
73	5–8	♦	73	6–7	♦	6–8	♦
72	6–9	♦	72	2–5	♦	1–4	♦
71	7–9	♦	71	9–10	♦	10	♦

N.B. Detailed charts will be found on pages 22, 23 (France), 100 (Germany).